Encyclopedia of
ADVANCED DRESSMAKING

Marshall Cavendish London & New York

Edited by Annie Woolridge
Published by Marshall Cavendish Books Limited
58 Old Compton Street, London W1V 5PA

© Marshall Cavendish Limited 1978

This material has previously appeared in
Golden Hands Monthly and *Fashion Maker*.

First printing 1978

ISBN 0 85685 452 2

Printed and bound in Great Britain by
Redwood Burn Limited
Trowbridge & Esher

FOREWORD

If you have opened this book, you have probably mastered the basic techniques of dressmaking. You have almost certainly put your knowledge into practice. Now you would like to explore more of the possibilities that dressmaking opens up.

Encyclopedia of Advanced Dressmaking will explain clearly and carefully the skills you need in order to graduate from making simple gathered skirts and easy, loose-fitting dresses and tops to more sophisticated garments like evening coats and tailored jackets, or beautifully tailored skirts, or a stunning man's shirt or safari jacket. In addition, it gives you the facts about working with difficult fabrics from leather to chiffon – and there are pages and pages of patterns to help you put your skills into practice. There is a vinyl raincoat and matching hat for a child, a "wardrobe" in suede – jacket, skirt and jerkin, clothes for a sunny summer or holiday and for a mother-to-be. In fact, the book includes more than thirty separate items for the entire family, and it gives all the information required to make each one. There are easy-to-use graph patterns and detailed step-by-step instructions for making every one, and even more important, there are explanations and diagrams of a more general nature to help you adapt the specific features of a garment or to alter the whole garment to fit rather more specific features of the human body. You'll find all you need to know about tucks and pleats, hems and belts, seams and sleeves, as well as fitting and lining a variety of garments, working with plaids, checks and stripes, and maintaining a professional finish when sewing on velvet or fur, the sheerest voile or the thickest Harris tweed.

Encyclopedia of Advanced Dressmaking is a complete reference book for every seamstress, whether you want to expand your existing skills or learn new ones to last a lifetime.

CONTENTS

SECTION 1
Techniques and methods for the advanced dressmaker

The section that follows is designed to explain the skills necessary to enable the novice seamstress to approach dressmaking in a more professional manner. It explores fully the methods for working with different, and difficult, fabrics, for altering garments to give a better fit and for adding finishing touches like unusual pockets or raglan sleeves to give your work an extra bit of flair without overlooking basic techniques.

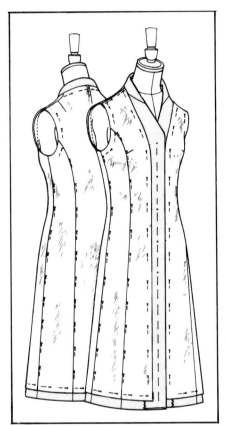

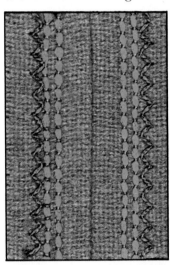

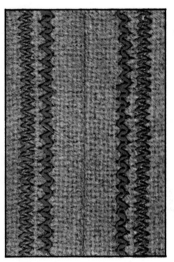

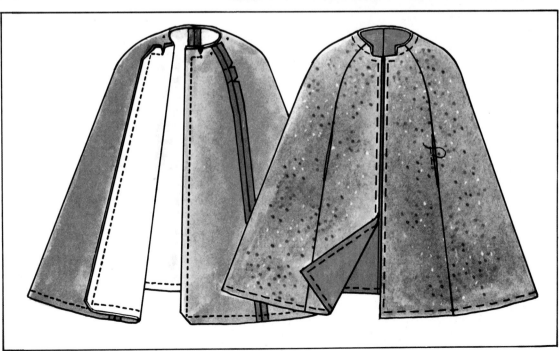

Professional hems

Beautifully finished hems are most important as they provide a professional finish to all the care given in the making of a garment. The length is dictated by fashion to a certain extent, but it must be right both for the garment and for the particular figure.

Wearing appropriate shoes, check the length of a garment before a mirror, and always wear the jacket when looking at a suit skirt to see that the proportion of jacket to skirt is correct.

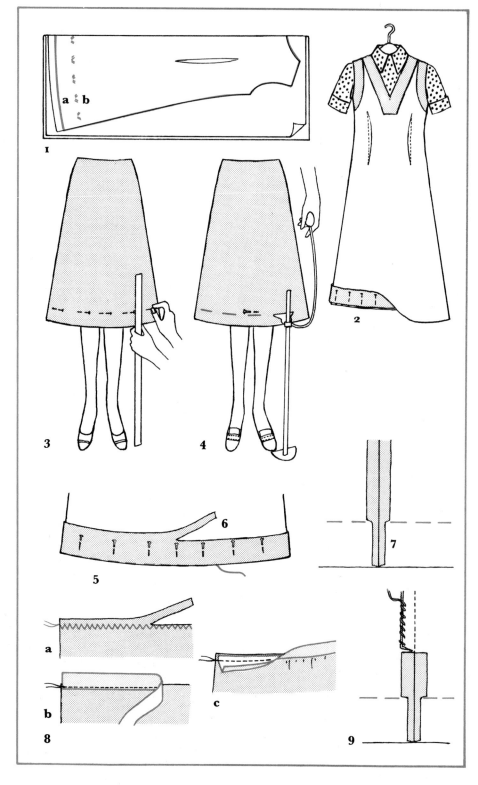

GENERAL POINTS
Hem length

There are various ways to get the right hem length:

From the back neck, measure the length of the pattern and adjust if necessary (Fig. 1a).

After cutting out, tailor tack along the hem line and pin the hem up to the line when fitting (Fig. 1b).

Place a dress of the right length on a hanger with the new dress over it. Pin up the new hem to match (Fig. 2).

Ask a friend to measure up from the ground and mark the line with pins (Fig. 3). Use a skirt marker. Be careful here; measure 1.3cm ($\frac{1}{2}$ inch) longer than needed to avoid the possibility of the chalk marking the fabric permanently. Turn up 1.3cm ($\frac{1}{2}$ inch) above the chalk line (Fig. 4).

Preparation before neatening

Trace tack along the hem fold and unpin (Fig. 5).

Most hems are 5 to 6.5cm (2 to $2\frac{1}{2}$ inches) deep, so trim evenly to the required depth (Fig. 6). Exceptions are for blouses, 2.5cm (1 inch); faced hems, 1.3cm ($\frac{1}{2}$ inch); long skirts of fine fabric, 1.3cm ($\frac{1}{2}$ inch).

Trim all seams to 0.6cm ($\frac{1}{4}$ inch) between the hem line and the hem edge (Fig. 7).

Hem neatening

For non-fray fabrics oversew or zigzag along the cut edge.

For fraying fabrics use one of the following methods:

Zigzag 0.6cm ($\frac{1}{4}$ inch) away from the cut edge and trim to the machining (Fig. 8a).

For straight hem lines, edge with straight binding (Fig. 8b).

For curved or bias edges, ease the hem and edge with bias binding (Fig. 8c).

For fine cottons (mainly children's clothes and summer dresses), fold under the raw edge for 1.3cm ($\frac{1}{2}$ inch).

For pleats which are seamed, the seam turnings are snipped the hem depth above the hem line and pressed open below the snip. Above the snip, the turnings are neatened and pressed together (Fig. 9).

After neatening the raw edge, press it, making sure it is away from the body of the garment.

Fold the hem up on the tacked line, slip a piece of card or brown paper inside the fold and press well. Use a damp cloth rather than a steam iron as it is easier to control the amount of steam this way. Tack through the folded edge to keep it firmly in place.

Plain
This is used for absolutely straight hems i.e. skirts and trousers.
Tack the hem 1.3cm ($\frac{1}{2}$ inch) below the neatened edge. Stitch into place using invisible hemming stitch (Fig. 10).

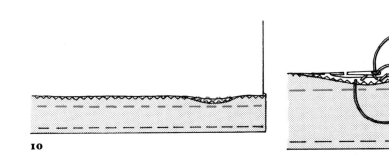

10

Slightly flared – A line skirts and flared trousers
After tacking the fold, run a gathering thread 0.6cm ($\frac{1}{4}$ inch) below the neatened edge. Pull up the gathering thread until the seams match and the hem lies in place. Ease out the fullness evenly (Fig. 11a).
For fabrics which will shrink, press as shown (Fig. 11b), and invisible hem stitch into place.
For fabrics which will not shrink, attach bias binding, stretching it slightly. Fold the binding over the raw edge and slip stitch in place (Fig. 11c).

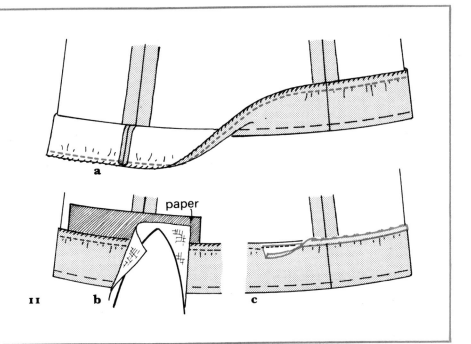

11   **a**   **b**   paper   **c**

Very flared skirts
It is not easy to make a deep hem for these, so they are usually finished either with a narrow or a faced hem.

Narrow hem for lightweight fabrics
Cut the hem depth to 2cm ($\frac{3}{4}$ inch). Do not neaten the edge. Run a gathering thread 0.6cm ($\frac{1}{4}$ inch) from the cut edge. Turn under 0.6cm ($\frac{1}{4}$ inch) and pull the gathering thread so it lies easily to the skirt. Slip stitch the hem through the fold (Fig. 12a).

Narrow hem for heavier fabrics
Cut the hem depth to 1.3cm ($\frac{1}{2}$ inch) and neaten the edge by oversewing or zigzag stitch. Press the hem up over paper and stitch with invisible hemming stitch (Fig. 12b).

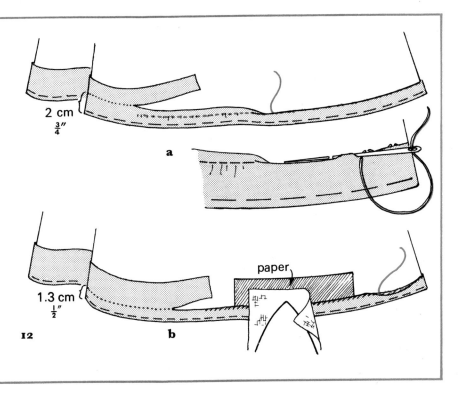

2 cm $\frac{3}{4}''$ **a**
1.3 cm $\frac{1}{2}''$ paper   **12**   **b**

Faced hem for all fabrics

If extra bulk is not desirable, then lining or net can be used for the facing fabric.

Cut a 5cm (2 inch) shaped facing from the skirt pattern (Fig. 13a).

Sew the seams together and neaten the shorter edge (Fig. 13b).

Place the facing to the right side of the skirt hem and stitch (Fig. 13c).

Turn up and press. Sew the facing to the skirt with invisible hemming stitch (Fig. 13d).

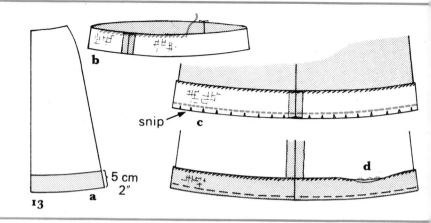

Rolled hem for sheer fabrics

Trim the hem to 0.6cm ($\frac{1}{4}$ inch). Turn under 0.3cm ($\frac{1}{8}$ inch) (Fig. 14a) and either slip stitch hem (Fig. 14b) or machine (Fig. 14c).

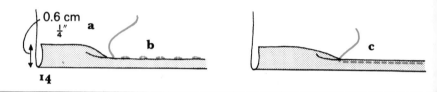

Tailored hem for jackets, coats and sleeves

A strip of canvas is used to support the weight of a coat or jacket hem and to give a good line.

Cut 5cm (2 inch) strips of canvas or shrunk duck on the true cross grain of the fabric (Fig. 15a).

Lay the canvas above the hem line and catch stitch to the garment (Fig. 15b). Turn up the hem and sew it to the canvas with invisible hemming stitch (Fig. 15c).

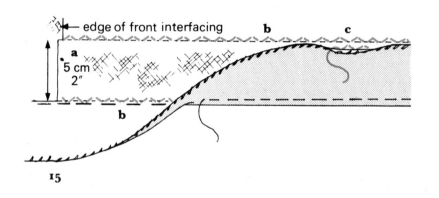

Lining hem finish for jackets and coats

Finish the coat or jacket and press it well. Make up the lining and press this too.

Pin the lining to the jacket, matching seam lines, armholes and style lines (Fig. 16a).

Fold under and pin the front edges (Fig. 16b).

Fold and pin the hem turning to the exact length of the jacket or coat (Fig. 16c).

Lift up the folded edge 2.5 to 3.8cm (1 to $1\frac{1}{2}$ inches) and re-pin (Fig. 16d).

Slip stitch the hem along the fold (Fig. 16e).

Fold down the pleat at the front edges and slip stitch hem all round (Fig. 16f).

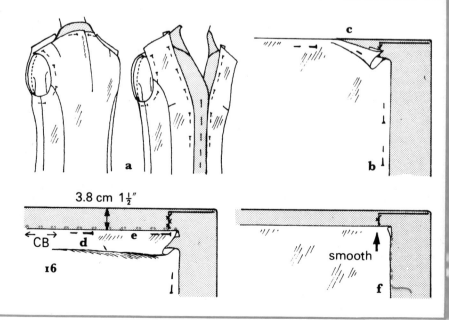

Interfacings

Interfacing is used to strengthen, to give a good shape to a garment and to prevent stretching. It adds body and crispness to areas such as collars, cuffs, necklines, belts and behind buttons. Interfacing can also be used to add firmness and roundness to the hems of skirts and sleeves made from medium or heavier-weight fabrics. There is a wide selection of interfacings to choose from, each suited to a certain process or type of fabric. Interfacings may be made especially for interfacing purposes, or they may be fabrics like organdie, taffeta or net.

GENERAL USAGE

First decide how crisp you want the interfaced areas to be and whether some areas require more body than others. Collars and pocket flaps, for instance, may look better with a slightly heavier interfacing than for areas such as front facings or hem lines. In general, it is advisable to choose an interfacing which is of the same weight or slightly lighter than the fabric being worked. Never use one that is thicker, because the interfacing should blend into the garment, doing its job without being noticeable. If in doubt, use a slightly lighter weight interfacing.

If a soft effect is desired, place the edge of the interfacing into the folded edge of the top fabric. If the fabric falls over the interfacing in a soft roll, it is the correct interfacing to use. If sharp points and a hard edge are formed, it is the wrong one. Another general rule is to match the fibre content of the interfacing to that of the fabric. For example, choose a silk interfacing such as organza for silk, and canvas for a woollen fabric.

Unless using an iron-on or non-woven type, the interfacing should be ironed before it is cut out. If a garment is washable, the interfacing should be washable too and must be pre-shrunk before use.

TYPES OF INTERFACING

Interfacings can be divided into three main groups – woven, non-woven and iron-on.

Non-woven interfacings

This type of interfacing is manufactured in a variety of weights and is available in either black or white, 84cm (33 inches) wide. Non-woven interfacings are best used where a stand-up, sculptured effect is required. These interfacings are tested and designed for use with special fabrics and usually carry the manufacturer's recommendations for use and combinations with fabrics. However, it is always advisable to test a piece on a scrap of the top fabric before using it on the garment. They are rarely suitable for use with sheer or semi-transparent fabrics, as they show through.

Iron-on non-woven interfacing

Iron-on non-woven interfacings are available in the same width and colours as the non-woven interfacings but not in such a variety of weights. They are useful for belts, pocket flaps and cuffs but great care must be taken when applying them, or the interfacing will 'bubble' and spoil the finished look of the garment. Lay the fabric piece (usually the facing) right side down on the ironing board and place the interfacing on this with the adhesive side facing downwards. Cover with a damp cloth and hold a medium hot iron over the cloth for 15 seconds. Lift the iron away and repeat the process until the whole surface has been ironed. The interfacing should now be fused to the fabric (Fig. 4). Unfortunately, once they are ironed on these interfacings do not always stay permanently in place and sometimes work loose unless they are held in position with a row of stitching round the edges.

Iron-on non-woven interfacings are not suitable for covering large areas, nor are they suitable for garments which receive frequent laundering as they will part from the fabric and cause 'bubbling'. Always test iron-on interfacings first on a spare piece of fabric in case the adhesive shows through.

Non-woven and iron-on interfacings should never be used on silks, 100 per cent synthetics or sheer fabrics.

Iron-on woven interfacings

This type of interfacing is made from a finely woven cotton with an adhesive backing. It has, to a certain extent, the same disadvantages as the non-woven iron-on interfacings but it is more pliable and blends better with the fabric. It can be used with cotton, linen, medium and heavy-weight rayons of the linen weave type. It can also be used quite successfully on certain fine cotton fabrics, but it is essential to test a piece on a scrap of the top fabric before using it on the garment. This type of interfacing is generally best ironed onto the facing fabric rather than the top fabric. The edges can then be held by the seam and the loose edge finished with the top fabric to hold it securely in position. This type of interfacing is most useful for stiffening blouse and shirt collars and cuffs because several layers (up to three or four) can be ironed on to achieve the required stiffness. These layers should be ironed onto the under collar and sleeve facings, and the interfacing should be cut just a fraction beyond the stitching line so that it can be caught in the seam. It is not possible to trim the interfacing back after stitching because it is usually stuck so firmly to the fabric.

INTERFACINGS	
Outside fabric	**correct interfacing**
Dress weight: cotton linen wool	pre-shrunk treated lawn iron-on or non-woven interfacing as recommended by the manufacturer
Suit-weight: cotton linen wool	treated cotton interfacing, such as bleached calico iron-on or non-woven interfacing as recommended by the manufacturer
Man-made fibre fabrics	non-woven interfacing as recommended by the manufacturer for very light fabrics (lawn, voile, etc.) pure silk or nylon organza
Pure silk	fine lawn or pure silk organza
See-through fabrics	soft organdie or pure silk organza

11

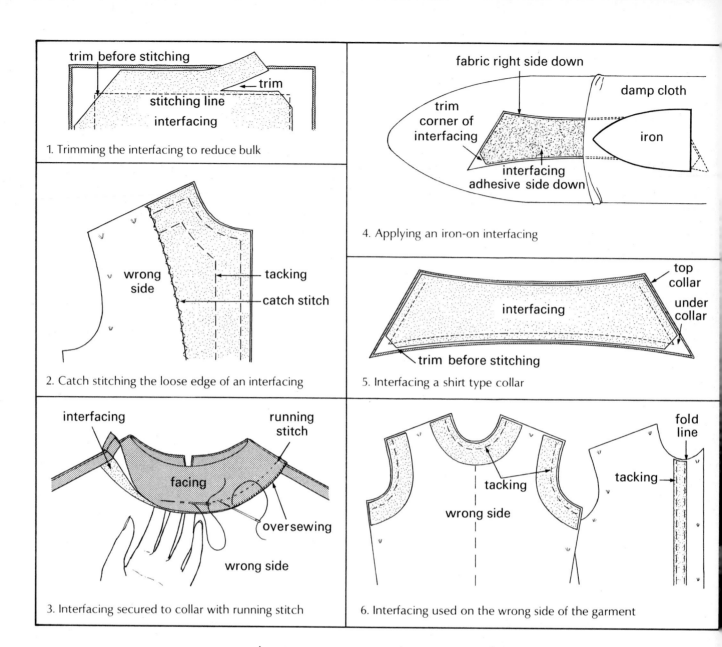

1. Trimming the interfacing to reduce bulk

2. Catch stitching the loose edge of an interfacing

3. Interfacing secured to collar with running stitch

4. Applying an iron-on interfacing

5. Interfacing a shirt type collar

6. Interfacing used on the wrong side of the garment

Woven interfacings are made in the same way as woven fabrics with lengthwise and crosswise threads, i.e. with a grain. They should therefore be cut on the same grain as the top fabric to which the piece is to be applied.

Woven interfacings are made from different types of canvas such as hair canvas, cotton canvas, linen canvas and a variety of finer weaves in varying degrees of stiffness. It is advisable to shrink these interfacings before use by pressing them well under a damp cloth. Woven canvas interfacings are suitable for woollen fabrics and tailoring weight linens.

Woven canvas interfacings

Cotton organdie, silk or nylon organza, lawn and cotton or nylon net are the types of interfacing best suited to use with lightweight fabrics such as fine cotton, silks, sheer and semi-transparent fabrics.

Other woven interfacings

Mark the pieces of interfacing with the same construction symbols as found on the pattern for easy matching with the top fabric. Darts should be marked on both the interfacing and the top fabric as they are stitched separately.

The interfacings are sewn into the seams when the garment is being made up, and trimmed back to the machine line to avoid bulky seams. To avoid excess bulk at the sharp corners on collars and cuffs, trim the corners off about 0.6cm ($\frac{1}{4}$ inch) inside the meeting point of the seam before stitching the interfacing in place (Fig. 1). Where one edge of the interfacing is not sewn into a seam it can either be left free, sewn onto the garment with catch stitching (Fig. 2) (not suitable for fine fabrics as the stitches show through), or sewn onto the facing with tiny running stitches after the facing has been sewn to the garment

and turned to the wrong side (Fig. 3).

When interfacing roll and shirt type collars, the interfacing is placed on the undercollar (Fig. 5).

For plain necklines, sleeveless armholes, behind buttonholes and buttons, the interfacing is placed to the wrong side of the garment (Fig. 6), not to the facing. The raw edges of the facings are caught onto the top fabric with a catch stitch. (Iron-on and non-woven interfacings are not suitable for this technique.)

For cuffs and stand-up collars the interfacing is placed to the wrong side of the top fabric. If a crisp effect is required, place the interfacing on the outer collar or cuff, and for a softer effect on the under collar or cuff facing.

Waistbands & Belts

WAISTBANDS

A properly sewn and fitted waistband never stretches, wrinkles or folds over, nor is it too tight or so loose that it slips down to the hips.

Personal preference and the style of the garment determine the width and type of waist finish and all waistbands need to be interfaced to prevent stretching, particularly where loosely woven fabrics are being used. Knits need an elastic section to ensure a proper fit. Petersham is used for interfacing; this comes in various widths and is either plain or stiffened with small 'bones' of plastic. If used in a washable garment, it should be pre-shrunk by washing and left to drip dry.

Unless the garment is gathered at the waist, the skirt is eased to the band to fit the curve of the body directly below the waist. For this reason the skirt waist measurement must be 2.5cm (1 inch) bigger than the waistband, which itself must be a comfortable fit. This is where personal preference comes in and it must be left to the individual to decide how much ease to allow.

For comfort and a smooth fit, the ends of the waistband should overlap by 3.8 to 5cm ($1\frac{1}{2}$ to 2 inches) with the back extending under the front for side openings, the left extending under the right for front openings and the right extending under the left for back openings.

The waistband is applied after the zip and zip guard if used and before the lining. If a waistband is not required, then the waist is finished by the addition of a shaped facing which should be interfaced with Vilene, or a firm woven interfacing. This is applied after the zip is sewn in and the lining tacked into place.

Tailored waistband

Cut the waistband with one long edge to the selvedge; if this is not possible neaten one long edge by overcasting by hand or machine. Make it 7.5cm (3 inches) longer than the waist measurement and twice as wide as the petersham, plus two turnings. Cut the petersham 3.2cm ($1\frac{1}{4}$ inches) shorter than the band (Fig. 1).

Ease the skirt onto the long cut edge of the waistband, leaving 6cm ($2\frac{3}{8}$ inches) underlap on the appropriate side. Tack through band and skirt and machine (Fig. 2).

Sew the petersham just above this line, placing it so that there is a 1.5cm ($\frac{5}{8}$ inch) turning left at both ends (Fig. 3).

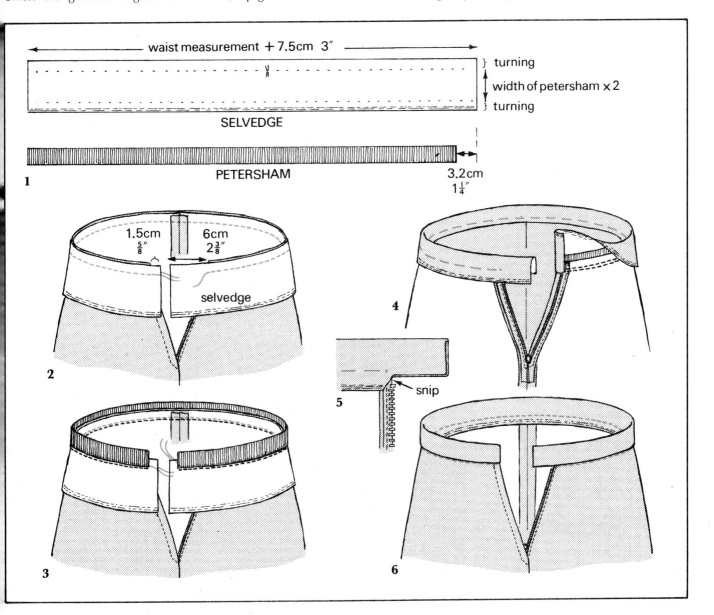

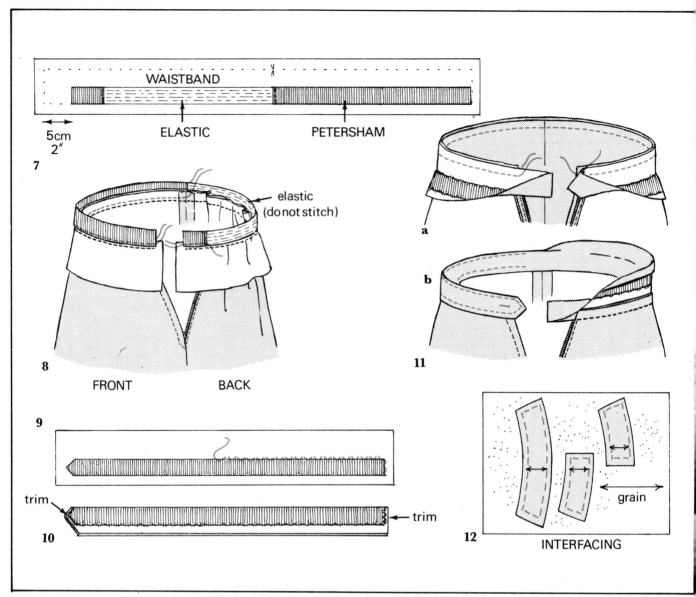

WAISTBAND

ELASTIC   PETERSHAM

5cm
2"

7

elastic
(do not stitch)

a

b

8

FRONT   BACK

9

11

trim   trim

10

grain

12   INTERFACING

Turn in the seam allowance at the ends of the petersham and fold the band over the petersham (Fig. 4).

Snip at the zip, turn under along the underlap and tack along the length of the band. Hem the extension and the front ends (Fig. 5).

Machine or stab stitch along the waist band seam, stitch through the skirt and inside waistband, not through the front of the band (Fig. 6).

Elasticised waistband

This is used for knitted fabrics and gives a smooth finish in front and a slight gather at the back to take up the ease and prevent stretching. Because elastic is used the back darts can be made smaller, or left out altogether, and the difference between skirt and band can be as much as 6.5cm ($2\frac{1}{2}$ inches), comprising of 1.3cm ($\frac{1}{2}$ inch) to ease in at the front and 5cm (2 inches) at the back.

Substitute the back half of the petersham with elastic of the same width, cut 5cm

(2 inches) shorter and stitch a 5cm (2 inch) length of petersham at the end to make the underlap (Fig. 7).

Sew the waistband to the skirt as shown in Fig. 2.

Sew the petersham sections as in Fig. 3 but do not sew the elastic (Fig. 8). Fold the waistband over and finish as shown in Figs. 4, 5 and 6, making sure that the elastic is stretched to allow the band to be folded and stitched evenly.

Strong machine finished waistband

This is a useful finish for children's clothes, denims etc., and where the machined effect adds to the style of the garment.

Lay the petersham to the wrong side of the band and shape end if required. Catch stitch all round (Fig. 9).

Fold the band with right sides together along the centre fold and machine each end. Do not stitch through the petersham. Trim the corner. Turn to the right side and press (Fig. 10).

Using the un-interfaced side, lay the right

side of the band to the wrong side of the garment, easing as before (Fig. 11a).

Machine and press the seam into the band (Fig. 11b).

Turn in the remaining long edge over the petersham and tack over the seam. Machine all round band (Fig. 11c).

If required, make a buttonhole by machine or hand.

Faced waistline using fabric

Some trousers or skirts are finished with a shaped facing, when comfort or style call for it. When there is a yoke to the garment, this is interfaced and the facing cut to match the yoke and not itself interfaced. Otherwise the facing is interfaced before being sewn to the skirt. Use the weight of interfacing suitable for the garment fabric. The garment is completed before the facing is sewn in, any lining is tacked in and any yoke seams pressed towards the waist.

Cut out the facing pieces, separate and place the wrong side to the interfacing.

Tack all round inside the sewing line and cut out. This ensures that the pieces match exactly (Fig. 12).

Join the seams and trim back the interfacing, press open (Fig. 13).

Finish the lower edge by overlocking the raw edge to the interfacing (Fig. 14a), or trim the interfacing back 0.6cm ($\frac{1}{4}$ inch), turn facing over interfacing and machine down (Fig. 14b).

Place the right side of the facing to the right side of the skirt, matching seams and easing garment to fit. Machine (Fig. 15).

Grade the seam (Fig. 16a).

Snip through to the stitching line (Fig. 16b). Understitch the facing to the seam to stop it rolling back (Fig. 16c). Turn the facing to the wrong side and press well. Fold under the end seam allowances, mitring slightly to avoid the zip, and hem to the zip tape (Fig. 17a).

Catch the facing to the seams and darts (Fig. 17b).

Sew hook and eye to the top of the facing to keep it in place and to prevent strain on the zip (Fig. 17c).

For a yoke facing, proceed as above but hem it all round the yoke seam to provide a neat finish (Fig. 18).

Faced waistline using shaped petersham

It is possible to purchase shaped petersham but if this is not available then shape a straight piece by pulling it under a medium hot iron, stretching one side slightly (Fig. 19).

When attaching the petersham, great care must be taken to make sure that the inside diameter is sewn to the garment.

Fit the petersham to the body allowing 1.3cm ($\frac{1}{2}$ inch) extra at each end. Finish the garment as for the faced waistline and trim the waist seam to 1.3cm ($\frac{1}{2}$ inch), neatening the edge by overlocking (Fig. 20).

Place the inside curve of the petersham over the waist seam line on the right side, ease the skirt and tack. Sew one line of machining along the edge of the petersham and a second line 0.3cm ($\frac{1}{8}$ inch)

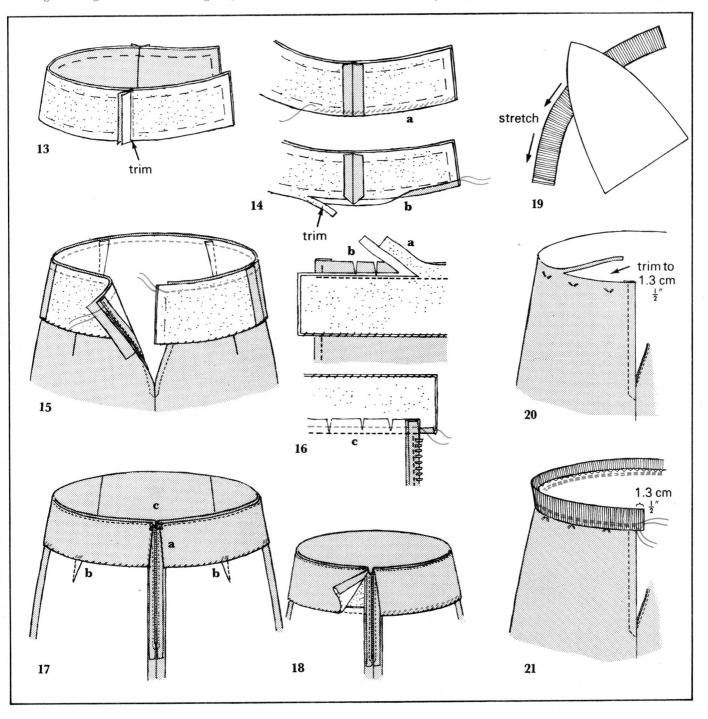

13 trim

14 a / b trim

b a

16 c

15

17 c a b b

18

19 stretch

20 trim to 1.3 cm $\frac{1}{2}''$

21 1.3 cm $\frac{1}{2}''$

away (Fig. 21).

Turn to the wrong side, fold under the petersham turnings and finish as Fig. 17.

BELTS

A belt made of fabric is a good alternative to a purchased one in that it does not 'break' the line of the garment. This can be disastrous if the figure is not all it should be, as the eye is drawn to the waist instead of taken away from it.

There are various interfacings which can be used to stiffen belts: petersham, boned petersham, Vilene, commercial belt stiffening. The latter is not suitable if the belt is to be finished by top stitching.

Cut the interfacing 15cm (6 *inches*) longer than the waist measurement, shaping the end to a point or curve as required (Fig. 22a).

Cut two pieces of fabric the length and width of the interfacing plus turnings (Fig. 22b).

Lay the petersham centrally on the wrong side of one piece of fabric and catch stitch the turnings in place, snipping the corners to enable the fabric to lie flat (Fig. 23).

Press the turnings of the other piece to the wrong side and lay it over the petersham. Either tack into place if the belt is to be top stitched (Fig. 24a), or ladder stitch together for a plain belt (Fig. 24b).

Make a hole for the buckle 3.8cm (1½ *inches*) from the plain end, buttonhole stitch round or apply an eyelet (Fig. 25a). (Kits are available in many colours and instructions are given with each set).

Place the prong of the buckle through the hole and hem the edge down to the wrong side (Fig. 25b).

Check for the correct position of the hole at the shaped end and make a hole (Fig. 25c).

Stab stitch

Working from the right side, push the needle down vertically, and pull the needle through from the wrong side. Then push the needle up vertically and pull through from the right side. The stitches should be very small and evenly spaced (Fig. 26).

Catch stitch

Working from the wrong side, pick up a thread of the fabric, then pick up a thread of the interfacing. The stitches must not go through to the right side (Fig. 27).

Ladder stitch

Slip the needle through each fold of fabric in turn, creating a series of straight stitches which should be invisible (Fig. 28).

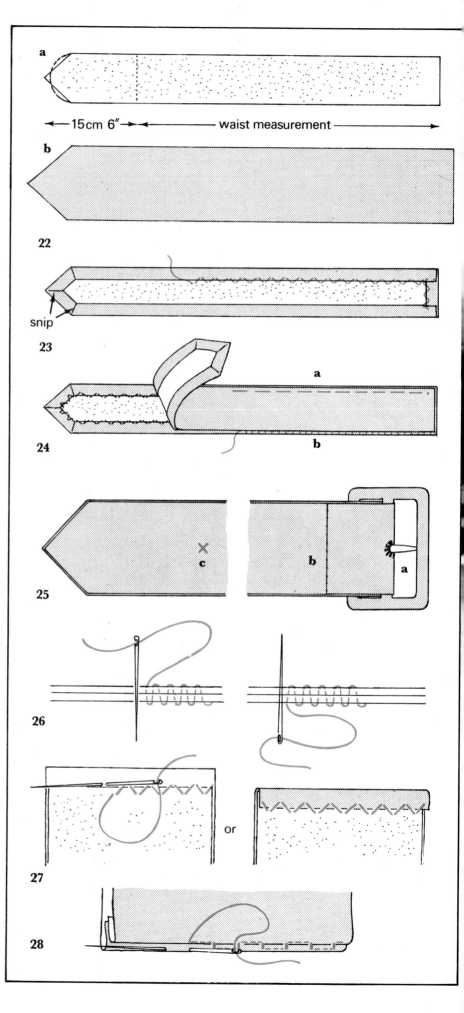

Shoulder pads

Shoulder pads are used to correct figure irregularities or to accentuate a prevailing fashion line. For example, in the 1940's, shoulder pads were used to support the darted sleeve heads which were then fashionable. During the 1950–60's, the smooth sleeve head which did not require such support, became fashionable. Today's designers are once again softening the look with ease and gathers so shoulder pads are now again needed to support these lines. They should not be obvious when so used but are definitely necessary to the look and line of the garment.

BASIC POINTS TO REMEMBER
If the pattern calls for shoulder pads, make them before fitting the garment, and pin them in each time it is tried on. This will ensure that the finished line of the garment is as the designer intended it to be.
Before making the pads two points have to be considered:

1. The figure
A figure with square shoulders will only need a thin pad to hold the desired shape. Sloping shoulders will need a thicker pad made with several layers of padding. For uneven shoulders it is necessary to build an individual pad for each shoulder to create a balanced look.

2. The garment fabric
If the garment is to be washed, then the pads should be made of 0.6cm ($\frac{1}{4}$ inch) thick foam plastic and covered either with self fabric or nylon fabric. If the garment is always to be dry cleaned, then tailors' wadding is ideal. The shoulder pads need not be covered if the garment is lined.

MAKING THE PATTERN FOR THE PADS
Remember that the shoulder pads should be unobtrusive and not leave a hard line where they end. To avoid this, cut the largest section of padding slightly larger than you think is necessary, it can always be trimmed a little afterwards.

PATTERN FOR A SET IN SLEEVE
Tailored jacket or coat shoulder pad
Take the front and back bodice pattern pieces and lay them down with the shoulder sewing lines matching. Over these place tissue or tracing paper to cover the armhole and shoulder lines. Trace along the shoulder line and extend for 1.3cm ($\frac{1}{2}$ inch). Follow the armhole line from notch to notch (Fig. 1, line A to B), extending gradually to 1.3cm ($\frac{1}{2}$ inch) at the shoulder.
Draw from A to B to the shoulder line at the neck in curved lines (Fig. 1).

Dress shoulder pad
Make the pattern as above but draw the armhole line from C and D, 7.5cm (3 inches) down from the shoulder line.

PATTERN FOR A RAGLAN SLEEVE
Take the front, back and sleeve pattern pieces and lay them in order, overlapping on the seam lines from the neck edge to the shoulder, as far as possible. Overlay with tissue or tracing paper. Trace the pad pattern as before, curving up from the notch to the shoulder and neck points (Fig. 2).
For a light shoulder pad these patterns would be sufficient if used with a single layer of padding.

MAKING A LAYERED PAD
Cut a base to the pattern in holland for heavy weight garments, or in fine canvas or mull for lightweight garments. Cut one piece of tailors' wadding or foam plastic to the size of the pattern. Also cut two or three other pieces successively 1.3cm ($\frac{1}{2}$ inch) smaller in length and width, but keeping them level at the shoulder edge. Tack each layer of padding to the base fabric as shown (Fig. 3).

To cover
Cut two pieces of fabric (self fabric or

nylon), with the cross-grain along the shoulder line. Make this 3.8cm (1½ inches) larger than the basic pattern (Fig. 4a). Sandwich the pad between the two layers of fabric and pin each layer along the shoulder line of the pad (Fig. 4b). Turn the raw edges under on the largest section of the pad and pull gently over the shoulder edge. Turn under the edge of the lower covering piece of fabric and pin and hem the two pieces of covering fabric together neatly all around the edge (Fig. 4c).

To use the pad

With the largest section of the pad towards the garment, pin it in place for fittings and only sew it in after the sleeve has been sewn in and pressed. Catch the pad at the neck edge and to the sleeve seam, making sure it extends for 1.3cm (½ inch) into the sleeve head (Fig. 5).

Padding the sleeve head

When making a tailored coat or jacket, another piece of wadding is placed in the sleeve head to soften the line. This will prevent the sleeve seam being impressed onto the sleeve. It will also help to support the shape of a darted or gathered sleeve. Measure the length between the back and front balance marks on the pattern and cut the wadding to that length by 5cm (2 inches) wide. Shape as shown (Fig. 6a).
Place the curved side to the sleeve so that the wadding extends 0.6cm (¼ inch) at the sleeve seam (Fig. 6b).
Using matching thread, hand stitch firmly in place inside the sleeve sewing line, working through all thicknesses (Fig. 6c).

Small pad

For a smaller pad to support gathers at the sleeve head in a dress or blouse, cut a piece of 0.6cm (¼ inch) thick foam plastic 10cm (4 inches) long and 3.8cm (1½ inches) wide and shape as shown (Fig. 7a).
Cut two pieces of dress or blouse fabric the same size plus 1.3cm (½ inch) seam allowance, the straight edge to be cut on the cross-grain (Fig. 7b). Cover in the same way as for the larger pads.
Pin the pad so that it is in the sleeve head with the straight edge standing on the seam. Stitch firmly to the seam by hand. As it is sewn in, it will curve and support the gathers (Fig. 7c).

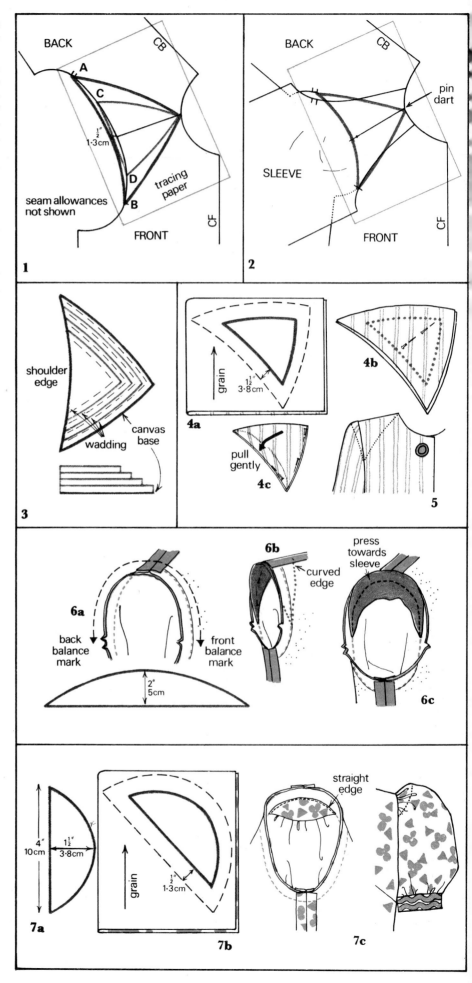

Decorative pockets

Pockets are made using one of two basic methods. They can be made from self fabric which is applied to the garment, or they can be made of lining fabric pushed to the inside through a seam or slash opening. These pockets are sometimes covered by a welt or a flap. All the pocket designs given here are variations of these two basic constructions.

Preparation of pockets

To achieve a crisp and professional finish, it is essential to plan the preparation and the placing of the pockets carefully. The positioning of pockets is most important, as they are often the main styling feature of the garment. For pockets to be positioned below the waist, the main rule is that they should be placed at a level where the hands can be slipped into them naturally and comfortably. If they are placed too close to the hem they will look and feel awkward. In certain cases, however, the rules are flexible. Pockets above the waistline, and patch pockets placed anywhere, are usually strictly decorative so it is better to concentrate on whether the position is flattering, regardless of how inaccessible the pocket may be.

When making any pattern adjustments, do not overlook the pockets as they may require repositioning.

Interfacing pockets

All types of pockets made in loosely woven or lightweight fabrics need to be interfaced. The interfacing preserves the pocket line, provides added strength and reinforces the opening. A lightweight interfacing, placed on the underside of the garment, has sufficient body to give the finished pocket a crisp feel and appearance. Welts and flaps should also be interfaced to preserve their shape and resilience. The interfacing is usually cut on the bias grain to extend 1.5cm ($\frac{5}{8}$ inch) beyond the foldline. Patch pockets are not usually interfaced, but are generally lined for a good finish. To achieve accurate shaping when making patch pockets it is worth tacking carefully round a paper template for both the shape of the pocket and the flap. This will ensure that all the pockets on a garment are of the same size and shape. It also makes the machining round curves much easier because it makes the fabric firmer. Any top-stitching lines should also be marked with tacking stitches before the pocket is made up. For top-stitching lines of an unusual shape such as in designs 12 and 16, make a separate template and mark the line with tacking stitches.

The top-stitching should, whenever possible, be worked before the pocket is stitched to the garment.

PATCH POCKETS
Patch pockets with a mock flap

Patch pockets can be made in virtually any shape desired and designs 1, 2, 3 and 4 are all based on a simple lined patch pocket

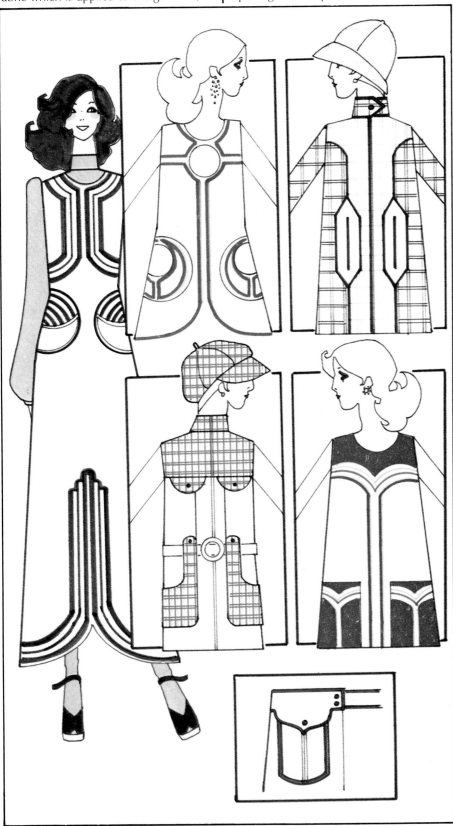

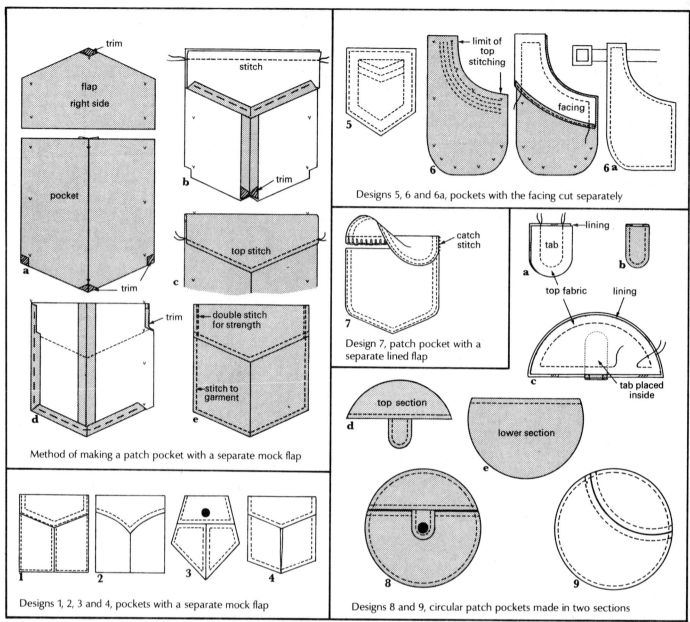

trim

flap

right side

stitch

pocket

b

top stitch

c

a

trim

d

trim

double stitch
for strength

stitch to
garment

e

Method of making a patch pocket with a separate mock flap

1

2

3

4

Designs 1, 2, 3 and 4, pockets with a separate mock flap

limit of
top
stitching

facing

5

6

6a

Designs 5, 6 and 6a, pockets with the facing cut separately

catch
stitch

7

Design 7, patch pocket with a
separate lined flap

lining

tab

a

b

top fabric

lining

c

tab placed
inside

top section

d

lower section

e

8

9

Designs 8 and 9, circular patch pockets made in two sections

with a mock flap. However, in the case of these pockets, the flap section is cut separately and turned over to the right side of the pocket, as they have either a seam or a pleat down the centre.

Patch pockets with a separate facing

Designs 5, 6 and 6a are based on a simple lined patch pocket with the facing cut separately, which in this case is turned and hemmed to the wrong side of the pocket and not the right. The top-stitching on design 6 is worked before the facing is applied.

Design 6a is made in the same way as design 6. A space is left when the pocket is stitched to the garment through which a belt can be slotted.

Patch pocket with a separate flap

Design 7 is based on a simple, lined patch pocket but the lined flap is worked

separately from the pocket and is fastened with a button and buttonhole. If the pocket is purely decorative then the button can be sewn on through all thicknesses of fabric, omitting the buttonhole.

Patch pockets based on circles

All these designs are based on the techniques of a simple, lined patch pocket. The opening of the pockets is either achieved by having a buttonhole type slit, two shapes made separately to form the circle, or a hole in the centre of the circle.

Pockets made from two shapes

Designs 8 and 9 are constructed from two separate shapes, as shown.

Pocket with contrast backing

For design 10, the main pocket is made as a simple, lined patch but the top-stitched pocket backing is made separately (un-

lined) and extends into the pocket. The raw edge of the backing section is finished with buttonhole stitch worked through to the garment and it is covered by the main pocket overlapping it as shown in the diagram above.

Pockets with buttonhole slit opening

For designs 11 and 12, the pocket and lining are cut in two halves and seamed at either end of the straight edge, leaving an opening in the centre to the required length. They are made up as shown. Alternatively, the same designs can be made by working a large bound buttonhole across a circular patch pocket for added strength.

On design 11, the inner line of top-stitching is marked round a template and worked first. The pocket is then top-stitched round the outer edge, directly onto the garment.

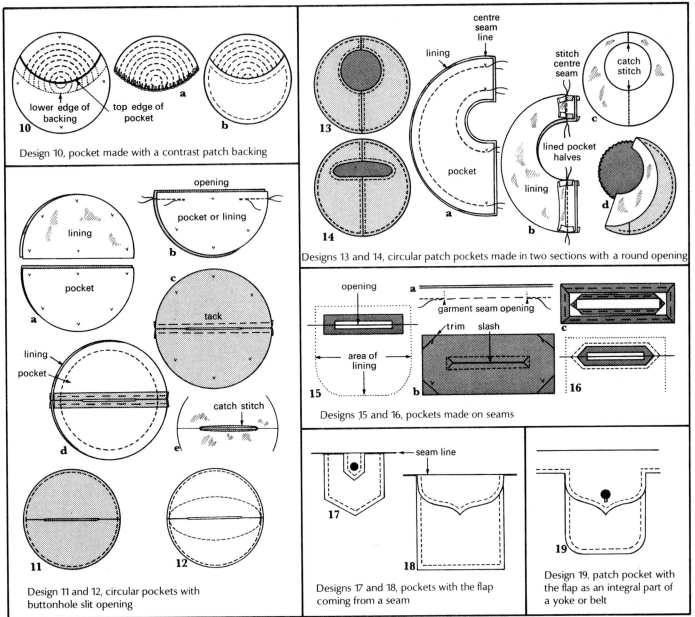

Design 10, pocket made with a contrast patch backing

Designs 13 and 14, circular patch pockets made in two sections with a round opening

Design 11 and 12, circular pockets with buttonhole slit opening

Designs 15 and 16, pockets made on seams

Designs 17 and 18, pockets with the flap coming from a seam

Design 19, patch pocket with the flap as an integral part of a yoke or belt

Pockets with a hole opening

Designs 13 and 14 are both based on two halves of a circle. A contrast backing is cut to a size larger than the intended circular opening and zigzag stitched in place directly onto the garment. The pocket is then placed centrally over the contrast fabric and top-stitched in position.

POCKETS IN A SEAM
Seam pockets with a patch

Designs 15 and 16 are made in the same way, using applied patches of different shapes over the seam as shown. Design 16 has a line of top-stitching worked the width of the machine foot away from the outer edge of the patch to give extra interest.

Cut a patch to the required shape and size, allowing 1.5cm ($\frac{5}{8}$ inch) turnings on the outer edges. Mark the size of the pocket opening on the patch and indicate the outer edge with tacking stitches.

Machine stay-stitch round the shape of the opening just inside the marked edge. Turn and tack all seam allowances to the back of the patch. Press carefully on the wrong side. Tack and slip-stitch the patch over the seam opening and press. Tack one piece of the lining fabric pocket to the wrong side of the opening and finish as for a bound buttonhole. Lay the second lining piece onto the first and stitch all round the edge. Press and remove tacking stitches from seam opening.

These pockets can be worked either into a seam across the garment or into a side seam. If the pocket is on a side seam, the pocket lining should be cut to the shape of a side pocket.

Flap or tab worked into seam

For designs 17 and 18, the main pocket is made as for a basic, lined patch pocket and the tab or flap is made separately and stitched into the seam of the garment,

for example the yoke seam on a dress or jacket.

Design 19 is made in the same way except the flap is integral with a belt, waistband or a yoke.

Working with pleats

Pleats are folds of fabric which provide controlled fullness in certain parts of a garment. They can be placed either singly or in a series, and can be pressed flat or left unpressed, as the style of the garment dictates. Pressed pleats give a smooth, slimming line to a garment and unpressed pleats a softer, fuller shape.

Fabrics

The type of fabric dictates how the pleats hang, so choose it carefully. Consider the grain and check the layout given with the pattern, remembering that pleats on the lengthwise grain fall well, while those on the crosswise grain tend to bunch out.

Any firmly woven fabric such as wool, gaberdine or linen will hold a pleat well, but pleats in loosely woven fabrics, knits and silk look better if they are top-stitched.

Patterns for pleated skirts should be bought by the hip measurement and patterns with pleated bodices by the bust measurement.

If any alteration in width is required, dis-tribute it evenly throughout all the pleats to keep them uniform. When tapering pleats to fit the waistline, keep the top fold on the same grain and make any adjustment to the under fold, remembering to distribute alterations evenly.

Preparing the fabric before cutting. Before you start cutting out a pleated skirt, it is essential that the fabric is perfectly square in the grain. Use the thread drawing method by drawing a thread out of the fabric and cutting the fabric along the line of the drawn thread.

Types of pleat

Box pleats. These are made by making two equal folds and turning them away from each other, the under folds meeting in the centre beneath the pleat (Fig. 1).

Inverted pleats. Inverted pleats are the reverse of box pleats. Two folds of equal depth are turned towards each other to meet at the centre, the fullness lying underneath (Fig. 2).

Knife pleats. These are narrow folds all running in the same direction. For com-fort, ease of movement and correct hang, knife pleats are sometimes cut 1.3 to 2cm ($\frac{1}{2}$ to $\frac{3}{4}$ inch) wider at the hem (Fig. 3).

Straight pleats. These pleats are the same width for their full length. They can be folded over each other to fit into a waist-band, or used as a decorative panel on a skirt or dress.

Unpressed pleats. Unpressed pleats can be folded in the same way as pressed pleats, but are left to hang free and take their own line.

If a bunchy effect is required for a particular design, the fabric should be cut on the crosswise grain. For example, a full-headed two-piece sleeve looks better if the top part is cut in this way (Fig. 4).

A bunchy effect is not generally suitable for unpressed pleats on a skirt, so cut on the lengthwise grain of the fabric. Never try to save material by cutting one skirt pattern piece on the lengthwise grain and the other on the crosswise grain of the fabric – the effect can be disastrous.

Contrast fabric inverted pleat. Inverted pleat underlays can look attractive in a contrast material. If the pattern does not have a separate piece for the underlay, adjust it as follows. Cut the pattern on the under fold line and add 1.5cm ($\frac{5}{8}$ inch) turning to all cut edges.

Sew the contrast fabric to the under fold

line before making the pleat (Fig. 5).

Top-stitching pleats

It is possible to make a fashion feature of top-stitched pleats. Tack the pleats flat through all the layers of fabric before stitching. A bold effect is required, so use a large needle in the sewing machine, set the machine to the longest stitch and use buttonhole twist for both threads.

Before working the top-stitching on a garment, take a spare piece of the fabric, make some pleats and practise the stitches, adjusting the tension until the desired effect is achieved.

Fine fabrics which do not hold a pleat well are best top-stitched along both top and under folds for the entire length of the pleat.

As long as the pleat is on the straight grain of the fabric, it can be stitched either from the top or the bottom. If the grain is not straight it is better to stitch from the bottom of the pleat upwards to avoid stretching the fabric (Fig. 6).

If the fabric is stretched it will create a slight fullness at the hem which means that the pleat will not hang straight.

The best stage at which to work the top-stitching is before the skirt is sewn onto the waistband or the bodice, and after the hemline is finished.

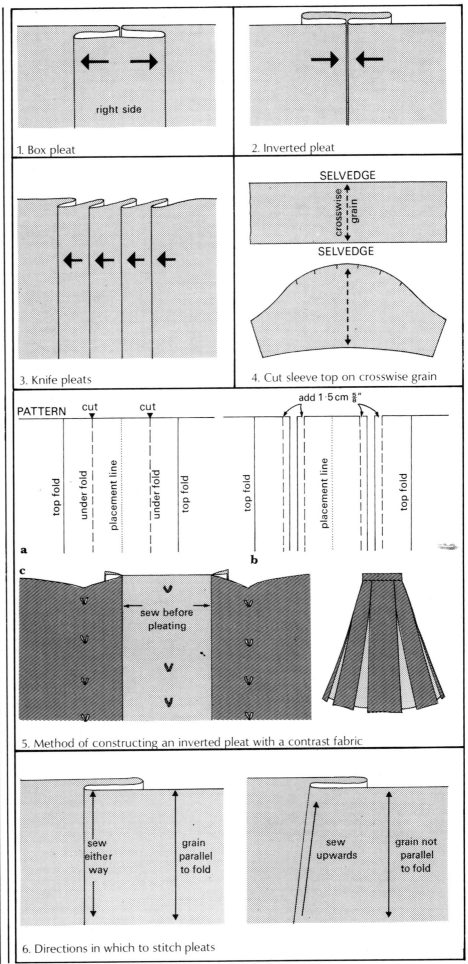

1. Box pleat

2. Inverted pleat

3. Knife pleats

4. Cut sleeve top on crosswise grain

5. Method of constructing an inverted pleat with a contrast fabric

6. Directions in which to stitch pleats

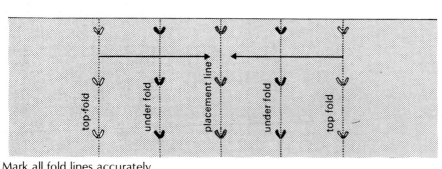

7. Mark all fold lines accurately

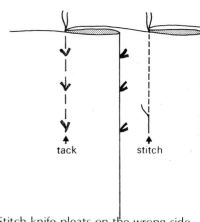

10. Stitch knife pleats on the wrong side

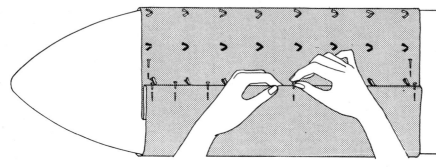

8. Pin each pleat at lower and upper ends and then along the length

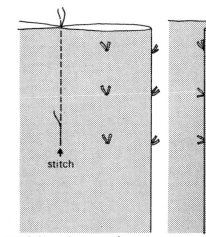

11. Stitch box pleats on the right side

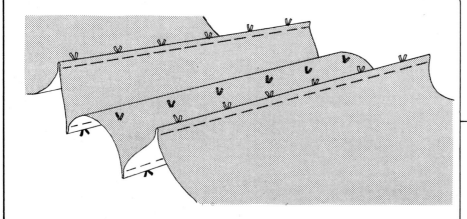

9. Tack the pleat folds on the right side, then tack those on the wrong side

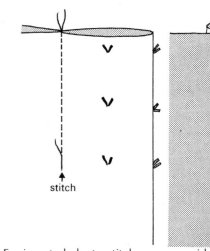

12. For inverted pleats, stitch on wrong side

The general construction of pleats

All pleats should be shaped with precision, so always transfer the pattern markings accurately, using different coloured tailor tacks for the top and under folds and for the placement line (Fig. 7). Lay the fabric on a flat surface. An ironing board is ideal, as the fabric can be pinned to the cover when the initial folding takes place. Pin each pleat at the upper and lower ends and then along the length, keeping it free from the under layer (Fig. 8).

Beginning at the lower edge, tack the pleat folds on the right side, then turn the fabric over and tack the folds on the wrong side. Tack down any which are to be top-stitched. Tack across pleats at waistline and tack up the garment for fitting (Fig. 9).

Fitting

When the skirt is tacked up, try it on to make sure that the pleats hang straight. If the skirt is tight over the hips or stomach, adjust each pleat under fold until it hangs correctly. However, the problem should not arise if the pattern has been adjusted correctly before cutting out.

If the pleats spring open at the hem, raise the waistline. Pin the skirt to a length of tape fastened round the waist, and raise the tape until the pleats hang straight. Adjust the under folds evenly. If the pleats overlap at the hem, lower the waist slightly in the same way and adjust the pleat under folds evenly.

Finishing the pleats

When finishing pleats always work with the front and back of the skirt separated. Mark any fitting alterations before un-tacking the side seams and starting work on the pleats.

Top-stitch knife pleats on the wrong side for a smooth effect, making sure to finish them securely at the lower end (Fig. 10).

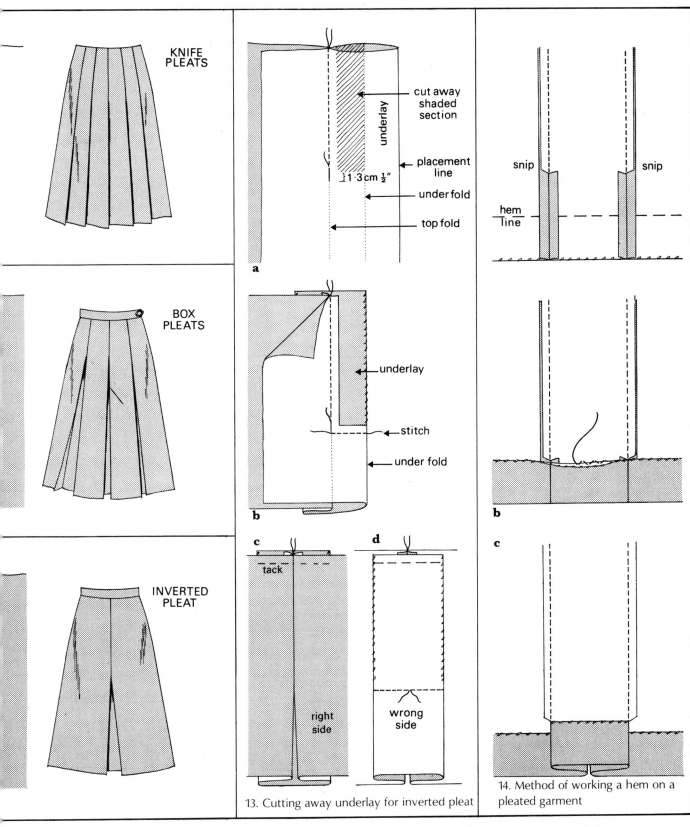

KNIFE PLEATS

BOX PLEATS

INVERTED PLEAT

cut away shaded section

underlay

placement line

1·3 cm ½"

under fold

top fold

a

underlay

stitch

under fold

b

c

tack

right side

d

wrong side

13. Cutting away underlay for inverted pleat

snip

snip

hem line

b

c

14. Method of working a hem on a pleated garment

Stitch box pleats on the right side for desired length and press pleat flat. (Fig. 11). Stitch inverted pleats on the wrong side and press flat (Fig. 12). If inverted pleats are being made in a heavy material, a section of the under fold can be cut away as shown, to reduce bulk (Figs. 13a–d). Machine stitch pleat to the length required and cut away half the under pleat as

shown. Neaten the outside raw edge and machine stitch across each side of the pleat, keeping the fold away from the background fabric. Tack across the top of the pleat.

Hemming pleated skirts

Run a line of tacking stitches along the hem line. Trim the hem evenly and over-sew the raw edge. Measure the hem depth above the hemline and snip seams at this point. Press the seam flat above the snip and open below it (Fig. 14). Slip stitch hem, retack pleats and press using a damp cloth.

All you need to know about tucks

TUCKS

A tuck is a fold of fabric used as a decorative feature, to hold fullness and to give shaping.

On children's garments tucks are useful for holding extra fabric allowed for growth, especially around a skirt hem or on a bodice.

Completely tucked fabric with no release for fullness, can be used for decorative panels, collars or cuffs.

Tucks are usually folded on the straight of grain, and for decorative purposes the fold is generally on the right side of the garment.

When used to control fullness, and shape the contour of the design, the fold is made on the inside of the garment. These tucks may be stitched on or off the grain and can be either straight or curved.

Fabric allowance

It is difficult to calculate the exact amount of extra fabric needed when tucking a section of garment not tucked in the original design. However, the extra allowance can be gauged at approximately twice the finished width of each tuck.

Decide on the width of the tuck, then work out how many will fit into the area required to be tucked. Multiply the width of the tuck by two, then multiply this by the total number of tucks to determine how much extra fabric will be needed.

It is important to work all the tucks across an area before marking out the pattern and cutting out.

Note: Remember to purchase sufficient extra fabric to that allowed on the pattern.

Pressing

Press each tuck after it has been stitched. First press the crease in the tuck from the underside of the fold on the right side of the fabric. Then press the entire tucked area on the wrong side. Avoid using too much steam as this tends to pucker the fabric and make indentations. To avoid this tendency to marking, with some fabrics it is necessary to use strips of brown paper under the fold of each tuck when pressing.

TYPES OF TUCKS
Pin tucks

These are very narrow tucks which can be arranged in groups or evenly spaced. They can be made automatically on many of the modern twin-needle sewing machines, which can also raise and cord the tucks, or they can be made on most other sewing machines by accurately top stitching 0.3cm ($\frac{1}{8}$ *inch*) away from the fold edge of the fabric (Fig. 1). For tuck gauge see Fig. 9. Suitable fabrics: Nun's veiling, voile, cotton lawn, Terylene lawn, silk, chiffon, cotton and lightweight wool or corduroy.

Wide tucks

These are made in a similar way to pin tucks but instead of stitching 0.3cm ($\frac{1}{8}$ *inch*) away from the fold edge, the stitching is usually 0.6 to 1.3cm ($\frac{1}{4}$ to $\frac{1}{2}$ *inch*) away from the fold edge.

The depth and spacing of these tucks will depend on the design of the garment, the type of fabric being tucked and the finished effect required. So experiment with some of the fabric being used before deciding on the depth of the tuck and the spacing required. Then make a double notched tuck guide to the required measurements (Fig. 8). Some suitable fabrics are the same ones as given for pin tucks, plus lightweight jersey fabrics and other knitted ones.

Corded tucks

Enclose the cord in the tuck and stitch, using a cording or zipper foot on the sewing machine.

If a slippery fabric is being used, it is advisable to tack the cord in place before stitching (Fig. 2).

Suitable fabrics: Corded tucks are best made on fabrics which are dry cleanable rather than washable because when the cord is inserted into the tuck it tends to be a little bulky, and if worked on a washable fabric, drying might be a problem. A fabric like PVC made into a raincoat would be ideal for tucking boldly around the hem and cuffs, or as decoration on patch pockets.

Cross tucks

These are a variation of normal pin tucks and when arranged in groups they can be a most attractive form of decoration on a garment.

Cross tucks consist of a second row of tucks made across a normal group of pin tucks. First work all the tucks across in one direction, then work the crossing tucks. Extra care must be taken with the second group of tucks to avoid the fabric slipping and to ensure that each crossing is true. (Fig. 3).

Suitable fabrics: Cross tucks are most effective when worked on fine fabrics such as lawn, lurex, voile and chiffon.

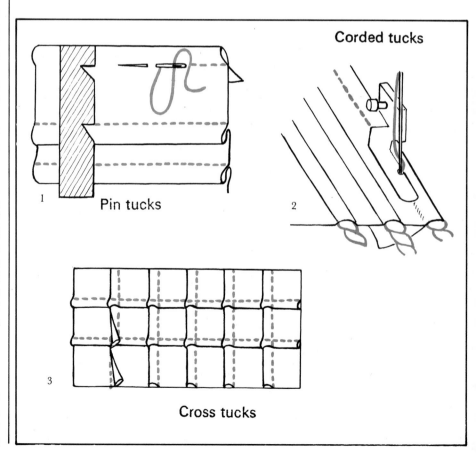

1   Pin tucks

Corded tucks

2

3

Cross tucks

Shell tucks

Crease the tuck and tack along the folded edge. Mark the length of each shell with a small dot at intervals. The length of the shell should be about twice the depth of the tuck.

Work running stitches along the tuck, and on reaching each dot, take two stitches over the tuck, drawing the thread up tight to form the shell pattern (Fig. 4).

Shell tucks can be used in groups, singly, running vertically or horizontally.

Suitable fabrics: These tucks are most successful when worked on very fine fabric such as lawn, cheesecloth, chiffon or any fine fabric which is normally difficult to work on and produce a neat finish.

Overhand tucks

Mark lines for the tiny tucks and work neat overhand stitches along the lines using either a self or contrast colour sewing thread.

These tucks can be worked in straight lines or in scallops (Fig. 5).

Suitable fabrics are the same ones given earlier for pin tucks.

Grouped tucks

Make several lines of tucks close together and press them all in one direction at the top. Stitch across the tucks in the direction they have been pressed. Then turn the tucks in the opposite direction and at the desired interval, stitch across them in the new direction. The tucks are turned alternately in this way until the required area has been completed (Fig. 6).

Suitable fabrics: this is a simple method of producing a decorative raised surface on a plain fabric and because the tucks are stitched alternatively from one direction to another, a striking effect can be obtained by using a fabric with a rich pile or sheen to produce a shaded texture, such as velvet or satin.

Hem stitched tucks

Mark the fold edge of the tuck along the grain of the fabric with tacking stitches. Draw out one or two threads for the finished width of the tuck at an even distance from either side of the fold line. Tack the tuck along the fold line and work the hem stitching from the underside of the tuck. Press the tuck flat in position and measure the distance to the fold line of the next tuck as shown for wide tucks. Mark the fold line with tacking stitches and repeat as for the first tuck (Fig. 7).

Suitable fabrics: Lightweight fabrics of a loose even weave where the threads can be withdrawn easily.

TUCK GUIDE
For wide tucks

Cut a 10 × 2.5cm (4 × 1 inch) strip of stiff cardboard, squaring the corners accurately. Measure the width of the tuck required down from the top and make a 0.6cm ($\frac{1}{4}$

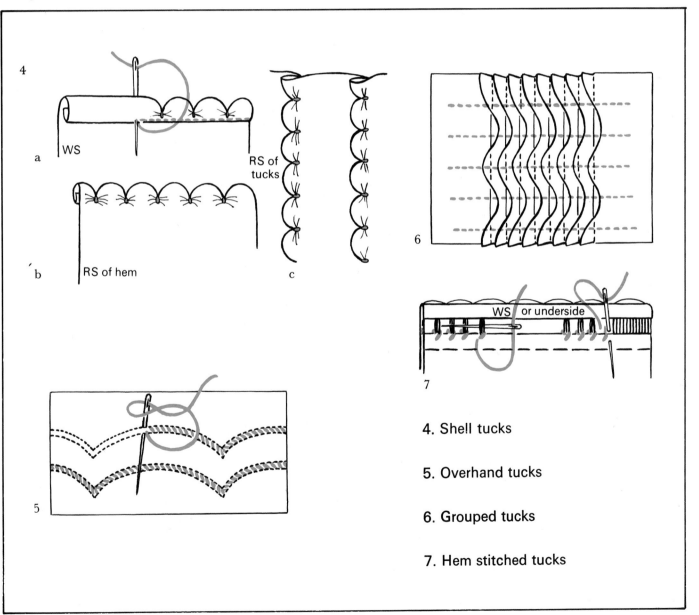

4. Shell tucks

5. Overhand tucks

6. Grouped tucks

7. Hem stitched tucks

inch) cut, parallel to the top. Make a second cut diagonally from below the first to make a triangular notch. Make another straight cut away from the first (the distance required between the tuck and the stitching), again notching out a diagonal (Fig. 8).

For pin tucks

Cut a rectangle of cardboard as for wide tucks. Mark the distance required between the fold edges and cut out a notch as described above (Fig. 9).

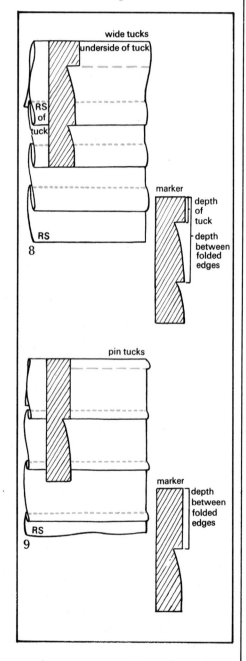

Sleeves

By altering the sleeve shape of a dress or a blouse it is quite easy to change the balance of the garment, to provide a new focus or to give a new importance to a plain-sleeved dress.

Here are a few ways of drafting sleeves, shown in the five illustrations below 1a, b, c, d, e. From a simple sleeve pattern you will be shown how to draft a variety of sleeves. Figures a and b both show a bell sleeve. Figure a is a simple bell sleeve which is cut wide. The bottom of the pattern is spread, and figure b has been gathered into a band.

Figure c is a gathered sleeve where the pattern is altered to give fullness to the head of the sleeve.

Figures d and e show both a long puff sleeve and a short puff sleeve. These are finished off with a cuff or gathered into a casing.

Choosing the sleeve

2a, b. Sleeves play a very important part in the design of a garment. They can add balance to a design (a), they are sometimes the focus of interest in a design (b). But before choosing the sleeve style there are a few points to be considered first.

3a, b. It is important not to add bulk or width to that part of your anatomy which is bulky enough already, like a large bosom with short puffed sleeves (a), and large hips with long, very full sleeves (b). Full sleeves can sometimes look ridiculous with a very full skirt.

4. Here the droopy sleeves accentuate the already droopy looking appearance. Always consider the bulk and character of the fabric to be used. The correct fullness for a jersey or a crepe fabric may be very skimpy in a voile.

Also consider the occasions when the garment is to be worn, and make sure that the sleeves chosen will not be unmanageable or a source of irritation. Will the garment be worn under a coat with tight sleeves and is the fabric for a full sleeve sufficiently crease resistant not to look crumpled and sad when it emerges?

Requirements

5. The following sleeve patterns can be drafted from a simple basic sleeve pattern. You will need a fresh piece of paper to draft the new pattern.

As in all pattern construction seam allowances are added only when the drafting is complete, so when adapting a commercial paper pattern make a copy without turnings to use in drafting the variations.

6a, b. If the basic pattern has an elbow dart cut up from the wrist to the dart point (a) then close the elbow dart (b).

7. Draw two lines parallel with the centre line from shoulder to wrist. Draw in both the lines about mid way between the centre line and the sleeve seam as shown.

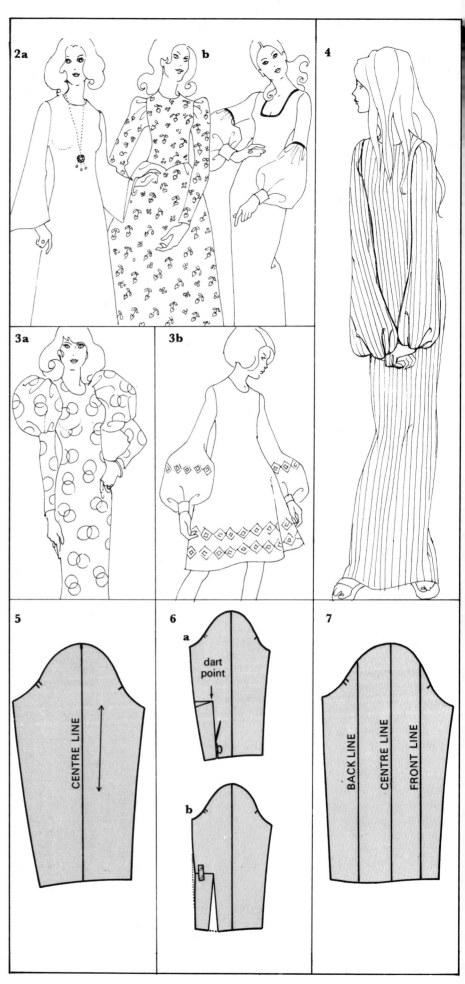

Bell sleeve

8. Slash the back and front lines and spread them at the bottom only for 3.8cm (1½ inches). The length of the sleeve armhole seam remains the same. Draw in the bottom edge of the sleeve in a smooth curve.

9. For a wider sleeve slash the centre line as well and spread to 3.8cm (1½ inches). Increase the spread of the back slash to 6.5cm (2½ inches).

10. If you want to gather this sleeve into a band, add a little to the length, adding more at the back than the front as shown. The length of the underarm seam remains the same, otherwise the sleeve would drop down over the hand.

11. Unless the wrist band is cut long enough for the hand to slip through, a bound opening will have to be made up the back line of the sleeve as shown.

Gathered sleeve head

12 a, b, c, d. For a sleeve with the head gathered into the armhole seam (a), slash the pattern across at the armhole points and then slash diagonally from points shown to centre line (b). Spread the pieces to give both extra height and width (c). Draw the new sleeve head with a good curve, not forgetting to add the original ease marks.

Whatever the fullness, the gathering is always between these marks, never below (d).

13. Further slashes will give more puff to the sleeve head.

Puffed sleeves

14. For a long puff, gathered top and bottom, slash and spread the pattern and add 2.5cm (1 inch) to the crown and to the wrist as shown.

15. For a short puff, gathered top and bottom, cut across the sleeve 7.5cm (3 inches) down from the armhole point. Slash and spread the pattern, then add to the height of the crown and the lower edge as shown.

16. Finish the puffs with a cuff or gather into a rouleau or elastic casing.

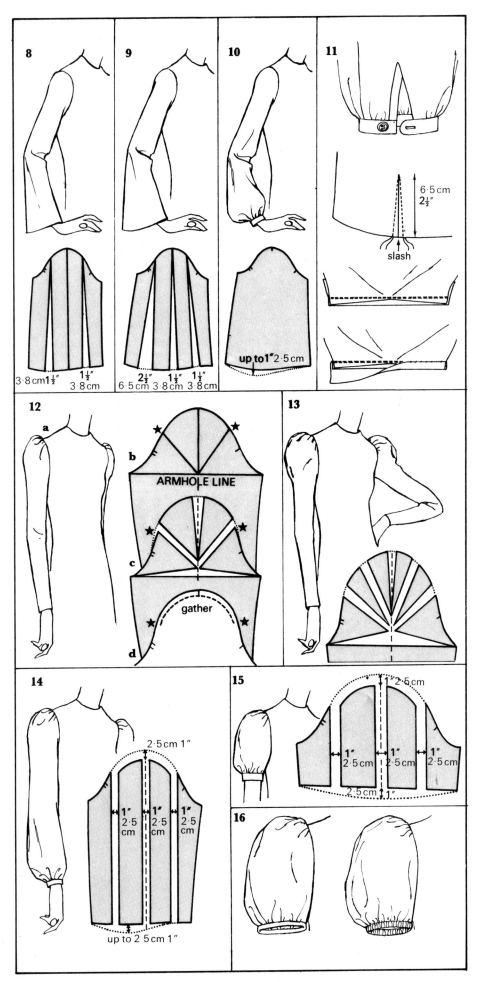

Cutting a raglan sleeve

Fashion trends show the emergence of a softer line. One way to achieve this is with the raglan sleeve. If the pattern you want to use is right in all details except for the sleeve, here's how to convert a simpl set-in sleeve to a raglan.

PREPARING THE PATTERN

Requirements

The pattern must have a simple bodice and plain set-in sleeves, without any shoulder detail and preferably with a high round neck. Before working on the pattern trim all seam allowances from it.

Patterns with contour bodice seaming are not suitable.

You will need a ruler, pencil, red crayon or felt tip pen, some large sheets of tracing paper and Sellotape.

Choosing the style

1a, b. You will need to decide on the depth of the raglan. You can have a simple raglan which runs into the original sleeve underarm line (a) or an extra deep raglan (b).

2a, b, c. If you are making a simple raglan you have a choice of sleeve line which can alter the appearance of your shoulder width. There is the raglan shape (a) or you can make the shoulders look wider (b) or narrower (c).

Back shoulder dart

A back shoulder dart has to be swung into the back neck before you cut the raglan sleeve.

3. Draw a line from the centre of the neck as shown. Cut along the line.

4. Close up the original dart. The cut opens up to form the new dart which should be drawn as shown.

Underarm bust darts

If the pattern front has an underarm bust dart it is usually best to swing this in to a front body dart. You can, if you wish, keep the underarm dart on the simple raglan version.

Mark the position of your bust point on the pattern. To do this measure the length from your shoulder to bust point and the distance from the centre front to bust point.

5. Extend the bust dart to the bust point as shown.

6. If the pattern already has a front body dart also extend that to the bust point as shown. Cut out the front body dart along these lines.

7. If the pattern does not have a body dart draw a line from bust point to waist and cut along this line.

8. Close the bust dart and stick a piece of paper behind the body dart that has opened up.

9. Draw in the new dart as shown: do not take it right up to the bust point as darts should never run right on to the bust.

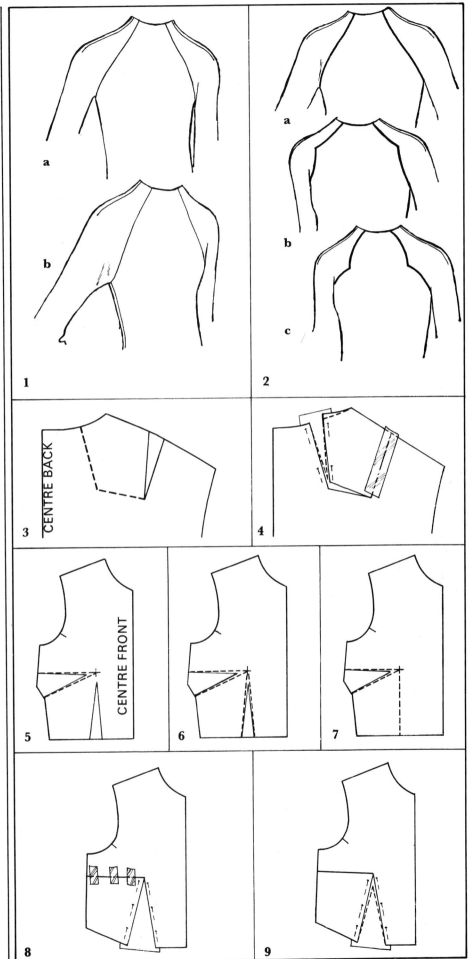

33

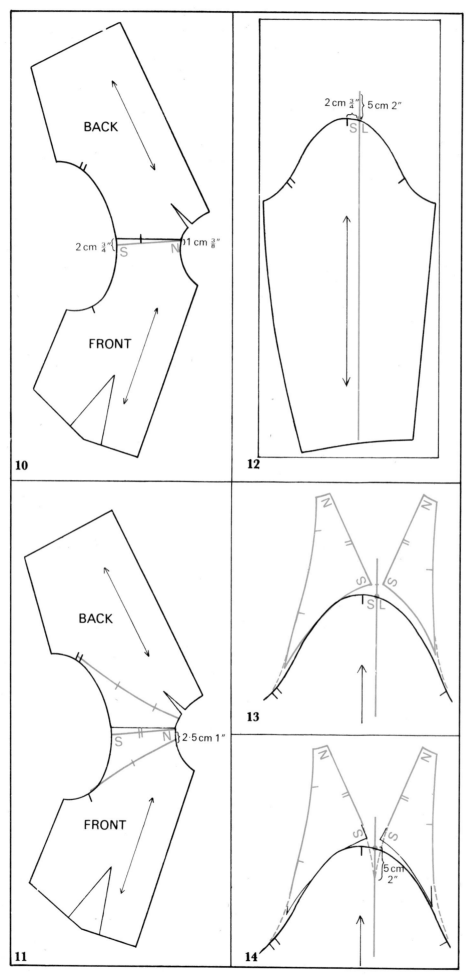

SIMPLE RAGLAN

10. Lay the bodice patterns out flat with the shoulder seams corresponding.
Draw new shoulder line on front 1cm ($\frac{3}{8}$ inch) down at neck and 2cm ($\frac{3}{4}$ inch) down at shoulder. Mark the new shoulder line N at neck edge and S at shoulder.

11. Outline the shape of the raglan. This line usually starts 2.5cm (1 inch) each side of N and goes down to the notches on the armhole. Mark the line in red and put in balance marks.
Lay a large sheet of tracing paper over the pattern. If the tracing paper is not large enough to cover the pattern stick pieces together with Sellotape.
Trace off the back, front and raglan sections, mark the raglan lines, the new shoulder line and put in the balance marks, grain lines and darts. Label.
Cut out the patterns along the outside lines and the raglan lines.

12. Make a tracing of the sleeve pattern, leaving 20cm (8 inches) of tracing paper clear above the crown. Trace off all sleeve markings such as darts, grain lines and balance marks.
To compensate for the alteration of the shoulder line on the bodice pattern, move the shoulder point 2cm ($\frac{3}{4}$ inch) to the front. Mark this point SL.
Draw a line parallel to the grain line through SL and extend the line for 5cm (2 inches) above the crown.
Cut the raglan section along the new shoulder line NS to separate the front raglan section from the back raglan.

13. Using these sections place the shoulder points S 1.3cm ($\frac{1}{2}$ inch) above SL and 0.6cm ($\frac{1}{4}$ inch) to each side of the extended line, with the armhole edge to the back and front crown line, as shown.

14. Draw all round new raglan line, curving gently into sleeve at armhole edge. Extend into the original sleeve head over the top of the sleeve head for 5cm (2 inches) to give a smooth narrow dart over the top of the arm.
Transfer balance marks, grain lines and darts to tracing. Cut out sleeve pattern. This gives a pattern without seam allowances, so mark this fact on all pattern pieces and remember to add 1.5cm ($\frac{5}{8}$ inch) all round when cutting out.
Having made the pattern it is a good idea to make it up in calico or cotton to check the fit before cutting into your fabric.

DEEP RAGLAN SLEEVES

First prepare the pattern as before, cutting off seam allowances and swinging under-arm and shoulder darts.

Set up the pattern as for a simple raglan and draw in a new shoulder line (Fig. 10).

15. Draw in the raglan line. This line should not be more than 3.8cm ($1\frac{1}{2}$ inches) to each side of N and not deeper than 5cm (2 inches) below the armhole point. Mark the lines in red and put in balance marks.

Lay a large sheet of tracing paper over the pattern. If the tracing paper is not large enough to cover the pattern stick pieces together with Sellotape. Trace off the back, front and raglan sections. Mark the raglan lines, the new shoulder line and put in the balance marks, grain lines and darts. Label each piece clearly.

Make a tracing of the sleeve pattern, leaving 20cm (8 inches) of tracing paper clear above the crown. Trace off all sleeve markings such as darts, grain lines and balance marks.

Find the point SL as in Fig. 12, and draw the line parallel to the grain line through this point as before.

16. Cut the raglan section along the new shoulder line to separate the front raglan section from the back raglan section.

Place the raglan pieces 1.3cm ($\frac{1}{2}$ inch) above SL and 0.6cm ($\frac{1}{4}$ inch) each side of extended line. Slash into raglan pieces as shown and spread close to crown line. Allow the under-armhole point to extend 5cm (2 inches) at back and front.

Join the new point to the elbow line in a gentle curve as shown.

17. Draw all round the new raglan line, curving into the sleeve and curving into the top of the sleeve head for 5cm (2 inches) to give a smooth narrow dart over the top of the arm.

Transfer balance marks, grain lines and darts to tracing. Cut out sleeve pattern.

You can either make a one piece sleeve following the outline or cut down the broken line illustrated and make a two piece sleeve. If you separate the pattern name each piece carefully.

This gives a pattern without seam allowances, so mark this fact on all pattern pieces and remember to add 1.5cm ($\frac{5}{8}$ inch) all round when cutting out.

Having made the pattern it is a good idea to make it up in calico or cotton to check the fit before cutting into your fabric.

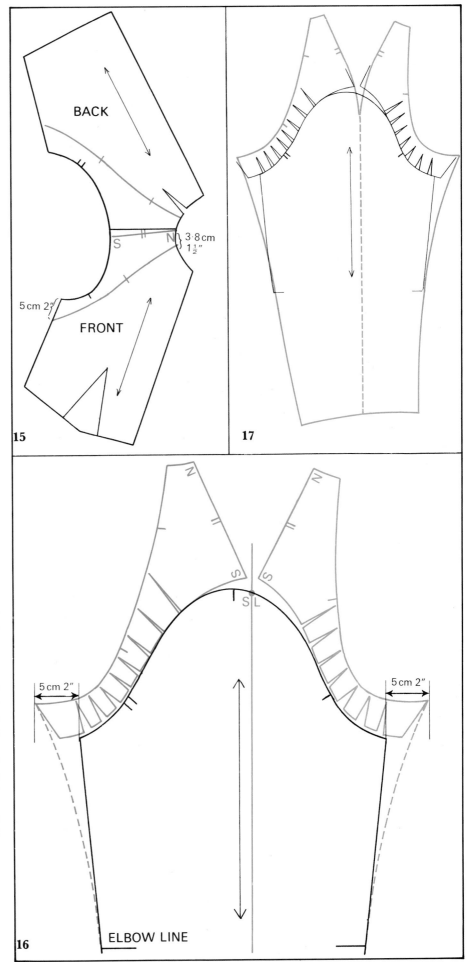

35

Decorative seams

Decorative seaming is a subtle way in which to add extra interest and individuality to a garment. Decorative seams are excellent for large or awkward figure shapes, for which a plain fabric is often more flattering. The plain fabric shows up the seams and reduces the overall impact of an ample figure. A small selection of decorated seams is shown on these pages but the variations are endless.

Here, a plain seam is decorated with top stitching worked with buttonhole twist wound onto the spool. Contrasting colours have been used for a bold effect.

This plain seam is simply decorated with spaced lines of straight stitching in a self colour. The stitching is worked using Sylko, both on the spool and on top of the sewing machine, and the stitches made fairly long. Further lines of stitching could be added and the stitch adjusted to an even longer length if desired. However, too many lines of stitching would not look so attractive.

The top stitching here is worked as a zigzag stitch, the line closest to the seam being more widely spaced than the outer line.

A plain seam, decorated with spaced lines of straight stitching in a contrasting colour. The contrasting colour stands out and shows up better at a distance.

For more textural interest, the straight lines of top stitching have been worked here in wool which is wound onto the spool, and the zigzag lines with buttonhole twist wound onto the spool, with the spoolcase tension loosened. Sylko is threaded on top of the machine with the tension set at normal. The thicker yarns should appear to be couched onto the fabric.

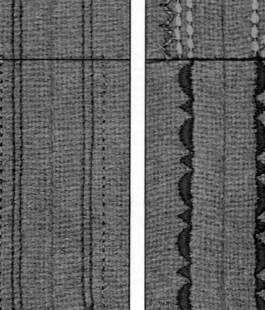

Several lines of straight stitching worked in different colours gives a softer effect.

Automatic patterns worked in a strong colour contrast using Sylko, make pretty seam decorations. When using automatic patterns to form decorative top stitching, follow the instructions supplied with the sewing machine.

The automatic patterns can be combined with lines of satin stitch of varying widths or lines of straight stitching. Avoid working too many lines of stitching or the effect of the individual patterns will be lost.

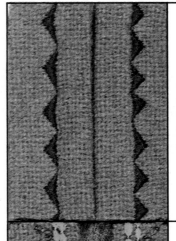

This channel seam is dramatically heightened when backed with a strong contrasting colour and top stitched with an automatic pattern in the same contrast.

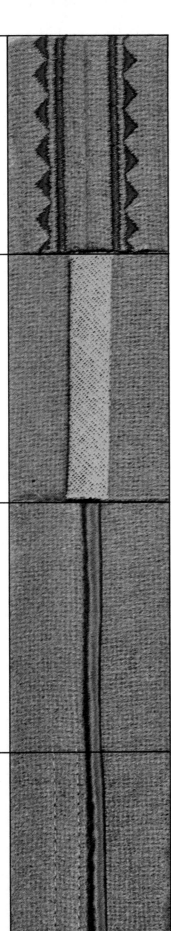

This bound seam relies on colour and textural contrast. Try using silk on wool; plain on patterned; bias weave (cut) and straight. Cut the bias binding strip approximately three times the width of the finished seam. With right sides together, stitch the binding along the stitch line on a single layer of fabric. Fold the binding over to the wrong side, tack and press. Place the inner edge of the binding on the right side of the seam line of the corresponding seam and work a line of stitching along the edge.

A channel seam takes on a new look when the space between the seam edge is widened and a fabric of a contrasting texture used for the backing. Here a heavy satin is used as a contrast to a firmly woven woollen fabric. The wool fabric is decorated with rows of straight stitching worked with wool on the spool, and with rows of widely spaced zigzag worked with buttonhole twist on the spool.

A piped seam can be successfully used for curved seams as the piping fabric is cut on the bias grain of the fabric. The piping can be of piping cord, quilting wool, chunky quilting wool, chunky knitting wool or similar yarns. If the piping cord is bulky, when joining a seam, cut it off level with the stitching line, leaving the binding fabric to continue under the seam. This is necessary to reduce bulk.

With the space between the seam edges widened to this extent, the backing fabric becomes more of an insertion than a seam. Great care must be taken in measuring the width of the backing fabric and the cutting down on the garment to allow for this new stitching line. Straight seams like the one shown are easier to handle than shaped ones. The top stitching used here is widely spaced zigzag stitch worked with buttonhole twist on the spool, and an automatic pattern worked with Sylko.

If the piping is narrow, some additional straight top stitching can be incorporated as extra decoration.
As this seam faces in one direction, the piping must be stitched to the top layer of the garment first to ensure a good line and then a second line of stitching next to the first, worked to join the seam.

Insertions make very pretty seam decorations. Here, Italian buttonhole insertion stitch has been worked in buttonhole twist in a bright contrasting colour for a striking effect. There are many insertion stitches to choose from, some of which form a stronger joining medium than others. The stitch and the type of yarn should be carefully chosen according to the type of fabric to be worked on. Heavy-weight insertions, for example, are not suitable for delicate fabrics.

Fitting trousers

TROUSER PATTERNS

Patterns generally conform to the measurements of a standard figure and it is often necessary to alter a pattern to accommodate individual figure proportions. Trousers create special fitting problems because of the complexity of the proportions involved.

It is important for all major alterations to be made on the pattern since little can be done once the garment has been cut out of the fabric. If there are a number of fitting problems, it would be advisable to test the pattern in calico first. Once a perfect fit has been achieved, use this as a basic pattern which can be adapted for all kinds of trousers.

Trouser patterns should be selected according to the hip measurement. However, there are other measurements which are required to alter the pattern correctly. Before locating the hip line on the pattern, make all the lengthwise adjustments; that is, the crutch length and the trouser length. Before cutting the fabric, check the pattern as described in stages below, and then make the alterations necessary for the figure. Although some further adjustments may be necessary in the first fitting, cutting out can be done with the assurance that the pattern has been proportioned to the individual body measurements.

Adjusting the length of the crutch

To determine the crutch length, sit on a hard chair and measure from the waistline to the seat (Fig. 1). To this measurement add 1.3cm (½ inch) ease if the hips are less then 89cm (35 inches), 2cm (¾ inch) if the hips are 89cm (35 inches) to 96.5cm (38 inches), and 2.5cm (1 inch) if the hips are more than 96.5cm (38 inches). The body measurement plus ease allowance is the total crutch length.

To adjust the length of the crutch, draw a line across the pattern at right angles to the grain line, from the widest part of the crutch to the side seam. The length of the pattern from the waistline to this line should be the same as the crutch length when taken in the sitting position, plus the ease allowance.

If the pattern is too long, then crease along the shortening line and fold a tuck to take up the desired amount. Tape in place. Redraw the seams and construction mark-

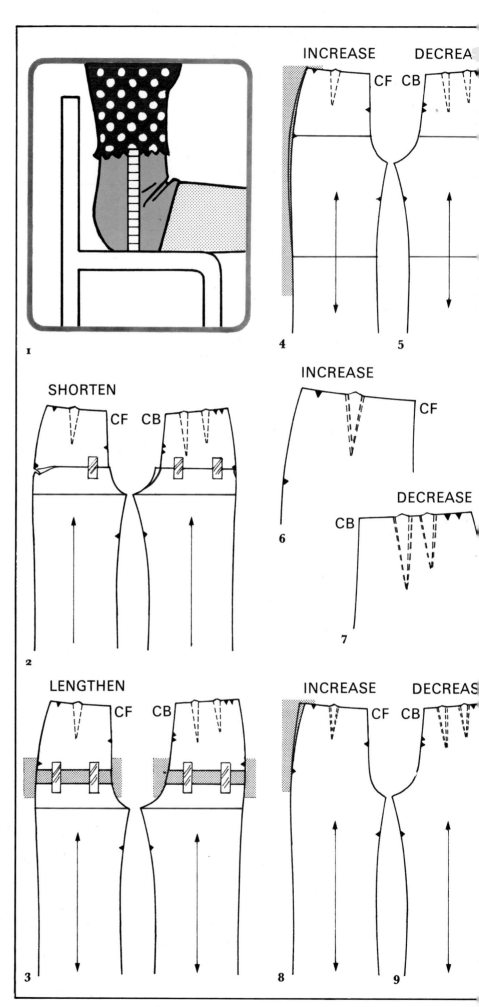

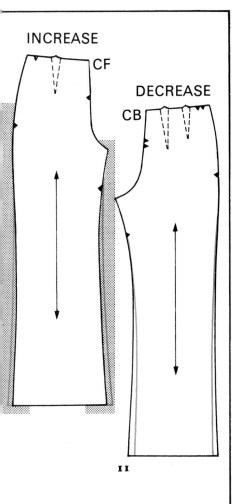

INCREASE
CF

DECREASE
CB

11

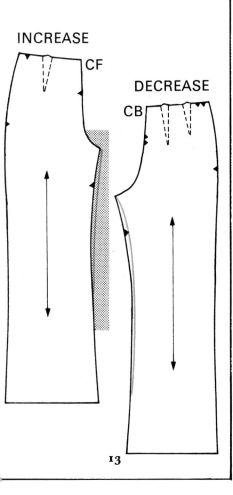

INCREASE
CF

DECREASE
CB

13

ings to retain the original shape of the side seam and the crutch seam (Fig. 2).

If the pattern is too short, cut along the lengthening line and open the pattern to the desired amount. Insert a piece of paper behind this section and tape in place. Redraw the seams and construction markings to retain the original shape of the side seam and the crutch seam.

Make. the same adjustment to the front and back pattern pieces (Fig. 3).

Adjusting the trouser length

Measure the length of the pattern from the waistline to the lower edge. This should be the same as the measurement from the waist to the ankle. If the pattern is too short or too long, use the same principle as shown in Figs. 2 and 3 to correct this. Make sure that there is adequate length for the hem allowance and for turn ups if these are required.

Locating the hip line

For the average figure the hip line is measured 20.5cm (8 inches) below the waistline. Measure down 20.5cm (8 inches) from the waist and draw a horizontal line on the pattern. The hip measurement will be taken at this point.

For the disproportionate figure, it is necessary to take three measurements on the body. First, measure 7.5cm (3 inches) below the waistline. Secondly, measure 18cm (7 inches) below the waistline and then 23cm (9 inches) below the waistline.

Draw three horizontal lines on the pattern at these points. The widest measurement will be showing at or in-between one of these points. The hip line on the pattern will be the larger measurement.

Adjusting the hip

Take the hip measurement on the pattern at the hip line. There should be 5cm (2 inches) ease allowance. If the pattern does not measure 5cm (2 inches) more than the body measurement, the pattern will need adjusting.

To increase the hip line, determine the amount needed, divide this total by four and increase each side seam by this amount. Measure the amount of adjustment out from the hip line edge at the side seam on both front and back pieces, and mark. Tape a piece of tissue under-

neath each pattern section. Taper from the mark at the hip line into the original cutting line both above the knee and at the waistline, retaining the shape of the leg and the width of the waist (Fig. 4).

To decrease the hip line, use the same principle as above but subtract the amount at the side seams (Fig. 5).

Adjusting the waistline

The ease allowance at the waistline should be 1.3 to 2cm ($\frac{1}{2}$ to $\frac{3}{4}$ inch). The waistline can be increased or decreased by adjusting the darts. Each dart can be increased or decreased by as much as 0.6cm ($\frac{1}{4}$ inch) but no more (Fig. 6 and 7).

If this adjustment is not sufficient, the side seams can also be altered. Divide the amount of increase or decrease by four, and adjust each side seam edge by this amount. Taper to the hipline, being careful not to change the hip measurement (Figs. 8 and 9).

Adjusting width of lower edge

If the lower edge of the pattern is too narrow, determine the amount to be added and divide this by four. Add this amount to the side and inside seam edges at the hemline. Taper from the hemline to the hipline on the side seams, also from the hemline to the crutch on the inside seams (Fig. 10).

If the pattern is too wide at this point, divide the total amount to be subtracted by four, using the same method as above, but subtracting and not adding (Fig. 11).

Adjusting the width of the leg

There is no standard amount of ease required for the width of the leg. This is a matter of personal preference and depends upon the size and shape of the leg.

If a leg is large thighed, then add to the front and back inside leg seams at the crutch point, tapering the line to the lower edge of the pattern. Do not add to the side seams. Tightness in the thigh area means that more width is required in the crutch as well as in the leg, and adding at this point will give both (Fig. 12).

Altering a pattern to accommodate thin thighs must never be done by decreasing at the side seams. If the thighs are thin, then decrease both the front and back inside leg seams at the crutch point and taper to the lower edge (Fig. 13).

ADDITIONAL ADJUSTMENTS
Alterations for a sway back
If the figure has a sway back this will cause folds in the trousers below the back waist. These folds can be eliminated by removing the extra fullness at the centre back. Slash straight across the back to the side seam about 9cm (3½ inches) below the waistline. Overlap the slash line to remove the necessary amount. Re-draw the centre back seam, and also the darts if they have been affected. Consequently the back waistline will have been decreased (Figs. 14a and 14b).

If the normal waistline width is required, add the material which has been trimmed from the centre back to the side seam and taper from the waistline to the hipline (Fig. 15).

Alterations for a large stomach
A person with a large stomach will find this adjustment most useful, especially if wishing to wear fitted trousers, because this style emphasises the slightest figure fault. To make this alteration, draw a line through the centre of the waistline dart to the knee. This line should be parallel to the grainline.

Then draw a horizontal line from the centre front to the side seam keeping the line 7.5cm (3 inches) below the waistline (Fig. 16).

Slash the horizontal line to the side seam and open the pattern a quarter of the amount required. Slash the vertical line and open the pattern a quarter of the amount required, keeping the centre front straight. Insert a piece of tissue under the slashes and tape in position. Adjust the waistline dart in the middle of the slash, returning it to its original position and size (Fig. 17).

Alteration for protruding hips
Extra dart fullness released at the point of the hip bones will solve this problem. The larger dart releases more fullness. Reposition and increase the width of the dart so that it is in line with the hip bone. For some figures the dart may need shortening (Fig. 18). As a result, the waistline becomes smaller, so add the difference to the side seam and taper to the hipline (Fig. 19).

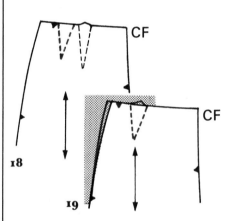

Alterations for a large seat
To make this alteration, the width and length at the fullest part of the seat must be increased.

Determine the amount of increase necessary for the adjustment. Slash the pattern vertically to the knee, between the centre back and the back dart, parallel to the grain line. Measure 20.5cm (8 inches) below the waistline and slash the pattern horizontally from the centre back to the side seam. Open the vertical and horizontal slashes each to a quarter of the amount required, keeping the centre back straight. Insert a piece of tissue and tape in place.

Re-draw the cutting lines. If the waistline becomes too large, divide the adjustment equally between the back darts and increase each one (Fig. 20).

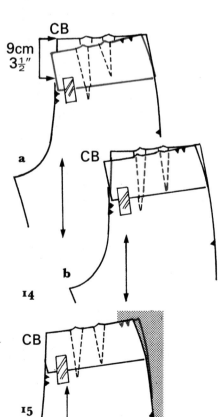

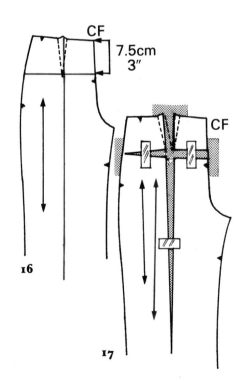

Alterations for a flat seat

In this case proceed as if making the alteration for a large seat, but instead of opening the vertical and horizontal slashes, overlap them each by a quarter of the amount required. If the waistline becomes too small, divide the vertical adjustment equally between all the back darts and decrease them by this amount (Fig. 21).

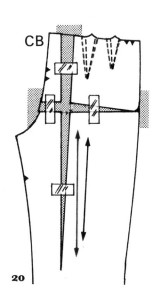

20

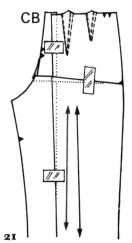

21

Alteration for one hip higher than natural hipline

Measure down 20.5cm (*8 inches*) from the waistline and draw a line through the centre of the dart, keeping in line with the straight grain. Square across at the hipline to the vertical line. At the side seam where the hip is higher, measure down from the waistline to the hip bone and mark. Draw a line from this mark to the point where the vertical and horizontal lines meet (Fig. 22).
Slash along this line and the horizontal line, and overlap the pattern. This will open the pattern at the new hip line.

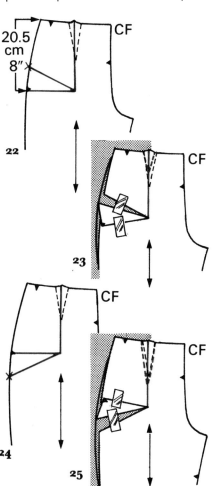

22

23

24

25

Adjust the amount overlapping to fit the hip and tape in place. Re-draw the side seam from the waistline, tapering to the new hipline. Make this adjustment to both front and back pattern pieces.
It will be found that after making this adjustment, the dart will need shortening to the level of the new hipline (Fig. 23).

Alteration for one hip lower than natural hipline

For this alteration, the same method is used as above. Having drawn the vertical and horizontal lines, measure down from the horizontal to the new hipline and mark. Draw a line from this mark to the point where the vertical and horizontal lines meet (Fig. 24).
Slash along this line and the horizontal line and overlap the pattern. This will open the pattern at the new hipline. Adjust the amount overlapping to fit the hip and tape in place. Re-draw the side seam from the waistline, tapering to the new hipline (Fig. 25).

A final tip on fitting trousers

After the pattern pieces have been cut out in the fabric and marked, fold each piece vertically in half with the wrong sides together. Press in the creases firmly. The front crease points to the first dart or pleat, and the back crease stops at the crutch seam.
During the first fitting, ensure that the creases hang straight. If a crease hangs inwards, raise the trousers at the waistline on the appropriate side until the crease hangs correctly. This occurs because the two hips are not exactly the same (Fig. 26).

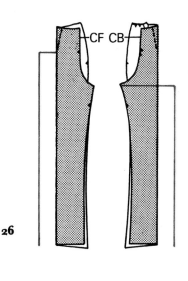

26

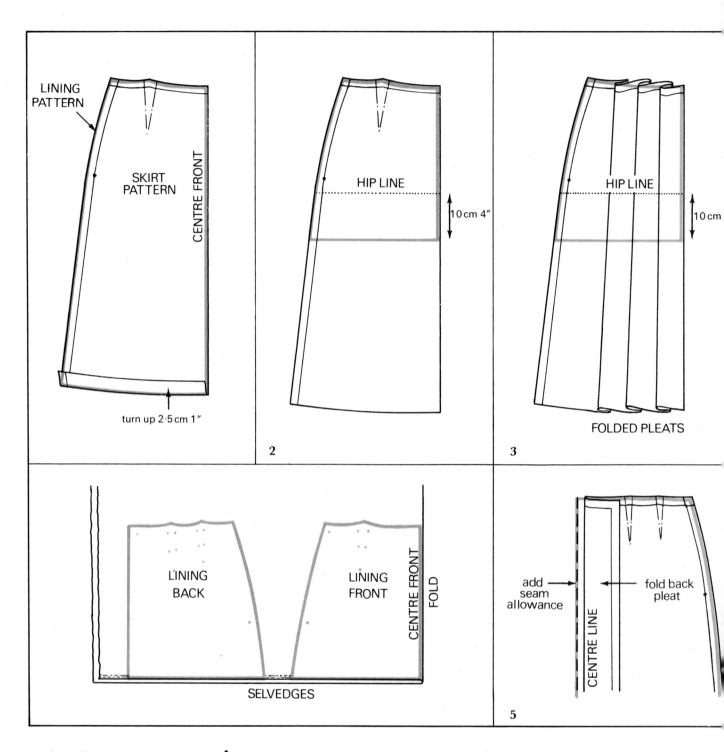

LINING PATTERN

SKIRT PATTERN

CENTRE FRONT

turn up 2·5 cm 1"

HIP LINE

10 cm 4"

2

HIP LINE

10 cm

FOLDED PLEATS

3

LINING BACK

LINING FRONT

CENTRE FRONT FOLD

SELVEDGES

add seam allowance

CENTRE LINE

fold back pleat

5

Lining & re-lining a skirt

A lining prolongs the life of a skirt by covering the seaming and protecting the fabric from wear and tear. In addition the lining prevents the skirt from stretching, helps to preserve its shape, reduces wrinkling and adds body to limp fabrics.

If a lining is not to affect the fit or appearance of the skirt it must always be lighter in weight and softer than the skirt fabric. The choice of lining material also depends on how the skirt fabric is to be cleaned; whether it is to be washed by hand or machine, whether it will need ironing or whether it must be dry cleaned. The lining must have similar characteristics. So check the labels for washing instructions when buying and, if in doubt, ask for advice.

Lining variations

The lining shape depends on the style of the skirt. For a simple straight or 'A' line skirt, the lining can be either full length or half length, falling just below the hip line. Alternatively, the skirt can be lined on the front or back only. For a skirt with a single pleat the lining should have a slit, and for a pleated skirt the best version is a half length smooth lining as for the simple or 'A' line skirts.

Cutting the lining

For a full length lining use the original

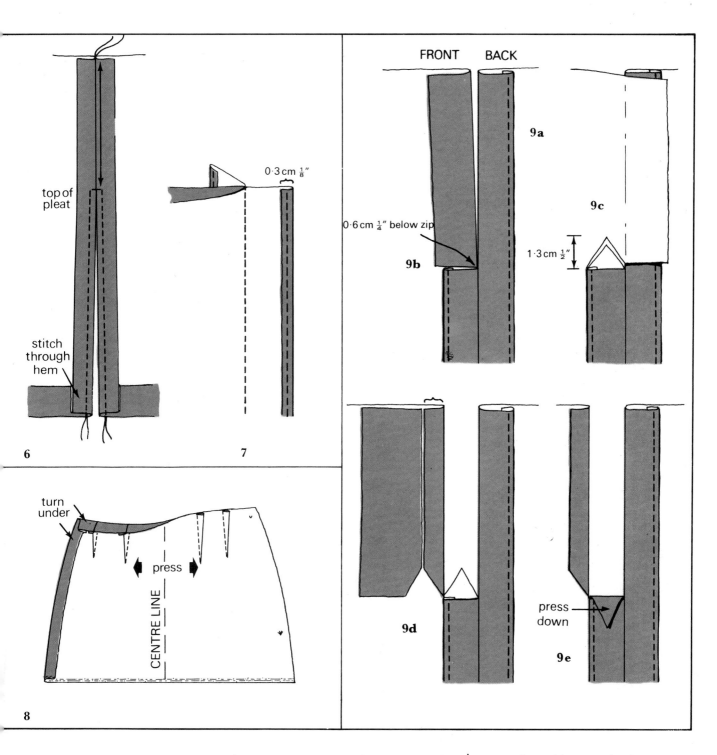

6

top of pleat

stitch through hem

7

0·3cm ⅛"

8

turn under

press

CENTRE LINE

FRONT   BACK

9a

0·6cm ¼" below zip

9b

9c

1·3cm ½"

9d

press down

9e

pattern pieces, cutting them 2.5cm (1 inch) shorter than for the skirt (Fig. 1). For a half length lining on a plain skirt, cut 10cm (4 inches) below the hip line (Fig. 2).

For a half length lining on a pleated skirt, fold the pleats in the paper pattern and cut the lining from this to 10cm (4 inches) below the hips (Fig. 3).

For lining the front or back only, cut the appropriate pieces as for a half length lining (Fig. 2).

When making a half length lining place the pattern piece on the lining fabric so that the lower edge is to the selvedge, thus avoiding the bulk caused by a hem (Fig. 4).

For a single pleat, omit the extension but be sure to leave a seam allowance (Fig. 5). If an old skirt is to be relined, remove the old lining carefully, unpick the seams and darts, press the pieces carefully and use as the pattern.

Making the lining

All full linings are made in exactly the same way as the skirt itself, leaving the zip opening 0.6cm (¼ inch) longer than for the skirt. Remember to position the zip opening at the right side for a left side opening. For single pleats, sew to the top of the pleat and neaten the opening with a narrow hem (Fig. 6).

Because lining fabrics tend to fray, neaten the seams by turning under 0.3cm (⅛ inch) of the seam allowance and top-stitch (Fig. 7).

For a single piece of lining sew the darts and press under the seam and waist allowances (Fig. 8).

Test the temperature of the iron on a spare piece of lining as too hot an iron distorts some man-made fibres. Press the lining carefully, making sure that the darts lie away from the back and front centre lines, thus avoiding bulk under the skirt darts as shown in Fig. 8.

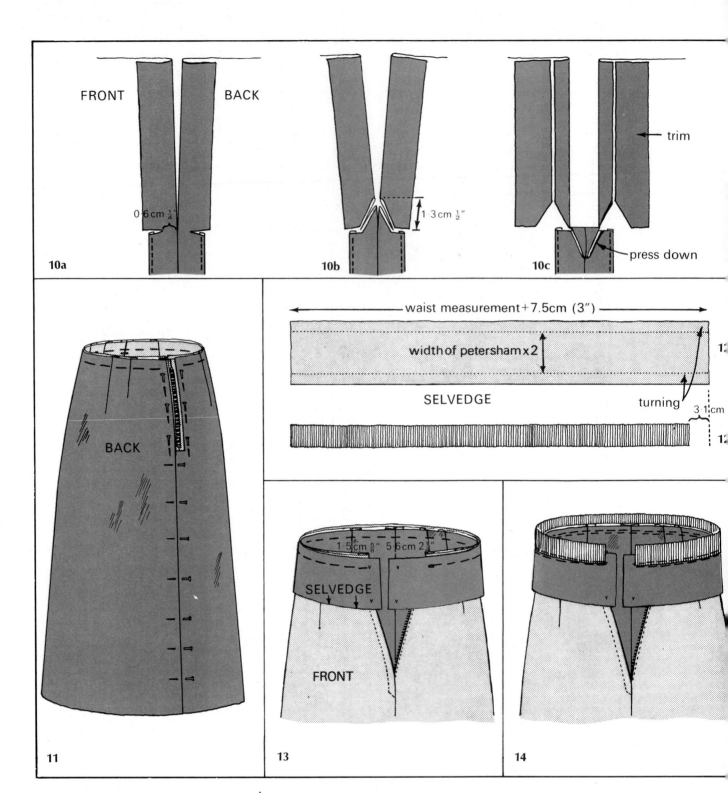

FRONT   BACK

0·6cm ¼″

10a

1·3cm ½″

10b

trim

press down

10c

BACK

11

waist measurement + 7.5cm (3″)

width of petersham x 2

SELVEDGE

turning

3·1cm

12

12

1·5cm ⅝″   5·6cm 2¼″

SELVEDGE

FRONT

13

14

Neatening the zip opening

The bottom of the seam opening on the lining can be neatened using either of two methods, depending upon the method chosen to sew the zip into the skirt.

Lapped or concealed zip

Press the back seam allowance to continue the seam line (Fig. 9a).
Cut straight through the seam allowance to the top of the seam (Fig. 9b)
Cut a mitre in the front lining fabric 1.2cm (½ inch) high and 1.2cm (½ inch) wide (Fig. 9c).

Fold the seam allowance back to the end of the mitre and trim to 0.6cm (¼ inch) (Fig. 9d).
Fold the mitre to the wrong side and press carefully (Fig. 9e).

Invisible or semi-concealed zip

Snip both seam allowances to within 0.6 cm (¼ inch) of the seam line (Fig. 10a).
From the folded edges of the allowances cut a half mitre 1.2cm (½ inch) high by 0.6 cm (¼ inch) wide (Fig. 10b).
Cut allowance back to original fold line, fold down the mitres and press (Fig. 10c).

Sewing the lining to the skirt

The lining can be sewn in before or after the waistband is attached. Remember that it is easier to re-line a skirt if the lining is not machined in at the waist.

Method 1: Before the band is attached. Place the skirt and lining with wrong sides together and pin and tack along the waist. Pin down the seams and round the zip (Fig. 11).

Place the waistband with one long edge to the selvedge, if at all possible, and cut it 7.5cm (3 inches) longer than the waist measurement and twice as wide as the

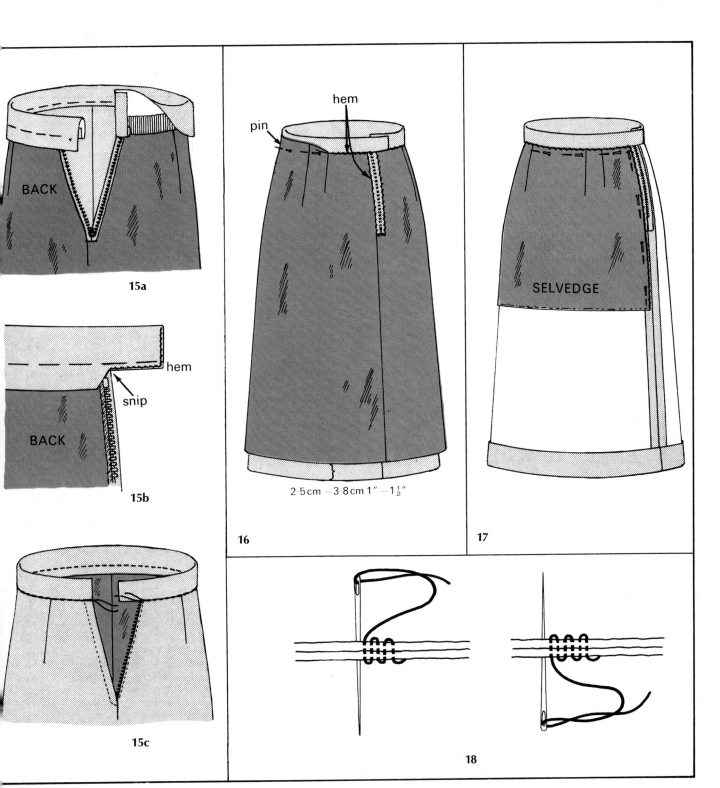

15a

BACK

15b

hem

snip

BACK

15c

16

hem

pin

2·5cm —3·8cm 1″—1½″

17

SELVEDGE

18

petersham stiffening, plus two turnings (Fig. 12a).

Cut the petersham 3.1cm (1¼ inches) shorter than the band (Fig. 12b).

Ease the skirt onto the long cut edge of the waistband leaving 1.5cm (⅝ inch) overlap at the front zip edge and 6cm (2⅜ inches) at the back. Tack through band, skirt and lining and machine (Fig. 13).

Sew the petersham just above this line, placing it so that there is a 1.5cm (⅝ inch) turning left at both ends (Fig. 14).

Turn in the seam allowance at the ends of the petersham and fold the band over

the petersham along the waistline (Fig. 15a). Snip at the zip and turn under along the extension and tack along the length of the band. Hem the extension and the front ends (Fig. 15b).

Machine or stab stitch (Fig. 18) along the waistband seam working from the right side (Fig. 15c).

Method 2: After the waistband is sewn on. Make the skirt and attach the waistband as above.

Place the lining to the skirt with wrong sides together and pin down the seams and round the zip (Fig. 16a).

Turn under the waist seam allowance to the waistband sewing line and hem all round (Fig. 16b).

For all full length linings, turn up the hem 2.5 to 3.8cm (1 to 1½ inches) shorter than the skirt and hem.

Method 3: Half lining either front or back. Make the skirt and attach the waistband. Place to the appropriate piece of the skirt, with wrong sides together, and pin (Fig. 17).

Hem down the side seams and along the waistband machine stitching line.

Lining a coat or a jacket

The lining in a tailored coat or jacket combines several important functions. It covers the internal canvassing and seams, prolongs the life of the coat and makes it much easier to wear, slipping easily over jumpers and dresses.

When a coat outlasts its lining it is possible to re-line it, using the original lining as a pattern. The treatment of the hem is the only difference between lining a coat and a jacket. A coat lining is usually left free, whereas a jacket lining is stitched down.

LINING FABRIC

There are many lining fabrics to choose from, all of which will give the required 'silky' finish to the coat; but do not be tempted to buy the cheapest types as these tend to split in wear. Always consider the weight of the coat fabric before making a final choice.

For heavy weight coats

Use Tricel or Dicel with a satin weave. For extra warmth use Milium, which has a satin weave face and is backed with a fine layer of aluminium.

For medium weight coats

Use Tricel or Dicel with a plain weave.

For light weight coats

Use Tricel or Dicel taffeta.

For a very special coat use a pure silk lining. This is expensive, but it gives a really luxurious finish. Avoid using crepe lining as this will stretch in wear and become very uncomfortable.

LINING A COAT OR JACKET
The pattern

When lining a new coat or jacket, use the lining pieces given with the pattern and cut them out according to the layout instructions.

To re-line an old coat or jacket, take out the lining carefully, unpick the seams and darts or pleats and iron the pieces flat. Using these pieces as patterns, lay them on the new lining fabric, matching the grains exactly (Fig. 1).

Making the lining

Before starting to make the lining, test iron a spare piece of the fabric to find the temperature needed to make a good flat seam without melting the fibres. This temperature can be quite critical, so if the

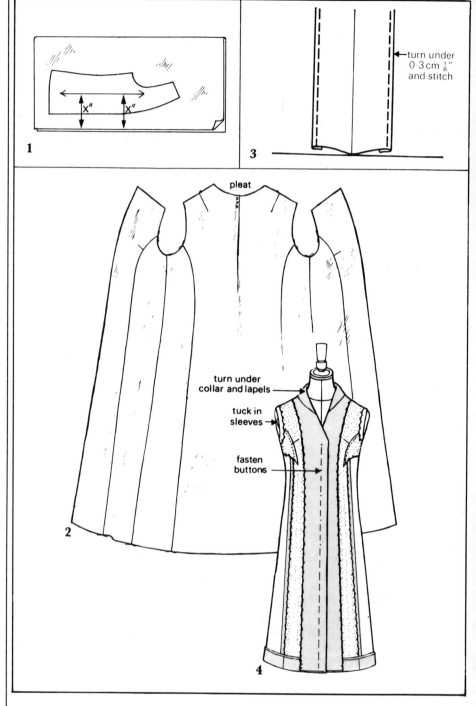

iron has been on for some time, re-test it before ironing the new lining.

Start by pinning, tacking, machining and ironing the darts and/or pleats. Then stitch all the seams except the shoulder and armholes (Fig. 2).

Most lining fabrics fray quickly when cut, so neaten the seam allowances by turning under 0.3cm ($\frac{1}{8}$ inch) and top-stitching (Fig. 3).

A new coat should be finished and pressed before the lining is sewn in. An old coat should be cleaned professionally or failing that should be brushed and pressed, before the new lining is sewn in. This will ensure the correct shaping.

Pinning in the lining

If you have a dressmaking dummy, put the coat onto it, wrong side out, turning the sleeves flat to the inside. Fasten the coat buttons and adjust it so that the seams are vertical and the hem line is straight (Fig. 4).

If a dummy is not available, lay the coat right side down on a flat surface and work with each section laid out as flat as can be managed.

Take the lining and place it to the coat, wrong sides together. The lining pieces should be pinned together first, so for best results do all work in the following order.

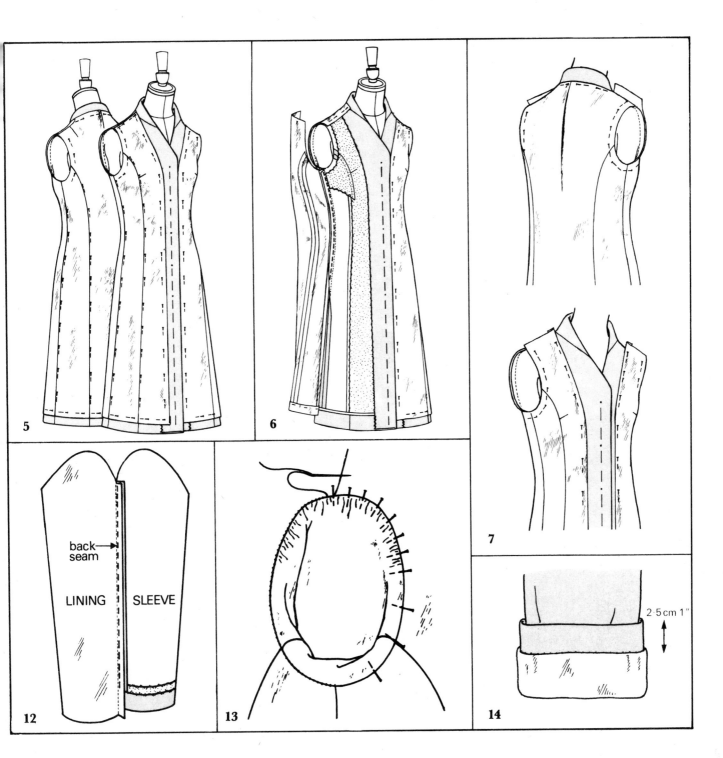

5

6

7

12

back seam

LINING   SLEEVE

13

14

2·5 cm 1"

Seams
Pin down from top to bottom of any style seams at the back, the side seams, the fronts from the centre back point and the centre pleat (if there is one).

Armhole
The canvassing should have held the armhole shape firmly but if there has been any stretching during the making do not cut the lining to match the stretching.

Instead, ease the coat to the lining, to regain the original line of the pattern. Then pin along the shoulder seams, over-lapping the front over the back.

Hem
For a coat, pin the lining up 2.5cm (1 inch) above the coat hem.

For a jacket, pin the lining hem the exact length of the jacket hem.

At this stage it is a good idea to slip the coat or jacket on to see if the lining is pulling at any point (Fig. 5).

Stitching the coat lining
The lining must be attached firmly inside the coat or jacket to stop it moving in wear, so lift the lining and tack the side seams of the coat and lining together from the underarm to the hip level, un-pinning where necessary. (Fig. 6).

Next, turn under the seam allowances along the neck, front edges and front shoulders and re-pin in smooth lines (Fig. 7). Level the hem to leave a 3.8 to 5cm (1½ to 2 inch) turning. Turn under 1.2cm (½ inch) and tack. Stitch the lining to the coat with felling stitch for a really professional finish (Fig. 8).

Hem. Press the hem before sewing in the rest of the lining.

Shoulder seams. Check that the front seam allowance laps over the back (Fig. 9).

Outer edge. Work each side from the centre back to the hem line to avoid any movement of the lining as you sew (Fig. 10).

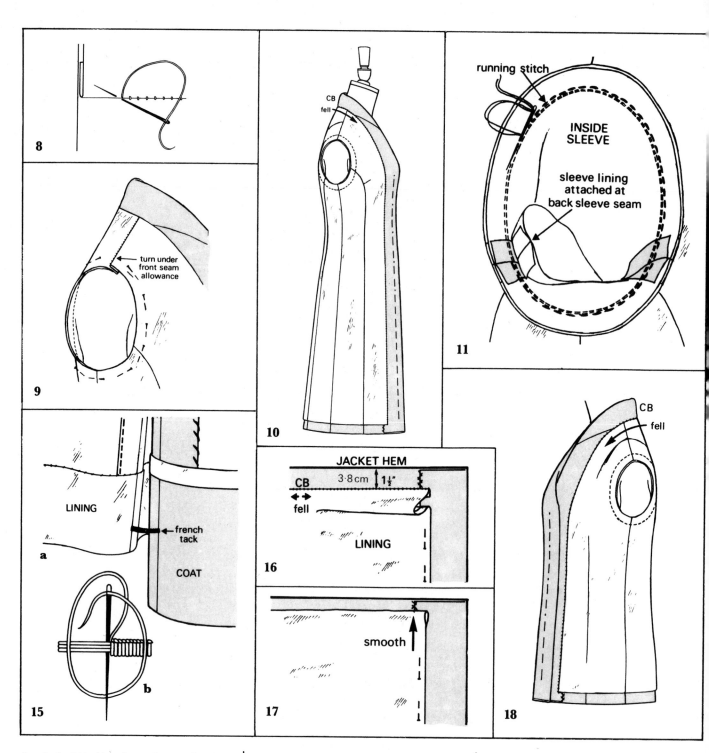

Armhole. Working from the inside of the sleeves, sew the lining to the coat 0.3 to 0.6cm ($\frac{1}{8}$ to $\frac{1}{4}$ inch) outside the coat stitching line. This stitching must be very firm, so use a double thread and a small running stitch (Fig. 11).

Stitching the sleeve lining

Turn the coat sleeve through to the wrong side and place the wrong side of the lining to the sleeve, matching the underarm seams, or the back seams with a two-piece sleeve. Tack together (Fig. 12).
Turn the sleeve back to the right side, taking the lining with it.
At the sleeve head, bring the sleeve lining up, turn under the seam allowance and pin to cover the small running stitches. Adjust the lining sleeve head fullness into tiny pleats and fell firmly (Fig. 13).
At the sleeve hem, turn under the lining hem 1.5cm ($\frac{5}{8}$ inch) and fell 2.5cm (1 inch) above the sleeve hem line (Fig. 14).

French tacks

To hold a lining at the hem, make French tacks between the lining and coat side seams (Fig. 15).

Stitching a jacket lining

Pin the lining into the jacket as described under 'Pinning in the lining' and try on to check that the lining is not pulling.
At the hem, lift the lining fold 2.5 to 3.8cm (1 to 1½ inches) above the jacket edge and turn the front seam allowances to the wrong side. Fell firmly (Fig. 16).
Continue as for the coat until shoulders and armholes have been stitched, and the outer edges turned under and pinned, smoothing the front lining down into a fold at the hem edge (Fig. 17).
Fell from the centre back as for the coat (Fig. 18).
The extra length in the lining provided by the fold at the hem allows for ease of movement when the jacket is worn. Fell the sleeve lining as for the coat.

Rouleau

The return of soft, feminine fashions has created interest in the finer points of dressmaking details. Here are some suggestions for using rouleau, one of the most versatile and decorative self-fabric trimmings in dressmaking.

Suitable fabrics

The most suitable fabrics for making rouleau are those which are reasonably fine and not too crisp in texture. Amongst these are wool, wool/synthetics and silk jerseys, crepes, fine woollens, silks and satins. Velvet can be used but is difficult to handle. Thick and heavy weight fabrics such as tweed and velour should be avoided.

Cutting the fabric

The golden rule for making rouleau is that all strips of fabric must be cut on the true bias.
Fig. 1 shows the fabric marked accurately with tailor's chalk and a ruler. When the strips have been cut cleanly, all the ends must be trimmed to the same angle if they require joining (Fig. 2).
The tubing can be made in lengths up to 90cm (36 inches) if the fabric is really supple. The secret of well rounded tubes is that when they are made up, sufficient turnings are left inside to fill them without making them over-stiff. So that the width of the crossway strips can be carefully planned to save trimming, note that the stretching during making up will narrow the tubing.
As a general guide, the strips of fabric are cut allowing one to one and a half times the width of turnings to the width of the rouleau. Therefore, for a fine silk or jersey rouleau of 0.6cm ($\frac{1}{4}$ inch), a seam allowance of 1cm ($\frac{3}{8}$ inch) should be allowed, making the strip cut measure 3.2cm ($1\frac{1}{4}$ inches). The thicker the fabric, the less the seam allowance required for filling the rouleau.

Sewing the strips

Make any necessary joins. Then, with right sides together, fold the strips in half lengthwise. Tack and stitch. The seam needs elasticity, so use a pure silk or polyester thread and a short stitch with a slight zigzag. If this is not possible, stretch the fabric slightly when stitching.

Turning through to the right side

Turning rouleau through to the right side presents no problems if one of the following methods is used.
Finish the stitching by widening it slightly and then thread the ends of the sewing thread into a bodkin or a needle with a rounded point. Thread the bodkin or needle through the tubing and pull the rouleau right side out (Fig. 3).
The second method (Fig. 4) is for rouleau filled with cord.
The cord must be cut twice the finished length of the rouleau.

With right sides together, fold the fabric in half over the cord and tack close to the cord. Using the zipper foot on the machine, stitch across the centre of the cording, then sew close to the cording as shown. Trim the turnings and then pull the cord gently out of the tubing so that the fabric is eased back over the other half of the cord to give a closely covered rouleau (Fig. 5). This method is used where extra strength is needed: perhaps for a narrow belt.

Using rouleau

Rouleau is often used in conjunction with piping or narrow bindings. A neckline may be bound and finished with a rouleau bow, or a sleeve finished with a binding at the wrist may have a small rouleau button loop.
Shown here are several ideas for making decorative trimmings which can give individual interest and distinction to home dressmaking.
If loops are used for a decorative edging or a practical fastening, they are always attached to the edge of a garment with a facing for neatness and strength in wear.

Button loops

Loops for buttons may be spaced singly, or made with a continuous strip of rouleau. The size of the button governs the size of each loop, and domed or small ball buttons look the most attractive for

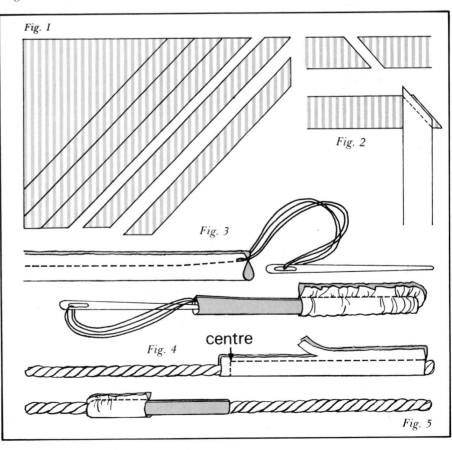

Fig. 1

Fig. 2

Fig. 3

Fig. 4

centre

Fig. 5

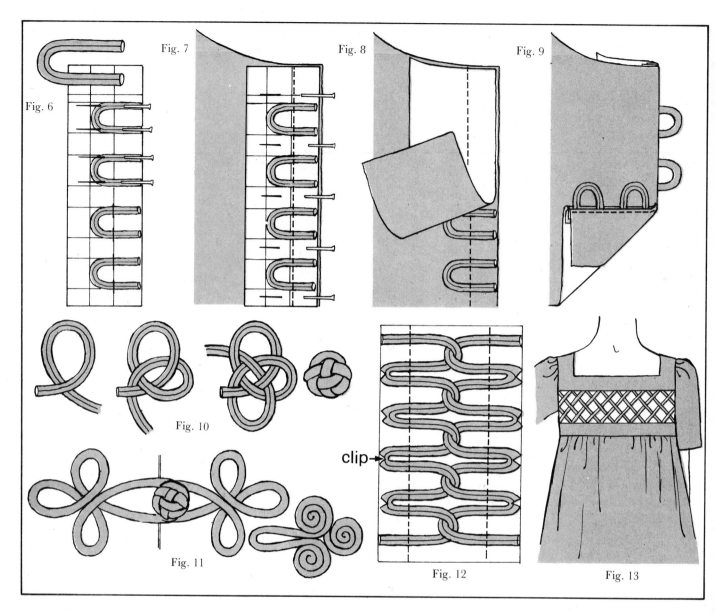

Fig. 6

Fig. 7

Fig. 8

Fig. 9

Fig. 10

Fig. 11

clip→

Fig. 12

Fig. 13

this type of fastening. Styles of loops can be varied and the main check point is that the button can slip through the loop comfortably.

To ensure an even thickness of rouleau, make sufficient tubing for a set of button loops in one strip.

To help make all the loops equal in size and shaping, arrange them over a paper guide. Cut a strip of firm paper the length of the seam and mark the layout accurately. Pin and tack the loops to the paper with the seam facing upwards (Fig. 6). Lay the paper over the garment with the loops facing away from the seam edge and machine just inside the seam line (Fig. 7). Tear the paper away and sew on the facing (Fig. 8). Layer the turnings and trim the rouleau ends back to 0.6cm ($\frac{1}{4}$ inch). Work a row of understitching.

If the loops are pinned directly onto the garment, use small stitches in matching thread to hold them in place, rather than tacking thread which is difficult to remove after the facing seam has been machined.

Chinese ball buttons

These are attractive trimmings traditionally used with frog fastenings, or to finish the end of a rouleau tie. They can be made of a purchased cord or self-fabric rouleau. Follow Fig. 10 to form the open knot, then gradually tighten by pulling both ends together. Clip off any spare rouleau and sew the ends firmly and neatly to the back of the knot to form the button.

Frogging

Frogging is another fashion detail which is far more rewarding to make.

Sew the loops of a frog together before applying it to the garment. Use small invisible stab stitches, working from what will be the wrong side. One loop must be long enough to extend over the edge of the garment and hold the button on the other side (Fig. 11).

Insertions and faggotting

Using a softer rouleau which is not too tightly filled, a decorative insertion can be

made to highlight a yoke or hem on a fine fabric. All this work must be tacked onto paper before it can be joined to the garment. Fig. 12 shows interlocking loops which would make an interesting panel down a dress bodice.

Faggoting can be done using a twisted herringbone stitch or with straight bars which can be twisted or overcast, or stitched with groups of sheaf stitch. A complete yoke or section of a garment can be made with rouleau, which must also be tacked to a paper guide before it is sewn and attached to the rest of the garment (Fig. 13).

If rouleau is applied as a decoration, it is better to choose a curving design rather than to force it to turn sharp angles. Tassles and fringes of rouleau can make unusual trimmings and these may be tied and grouped with macramé knots and given extra swing if beads are attached to weight the ends.

Rouleau from fabrics like voile and organza filled with coloured wools looks delightful.

Tailoring techniques

Tailoring demands a certain amount of time and effort, as well as a knowledge of specialist techniques. The methods dealt with here include moulding and shaping by pressing and with the aid of supporting canvases, plus the special stitches used in sewing.

CANVASING THE COAT

Two groups of canvases or interfacings are used in tailoring. Both groups are made up of woven fibres so that the grain lines of the main fabric and the interfacing can be exactly matched.

Mixed fibre hair canvases

Wool and hair. A smooth, greyish fabric which is very springy and does not crease. It keeps the shapes moulded into it better than any other canvas. This is due to its natural springy quality.

Cotton and hair. This type of canvas is slightly springy, but it can crease.

Single fibre interfacings

Pure wool. A smooth, creamy-coloured fabric which is very springy and soft. It is useful for lightweight tweeds and also for completely interlining a garment where extra warmth is needed.

Linen canvas (or shrunk duck). A soft canvas which will maintain a crease. It is used with lightweight fabrics or linens as a backing for pockets and hems.

French canvas (or collar canvas). This canvas is made with the warp and weft threads of equal weight to give firm control to the undercollar.

Shrinking

Canvases should always be pre-shrunk before use, either by wrapping in a damp sheet overnight and ironing the next day, or by pressing all over with a hot iron and a wet cloth and leaving to dry.

Linen stay tape 1.3cm ($\frac{1}{2}$ inch) wide should also be pre-shrunk. This can be done by washing the tape and then ironing dry.

Canvas pattern pieces

Use the appropriate pieces given with the pattern, or cut your own from the front and back pieces.

For each front cut one piece of canvas as for the facing, adding an extra 2.5cm (1 inch) seam allowance at the inner edge (Fig. 1), or if the pattern has a side front seam, use the front pattern complete instead of the facing pattern (Fig. 2).

Cut a second piece of interfacing for each front to include the armhole as shown, using the front or side front piece as a guide (Figs. 3a and b).

For the back, cut the canvas to include the neck and armhole using the back pattern as a guide, and curving the lower edge as shown (Fig. 4a).

If there is a centre back seam, cut two pieces and join by overlapping on the seam line (Fig. 4b).

Where there are side back seams, overlap the pattern pieces on the stitching line (Fig. 4c). Always keep to the pattern grain lines.

Before any machining is attempted, the coat shell must be tacked together, the canvas tacked into the shell with the grain

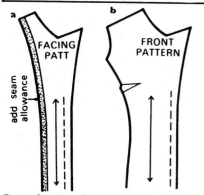

Centre front interfacing: 1. using facing pattern; 2. using front pattern

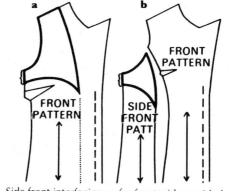

3. Side front interfacing: a. for front without side front seams; b. for front with side front seam

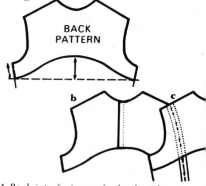

4. Back interfacing: a. for back without seams; b. for back with centre back seams; c. for back with side back seams

8. Stitching interfacing seams

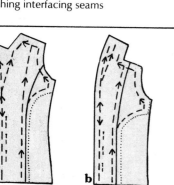

9a and b. Step collar and shawl collar

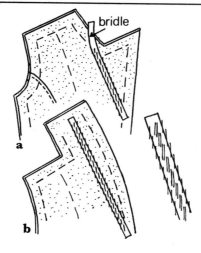

10a and b. Pad stitch the stay tape to the crease line

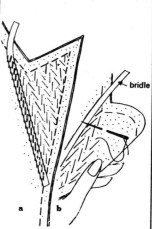

11a and b. Pad stitching the step collar

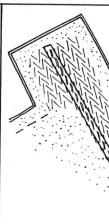

12. For a shawl collar stitch between the crease and the neck edge

lines matching, and the coat must be tried on for fit (Fig. 5). Mark where the lapel crease lines fall (Fig. 6).

Shaping the canvas

Darts. Cut out the dart shape along the stitching line, place the cut edges over stay tape and machine (Fig. 7).

Seams. Overlay the seams on the stitching lines and machine. Trim the seam allowance back to 0.6cm (¼ inch) (Fig. 8). Press over a tailor's ham to retain the shapes thus created.

Canvasing the front and back

The canvas is sewn in place after any style seams, darts and back seams have been stitched and pressed, but before the shoulder and side seams are stitched.

Front. Lay the interfacing flat on the table, over it lay the corresponding coat front, with the wrong side of the coat fabric towards the canvas (Figs. 9a and b). Match and pin the centre and crease lines together (Fig. 9i).

Working from the bust line upwards, baste the front edge to the canvas, smoothing it to prevent wrinkles (Fig. 9ii). Repeat from the bust line downwards (Fig. 9iii). Baste the opposite edge of the canvas from hem to shoulder (Fig. 9iv). Finally baste round armhole, shoulder, neck and along the crease line (Fig. 9v).

A bridle. This is a length of stay tape used to support the crease line. This goes right along the crease line for a shawl collar, and 5cm (2 inches) beyond for a step collar. Pin the stay tape centrally along the crease line, keeping it taut. Using a double matching silk thread, pad stitch and stay tape centrally in place. Pad stitch each edge with single thread (Figs. 10a and b).

Remove the collar or lapel edge tacking and continue to work rows of staggered pad stitching, keeping the rows in line with the bridle. Roll the work over the hand to help create the 'roll' which will enable the collar or lapel to lie correctly (Figs. 11a and b).

For a shawl collar, pad stitch between the crease line and the neck edge (Fig. 12). Another length of stay tape is sewn to the front seam edge to retain its shape. Trim the front edge of the canvas just within the sewing line of the coat to reduce bulk in the seam. Cut the stay tape

to the required length and centralize it over the sewing line (Figs. 13a, b and c). Tack the tape firmly along the outside edge and catch stitch the inner edge to the canvas (Fig. 14).

To finish attaching the canvas to the coat, trim the shoulder and underarm seams to just within the sewing line of the coat. Catch stitch down carefully (Figs. 15a and b).

To press the lapel, steam it firmly over the pad stitching and roll it on the crease line – do not press it flat.

Back. Lay the canvas to the wrong side of the coat and tack. Trim the shoulder and underarm seams and catch stitch as for the front (Figs. 16a and b).

Canvasing the step under collar

This type of collar should be smooth and well fitting, so great care must be taken not to distort it when stitching and pressing. Ideally, the collar should be sewn to the coat by hand to ensure a perfect fit.

Sew the centre back seam on the fabric, trim seam allowance to 0.6cm (¼ inch) and press. Overlap the canvas seam (Fig. 17). Lay the canvas to the wrong side of the

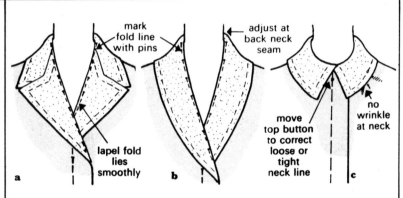

6. Fitting a collar: a. step collar; b. shawl collar, c. coat without lapels

mark fold line with pins
lapel fold lies smoothly

adjust at back neck seam
move top button to correct loose or tight neck line
no wrinkle at neck

...paring for first fitting: a. back; ...nt; c. under collar; d. overbasting ...der side and neck seams

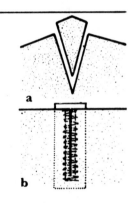

7. Interfacing darts: a. cutting out dart; b. stitching dart together on stay tape

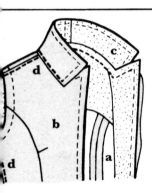

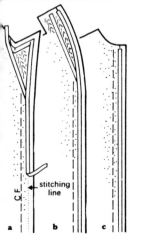

Stay tape stitched to front of ...at with: a. step collar; b. shawl ...lar; c. coat without revers

stitching line

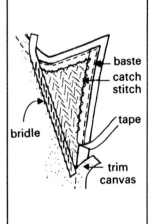

baste
catch stitch
tape
bridle
trim canvas

14. Sewing on stay tape

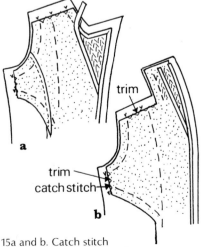

trim
trim
catch stitch

15a and b. Catch stitch the canvas at shoulder and underarm seams on front

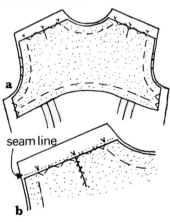

seam line

16a and b. Catch stitch the canvas at shoulder and underarm seams on back

53

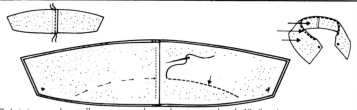

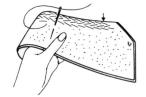

17. Joining under collar canvas along the centre back 18. Sewing canvas to under collar along crease line 19. The stand and fall of the collar

20. Pad stitching the canvas to the under collar on the fall

21. Pad stitching the canvas to under collar on the stand

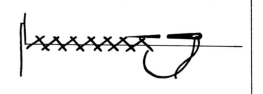

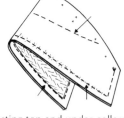

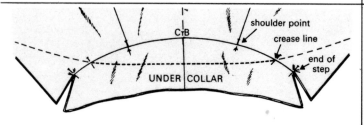

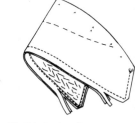

25. Trimming the canvas on the under collar

26. Checking the fit of the under collar

27. Basting top and under collars together

28. Stitched collar seams re for turning

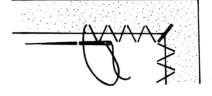

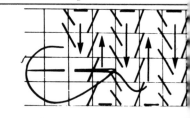

31. Pinning the under collar to the coat neck edge

32. Felling the under collar to the coat neck edge

36. Herringbone stitch

37. Catch stitch

38. Pad stitch

undercollar with the centre backs matching. Pin along the crease line, then run a taut thread along the crease line in matching thread (Fig. 18).

This crease line divides the stand and fall of the collar (Fig. 19).

With the canvas side up, pad stitch the fall and stand in lines of staggered pad stitching. Hold the work as shown in Figs. 20 and 21, so that the crease line is away from you.

Pressing the collar pieces

To fit the coat correctly, the under and top collar need to be pressed and moulded before being stitched together. Lay the under collar, right side down, on an ironing board. Using a damp cloth, press the fall, gently pulling the outer edge of the collar slightly just above the shoulder position. Always pull towards the centre back as this must not be stretched. Do not stretch for more than 1.3cm ($\frac{1}{2}$ inch) (Figs. 22a and b). Repeat for the stand.

Turn right side up and lay it flat with the stand folded over on the crease line. Using a damp cloth, press firmly without stretching (Fig. 23).

While the under collar is still damp curve it round a pudding basin, with the stand turned in, to dry in a curve (Fig. 24). Prepare the top collar similarly, but turning the stand under to the wrong side.

Making the collar

Trim the canvas to inside the fabric seam line and check that the under collar fits the coat (Figs. 25 and 26). Place the two collar pieces right sides together and baste along the crease line. Baste on outside and step edges. There should be a slight ease on the outside edge to allow the seam to lie on the underside of the finished collar (Fig. 27).

Machine, layer the seams and snip the corners (Fig. 28).

Turn the collar to the right side and work the corners or curves into a good shape.

Working on the underside, baste along the stitched edges, keeping the seam rolled to the underside. Side stitch the seam edges to keep them in place (Fig. 29). Turn under the seam allowance on the neck edge of the under collar and baste. Snip into the neck edge seam allowance of the top collar at the shoulder points. Turn under the seam allowance from the front edges to the shoulder point as shown and baste (Fig. 30).

Press very carefully without destroying the crease line.

Attaching the collar to the coat

Lay the coat, right side up, over the knees with the neck line towards you. Lay the under collar to the neck edge of the coat, right side up, with the folded edge of the under collar meeting the sewing line of the coat neck edge.

Carefully match centre backs, shoulder points and crease line. Pin along neck edge distributing the crease evenly (Fig. 31).

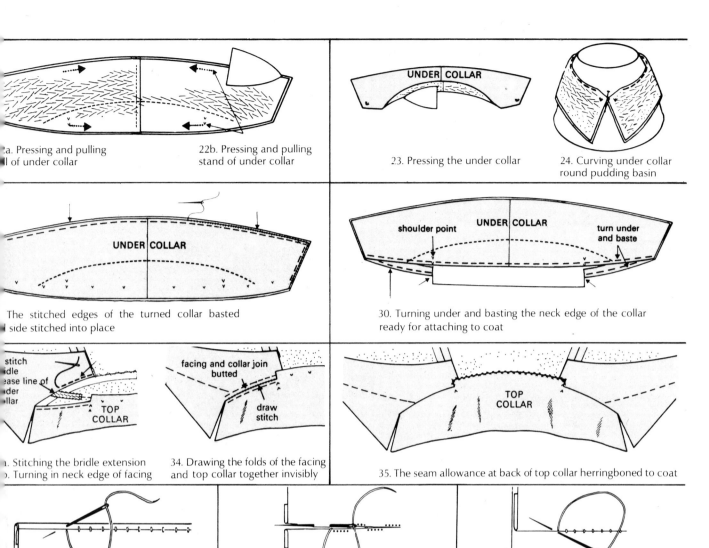

a. Pressing and pulling l of under collar

22b. Pressing and pulling stand of under collar

23. Pressing the under collar

24. Curving under collar round pudding basin

The stitched edges of the turned collar basted side stitched into place

30. Turning under and basting the neck edge of the collar ready for attaching to coat

stitch dle ease line of der llar

facing and collar join butted

draw stitch

TOP COLLAR

TOP COLLAR

. Stitching the bridle extension . Turning in neck edge of facing

34. Drawing the folds of the facing and top collar together invisibly

35. The seam allowance at back of top collar herringboned to coat

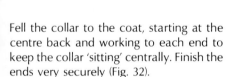

. Side stitch

40. Draw stitch

41. Felling

Fell the collar to the coat, starting at the centre back and working to each end to keep the collar 'sitting' centrally. Finish the ends very securely (Fig. 32).

Still with the coat over your knees, turn it over to the wrong side. Pad stitch the end of the bridle firmly to the under collar crease line (Fig. 33a). Turn in the seam allowance of the facings along the neck edge in a smooth line and baste to the coat (Fig. 33b).

Put the folded edges of the top collar to the folds of the facing. Using a draw stitch, draw the folds together making the stitches invisible (Fig. 34). The raw edge is herringboned down and eventually covered by the lining (Fig. 35). Press carefully over a tailor's ham.

Herringbone

This stitch is similar to catch stitch and is used in hems or areas where the edges need to be held down flat (Fig. 36) with minimum show through.

Catch stitch

This is used to catch one fabric to another where bulk is to be avoided. Lift one thread of fabric with each stitch so as to be invisible on the right side. Do not pull the stitches tight (Fig. 37).

Pad stitching

Work the stitch as shown, the needle to be inserted carefully at right angles to the stitching line.

Work with an imaginary grid, coming down one line and going up to the next, without turning the work. Stagger the lines to prevent pleats being formed. Use small stitches 0.6 to 1.2cm ($\frac{1}{4}$ to $\frac{1}{2}$ inch) long (Fig. 38).

Side stitch

This is used to flatten edges of lapels and collars. Make a tiny stitch at right angles to the line of stitching. The stitches should not appear on the right side of the garment (Fig. 39).

Draw stitch

This stitch is used to close two folds of fabric together. Slip the needle through the top fold for 0.6cm ($\frac{1}{4}$ inch), then directly under the end of the first stitch slip the needle through the lower fold for 0.6cm ($\frac{1}{4}$ inch) (Fig. 40).

Felling

This is a firm form of hemming, with a stitch at right angles to the hem or fold (Fig. 41).

Mounting fabrics

When designing a garment, the designer will depend either on the natural qualities of the fabric to keep the required shape, or on an inner mounting to support the fabric. Apart from this support, the mountings, underlinings and interfacings help the garment to last longer, prevent creasing and stretching out of shape, and give added warmth where required.

Hence the fabrics used for mounting should be lighter than, but as durable as, the fashion fabric, and of a similar fibre to avoid the tearing or splitting which sometimes occurs when the garment itself is not worn out.

WHEN TO MOUNT

Almost all garments are improved by having the main parts mounted, especially crisp, tailored ones i.e. shirt waisters with unpleated skirts, pinafore dresses, straight or A-line skirts.

Loose weave fabrics should always be mounted, especially the novelty tweeds used in tailoring, as it stops the interfacings and linings showing through. Fashion details such as cuffs, shirt style collars and high necklines are also all improved by mounting.

Tie collars, cowl necklines and slight drapes are often mounted on self fabric to avoid any possibility of distortion, which might occur by using too heavy a mounting fabric or one of a different fibre content.

When not to mount

The shaping influence of mounting is not always required and can, in some cases, actually spoil the look of the garment.

Where the fabric is sheer, the delicate look must be kept, especially where the underdress is meant to be seen.

Whatever fabric is used, sleeves which flow loosely or blouse into a cuff, must be unmounted. Similarly, drapes which flow into folds or unpressed pleats should be left unmounted.

Pleats needing a sharply pressed or edged stitched finish are unmounted, as the inner fabric could cause ripping or puckering, thus making it impossible for the pleats to lie flat.

The inherent quality of knitted fabrics is their ability to stretch, and this would be lost with mounting, especially on trousers and skirts.

How to use the mounting fabric

If the finished garment is to be washed, the

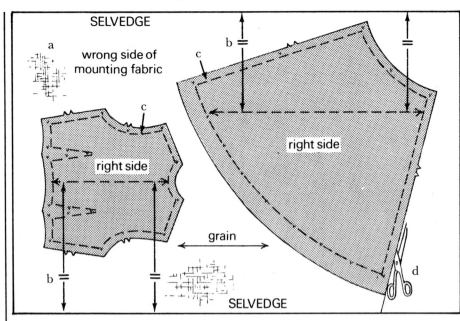

1

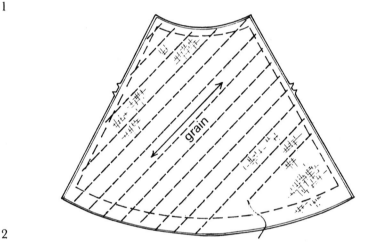

2

SUITABLE MOUNTINGS	
Outside fabric	**Mounting**
Silk, fine wool	pure silk organza Jap silk
Cotton, fine wool, Linen	soft lawn Organdie
Medium weight wool, suit weight	cream wool (usually for extra warmth)
Heavy weight wool, loose weave novelty tweeds	soft lawn or mull
Terylene, Rayon, Nylon etc. Mixtures of these, Mixtures of natural/man-made fibres	terylene lawn or soft woven nylon

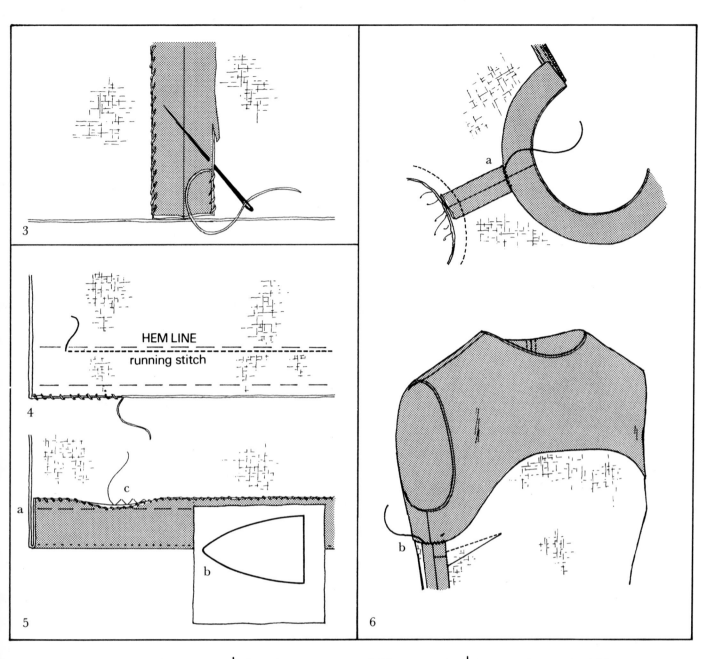

3

HEM LINE
running stitch

4

5

a

c

b

6

a

b

mounting must be pre-shrunk. Soak it in cold water for 10 minutes, hang out to dry and press flat.

Cut out the main fabric and tailor tack all markings and the centre lines. For bias cut pieces, mark the grain line as well.

Only the main body pieces are mounted; fronts, backs and sometimes sleeves.

Lay the mounting fabric wrong side up, flat on a table (Fig. 1). Place the body pieces singly with the wrong side to the mounting, matching the grains exactly, using the centre lines as a measure. Take great care with pieces cut on the bias as any un-evenness of grain will result in the finished article 'pulling' in a disappointing way (Fig. 1a).

Tack all round each piece just inside the stitching lines, and down the centre lines of the large pieces (Fig. 1b). Cut out and use as one piece of fabric. For large bias cut pieces on loose weave fabrics, i.e. the

skirt, the mounting and fabric must be permanently stitched together (Fig. 2). Lay the tacked pieces flat with the mounted side upwards. Stitch parallel lines along the grain, using matching thread and tiny stitches 2.5cm (1 inch) apart, which just catch the main fabric. The rows should be 5cm (2 inches) to 7.5cm (3 inches) apart.

FINISHING
Seam and hem neatening

Avoid machine neatening, as this tends to curl the two layers of fabric, and creates a hard edge which could mark the main fabric. Instead, trim the two layers evenly and oversew by hand (Fig. 3).

Hems

To avoid the mounting bunching in the hem, work a line of running stitches just above the hemline (Fig. 4).

One of the advantages of mounting is that

hems can be sewn invisibly.

Fold on the hemline and tack 1.3cm ($\frac{1}{2}$ inch) below the hem edge (Fig. 5a). Press on the fold, with the cloth between the iron and the fabric (Fig. 5b). Catch stitch the hem, taking great care to stitch to the mounting only (Fig. 5c).

Facings

Facings should be caught lightly at the shoulder (a), or the underarm seams (b), not stitched all round (Fig. 6).

Reversible garments

Reversible garments can be made with two separate layers of fabric, or with one in which two fabrics have been woven on one loom and held together by some joining threads.

Because of the bulk involved these fabrics are best made into capes, coats, waistcoats or skirts.

Choice of pattern

The choice of pattern is important as seams and fashion details must be kept to a minimum. Try to find a coat or cape design with a raglan sleeve line and a simple 'A' line skirt with no pleats or yokes. It is usually indicated on the pattern envelope whether the design is suitable for reversible fabrics.

Choice of fabric

If using two separate fabrics they must be of the same fibre content and weight, otherwise distortion could occur. The true reversible fabrics often have a check pattern on one side. Look at this very carefully as easy seam matching and economy of cut are only possible where the check is an exact square. If it is not then extra fabric must be bought to allow for pattern matching.

Cutting out

Place the trimmed pattern very carefully allowing 2.5cm (1 inch) seams, unless this has already been put onto the pattern by the designer (Fig. 1).

If using two separate fabrics, then make sure that the grain lines of each pair of pieces match exactly.

Tailor tack (Fig. 2), or thread mark all seam lines and balance points (Fig. 3a and b).

MAKING UP USING TWO SEPARATE FABRICS
Coats and capes

Make up each side of the garment according to the instructions given with the pattern, leaving the collar until later.

With right sides together, tack and stitch all round fronts and hem, leaving the collar space open. Snip any curves and cut across corners. Press the seam open over a sleeve board (Fig. 4).

Turn the garment through the neck opening and tack all round neck, front and hem edges (Fig. 5).

Turn under the seam allowance on sleeve hems or cape arm slits and ladder stitch together (Fig. 6).

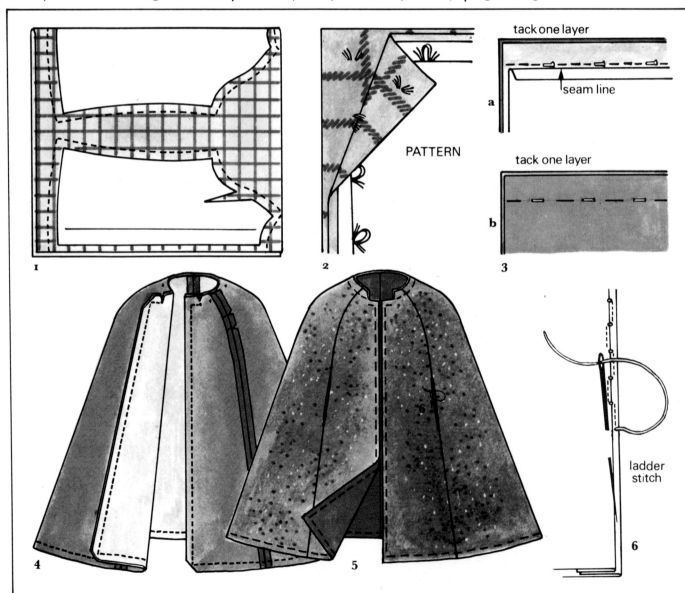

Sew on the collar as shown for the plain finish reversible collar.

To finish, saddle or top stitch round all edges.

Waistcoat

Machine and press darts and shoulder seams.

With right sides together, tack and stitch armholes and front, neck and front edge (Fig. 7).

Snip curves, cut corners and press the seams open. Turn right side out.

With right sides together, tack and stitch the side seams, making sure that the underarms match exactly (Fig. 8).

Turn under hems, place together and ladder stitch together (Fig. 6).

Top stitch if desired.

Skirt

Make two skirts, making sure that the correct side seams are left open for inserting the zip fastener.

Hand stitch the zip into one skirt using the semi-concealed method (Figs. 9a and b).

Check the skirt length. Place the skirts right sides together and machine along the hem line. Trim to 1.3cm (½ inch). Turn right side out and tack round the hem line. Fold back the zip opening and sew by hand to match the first side (Fig. 10). Cut the waistband 5cm (2 inches) longer than the waist, plus turnings.

Catch stitch petersham to one side of centre fold and make a bound buttonhole at one end (Fig. 11a).

Fold the waistband with right sides together and machine as shown (Fig. 11b).

Turn right side out and tack around the stitched edges. Turn the seam allowance under on the long edges and tack.

Slip the skirts into the band and hem both sides (Fig. 11c).

Complete the reverse side of the bound buttonhole as neatly as possible.

Alternatively, all these garments made in two separate fabrics can be trimmed on the outside sewing lines, tacked together and the edge bound as for the reversible fabrics.

MAKING UP USING REVERSIBLE FABRICS
Darts

Machine stitch darts as usual (Fig. 12). Fold the dart to centre front, centre back, or towards the hem. Trim away half of the underside as shown (Fig. 12a). Tack down to garment and hem or top stitch (Fig. 12b).

Patch pockets

Plain. Turn under seam allowance, snip or cut corners and tack (Fig. 13a).

Hem top edge (Fig. 13b).

Place onto coat and hem (Fig. 13c).

Bound. Trim to sewing lines (Fig. 14a). Press binding in half. Slip pocket into binding and hem both sides (mitre corners) (Fig. 14b).

Place onto coat and hem in position carefully.

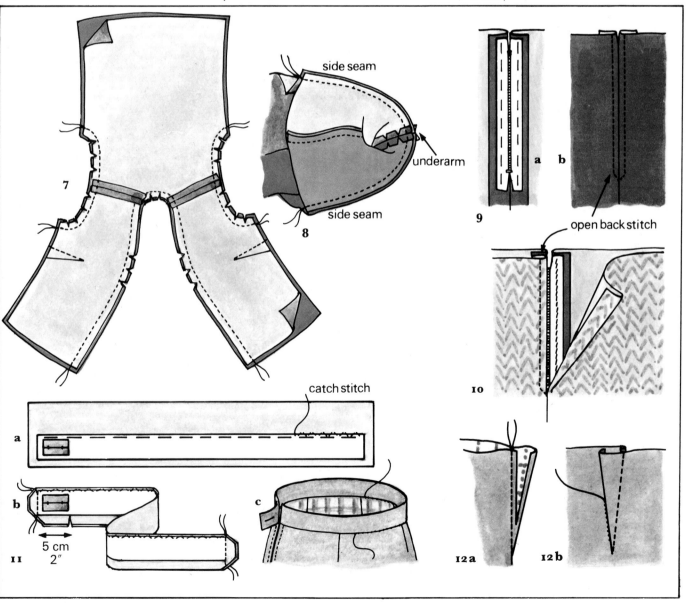

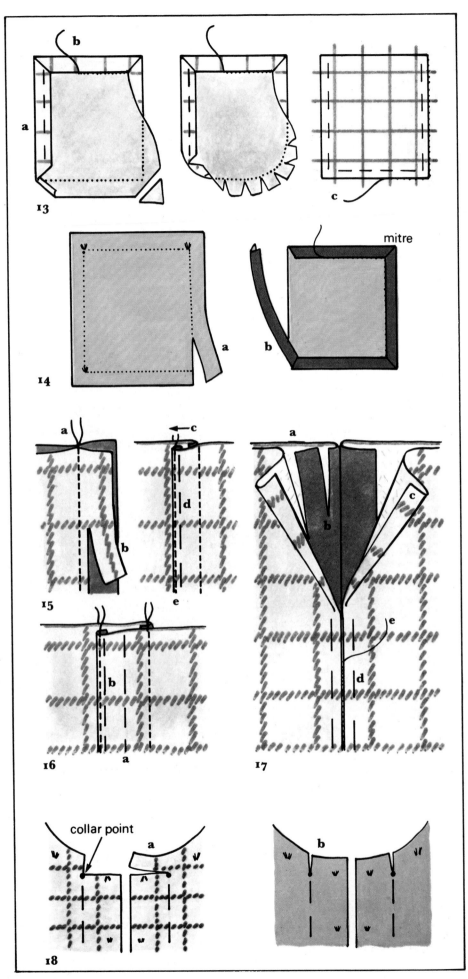

13

14

15

16

17

18

collar point

mitre

a

b

c

d

e

Seams

The following three methods of seaming are all used when making reversible garments. It depends on the design as to which method is used.

Run and fell. With wrong sides together, tack and stitch on the seam line, making sure that checks match exactly (Fig. 15a). Trim away the seam allowance nearest the centre back (Fig. 15b).

Press the seam towards the centre back (Fig. 15c).

Turn under 0.6cm ($\frac{1}{4}$ inch) on the remaining seam allowance and tack down to the garment (Fig. 15d).

Hem, top stitch or saddle stitch down (Fig. 15e).

Mock run and fell. Overlap and tack on the seam line (Fig. 16a).

Turn under each seam allowance and tack (Fig. 16b).

Hem, top stitch or saddle stitch the seams.

Plain seam. Divide the fabric for 3.8cm ($1\frac{1}{2}$ inches) along the length of the seam (Fig. 17a).

Lay two matching sides together and stitch a plain seam. Trim the seam allowance to 0.6cm ($\frac{1}{4}$ inch) and press open (Fig. 17b).

Turn under the remaining edges on the sewing lines and trim to 1.3cm ($\frac{1}{2}$ inch) (Fig. 17c).

Tack the folds exactly over the seam line (Fig. 17d).

Ladder stitch together (Fig. 17e).

Collars

Neck edge preparation

Bound edges. Trim away the front neck edge along the sewing line to the collar point (Fig. 18a).

Plain edges. Snip to collar point (Fig. 18b).

Collar pieces. Cut two pieces of fabric for the collar exactly the same, using the top collar pattern.

For bound edge. Trim off all but the neck edges to the seam lines (Fig. 19). Place the collars with right sides together to the coat, matching or contrasting colours or checks (Fig. 20a). Machine along the neck line (Fig. 20b). Trim the coat seam to 0.6cm ($\frac{1}{4}$ inch).

Press the collars up and tack together (Fig. 20c).

Bind the edge as instructed in edge finishes.

For plain seam. Pull away and trim the inside of the collar pieces to the collar seam lines. Cut corners of remaining layer away (Fig. 21a).

Fold under to seam lines, tack and press (Fig. 21b).

Take each piece in turn and hem the neck edge to the coat matching ends exactly (Fig. 21c).

Tack the collar edges together and ladder stitch (Fig. 21d). Top stitch or saddle stitch.

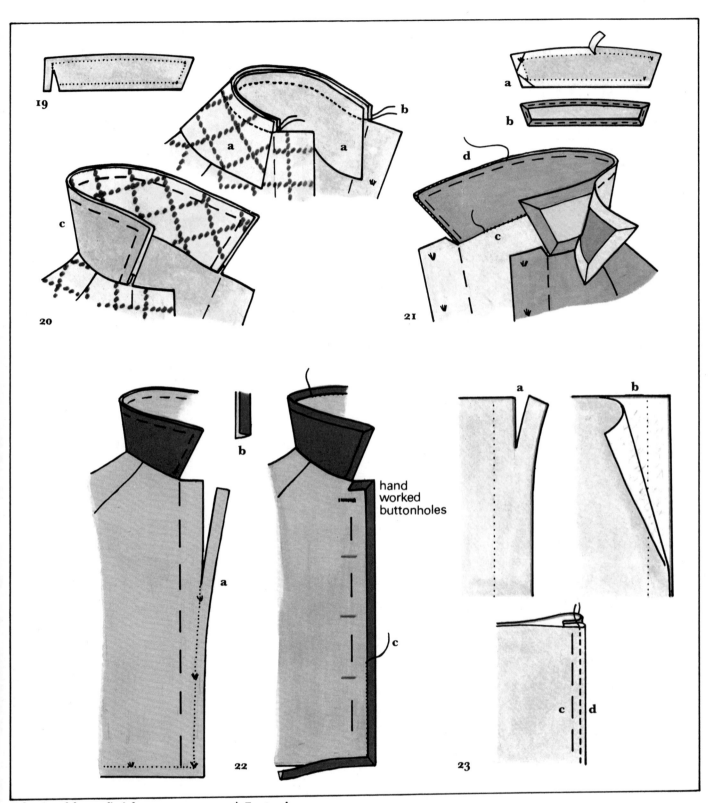

Edge and hem finishes

Bound. Trim to seam lines (Fig. 22a).
Press bindings in half (Fig. 22b).
Sandwich the coat into the fold and hem both sides (Fig. 22c).

Plain. Trim the seam allowance to 1.3cm ($\frac{1}{2}$ *inch*) (Fig. 23a). Divide the fabric for 3.2cm ($1\frac{1}{4}$ *inches*) (Fig. 23b).
Fold in separate layers to the seam line and tack the folds together (Fig. 23c).
Ladder, top stitch or saddle stitch (Fig. 23d).

Fastenings

Use frogs for both reversible and two layers of fabric, and zip fasteners for two layers of fabric only.

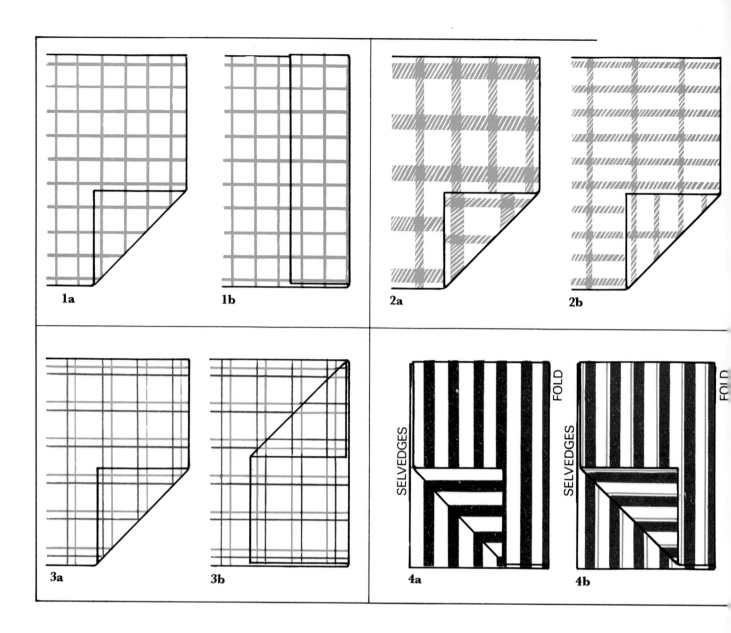

1a   1b   2a   2b

3a   3b   4a   4b

Plaids, checks & stripes

When using plaid, check or stripe fabrics, the aim is to achieve a balanced, harmonious effect in proportion to the figure. Vertical lines tend to lengthen a figure and horizontal lines have a broadening effect, but, bearing this in mind, very pleasing results can be achieved when using modern fabric designs and fashion styles. When choosing a pattern for these fabrics, give careful attention to the layout of the pattern pieces. Once this is done, the actual construction of the garment should be straightforward.

Plaids

Plaids are made from stripes crossing each other at right angles, spaced as the designer desires and repeated to form a length of fabric. In all plaids the main outlines of the design are formed by two dominant stripes, one vertical and one horizontal.

In even plaids these stripes form perfect squares, and when any square is folded diagonally or vertically in half, it forms a mirror image of itself (Figs. 1a and b). Even plaids are easy to use and ideal for those using these designs for the first time. In uneven plaids the stripes and designs can be different either lengthwise or crosswise or in both directions (Figs. 2a and b). It is not always easy to see if a plaid is a true square or not.

To check this, fold the fabric diagonally through the centre of the repeat, then horizontally or vertically as a double check, because some plaids have a subtle repeat which matches diagonally but not in other directions (Figs. 3a and b).

Checks

These are made in the same way as plaids and most are formed from complete squares. Some checks are oblongs, however, so fold the fabric as shown in the figure above to check their shape and accuracy.

Stripes

Stripes can be even or unevenly balanced and of varying widths. Fold across the true bias to see this clearly (Figs. 4a and b).

62

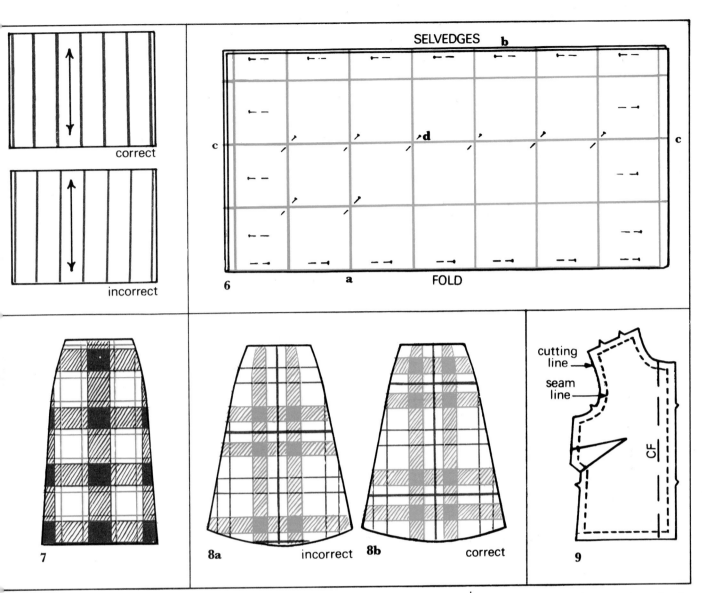

correct

incorrect

SELVEDGES b

c   c

6   a   FOLD

7

8a   incorrect   8b   correct

cutting line
seam line

CF

9

Striped fabrics can often be cut to create exciting visual effects; they can be used as bias bindings for pockets and cuffs, or to give a chevron effect when cut on the bias and seamed centrally. Be very careful to match precisely when stitching.

The best and most accurate of all plaids, checks and striped fabrics are those which have the designs woven into them.

When working with printed fabrics it is essential to test the pattern as shown (Figs. 1a–4b), and also to make sure that the designs are printed in line with the grain (Figs. 5a and b).

To find the dominant line or lines, half close the eyes and squint at the fabric, to blur the design and allow these lines to become obvious. Because a small piece of fabric does not always show a complete repeat of a design, it is best to buy from a roll and to allow extra for matching. The amount needed will depend on the size of the design, but allowing 22.5cm (¼ yard) extra for small designs and 45cm (½ yard) for larger patterns should prove to be sufficient.

Styles to consider

Stripe or plaid fabrics can be used to make a whole garment, or as a contrast. Study patterns to see how the designers drew their ideas and imagine how individual touches could be added. It is a good idea to take a tracing of the garment, and to add these touches to it to see if they are suitable.

Always make sure that the pattern used is designed for plaids, checks or stripes. If it has been found that seam lines cannot be matched owing to differing angles or style lines, then this information will be given on the pattern envelope.

Preparation of fabric

This is most important as the underneath piece of the folded fabric must exactly match the top piece.

Pin down the fold, having decided where this is to be after reference to the pattern, i.e. which part of the design is to be at the centre back or centre front, making sure that the fold is either at the centre of a design or on a dominant line (Fig. 6a).

Pin along the selvedge, matching the design every 5cm (2 inches) (Fig. 6b), and across the ends of the fabric, matching the design (Fig. 6c).

Pin at intervals all over the fabric, checking underneath to see that the pattern matches exactly (Fig. 6d).

If the fabric has to be refolded to cut specific pattern pieces, this process should be repeated every time. Even with quite small checks, this procedure should be followed.

Layout

Because a great deal of time and thought has to be given to the layout of the pattern, it is essential that the pattern should fit the figure. Pin it together along seam lines, try on and make any necessary alterations. Consider the following points before starting the layout:

For a straight hemline, the dominant stripe should be at the hem (Fig. 7).

For a curved hemline the dominant stripe should be above the hemline to avoid the impression it is falling out of the skirt (Figs. 8a and b).

63

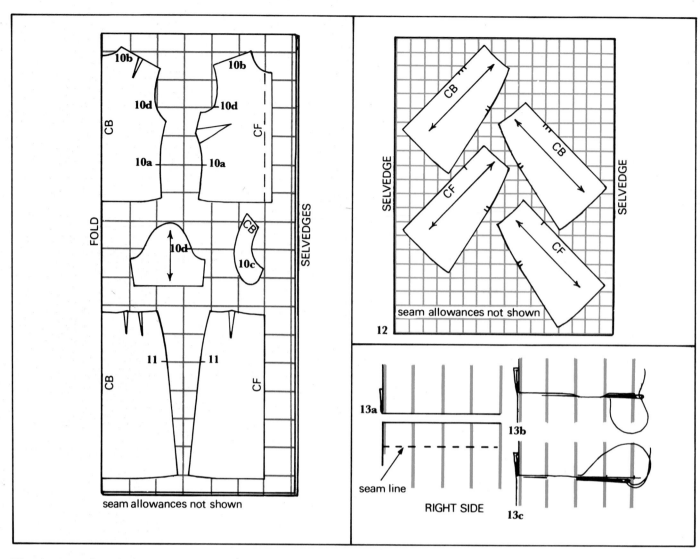

seam allowances not shown

seam allowances not shown

RIGHT SIDE

The dominant line should not fall across the widest part of the garment.

Always remember to match seam lines, not cutting lines. If this is found to be difficult then cut the pattern along the seam lines, but remember the seam allowance when cutting out the pattern pieces (Fig. 9).

For even designs, match the pattern at the following points:

On bodice or blouse

Side seam notches. If there is an underarm dart or style line it is impossible to match the complete side seam, so use the notches so that the part that shows in wear is correct. (Fig. 10a).

Shoulder seams. These are difficult to match because of the dart or ease that is sometimes included in the back shoulder line (Fig. 10b).

Centre back of collar to back bodice. This should be planned carefully so that there is a horizontal as well as a vertical match. Cutting the top collar can be left until the bodice is made up because it can then be seen whether it is better to match up the pattern at the centre front.

Cutting the top collar with the centre back on the bias (with a seam), can sometimes solve a difficult matching problem (Fig. 10c).

Setting in sleeves. Match the front sleeve head notch to the front bodice armhole notch. Because of the ease at the sleeve head it is impossible to match the complete armhole and with large plaids it is also impossible to match the pattern at the back (Fig. 10d).

For kimono or raglan sleeves, match below sleeve notches at shoulder point.

On skirts

Match the centre front, centre back and hem lines. Side seams can only match vertically where the slant on both is the same (Fig. 11).

On dresses

Match the full length of the centres front and back and at the hemlines.

On suits

Match the centres of the jacket to the skirt and the jacket hemline to the point where it overlaps the skirt.

On trousers

Work from the side seam notches, making sure that the hemline matches at the side.

Cutting on the bias

Very pleasing effects can be obtained by cutting the fabric on the bias. To do this, cut each piece singly, matching carefully each time. Remember to reverse the pattern piece for the second piece of a pair (Fig. 12).

Uneven plaids are more difficult and cannot be matched in both directions. Choose the design that is to be emphasised both vertically and horizontally and match this for the centres and hemline.

Slip tacking

This method of tacking is the easiest way in which to match the designs accurately. Lay two pieces side by side, right side up. Turn under the seam allowance on one piece (Fig. 13a).

Lay the folded edge to the sewing line of the other piece (Fig. 13b).

Take a stitch through the fold (Fig. 13c).

Pick up the under piece exactly on the sewing line (Fig. 13d).

ALTERATIONS

Grading patterns

Clothing manufacturers each have their own standard size charts, depending on the class of trade with which they are involved, whether it be outsizes, half sizes, women's sizes or children's sizes. Whichever class is involved it must comply with the size charts, for they state the actual measurements of an average figure or dress stand.

For example, size 12 has the following measurements:

Bust 87cm (*34 inches*)
Waist 67cm (*26½ inches*)
Hips 92cm (*36 inches*)
Back neck to waist 41.5cm (*16¼ inches*)

Other measurements such as shoulder, shoulder to elbow, elbow to wrist, across back etc., are not mentioned on the charts but the basic blocks used in the manufacturing industry are comprised of these measurements, which are proportionate to the average figure in the different classes of trade. However, in drafting for an individual, these measurements must obviously be made to conform to the particular requirements of the person in question.

One must understand that it is impossible for manufacturers to cater for every individual figure type.

GRADING
General instructions

The term grading is the name given to the process of increasing or decreasing a sample size pattern proportionately, according to the average (standard) body measurements, while retaining the original fashion features. The most important thing when grading is accuracy, both of the marks and measurements themselves and their placing. A detailed knowledge of a size chart is essential.

To grade a pattern from one size to another, one moves the pattern piece from point to point, tracing each step as one proceeds.

Once the master pattern or block has been drafted, showing all important markings – for example, dart points, straight

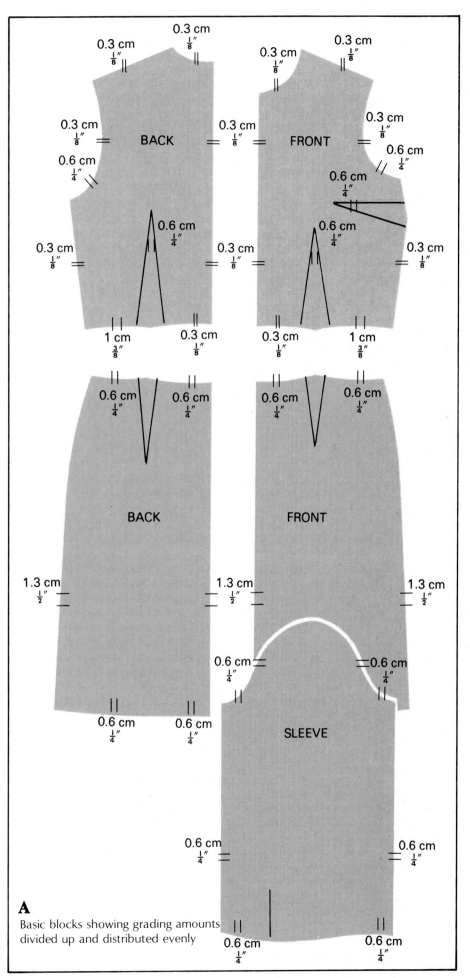

A
Basic blocks showing grading amounts divided up and distributed evenly

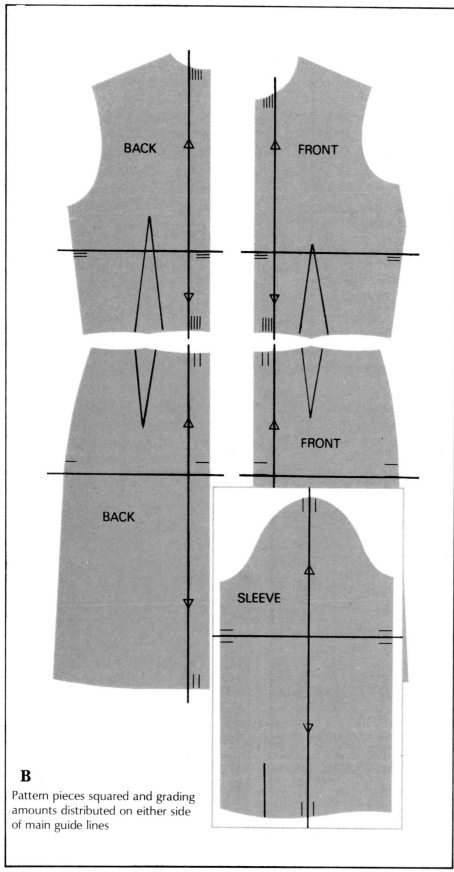

B
Pattern pieces squared and grading amounts distributed on either side of main guide lines

quired amounts afterwards. This is, however, a matter of personal preference.

Next, perforate all the dart points and any other main construction points using an especially designed paper punch (single punch) or any other similar sharp implement.

When these stages are complete, the pattern is then ready to grade. The directions for a simple method of grading are set out in this chapter. This method is ideal for multisize patterns which include a range of up to four sizes, and sometimes five sizes, conveniently placed on one sheet of paper.

By consulting the size chart, the pattern cutter decides how the increase or decrease at any one place is divided and distributed to give the required amount, whilst preserving the proportion of the design.

Sample standard size chart
The sample standard size chart includes four sizes, 10, 12, 14 and 16, with a separate column giving the amounts of increase or decrease (grade) between sizes.

Grading on basic blocks
Diagram A shows the blocks: back and front bodice, back and front skirt and sleeve, and the grading amounts which have been divided up and distributed evenly.

TO GRADE THE PATTERN
Beginning with the back bodice and then the front bodice, grade one piece at a time.

Pin or weight down a sheet of paper on a flat surface. Trace around the pattern piece leaving sufficient space at the edges for grading.

It is also advisable to weight the pattern piece down when doing this.

Having traced the pattern piece on to the paper, use a set square and square up and down and across through the grain lines, continuing these lines off the edge of the pattern. These act as guide lines enabling one to ensure that the pattern is kept square, which is essential for accuracy.

Diagram B shows the pattern piece squared up and down and across, and the new guide lines divided and distributed on either side of the main guide lines.

Remove the pattern and connect these lines. The amount of increase or decrease is divided and distributed on either side of the guide lines on the master pattern or block, to provide new guide lines with respect to the amount graded.

The pattern is then moved either up and out or down and in on these new guide lines to produce the new size of pattern.

grain lines, centre front and centre back lines, notches and if required, button, buttonhole and pocket positions – the pattern is then attached to card by pinning or stapling. This step is not necessary if the master pattern block is drafted directly on to the card. Trim off the excess card by cutting round the outer edge of the pattern shapes.

It is perhaps easier to include seam and hem allowances on the master pattern before grading, rather than add the re-

Grading the back bodice from size 10 to 12 (diagram C)

With the pattern square on the guide lines, first move the pattern up 0.3cm ($\frac{1}{8}$ inch) and draw part of the neck curve (Fig. 1)A. Move the pattern up another 0.3cm ($\frac{1}{8}$ inch), and at the same time out 0.3cm ($\frac{1}{8}$ inch). Draw the top of the neck and the shoulder (Fig. 1)B. With the pattern held at this position, move it out another 0.3cm ($\frac{1}{8}$ inch) and draw the shoulder and the armhole, stopping about 5cm (2 inches) above the lower edge of the armhole (Fig. 1)C.

Bring the pattern back to align with the guide lines and move it out 0.6cm ($\frac{1}{4}$ inch), ensuring that the pattern is square with the across guide line, and redraw the dart at this position, move it out another 0.6cm ($\frac{1}{4}$ inch), making the total grade at the side seam 1.3cm ($\frac{1}{2}$ inch), and draw the side seam from E to F (Fig. 2). With the pattern back in the original position, move it down 0.3cm ($\frac{1}{8}$ inch) and redraw the lower edge of the back from G to H (Fig. 2). Continue the dart lines from their new position.

Connect the lines up at points A to B, B to C and C to E (Fig. 3). This completes the grade.

Grading the front bodice from size 10 to 12

To grade the front bodice, use the same method of moving the pattern as instructed for grading the back.

At the stage of marking the waist dart D, mark also the point of the bust dart, that is the grade of 0.6cm ($\frac{1}{4}$ inch) out towards the side seam G.

Move the pattern out another 0.6cm ($\frac{1}{4}$ inch), making a total of 1.3cm ($\frac{1}{2}$ inch) at the side seam. Re-mark the dart and side seam (Fig. 4).

Note: The bust dart does not alter in width, only in length.

Grading the back skirt from size 10 to 12

To grade the back skirt, place the pattern square with the guide lines. Move the pattern out 0.6cm ($\frac{1}{4}$ inch), keeping the across guide line square and mark the waist dart (Fig. 5)A.

With the pattern held at this point, move it out another 0.6cm ($\frac{1}{4}$ inch) and draw the side seam line from B to C. Move the pattern back to the original position and move down 1.3cm ($\frac{1}{2}$ inch), keeping the up and down guide line square. Re-draw the hem line from C to D (Fig. 5). This completes the grade.

Note: To grade the front skirt, use exactly the same method as for the back skirt.

Grading the sleeve from size 10 to 12

To grade the sleeve, use the same method of moving the pattern as shown for the back and front bodice and skirt, beginning from A, then B to C, then D to E.

Move the pattern up 0.6cm ($\frac{1}{4}$ inch), keeping the up and down guide line square (Fig. 6)A.

Draw the crown of the sleeve to within 5cm (2 inches) of the underarm seam.

Bring the pattern back to the original position and move out 0.6cm ($\frac{1}{4}$ inches), and redraw the underarm seam B to C. The same applies to points D to E.

For the lower edge of the sleeve, place the pattern in the original position and move down 0.6cm ($\frac{1}{4}$ inch) and redraw line C to E. Connect these points to complete the grade.

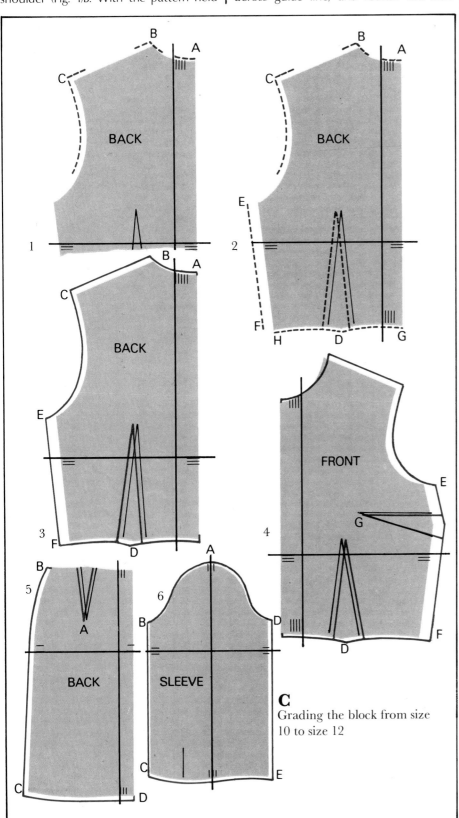

C
Grading the block from size 10 to size 12

Grading style lines

This chapter explains the methods of grading the following pattern shapes:

A. Two piece bodice with a seam line from the shoulder to the waistline.
B. Front bodice with a seam from the armhole to the waistline.
C. Back bodice with shaped yoke.
D. One piece front and back yoke.
E. Two piece sleeve.
F. Straight cuff.
G. Shirt collar.

General instructions for grading a two piece bodice with a seam line from the shoulder to the waistline

The amounts of increase or decrease when grading a two piece bodice are the same as those for grading a basic block. In the case of a two piece bodice, these amounts are divided and distributed between each pattern piece. The total grade of 1.3cm (½ inch) from the centre front to the side seam is divided between the front piece and the side front piece. For grading up or down a size, 0.6cm (¼ inch) is either added or subtracted to the front piece, from the line of the bust point to the waistline; this amount of grade is for the bust and waist dart on the basic blocks. When grading above the bust point on a basic block, the amount of increase or decrease, which is 0.6cm (¼ inch), is distributed between the neck and the armhole. Whereas here, when grading a two piece bodice above the bust point, the amount is divided equally between the front and side front pieces, so that each piece is graded by 0.3cm (⅛ inch). The side seam is graded by 0.6cm (¼ inch), thus making a total grade from the centre front to the side seam of 1.3cm (½ inch). The same method of grading also applies to the back pattern pieces.

As a general principle, attach the pattern to card by pinning or stapling. Trim off the excess card by carefully cutting round the pattern shapes and perforate all important markings and construction points. Pin or weigh down a sheet of paper, place one pattern piece on the sheet (grade only one piece at a time) and trace around the outer edge. Having traced the pattern piece onto the paper, use a set square and square up and down and across through the grain line, continuing these lines off the edge of the pattern. These act as guide lines. Remove the pattern and connect these lines. On the pattern, the amount of increase or decrease is divided and distributed on either side of the guide lines.

A. TWO PIECE BODICE WITH SEAM LINE FROM SHOULDER TO WAISTLINE

To grade the front pattern piece

Diagrams A1 and Ā2 show the front pattern pieces squared up, down and across, and the amounts of grade divided and distributed on either side of the guide lines.

With the pattern ready to grade, position the front pattern piece on the guide lines. Begin by moving the pattern up 0.3cm (⅛ inch) and draw part of the neck curve (Fig. 1a). Move the pattern up a further 0.3cm (⅛ inch) and at the same time out 0.3cm (⅛ inch). Draw the top of the neck and shoulder (Fig. 1b). With the pattern held in this position, draw the panel seam line at the shoulder (Fig. 1c). Bring the pattern back to align with the guide lines, move it out 0.6cm (¼ inch) and at the same time down 0.3cm (⅛ inch), and draw the lower edge of the panel seam line and the waistline (Fig. 1d and e). Remove the pattern and connect up the lines from points a to b, c to d and d to e (Fig. 2). This completes the grade.

To grade the side front piece

With the pattern positioned on the guide lines, move it up 0.6cm (¼ inch) and draw the shoulder (Fig. 1f). Hold the pattern in this position, move it out 0.3cm (⅛ inch) and draw the armhole to within 5cm (2 inches) of the lower curve (Fig. 1g). Return the pattern to its original position, then move it out 0.6cm (¼ inch) and at the same time down 0.3cm (⅛ inch). Draw the side seam and the waistline (Fig. 1h, j and k). Remove the pattern and connect up the lines from points f to g, g to h, h to j and j to k (Fig. 2). This completes the grade. For grading the back pattern pieces, use the same method and amounts of grade as for the front pattern pieces.

B. FRONT BODICE WITH A SEAM FROM THE ARMHOLE TO THE WAISTLINE

To grade the front pattern piece

Diagrams B1 and B2 show the front and side front pieces with the guide lines marked, and the increase of grade divided and distributed on either side of the guide lines.

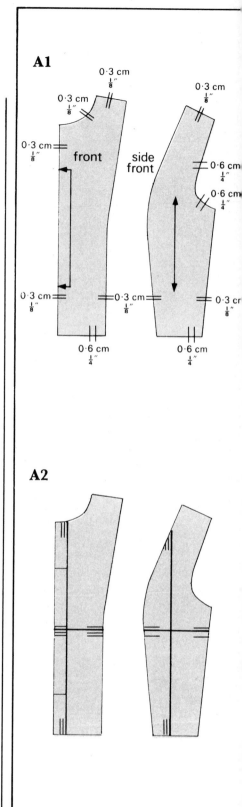

A1

0.3 cm ⅛"
0.3 cm ⅛"
0.3 cm ⅛"
0.3 cm ⅛"
0.3 cm ⅛"
0.3 cm ⅛"
0.3 cm ⅛"
0.6 cm ¼"
0.6 cm ¼"
0.6 cm ¼"
0.6 cm ¼"

front
side front

A2

To grade the front piece

With the pattern positioned on the guide lines, move it up 0.3cm (⅛ inch) and draw part of the neck curve (Fig. 3a). Move the pattern up another 0.3cm (⅛ inch) and at the same time, out 0.3cm (⅛ inch). Draw the top of the neck and shoulder (Fig. 3b). With the pattern held in this position, move it out 0.3cm (⅛ inch) and draw the

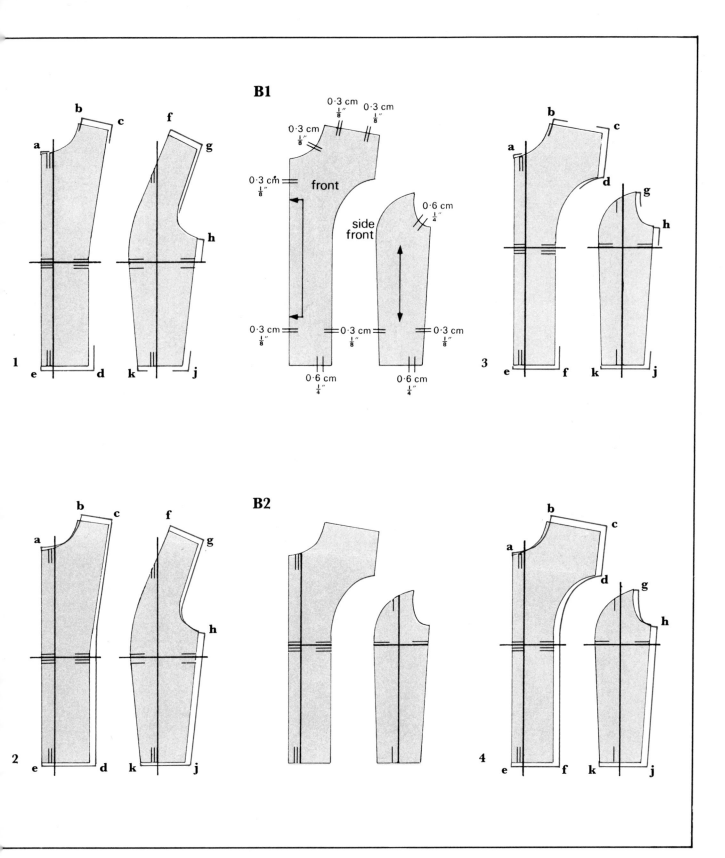

B1

0·3 cm $\frac{1}{8}''$ 0·3 cm $\frac{1}{8}''$

0·3 cm $\frac{1}{8}''$

0·3 cm $\frac{1}{8}''$ front

side front   0·6 cm $\frac{1}{4}''$

0·3 cm $\frac{1}{8}''$ 0·3 cm $\frac{1}{8}''$ 0·3 cm $\frac{1}{8}''$

0·6 cm $\frac{1}{4}''$ 0·6 cm $\frac{1}{4}''$

B2

shoulder and armhole (Fig. 3c and d). Re-align the pattern with the guide lines, then move it out 0.6cm ($\frac{1}{4}$ inch) and draw the curve of the panel seam at the armhole edge. (Fig. 3d). From this position, move the pattern down 0.3cm ($\frac{1}{8}$ inch) and draw the waistline and the lower edge of the panel seam (Fig. 3e and f). Remove the pattern and connect the lines up from points a to b, b to c, c to d, d to f and e to f (Fig. 4). This completes the grade.

To grade the side front piece
Position the pattern on the guide lines, then move it out 0.6cm ($\frac{1}{4}$ inch) and draw the lower part of the armhole to within 5cm (2 inches) of the lower curve (Fig. 3g). With the pattern held in this position,

move it down 0.3cm ($\frac{1}{8}$ inch) and draw the side seam (Fig. 3h), the waistline and the lower edge of the side seam (Fig. 3j and k). Remove the pattern and connect up the lines from points g to h, h to j, and j to k (Fig. 4). This completes the grade.
For grading the back pattern pieces, use the same method and amounts of grade as for the front pieces.

C. BACK BODICE WITH A SHAPED YOKE

Diagrams C1 and C2 show the back yoke and bodice with the guide lines marked, and the increase of grade divided and distributed on either side of the guide lines.

To grade the yoke piece

Position the pattern on the guide lines, move it up 0.3cm ($\frac{1}{8}$ inch) and draw part of the neck curve (Fig. 5a). Move the pattern up a further 0.3cm ($\frac{1}{8}$ inch) and at the same time out 0.3cm ($\frac{1}{8}$ inch), and draw the top of the neck and shoulder (Fig. 5b). Keeping the pattern in this position, move it out 0.3cm ($\frac{1}{8}$ inch) and draw the armhole to the lower edge of the yoke (Fig. 5c and d). Remove the pattern and connect up the lines from points a to b,

b to c and c to d (Fig. 6).
This completes the grade of the yoke.

To grade the bodice

Align the bodice pattern with the guide lines, then move the pattern out 0.6cm ($\frac{1}{4}$ inch) and draw the armhole to within 5cm (2 inches) of the lower curve (Fig. 5e). With the pattern held in this position, mark the dart (Fig. 5f), then move it out a further 0.6cm ($\frac{1}{4}$ inch) and at the same time down 0.3cm ($\frac{1}{8}$ inch), and draw the side seams and the waistline (Fig. 5g, h and j).
Remove the pattern and connect up the lines from points e to g, g to h and j to h, and connect the dart lines in the new position (Fig. 6).
This completes the grade.

D. ONE PIECE FRONT AND BACK YOKE

Diagrams D1 and D2 show the yoke with the guide lines marked and the grade divided and distributed on either side of the guide lines. One must remember that the shoulder line on a front and back basic block is graded by 0.6cm ($\frac{1}{4}$ inch), making a total grade of 1.3cm ($\frac{1}{2}$ inch), therefore this amount must be distributed through the shoulder line of the yoke as shown in diagram D1.

To grade the yoke

Position the yoke pattern on the guide lines in the manner shown in diagram D2. Move the pattern up 0.3cm ($\frac{1}{8}$ inch) and draw part of the neck curve (Fig. 7a). Move the pattern up a further 0.3cm ($\frac{1}{8}$ inch) and at the same time out 0.3cm ($\frac{1}{8}$ inch).

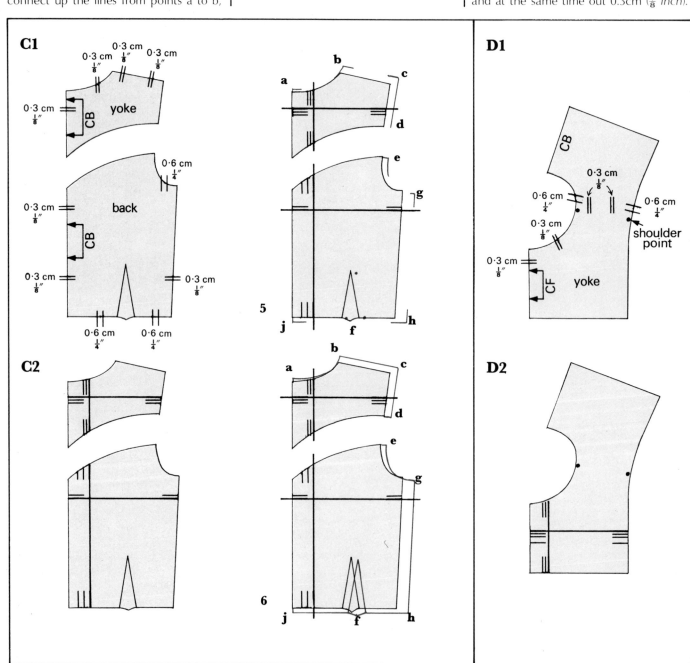

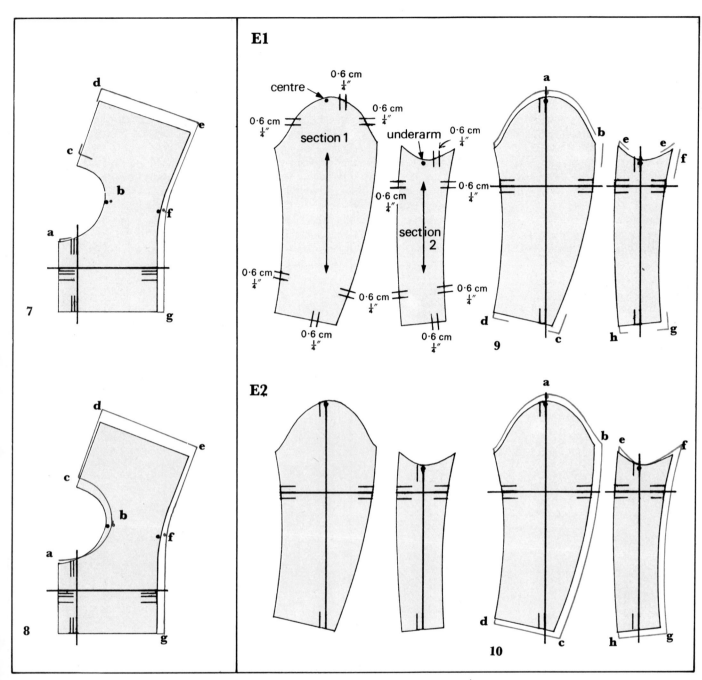

Mark the shoulder point at the neck edge (Fig. 7b). From this position, move the pattern up to 0.6cm ($\frac{1}{4}$ inch), and draw part of the back neck curve and the lower edge of the back yoke (Fig. 7c, d and e). The total amount of grade through the shoulder is shown at point d. With the pattern back in the original position, move it up 0.6cm ($\frac{1}{4}$ inch), at the same time move it out 0.6cm ($\frac{1}{4}$ inch), and draw the front armhole from the shoulder to the lower edge of the yoke (Fig. 7f and g) shown below.

Mark shoulder point.

Now move the pattern up a further 0.6cm ($\frac{1}{4}$ inch) and draw the back armhole from point f to e. Remove the pattern and connect up the lines from points a to b, b to c, c to d and d to e (Fig. 8). This completes the grade.

E. TWO PIECE SLEEVE
The increase of grade for a two piece sleeve is the same as that for a basic block. Diagrams E1 and E2 show the two piece sleeve with the guide lines marked and the grade divided and distributed on either side of the guide lines.

To grade the first section of the sleeve
Grade the larger section of the sleeve first. Position the pattern on the guide lines and move it up 0.6cm ($\frac{1}{4}$ inch). Draw the crown of the sleeve and mark the point of the sleeve head (Fig. 9a). Re-align the pattern with the guide lines, move it out 0.6cm ($\frac{1}{4}$ inch) and draw the top of the seam line (Fig. 9b). Then move the pattern down 0.6cm ($\frac{1}{4}$ inch) and draw the lower edge of the sleeve and the seam line

(Fig. 9c and d). Remove the pattern and connect up the lines from points a to b, b to c and c to d (Fig. 10). This completes the grade for this section.

To grade the second section of the sleeve
Align the pattern with the guide lines, then move it up 0.6cm ($\frac{1}{4}$ inch) and draw the curves to within 3.8cm ($1\frac{1}{2}$ inches) of the underarm point (Fig. 9e). After returning the pattern to its original position, move it out 0.6cm ($\frac{1}{4}$ inch) and draw the top of the seam line (Fig. 9f). Then move the pattern down 0.6cm ($\frac{1}{4}$ inch) and draw the lower edge of the sleeve and seam line (Fig. 9g and h). Remove the pattern and connect up the lines from e to f, f to g and g to h (Fig. 10). This completes the grade.

F. A STRAIGHT CUFF

The cuff grade must correspond with the grade of the lower part of the sleeve where the total amount is 1.3cm ($\frac{1}{2}$ inch), and this is divided to give 0.6cm ($\frac{1}{4}$ inch) on either side of the sleeve.

Square the pattern up, down and across with the grain line, and divide and distribute the grade on either side of the guide lines as shown in diagram F.

Align the pattern with the guide lines, move it out 0.6cm ($\frac{1}{4}$ inch) and draw the side of the cuff (Fig. 11a and b) and any buttonhole positions where necessary (Fig. 11c). Having returned the pattern to its original position, move it out to the other side 0.6cm ($\frac{1}{4}$ inch), and draw this edge of the cuff (Fig. 11d and e), and also any button positions which correspond to the buttonholes (Fig. 11f). Remove the pattern and connect up the lines from points a to b and d to e (Fig. 12). This completes the grade.

G. SHIRT COLLAR

When grading a collar, the amount of increase is the same as that for the front and back neck at the shoulder point. This amount is 1.3cm ($\frac{1}{2}$ inch).

Square the pattern piece up, down and across.

As a result of the grading, the collar is increased in length but is not increased in width.

The amount of grade is divided and distributed only on either side of the up and down guide lines as shown in diagram G. This being completed, position the pattern on the guide lines and then move it out 0.6cm ($\frac{1}{4}$ inch) and mark the shoulder point (Fig. 13a).

Now move it out a further 0.6cm ($\frac{1}{4}$ inch) and draw the outline of the collar (Fig. 13b, c and d).

Remove the pattern and connect up the lines from points b to c as shown in Fig 14.

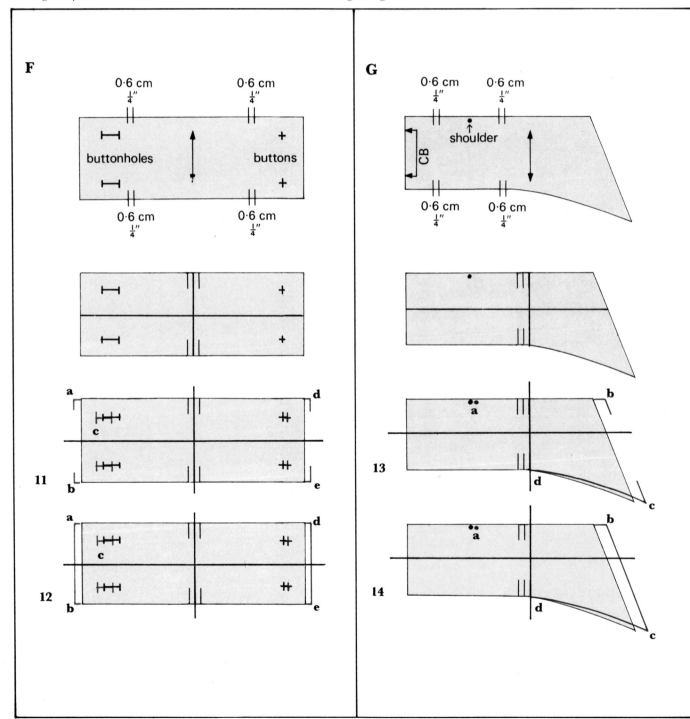

Grading styled skirts

This chapter explains the methods of grading the following pattern shapes:

A. Panelled skirt attached to a two piece bodice.
B. A four panelled skirt.
C. A skirt with a front yoke.
D. A pleated skirt.

Note: As an example, all grading instructions in this chapter are for grading a size 12 to a size 14. For grading other sizes, see Golden Hands Monthly, issue 20.

A. PANELLED SKIRT ATTACHED TO A TWO PIECE BODICE

The total grade on the skirt must be divided and distributed by the same amounts and between the same seams as on the bodice pattern pieces, thus enabling the seams to form a continuous line. Use the same method to square the skirt pattern pieces as that used for the bodice. The amounts of grade are then divided and distributed on either side of the guide lines. Diagrams A1 and A2 show the skirt front and side front, with the amounts of grade divided and distributed on the same seam lines as those on the bodice, as shown in diagrams A1 and A2.

To grade the skirt front piece

Position the pattern piece on the guide lines and move it out 0.6cm ($\frac{1}{4}$ inch). Draw the seamline at the waistline edge and at the lower edge of the seam (Fig. 1a and b). With the pattern held in this position, move it down 1.3cm ($\frac{1}{2}$ inch) and draw the lower edge of the pattern (Fig. 1b and c). Remove the pattern and connect up the lines from points a to b and b to c.

To grade the side front piece

Align the pattern on the guide lines, then move it out 0.6cm ($\frac{1}{4}$ inch). Draw the side seam at the waistline edge and the lower edge of the side seam (Fig. 1d and e). Then move it down 1.3cm ($\frac{1}{2}$ inch) and draw the lower edge of the pattern (Fig. 1e and f). Remove the pattern and connect up the lines from points d to e and e to f (Fig. 2). This completes the grade of both pattern pieces. The back pattern pieces are graded using the same method.

When the grading of both the bodice and the skirt pieces is complete, partly pin them together at the seam lines and around the waistline. Then, in order to ensure the accuracy of the grading, check that the seams form continuous lines.

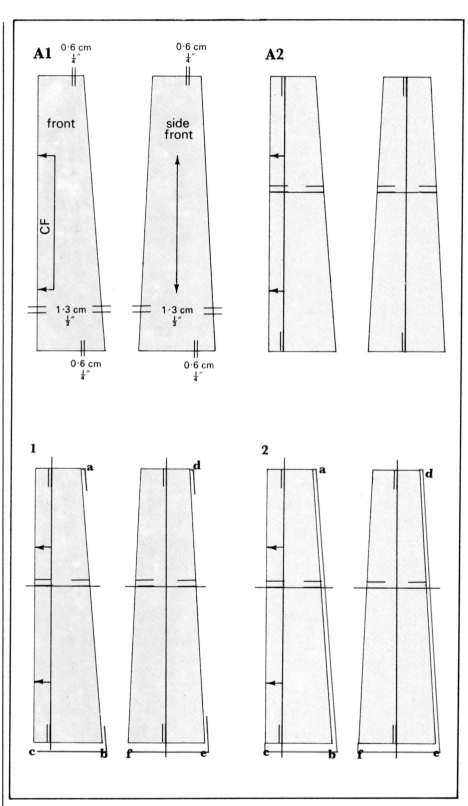

B. A FOUR PANELLED SKIRT

Diagrams B1 and B2 show the skirt pattern in two sections, (both of which are to be cut twice), and also show how much each section is to be graded. This amount has been divided and distributed evenly on either side of the guide lines.

The amount of increase at the waistline and at the hipline, when grading from size 12 to 14, is 5cm (2 inches). This amount is divided equally between the eight sides of the four sections, thus giving 1.3cm ($\frac{1}{2}$ inch) to each section and 0.6cm ($\frac{1}{4}$ inch) to each side.

Diagrams B1 and B2 show the guide lines marked and the grade divided and distributed on either side of the guide lines.

To grade the front skirt piece

Position the pattern on the guide lines, move it out to one side by 0.6cm ($\frac{1}{4}$ inch), and draw the side edge of the pattern at the waistline and at the lower edge (Fig. 3a). From this position move the pattern down 1.3cm ($\frac{1}{2}$ inch) and draw part of the lower edge (Fig. 3b). Re-align the pattern with the guide lines, then move it out to the other side by 0.6cm ($\frac{1}{4}$ inch) and draw the side edge of the pattern at the waistline and at the lower edge (Fig. 3c). Hold the pattern in this position, move it down 1.3cm ($\frac{1}{2}$ inch), and draw the lower edge of the pattern (Fig. 3d).

Remove the pattern and connect up the lines from points a to b, c to d and b to d (Fig. 4).

This completes the grade.

Grade the back skirt piece using the same method.

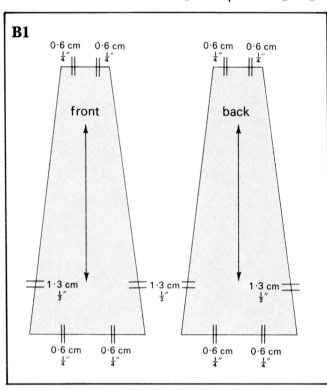

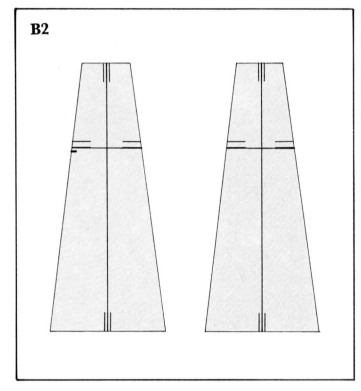

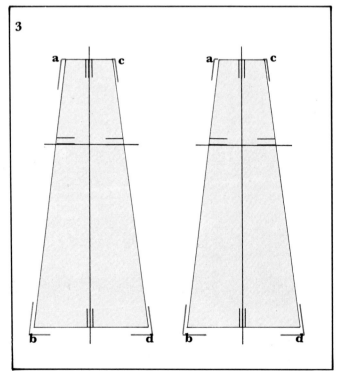

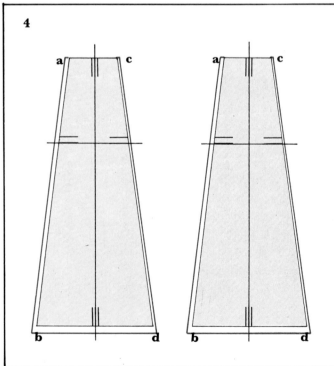

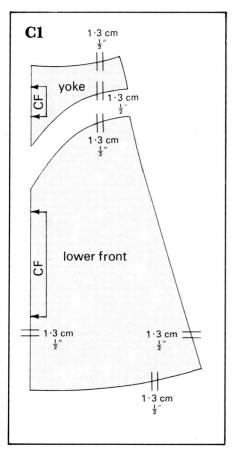

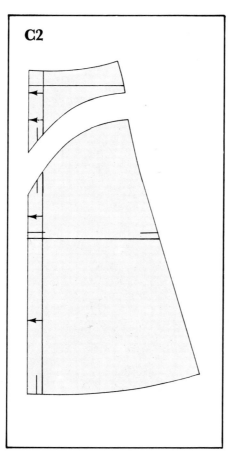

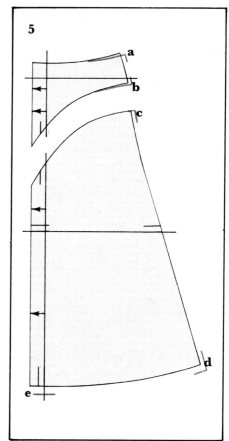

C. SKIRT WITH FRONT YOKE

Diagrams C1 and C2 show the skirt front yoke and skirt lower front (both of which are to be cut on the fold) with the guide lines marked and the increase of the grade divided and distributed on either side of the guide lines.

To grade the skirt yoke

Position the pattern on the guide lines, then move it out 1.3cm ($\frac{1}{2}$ inch) and draw the yoke side seam at the waistline and at the lower edge (Fig. 5a and b).
Remove the pattern and connect the lines up from points a to b (Fig. 6). This completes the grade.

To grade the skirt lower front

Align the pattern with the guide lines, then move it out 1.3cm ($\frac{1}{2}$ inch) and draw part of the side seam at the upper and lower edge (Fig. 5c). With the pattern held at this position, move it down 1.3cm ($\frac{1}{2}$ inch) and draw part of the lower edge of the pattern piece (Fig. 5d and e). Remove the pattern and connect the lines up at points c to d and d to e (Fig. 6). This completes the grade.

D. PLEATED SKIRT

For the sizes 10 to 16, the pleat lines remain in the same position and the increase or decrease of grade is distributed at the side seam.
Diagrams D1 and D2 show the skirt front with the guide lines and the pleat lines

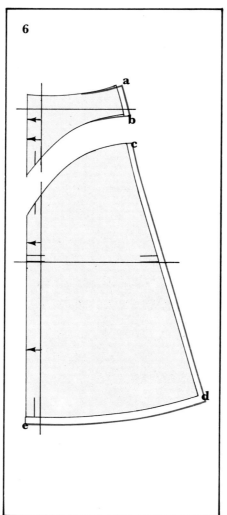

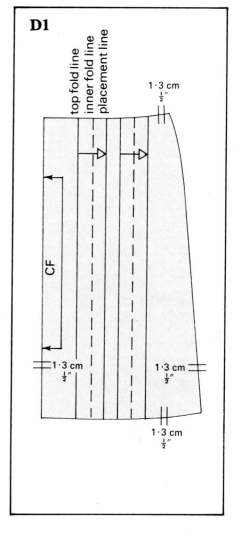

marked. The grade is divided and distributed each side of the guide lines. With the pattern positioned on the guide lines, move it out 1.3cm ($\frac{1}{2}$ *inch*) and draw the side seam at the waistline and at the lower edge (Fig. 7a). Hold the pattern in this position, then move it down 1.3cm ($\frac{1}{2}$ *inch*) and draw part of the lower edge of the pattern piece (Figs. 7b and c). Remove the pattern and connect up points a to b and b to c (Fig. 8). This completes the grade.

For sizes larger than size 16 or smaller than size 10, the pleat lines are repositioned but do not affect the grade: they are moved out 0.6cm ($\frac{1}{4}$ *inch*) or in 0.6cm ($\frac{1}{4}$ *inch*) and the increase or decrease of grade is distributed at the side seam.

The pattern is graded using the same method as above but first move the pattern out 0.6cm ($\frac{1}{4}$ *inch*) and mark each pleat line at the waistline edge and at the lower edge of the pattern (Figs. 9a and b). With the pattern held in this position, move it out a further 0.6cm ($\frac{1}{4}$ *inch*), making a total grade of 1.3cm ($\frac{1}{2}$ *inch*).

Proceed to grade the lower edge of the pattern as above.

When the pattern has been removed, connect each pleat line up at points a to b, and the side seam and the lower edge (Fig. 10).

This completes the grade.

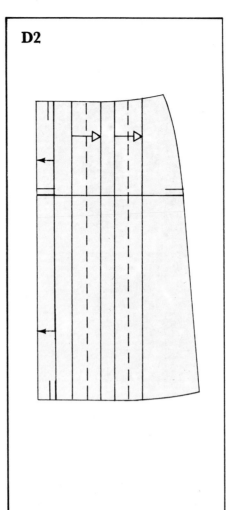

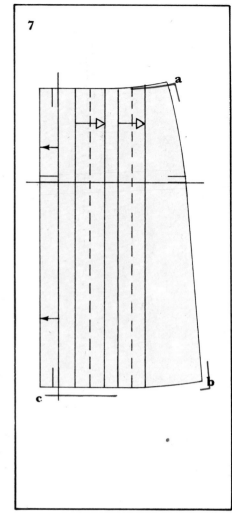

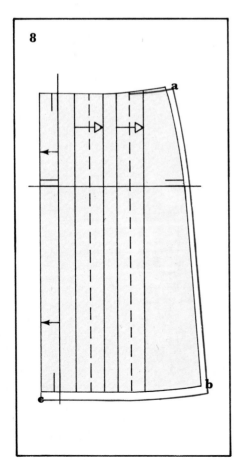

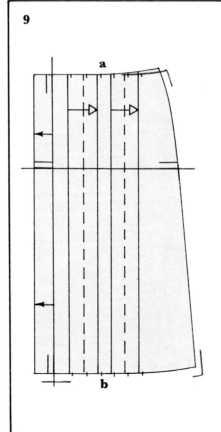

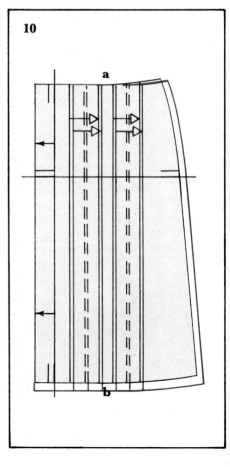

Further pattern grading

This chapter explains the method of grading the following pattern shapes:
A. Kimono sleeve and bodice
B. Raglan sleeve and bodice
C. Dolman sleeve and bodice
D. Trousers and waistband

As an example, all grading instructions in this chapter are for tackling grading on a size 12 to a size 14.

A. KIMONO SLEEVE AND BODICE

Diagram A1 and diagram A2 show the kimono sleeve and front and back bodice pattern pieces, squared up, down and across. The amounts of grade are divided and distributed evenly on either side of the guide lines.

To grade the front and back bodice

With the pattern ready to grade, position the front bodice pattern piece on the guide lines. Begin by moving the pattern up 0.3cm ($\frac{1}{8}$ inch) and draw part of the neck curve (Fig. 1a). Move the pattern up a further 0.3cm ($\frac{1}{8}$ inch) and at the same time out 0.3cm ($\frac{1}{8}$ inch). Draw the top of the neck edge and shoulder (Fig. 1b). With the pattern held in this position move it out another 0.3cm ($\frac{1}{8}$ inch) and draw the armhole edge (Fig. 1c). Bring the pattern back to align with the guide lines, move it out 1.3cm ($\frac{1}{2}$ inch) then draw the side seam edge and lower curve of the armhole edge (Figs. 1d and f). With the pattern in this position move it down 0.3cm ($\frac{1}{8}$ inch) and draw the waistline edge (Figs. 1e and f). Remove the pattern and connect the lines

up at points a to b, c to d and d to f (Fig. 2). This completes the grade. Use this method for grading the back bodice.

To grade the sleeve

Position the sleeve pattern piece on the guide lines, move it up 0.6cm ($\frac{1}{4}$ inch) and then draw the crown of the sleeve and mark the sleeve head (Figs. 1g, h and j). Bring the pattern back to align with the guide lines, move it out 0.6cm ($\frac{1}{4}$ inch) and draw the underarm seam line (Fig. 1k). With the pattern held in this position, move it down 0.6cm ($\frac{1}{4}$ inch) and draw part of the lower edge of the sleeve (Fig. 1l). Reposition the pattern on the guide lines, move it out in the opposite direction by 0.6cm ($\frac{1}{4}$ inch) and draw the underarm seam line (Fig. 1m). Hold the pattern in this position, move it down 0.6cm ($\frac{1}{4}$ inch) and draw part of the lower edge of the sleeve (Fig. 1n). Remove the pattern and connect the lines up at points g to k, h to m, k to l, m to n and l to n (Fig. 2). This completes the grade.

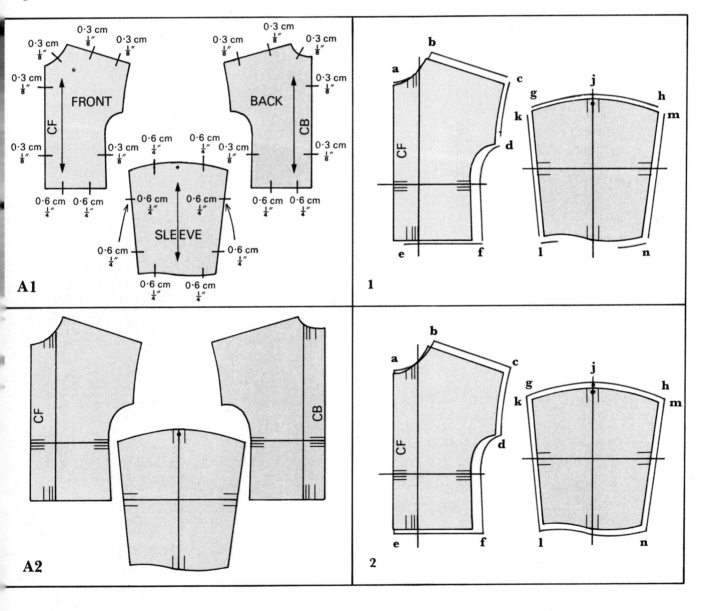

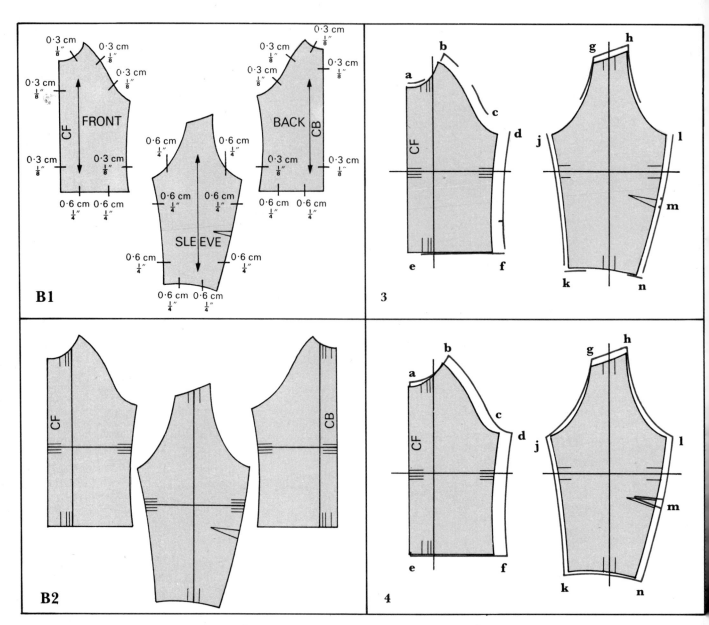

B. RAGLAN SLEEVE AND BODICE

When grading a raglan sleeve and a raglan armhole of the front and back bodice, it is important not only that the amounts of grade for the sleeve and the armhole be the same but also that their positions correspond with one another. The amounts of grade must be the same as that for a regular armhole and set in sleeve. The width of the sleeve at the neck edge remains the same for all sizes. When increasing or decreasing the size of the neck, the usual amount of grade is made but only on the front and back bodice pieces. Diagrams B1 and B2 show the raglan sleeve and bodice pieces squared up, down and across, with the amounts of grade divided and distributed on either side of the guide lines. The amounts on the bodice and sleeve pieces correspond with one another.

To grade the front and back bodice

With the pattern ready to grade, position it on the guide lines, move it up 0.3cm ($\frac{1}{8}$ inch) and draw part of the neck curve (Fig. 3a). Move the pattern up a further 0.3cm ($\frac{1}{8}$ inch) and at the same time out by 0.3cm ($\frac{1}{8}$ inch), then draw the top of the neck edge and raglan armhole (Fig. 3b). With the pattern held in this position, move it out another 0.3cm ($\frac{1}{8}$ inch) and draw the raglan armhole to within 5cm (2 inches) of the armhole curve (Fig. 3c). Bring the pattern back to align with the guide lines, move it out 1.3cm ($\frac{1}{2}$ inch) and draw the side seam edge (Fig. 3d). With the pattern held in this position move it down 0.3cm ($\frac{1}{8}$ inch) and draw the waistline edge (Fig. 3e and f). Remove the pattern and connect the lines up at points a to b, b to c, c to d, d to f and e to f (Fig. 4). The same method used for grading the front bodice is used for grading the back.

To grade the sleeve

With the pattern positioned on the guide lines, move it up 0.6cm ($\frac{1}{4}$ inch) and draw the neck edge of the sleeve and the sleeve armhole seam lines to within 5cm (2 inches) of the lower curve (Fig. 3g and h). Bring the pattern back to align with the guide lines, move it out to one side 0.6cm ($\frac{1}{4}$ inch) and draw the underarm seamline (Fig. 3j). With the pattern held in this position, move it down 0.6cm ($\frac{1}{4}$ inch) and draw part of the lower edge of the sleeve (Fig. 3k). Bring the pattern back to the original position, move it out in the opposite direction 0.6cm ($\frac{1}{4}$ inch), then draw the underarm seamline and also mark the new position of the dart (Fig. 3 l and m). Hold the pattern in this position, move it down 0.6cm ($\frac{1}{4}$ inch) and draw part of the lower edge of the sleeve (Fig. 3n). Remove the pattern and connect the lines up at points g to j, h to l, l to m, j to k and k to n. Connect the lines up at the dart points (Fig. 4m). This completes the grade.

C. DOLMAN SLEEVE AND BODICE

Diagrams C1 and C2 show the dolman sleeve and front and back bodice with the

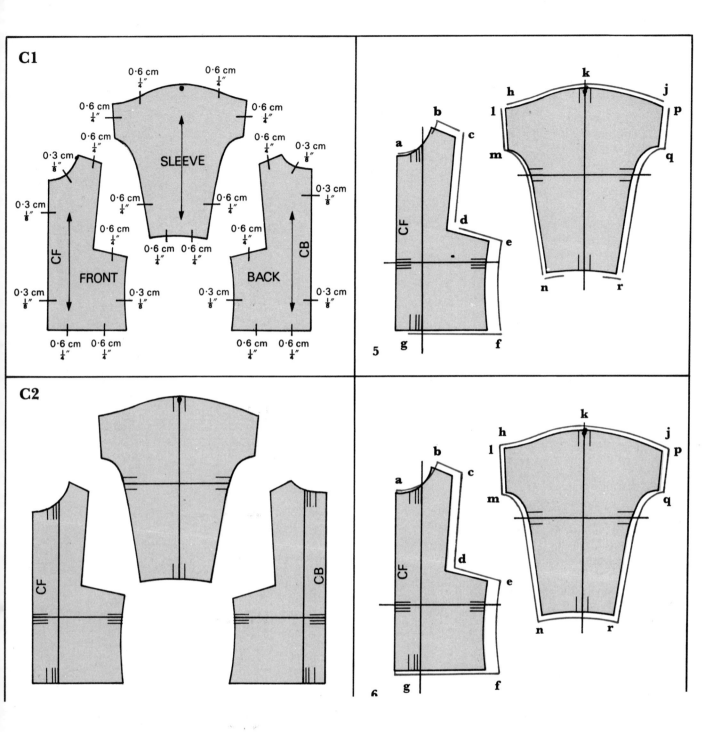

guide lines marked and the increase of grade divided and distributed on either side of the guide lines.

To grade the front and back bodice

Position the front pattern piece on the guide lines, move it up 0.3cm ($\frac{1}{8}$ inch) and draw part of the neck curve (Fig. 5a). Move the pattern up a further 0.3cm ($\frac{1}{8}$ inch) and at the same time out 0.3cm ($\frac{1}{8}$ inch) and draw the top of the neck edge and shoulder (Fig. 5b). With the pattern held in this position, move it out another 0.3cm ($\frac{1}{8}$ inch) and draw the vertical seam line to the lower corner (Figs. 5c and d). Align the pattern with the guide lines, then move it out 1.3cm ($\frac{1}{2}$ inch) and draw the

side seam edge and the horizontal seam line (Fig. 5e). Holding the pattern in this position, move it down 0.3cm ($\frac{1}{8}$ inch) and draw the waistline edge (Figs. 5f and g). Remove the pattern and connect the lines up at points a to b, b to c, d to e, e to f and f to g (Fig. 6). This completes the grade.
To grade the back bodice, follow the same method used for grading the front bodice.

To grade the sleeve

Align the pattern with the guide lines, then move it up 0.6cm ($\frac{1}{4}$ inch) and draw the crown of the sleeve marking the point of the sleeve and the point of the sleeve head (Fig. 5h, j and k). Re-align the pattern with the guide lines and move it out 0.6cm ($\frac{1}{4}$

inch). Draw the front vertical line, which corresponds with the bodice seam line, and then draw the underarm seam line (Figs. 5 l and m). With the pattern held in this position, move it down 0.6cm ($\frac{1}{4}$ inch) and draw part of the lower edge of the sleeve (Fig. 5n). Bring the pattern back to the original position, move it out towards the other side by 0.6cm ($\frac{1}{4}$ inch) and draw the back vertical line and the underarm seamline (Fig. 5p and q). With the pattern held in this position move it down 0.6cm ($\frac{1}{4}$ inch) and draw part of the lower edge of the sleeve (Fig. 5r). Remove the pattern and connect the lines up at points h to l, j to p, m to n, q to r and n to r (Fig. 6). This completes the grade.

D. TROUSERS AND WAISTBAND

Diagrams D1 and D2 show the trouser front and back pattern pieces squared up, down and across, and the amounts of grade divided and distributed on either side of the guide lines.

Diagram D3 shows the waistband (centre back to fold) with the guide lines marked and the grade divided and distributed on either side of the guide lines.

To grade the trouser front and back

With the front pattern positioned on the guide lines, move it out 0.6cm ($\frac{1}{4}$ inch) and mark the dart position (Fig. 7a). Move the pattern out a further 0.6cm ($\frac{1}{4}$ inch) and draw the side seam edge (Fig. 7b). With the pattern held in this position, move it down 1.3cm ($\frac{1}{2}$ inch) and draw part of the lower edge (Fig. 7c). Bring the pattern back to align with the guide lines, move it down 0.3cm ($\frac{1}{8}$ inch) and draw the crutch curve, tapering into the inside leg seam (Fig. 7d). Hold the pattern in this position, move it down a further 1cm ($\frac{3}{8}$ inch) (making a total grade of 1.3cm ($\frac{1}{2}$ inch) at the lower edge), and draw part of the lower edge (Fig. 7e). Remove the pattern, connect the lines up at points b to c, c to e and connect the dart lines at their new position (Fig. 8). This completes the grade.

The same method used for grading the trouser front is used for grading the trouser back. If there are two waist darts, mark them simultaneously before completing the total grade at the side seam.

To grade the waistband

The grade on the waistband must correspond with the grade at the waistline of the trousers, the total grade being 5cm (2 inches). As shown in Diagram D3, the grade is divided and distributed on either side of the side seam line by 1.3cm ($\frac{1}{2}$ inch), making a total of 2.5cm (1 inch) at each side seam.

Position the pattern on the guide lines, then move it out towards the centre front 1.3cm ($\frac{1}{2}$ inch) and re-mark the side seam (Fig. 9a). Then move the pattern out a further 1.3cm ($\frac{1}{2}$ inch) and draw the centre front line and the adjoining lines (Fig. 9b and c). Remove the pattern. This completes the grade.

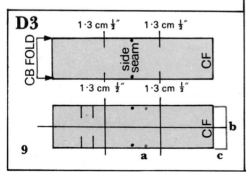

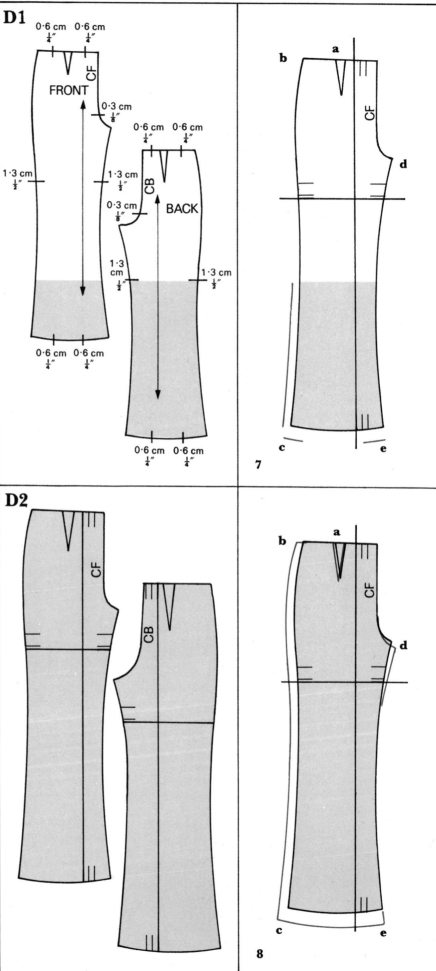

Unusual alterations 1

Paper patterns are made for a figure of average proportions in each size, but since actual figure proportions vary, often considerably, it is frequently necessary to alter a pattern to accommodate individual measurements. A comparison of your own measurements with those of the paper pattern will show which alterations are necessary.

All major alterations should be made on the pattern since much less can be done once the garment has been cut out of the fabric.

If there are a number of fitting problems it is advisable to purchase a simple basic dress pattern in the nearest figure type and size, and test the pattern in calico or cotton. By constructing this garment the specific amounts necessary for each adjustment can be determined. Once the basic pattern has been fitted, use the corrected measurements for adjusting other individual patterns. This ensures accuracy of measurement and thus gives assurance of a perfect fit.

Another way of determining which alterations are necessary is to measure each pattern piece and compare these measurements with your own. This will also give the amount of adjustment required for each alteration.

Before making this comparison, pin in any darts, pleats or gathers indicated on the pattern. The measurements are taken from seamline to seamline. Remember that body ease allowance is included in each pattern piece measurement.

The figure problems, and how to solve them, featured in this chapter are:

A. High bust
B. Low bust
C. Large bust
D. Smaller than average bust
E. Hollow chest

BUSTLINE ADJUSTMENTS

The bust area of the bodice should provide a smooth fit but with enough ease for comfortable movement. The bust and waistline darts should point towards the fullest part of the bust.

To determine whether the bust is high or low, measure from the middle of the shoulder to the tip of the bust. On the pattern, draw intersecting lines through the bust darts to locate the bust point (Fig. 1). Compare your own measurement from the middle of the shoulder to the bust point, with the distance on the pattern piece. If they are not the same, then an adjustment is necessary.

A. High bust
If the bust is high, the bodice fullness will fall below the bust, causing pulling across the actual bustline as shown in Fig. 2. The bust dart is therefore too low and must be raised.

To raise the bust dart
Having determined the amount of adjustment required, measure up from the original dart point and mark. Raise each of the dart lines by the same amount and mark them at the side seam. Re-draw the dart lines in their new positions; the new dart should be parallel to the original (Fig. 3).

To obtain the correct shape of the dart at the side seam, tape a piece of tissue underneath the side seam edge, fold the new dart and pin it in place. Cut along the side cutting line (Fig. 4).

If the bodice has a waistline dart, an equal adjustment is made. The point of the dart is raised by the same amount as the bust dart and the lines extended to this point (Fig. 5).

B. Low bust
If the bust is lower than the average bustline, the fullness will fall above the bustline, causing pulling across the actual bust as shown in Fig. 6. This indicates that the bust dart is too high and must therefore be lowered.

To lower the bust dart
When the amount of adjustment has been determined, measure the distance that the dart is to be lowered from the bust point and mark. Lower each of the dart lines by the same amount and mark them at the side seam. Re-draw the dart lines so that they form the new dart which should be parallel to the original dart (Fig. 7).

To obtain the correct shape at the side seam, follow the instructions given for Fig. 4.

An equal adjustment is also made to the waistline dart as shown in Fig. 5, but here the dart point is lowered, not raised.

If one has a large bust, the bodice fullness allowed on the pattern will not be sufficient. This will cause pulling across the bust area as shown in Fig. 8.

C. Large bust
First, draw a line through the centre of the underarm and waistline dart (Fig. 9a and b). The bust point is located at the intersection of the two lines (Fig. 9c).

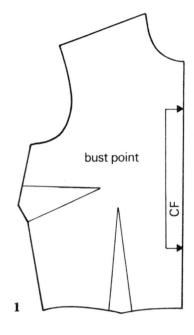

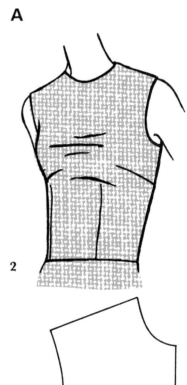

1

A

bust point

2

3

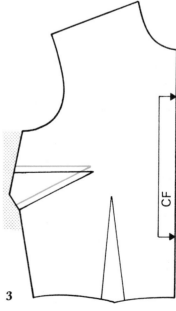

To increase the bust area

From this point, draw a line to the centre of the shoulder (Fig. 9d). Slash along the vertical line from the waist line to within 0.3cm ($\frac{1}{8}$ *inch*) of the shoulder seam (Fig. 10a). Then slash on the horizontal line to within 0.3cm ($\frac{1}{8}$ *inch*) of the centre front line (Fig. 10b). Place the pattern onto a sheet of tissue paper and spread the pattern on the vertical slash at the bust point by half the amount required. Next, spread the pattern on the horizontal slash at the bust point by half the amount required. Tape in place (Fig. 10).

Both bust and waistline darts have now been increased. Mark the new dart positions in the centre of each slash (Fig. 11), and shorten each dart from this point by 2.5cm (*1 inch*).

Re-draw the darts from the new points to the original dart lines at the side seam and at the waistline as shown in (Fig. 11).

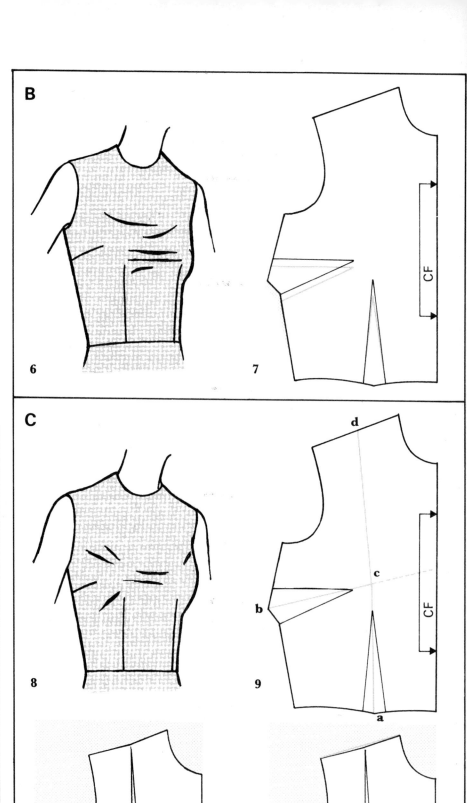

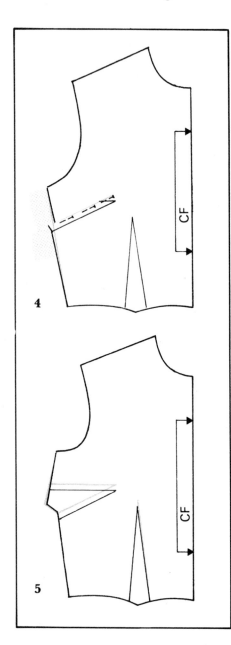

D. Smaller than average bust

The smaller bust requires less shaping than is allowed on the pattern. If the pattern is used without alteration, folds of fabric will fall across the bust area as shown in Fig. 12.

To obtain less shaping across the bust, the bust dart must be decreased. To do this, first draw a line through the centre of the underarm dart and the waistline dart (Fig. 13a and b). The bust point lies at the intersection of the lines. Draw a line from the bust point to the centre of the shoulder (Fig. 13c). Slash along the vertical line from the waistline to within 0.3cm ($\frac{1}{8}$ inch) of the shoulder seam. Then slash along the horizontal line to within 0.3cm ($\frac{1}{8}$ inch) of the centre front. Overlap both the vertical and horizontal slashes at the bust point, each by half the required amount, and tape in place. This has decreased both darts. The new dart point should now be located where the dart stitching lines intersect (Fig. 14a, b, c and d). Re-draw the centre front line (Fig. 14e).

E. Hollow chest

If you have a hollow chest, there will be too much fullness between the neckline and the bust, causing folds in the fabric as shown in Fig. 15. The distance from the neckline to the bust must be shortened on the pattern to eliminate the excess fullness.

When the amount of adjustment has been determined, trace the outline of the pattern at the centre front neckline, shoulder and armhole edges onto tissue paper and draw a line square with the grain line from the underarm edge to the centre front. Leave this aside until it is required. Slash the bodice front horizontally from the centre front to the armhole seamline (about 10cm (4 inches)) below the neckline edge. Overlap the slash line at the centre front by the necessary amount and tape in place (Fig. 16a).

Place the tracing of the front pattern over the pattern piece to obtain a straight centre front line above the slash line (Fig. 17a). Tape in place. Use the traced neckline, shoulder and armhole to obtain the original size of the pattern at the armhole and shoulder.

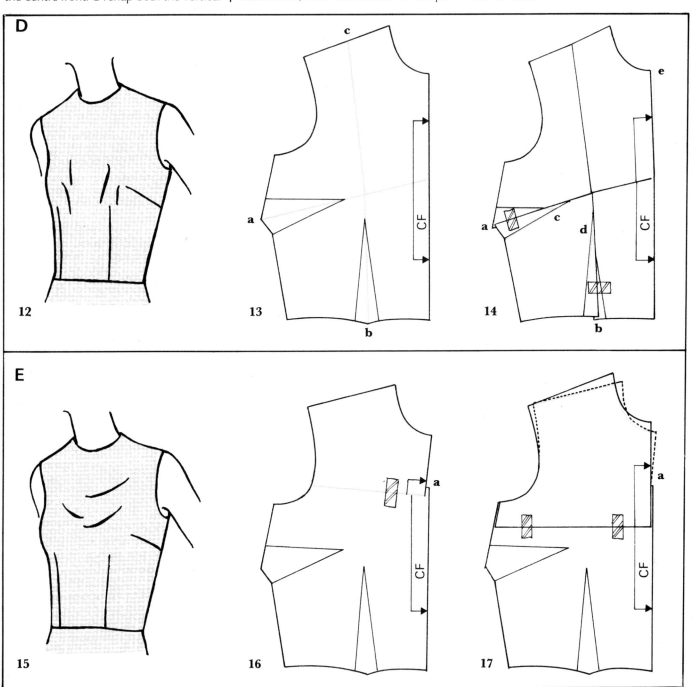

D

12   13   14

E

15   16   17

Unusual alterations 2

Paper patterns are made for a figure of average proportions in each size, but since actual figure proportions vary, often considerably, from these averages, it is frequently necessary to alter a pattern to accommodate individual measurements. A comparison of these measurements with those of the paper pattern will show which alterations are necessary.

All major alterations should be made on the pattern since much less can be done once the garment has been cut out of the fabric.

The figure problems, and how to solve them, featured in this chapter are:

A. Round shoulders
B. Narrow shoulders with a set in sleeve
C. Square shoulders with a set in sleeve
D. Uneven shoulders
E. Broad back.

A. Round shoulders

Round shoulders cause the back bodice to wrinkle and pull from the neckline towards the shoulders as shown in Fig. 1. To prevent this, extra length is required at the centre back. Trace the outline of the back bodice pattern at the centre back, neckline, shoulder and armhole edges onto tissue paper. Leave this aside until it is required.

Determine the amount necessary for the adjustment. Draw a horizontal line from the centre back to the armhole seam line about 10cm (4 inches) below the neckline edge. Slash the pattern along this line and spread the slash at the centre back by the necessary amount. Insert a piece of paper underneath the slash and tape in place (Fig. 2).

Place the tracing of the pattern *over* the adjusted pattern piece to obtain a straight centre back above the slash line. Tape in place (Fig. 3a). Use the traced neckline, shoulder and armhole to obtain the original shape and size of the pattern.

B. Narrow shoulders with a set in sleeve

If one has narrow shoulders, the shoulder seamline will extend beyond the top of the shoulder, and the sleeve seam will fall over the edge of the shoulder, as shown in Fig. 4. The width of the pattern across the shoulder is greater than the width of the body at this point and therefore the distance from the neck to the shoulder must be decreased.

The difference between your shoulder width at the sleeve seamline and that given on the pattern is the amount by which the shoulder width has to be decreased.

To make this adjustment, draw a horizontal line from the armhole notch of the centre front and centre back bodice to the centre front and centre back lines (Fig. 5a). Draw a line at right angles to the shoulder line from the centre of the shoulder to the horizontal line (Fig. 5b and c). Slash from points a and b to c. Lap the shoulder seam edges to decrease the necessary amount and tape in place. Redraw the shoulder line from the neck edge to the armhole, re-draw the armhole cutting line (Fig. 6) and re-position the shoulder in the centre of the shoulder line, using the original size dart. Ensure that the width of the shoulders at both front and back are equal. The size and shape of the armhole has not been altered and

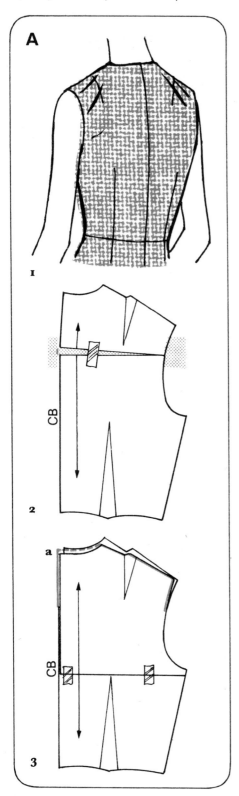

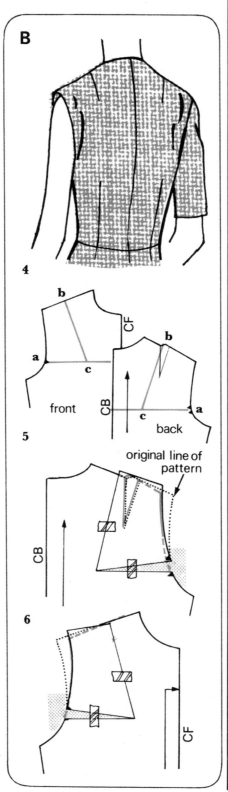

consequently, no sleeve alteration is necessary.

C. Square shoulders with a set in sleeve

Square shoulders will cause wrinkling and pulling from the shoulder to the bust area and at the shoulder blades as shown in Fig. 7.

To achieve a good fit at the shoulder, the slant of the shoulder seam must be altered to increase the length between the armhole and the top of the shoulder. Having determined the amount required to raise the shoulder seam, measure this amount from the armhole edge to the shoulder seam and mark (Fig. 8a). Re-draw the should seam from this mark to the neckline edge (Fig. 8a and b). Make this adjustment on both front and back bodice pattern pieces. The lowest part of the armhole is not altered unless this is necessary. If the armhole is raised then make the corresponding alteration to the sleeve curve. Extend the cutting lines of the underarm sleeve seam by the same amount as the armhole is raised. Re-draw the sleeve curves and taper them into the cutting line of the sleeve crown (Fig. 9a and b).

D. Uneven shoulders

Uneven shoulders will cause the fabric to wrinkle at the armhole as shown in Fig. 10. Solve this problem by inserting a small shoulder pad on the side of the low shoulder to conform to the higher side.

If this is not successful, the pattern will have to be altered. If the bodice fits correctly on the lower side, using the alteration for square shoulders, alter the higher side; if the bodice fits the higher shoulder, make the sloping shoulder alteration on the side of the lower shoulder.

E. Broad back

This will restrict movement in the bodice and the garment will pull across the back as shown in Fig. 11.

To correct this, the width of the back must be increased. Determine the amount required to increase the width of the back bodice. Draw a line across the bodice 5cm (2 inches) below the armhole to the centre back line. This line must be square with the grain line. From the shoulder seam line, draw a vertical line to meet the horizontal line (Fig. 12a, b and c). Then slash both horizontal and vertical lines, the latter to 0.3cm ($\frac{1}{8}$ inch) from the shoulder seam. Spread the vertical slash by half the required adjustment. Insert a piece of tissue underneath the slash and tape in place. Re-draw the side seam line (Fig. 13a and b).

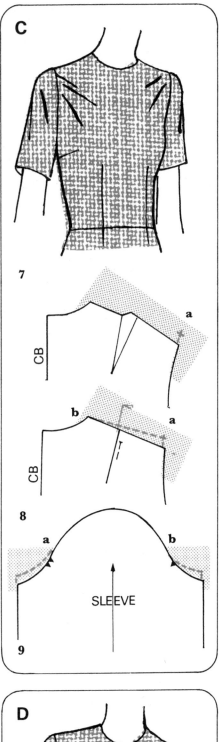

C

7

8

9 SLEEVE

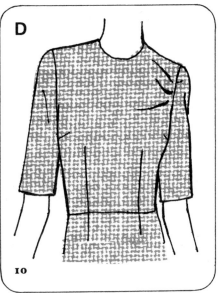

D

10

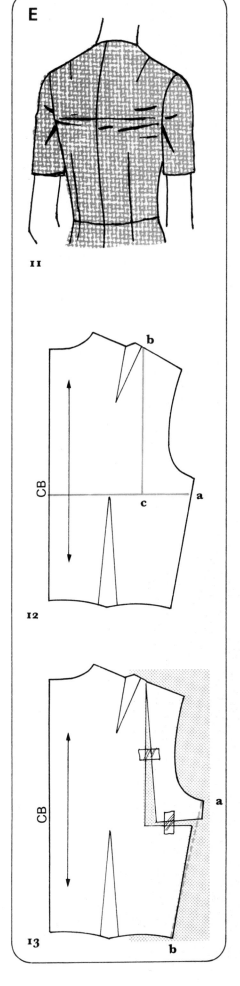

E

11

12

13

DIFFICULT FABRICS

Sewing with sheers

The soft feminine look in fashion could well be with us for several seasons and apart from lingerie and nightwear, sheer fabrics are very much part of the fashion scene. There are many different types of sheers ranging from soft fabrics to very stiff ones.

They are so fine and dainty that the usual dressmaking methods are too clumsy to use and new ones must be learnt. Because these fabrics are see-through, seam allowances show on the right side as do the usual interfacings and the whole sewing approach has to be changed. The methods used, however, are not so much difficult as different.

PATTERN, FABRICS, NOTIONS
Choosing the pattern

Select a pattern with fullness and soft flowing lines, preferably with a skirt cut on the straight of grain. Bias cut skirts in these fabrics tend to drop badly. If the skirt has a pronounced flare, it is wise to hang it for 24 hours to drop before marking the hem finally.

Very full sleeves look particularly good in sheer fabric. Take care when choosing a pattern with a full sleeve, for one that looks generous in a thicker fabric may look skimpy in a very fine one.

As these fabrics are fragile it is best to avoid a tight fitting bodice or tight sleeves. If the pattern you wish to make does have a fitted bodice you can interline the bodice and combine it with full inlined sleeves. This way will also solve the problem of what to wear underneath.

1. If you have chosen a garment with front buttoning and a front facing seam, eliminate the seam by cutting the facing in one with the bodice as shown.

Inter or underlining

A mounted interlining is often used with sheer fabrics on those areas you wish to be opaque. Here interlining and top fabric are tacked together before making up and the two fabrics are made up as one.

Unlike a separate lining, there has to be a perfect marriage between lining and interlining fabric, therefore the correct combination is important. Use a soft natural fibre interlining with a natural fibre top fabric, such as a soft jap silk.

A synthetic underlining should only be used with a synthetic top fabric, otherwise you cannot work the outside fabric properly. For instance when pressing, the outside fabric may require greater heat than the lining can withstand.

Alternatively, if you are after a translucent effect, use a double layer of the top fabric if it is plain. Or, if patterned, mount with a similar but matching plain fabric.

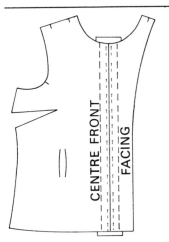

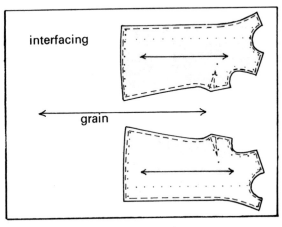

1. Combined front and front facing   2. Cutting out the interlining

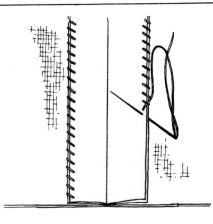

3. Overcasting interlined seam allowances

4. Prick stitching just below hem line on interlined garment

Cutting out: cut out top fabric and mark details. Place pieces to be underlined singly onto single interlining fabric. Make sure that the grain lines match exactly and take care not to stretch the fabric.

2. Tack all round each piece within the seam allowance or darts to avoid marking the fabric.

Cut out and work top fabric and interlining as one.

Seams. Seams in mounted fabrics are stitched as usual and not as for unmounted sheers.

3. When finishing off the raw seam allowances it is most important that they be oversewn by hand. A machine finish on a mounted fabric tends to curl the two layers, creating a thick and hard seam edge which makes an impression through the fabric on the outside and this should be avoided.

4. To stop the interlining folding up inside a hem, prick stitch fabric and interlining together just below the hem line before the hem is turned up.

When sewing up the hem do not sew through to the outside fabric, but catch the interlining fabric only to give the outside a smooth finish.

Interfacing

Interfacing of the usual type will be too heavy for sheer fabrics. Use either a lining fabric or a pure silk organza as interfacing. Pure silk organza is so colourless it can be used for most transparent fabrics.

If you still find that the interfacing shows through and changes the colour of the fabric it is best to leave it out, provided the fabric has enough substance to support itself.

Notions

Thread: Use a fine thread for sewing sheers. If the thread is used with a very fine needle this will make only tiny holes in the fabric and cause minimal damage to the fibres. Fine material can run very easily so great care should be taken to treat the material gently and not draw the thread through roughly.

Needles and pins: These should be very fine so as not to make large holes in the fabric which will be damaged very easily. Any breaks in the fabric would be seen quite easily. Use dressmakers silk pins or glass head pins. Glass head pins are made from needle discards, and consequently are good for using with fine delicate fibre.

87

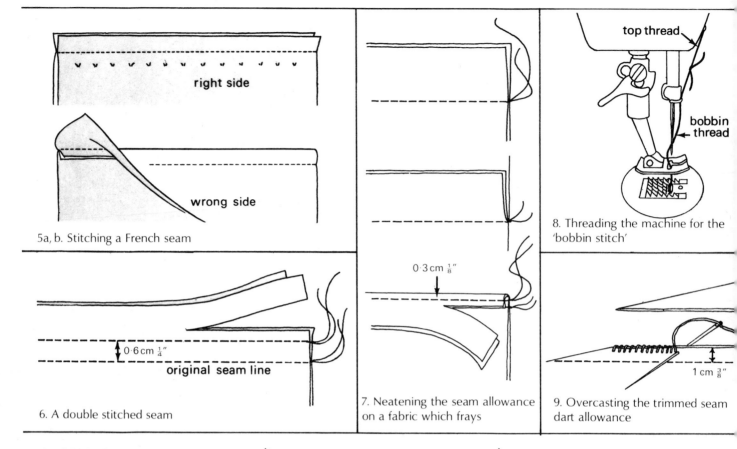

5a, b. Stitching a French seam

6. A double stitched seam

0.6cm ¼"
original seam line

0.3cm ⅛"

7. Neatening the seam allowance on a fabric which frays

top thread

bobbin thread

8. Threading the machine for the 'bobbin stitch'

1 cm ⅜"

9. Overcasting the trimmed seam dart allowance

WORKING THE FABRIC
Cutting out
If the selvedge is tight, snip it at 10cm (4 inch) intervals.

As the fabric is slippery it is a good idea to lay it out on a sheet.

Take care not to stretch the fabric when folding and laying it out.

Use fine pins and pin the pattern down at frequent intervals. When cutting out, hold the fabric securely with your free hand.

Tailor's tacks are best for marking pattern details as chalk and carbon markings are difficult to remove on these fabrics.

Machine stitching
Use a new fine needle on the machine and a fine thread. Test the machine for pressure, stitch length and tension on a double piece of fabric before starting on the garment.

If you find that the fabric puckers as you stitch it, place the fabric over tissue paper when stitching. The paper can easily be torn away afterwards.

Seams
There are several alternatives for stitching the seams on sheer fabrics. The object being to combine a strong seam, for a fabric which frays, with a narrow neat seam allowance, as this is visible from the right side of the garment.

A French seam is often used on fine fabrics

but is only suitable if the seam is straight. To make a French seam work as follows:

5a. With wrong sides together, machine 0.6cm (¼ inch) from seam line in seam allowance. Trim as close to stitching line as possible and press the seam allowance to one side.

5b. Turn the garment to the wrong side. With right sides together stitch along the original line, encasing the raw edges in the seam.

Decide if you wish to use French seams before you start tacking a garment for fitting. If you do, then tack as in 5a and pin along the seam line.

Double stitching (6). Stitch along the seam line, with right sides together. Make another row of stitching in the seam allowance through both layers, 0.6cm (¼ inch) from the first row. Trim seam allowance to 0.3cm (⅛ inch) from second row.

Fraying fabrics: if your fabric frays badly here are two good ways of dealing with the seam allowance. Stitch the seam on the seam line with right sides together. Trim seam allowance to 1cm (⅜ inch) and finely overcast the edges together.

7. Alternatively, after you have stitched the seam, press the seam allowance to one side. Fold under the seam allowance 0.3cm (⅛ inch) from the stitching line and stitch through fold with a straight stitch or zigzag. Trim as close to the second line as possible.

Darts
To avoid a knot or back stitch showing at the point of a dart, sew the dart by the 'bobbin stitch' method.

Thread the machine as usual except for the needle.

8. Draw the bobbin thread through the hole in the needle plate as usual then thread it through the needle, reversing the threading order you would use with the top thread. Knot the two threads together as shown.

Pull the bobbin thread until it is twice the length of the dart plus 5 to 7.5cm (2 to 3 inches), then wind the cotton reel until the slack is taken up.

Stitch the dart starting at the point. If the fabric does not fray, rethread the needle in the same way and work another row of stitches 0.6cm (¼ inch) from the first. Trim close to this line.

9. Alternatively, trim the dart seam allowance to 1cm (⅜ inch) and overcast the raw edges very finely together.

Armhole seams
Here are two good ways to finish the armhole seam:

Trim the armhole seam allowances to 1cm (⅜ inch) and oversew finely.

10. Alternatively the armhole seam can be self bound. Stitch the armhole seam along the seam line in the usual way. Trim seam allowance of sleeve only to 0.6cm (¼ inch). Fold bodice seam allowance under 0.3cm

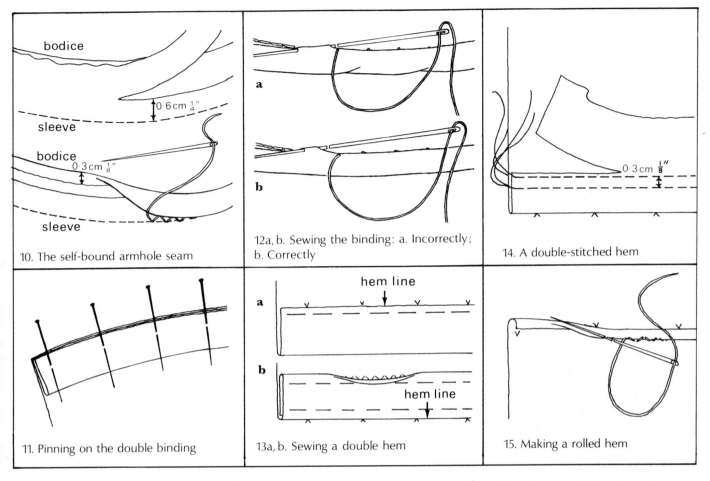

10. The self-bound armhole seam

12a, b. Sewing the binding: a. Incorrectly; b. Correctly

14. A double-stitched hem

11. Pinning on the double binding

13a, b. Sewing a double hem

15. Making a rolled hem

($\frac{1}{8}$ inch). Place fold to seam line and slip stitch loosely to machine stitches thus covering the sleeve seam.

Bound edges

Binding is a particularly good way to finish a neck edge if you do not want a bulky facing finish. A double binding is much easier to work on a fine fabric than a single one.

Here is how to work a double binding. It is a good idea to experiment on the width before working on the garment itself.

Decide on the width you would like the finished binding. Cut strips of bias fabric to the required length and slightly more than 6 times the width of the finished binding.

Fold strip in half lengthways, wrong sides together, and press carefully along the folded edge by placing the iron on it section by section. (You will find that the fabric stretches a bit and loses some of its width.)

11. Trim off the seam allowance of the edge to be bound. With right sides together, pin the double raw edge to the trimmed seam edge. As sheer fabrics often have a tendency to stretch work very carefully, resting the work on a flat surface.

After pinning, tack in place with a fine thread and small stitches.

Machine stitch, taking a seam allowance

which is $\frac{1}{3}$ of the width of the folded strip. Remove the tacking. With the work still resting on a flat surface, bring the folded bias edge over the seam allowance onto the seam line. Pin.

12a, b. Using a fine thread hand sew as shown. Do not tighten the stitches. Never insert the needle into the fabric for a new stitch exactly opposite the end of the previous one (a) but insert it a grain or two further on (b).

Hem

If your hem edge is straight and you want to make the usual type of hem, it is a good idea to make it double.

13a, b. To do this fold the raw edge up to the hem line and tack (a). Fold again, on hem line, and tack (b). Stitch very neatly with an invisible hemming stitch.

14. An alternative hem finish, suitable for any type of hem, is to turn it up on the hem edge and stitch with two rows of stitches about 0.3cm ($\frac{1}{8}$ inch) apart. Trim off seam allowance close to top row of stitches.

Hand rolled hem

Another way of finishing the hem edge is to hand roll it. Here are two ways of doing this, try both first on a scrap of fabric to see which you have more success with.

15. Trim the seam allowance to 0.6cm ($\frac{1}{4}$

inch). Rolling the edge a few inches at a time between thumb and forefinger, first turn under 0.3cm ($\frac{1}{8}$ inch) then roll up a further 0.3cm ($\frac{1}{8}$ inch) and slip stitch in place to complete the roll. The slip stitches should be closely placed to hold the roll firmly, but make sure that the stitches don't show on either side. Take a single thread for each stitch.

The second method is to stitch a line of machine stitching in the hem allowance 0.6cm ($\frac{1}{4}$ inch) from the hem line. Trim close to this, then proceed as before.

Fastenings

Avoid heavy buttons or zips as these can drag and distort the fabric and are quite out of character with very lightweight sheers.

Try light-weight buttons with loops or tiny buttonholes as these will give a fine delicate finish appropriate to the fabric. Use hooks and eyes and small press fasteners for hidden fastenings.

Working with velvets

Every type of fabric presents its own individual problems to both the home and the professional dressmaker. Velvet is one of the most difficult fabrics to handle and requires special care. Advice is given here on how to overcome the main problems of working with velvet.

FABRIC, PATTERNS AND NOTIONS

Velvet is a beautiful fabric with depth and colour. It is constructed either on a double shuttle loom, where extra warp yarns are interwoven between the two layers of fabric and then cut to make two separate lengths of velvet; or on a single loom, the threads forming the pile being woven over cutting wires so that when they are withdrawn they cut the loops to form velvet tufts (Fig. 1a and b). Velvet is a 'pile' fabric, and should be handled in the same way as a fabric with 'nap'. Lay the fabric on a table and run a hand gently up and down the surface. When you are moving with the pile or nap the feel is smooth – in the opposite direction the feel is rough.

Then hold the fabric up – when the nap is running from the top to bottom the colour is light and flat and sometimes shiny as well, when the nap is running from bottom to top a rich deep colour is apparent and this is the way velvet should be used for dress and formal wear. Having found the direction of the nap, mark it on the wrong side of the fabric with chalk arrows.

Modern velvets are made from 100% cotton, nylon, polyester or rayon, or a mixture of these. They vary from a long pile with definite nap to a short pile with hardly any appreciable nap. With the latter, decide which direction is correct by hanging it up both ways and choosing the one which gives the richest tone.

Pattern selection

The correct selection of a pattern for use with velvet is very important. Styles with simple lines and with the minimum of detail are the best, so look for a pattern with this in mind. Never choose a design with top-stitching as the pressure of the machine foot on the right side of the fabric can damage the pile, and the stitching gets lost in the pile.

Because of the nap, all the pattern pieces must be placed on the fabric in the same direction, so check that the pattern suggests the use of napped fabrics and gives the yardage for them. Compare the pattern piece measurements with your own, remembering to allow for ease, pin the pattern pieces together and try on. If there is any doubt as to the fit, make the garment first in calico and transfer any alterations to the pattern before cutting out. It is advisable to avoid overhandling of the velvet as unpicking damages the pile and this is almost impossible to repair.

Interfacing

Interfacing is used to give body to and maintain the shape of the parts interfaced. It should enhance the desired shape not dictate a new one, so where absolutely necessary use a lightweight woven interfacing to match the fibre content of the velvet.

Mounting

Mounting is used to give support to folds and body to skirts and bodices. It must also be woven and be of the same fibre as the velvet. Use a very lightweight fabric, such as organdie or voile.

Threads

The threads should be elastic and silk is the best for machining and all hand work.

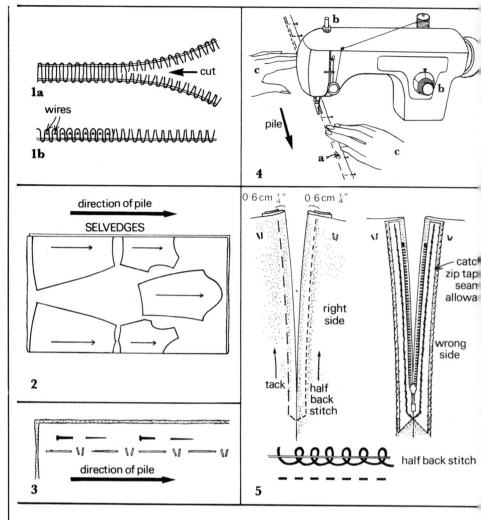

Layout

Lay the pattern pieces carefully with the nap running up from the hem to waist to neck, sleeve hem to sleeve head (Fig. 2). Transfer the pattern markings with silk thread.

If the garment is to be mounted, cut this first and transfer all markings. The mounting pieces can then be laid onto the wrong side of the velvet, tacked in the seam allowance and the velvet cut. Working with the pile, pin and tack inside the seam allowance to avoid marking the fabric (Fig. 3). Having checked the pattern before cutting out, only small alterations should be necessary at this stage.

Machining

At this point problems begin to appear. Sometimes seams 'bunch' along their length or 'creep' so that one side ends up longer than the other.

It is always a good idea to try a long sample seam before starting to machine the garment, following the suggestions given below:

a. Tack firmly with the pile just inside the sewing line and place the pins at right angles along the length of the seam (Fig. 4a).

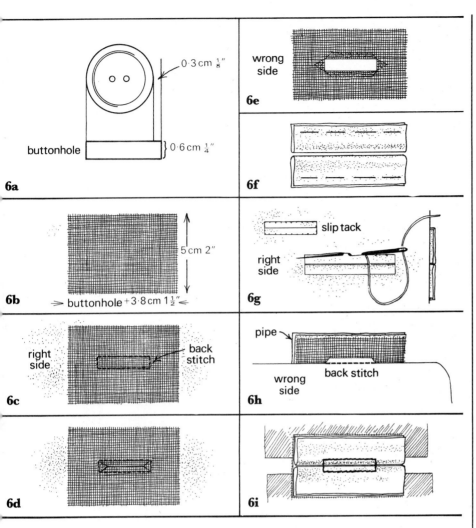

6a

0.3 cm ⅛"

buttonhole ⎱0.6 cm ¼"

6b

5 cm 2"

buttonhole + 3·8 cm 1½"

6c

right side — back stitch

6d

6e

wrong side

6f

6g

slip tack

right side

6h

pipe

wrong side — back stitch

6i

---

b. Decrease the machine foot pressure slightly unless you have a self adjusting one (Fig. 4b). Set a longer machine stitch than usual, 8–10 sts per inch and use a new fine needle.

c. Hold the seam firmly both at the back and at the front whilst machining slowly and evenly along the direction of pile. It is when machining is done quickly and in short bursts that puckering usually occurs (Fig. 4c).

d. If seams still 'creep' then try putting tissue paper under the seam and machine through this, tearing it away afterwards.

e. Oversew the seam edges by hand or machine.

Pressing

Always press as you work – if possible using a velvet board, which has a heavy canvas backing with hundreds of needle-like projections which allow the seam to be pressed without damaging the garment pile. Use a heavy Turkish towel or spare piece of velvet over your ironing board as a substitute.

If it is possible to use steam, do so, but do check first with the practice seam as steaming does leave marks on some man-made fabrics.

Lay the seam right side down on the velvet board and press open with the fingers. Working with the pile press lightly by touching the seam with the point of the iron, and let the steam penetrate and set the seam. Remove carefully from the board and leave to dry before touching the pile. Do not expect to achieve perfectly flat seams as this would be out of character with velvet. They should correctly have a slight bounce.

Many modern velvets have crease resisting finishes, but in the case of an accident, the pile can be raised by careful steaming. Hang the garment on a hanger and apply steam to the back of the fabric, taking care not to touch the pile with wet hands or whilst it is damp. If this does not raise the pile, gently brush the velvet against the pile whilst it is still damp, using a very soft brush or a piece of velvet.

FASTENINGS
Zips

Zips should always have a cotton tape because the pull of the velvet will distort finer ones.

Press the turnings back carefully and, working on the right side, tack each side to the open zip with the teeth just hidden

by the fabric fold. Close the zip to check that it is covered by the velvet. Then, with a half back stitch, sew up from the bottom to the top on each side (Fig. 5a and b).

Frog fastenings

Frogs for coats and jackets look attractive on velvet. They obviate the need for buttons and can be bought in many colours. Sew them on invisibly by hand, placing a piece of interfacing on the wrong side of the fabric for strength.

Buttonholes

If buttonholes must be used they should be made in the following way (Fig. 6a–i):

a. The buttonhole should be the button diameter plus 0.3cm (⅛ inch) long, by 0.6cm (¼ inch) wide.

b. Cut a rectangle of muslin or lining 3.8cm (1½ inches) longer than the buttonhole and 5cm (2 inches) wide.

c. Place centrally over the buttonhole position on the right side and back stitch buttonhole shape.

d. Cut along the centre through muslin and velvet and mitre neatly into the corners.

e. Turn the muslin to the wrong side and press seams back.

f. Make pipes by cutting two pieces of velvet to the length of the buttonhole plus 3.8cm (1½ inches) wide. Fold in half wrong side together and tack edges.

g. Place folds centrally behind the buttonhole, slip tack securely all round hole.

h. Fold the garment away from the hole and back stitch all round through pipes, muslin and seam.

i. Press lightly, placing brown paper behind the pipes to avoid impressing the garment.

Facings

Facings should be made in the lining fabric to avoid bulk.

Hems

Hems should be cut to a depth of 3.8cm (1½ inches), the fullness eased in, and the raw edge overcast and slip stitched lightly to the garment.

If the hem is very flared it should be faced with lining cut to the shape of the hem and on the same grain.

Working with thicker fabrics

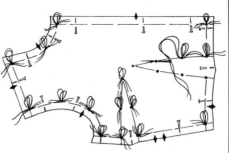

2. Tailor's tacks worked on wrong side of fabric through pattern symbols

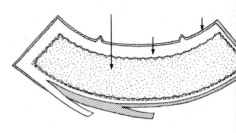

4. Layered seams on a collar

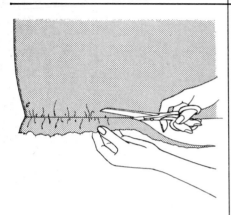

1. Straightening the fabric ends

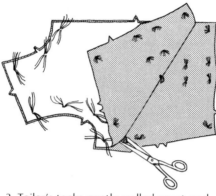

3. Tailor's tacks gently pulled apart and snipped between the right sides of the fabric

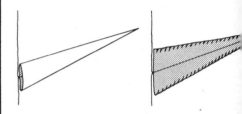

5. Darts slashed and pressed open after stitching: raw edges overcast

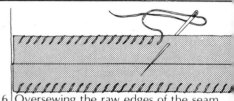

6. Oversewing the raw edges of the seam allowance

The main objective when sewing heavier fabrics in dressmaking is to reduce bulk on seams and hems. The techniques described here are recommended for use on suit- and coat-weight fabrics.

Preparation of fabric

The cut edges of all woven fabrics should be straightened by pulling tight a crosswise thread of fabric. Then, using the tightened thread as a guide, cut carefully along it (Fig. 1). If the fabric is to be folded in half across the width, the folded cut edge and the selvedges must meet exactly. When the length of the fabric is to be folded in half, it is necessary to straighten both ends of the fabric, folding and pinning the straightened cut edges, right sides facing, ready for the pattern pieces to be pinned in position.

All fabrics should be pressed before cutting out and special care taken to remove the fold marks by pressing over a damp, but not wet, cloth.

Woollen fabrics or wool and man-made fibre mixtures should be shrunk before cutting out or the garment may shrink when dry cleaned. It is also advisable to shrink any woven interfacings as many of these are not pre-shrunk.

The entire piece of fabric must be pressed evenly under a damp cloth.

Marking pattern symbols

If you are working on a smooth, firmly woven fabric which will be stitched up immediately after cutting out, the pattern symbols can be marked on to the main fabric with tailor's chalk. This method is not suitable for use on fabric which is to be left for some time before being made up, nor is it suitable for loosely woven fabrics, fabrics with a pile or nap, or fabrics with an uneven textured surface such as tweed. The pattern symbols should be marked on these fabrics with tailor's tacks (Figs. 2 and 3).

Stitching heavier fabrics

Use a heavy-duty mercerised cotton, gauge 36 to 40, for sewing, one shade darker than the fabric. The best needle size to use for these types of fabrics is a No. 6 crewel for hand sewing and a medium coarse needle (size 14 or 16) in the sewing machine, with the machine set to 10–12 stitches to 2.5cm (1 inch). To avoid missed stitches and to prevent the top fabric from riding, lessen the pressure of the machine foot according to the instructions given with the sewing machine. The pressure will depend on the thickness of the fabric: the thicker the fabric, the more the pressure should be released. Always work a practice seam over two thicknesses

of the fabric to check the size of stitch, the tension and the required foot pressure. The main thing to avoid when working on heavier fabrics is unnecessary bulk. To reduce bulk on all seams and hems as much as possible, seams should be well layered (Fig. 4).

Darts

On heavier fabrics, darts are generally best slashed open on the wrong side after stitching. Cut on the fold of the dart fabric to within about 2cm ($\frac{3}{4}$ inch) of the dart point. Press open and oversew the raw edges (Fig. 5).

Finishing seam edges

Oversewing by hand (Fig. 6) or machine zigzag stitch are the best methods to use for finishing raw edges of thicker fabrics since these methods add the least bulk. Bound edges are necessary on fabrics which are loosely woven or inclined to fray easily. Bind seam edges with 2.5cm (1 inch) wide crossway strips cut from Jap silk, pure silk or fine crepe in a colour chosen to match the fabric (Figs. 7 and 8). Purchased straight or bias bindings should not be used as these tend to add too much bulk to the seam edge.

Whichever seam finish is chosen, it should be used on all edges throughout the gar-

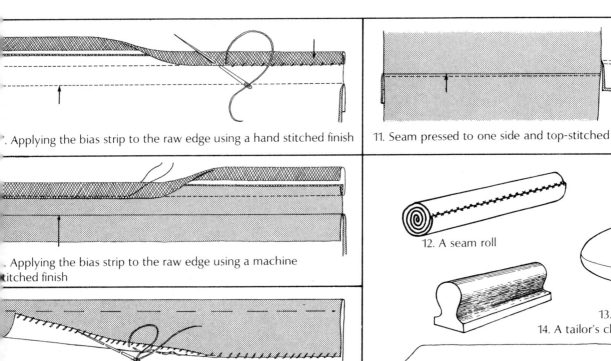

. Applying the bias strip to the raw edge using a hand stitched finish

11. Seam pressed to one side and top-stitched

. Applying the bias strip to the raw edge using a machine stitched finish

. Catch-stitching the hem 0.2cm ($\frac{3}{16}$ inch) below the finished edge

0. Top-stitching on either side of the seam

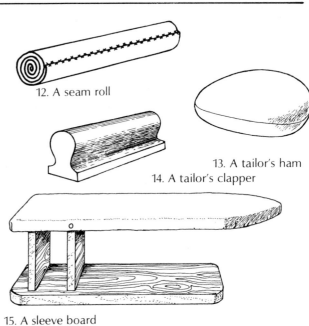

12. A seam roll

13. A tailor's ham

14. A tailor's clapper

15. A sleeve board

ment for a clean finish throughout.

If the seam edges are bound, particular care must be taken when pressing. Press seams over a seam roll to avoid an impression of the bound edges showing through to the right side of the garment. If you do not have a seam roll and the seam has to be pressed on a flat surface, place a 10cm (4 inch) wide strip of strong paper between the seam edge and the main fabric. This should prevent the seam edge from being pressed onto the main fabric.

Finishing hems

As a general rule, the hem edge is finished in the same way as the seam edges of the garment. If the seams are oversewn, finish the hem with oversewing, and if the seams are bound, bind the hem also

Whether oversewn or bound, the hem method best suited to thicker fabrics is an invisible catch-stitch hem. The catch-stitch should be worked about 0.2cm ($\frac{3}{16}$ inch) from the raw edge of the fabric or immediately below the binding on the edge (Fig. 9).

Care must be taken when pressing the hem to avoid pressing the finished edge. Press along the fold of the hemline only.

Finishes for seams

On certain man-made and natural fibre mixture fabrics, it is not always possible to press the seams completely flat due to the built-in crease resistance of the fabric. The best way to deal with these fabrics is to top-stitch the seams to hold them securely in place. Both sides of the seam can be top-stitched (Fig. 10) or the seam pressed to one side with one line of stitching (Fig. 11).

Top-stitching

Top-stitching looks most effective when worked with a thicker thread on the right side of the fabric. Wind two thicknesses of sewing thread or a single thread of buttonhole twist onto the spool. The spool-case tension should be loosened slightly and the top tension tightened to give a good even stitch on the right side. The stitch should be lengthened to the required length. The row of top-stitching is usually worked the width of the machine foot from the seam.

Pressing aids

Heavier fabrics require special handling when pressing. Care should always be taken to ensure that the garment is not over-pressed and that the seam and hem edges are not pressed through to make ridges on the right side of the fabric. Once such ridges are made, it is extremely

difficult to remove them. The flat fabric either side of the seam should be pressed up to the line of stitching, and then the actual seam pressed open over a seam roll (Fig. 12) for straight seams, and over a tailor's ham for curved seams (Fig. 13). Pressure is placed on the seam line itself and not on the seam allowance, thus preventing the outline of the seam from being pressed through to the right side of the fabric.

A tailor's clapper is used to flatten a seam after it has been steamed. The clapper is slapped down on the seam and held in place for a second or two. If a tailor's clapper is not available, the back of a strong clothes brush makes a good substitute. This is especially useful on hard-to-press seams (Fig. 14).

Use a sleeve board for pressing sleeves and sleeve seams (Fig. 15).

Working with fur fabrics

CHOOSING YOUR FABRIC

Before you begin to think about the style and design details of the garment you have in mind, make sure that you are familiar with the different types of pile and fur fabrics available in the shops. These can be classified into five main categories:
1. Sheepskin or shearling effect
2. Short smooth
3. Long smooth
4. Long shaggy
5. Two-height pile

The really deep pile fabrics are generally rather difficult to handle and often need a furrier's approach to design and marking up, so if you are a novice, use them sparingly to begin with. Create an elegant look with collar and cuffs, or a wide band of fur at the hem of a winter coat. There are some very convincing mink and fox type fabrics now available. The less dense pile fabrics present few problems if you bear in mind the following points:

Choosing your pattern

Remember that you want to show the fur fabric to the best advantage. It already has a distinctive look so you can dispense with tricky seams and construction details.

Choose a simple style with few seams, into which you can incorporate any pockets or buttonholes.

There are many alternatives to buttonholes, such as loops and zip fasteners, and a wrapover style with a tie-belt can eliminate all other forms of fastening.

Laying out the pattern

Check your pattern yardage for pile fabrics. The pile should lie along the length of the garment, running down from neck to hem, with every pattern piece laying in the same direction (Fig. 1). Do not be tempted to save fabric by turning a pattern piece round, either in the opposite direction, or by laying it from side to side. The result is that the pile will handle differently and secondly, the colour of the garment will be altered. This is called shading and also applies to short pile fabrics such as velvet and corduroy Remember to make a single lay. Do not cut on the fold of the fabric unless the pile is a very short one.

Open the fabric out flat and lay the pattern on the wrong side after making any necessary adjustments.

Pattern pieces to be cut on the fold must be pinned, outlined with chalk or coloured pencil and then reversed to complete the whole shape (Fig. 2).

Try to reduce any unnecessary bulk at this stage by cutting any facings in one with the body of the garment where possible, instead of cutting and seaming separately (Fig. 3).

Cutting the fabric

Do not attempt to cut through double fabric. After marking out the pattern pieces, remove them and cut through the backing only, with a single edged razor blade or electric scissors. On some short pile fabrics it is possible to use shears and cut through the backing and the pile in one operation. Test your particular fabric first on a small sample to find the best method.

SEWING FUR FABRIC

Choose a needle and sewing thread that will match the weight of your fabric; a size 14 needle is a medium size and is suitable for use with a synthetic thread which is stronger than a regular cotton thread, and will not wear out before the garment itself.

Remember that the main seams on the shoulder, neckline and armhole will take the whole weight of the garment and must be stitched with a 0.6cm ($\frac{1}{4}$ inch) pre-shrunk straight tape for stability and re-inforcement (Fig. 4). A useful stitch length is 8–10 stitches per 2.5cm (1 inch). Test the needle and stitch on a sample of fabric

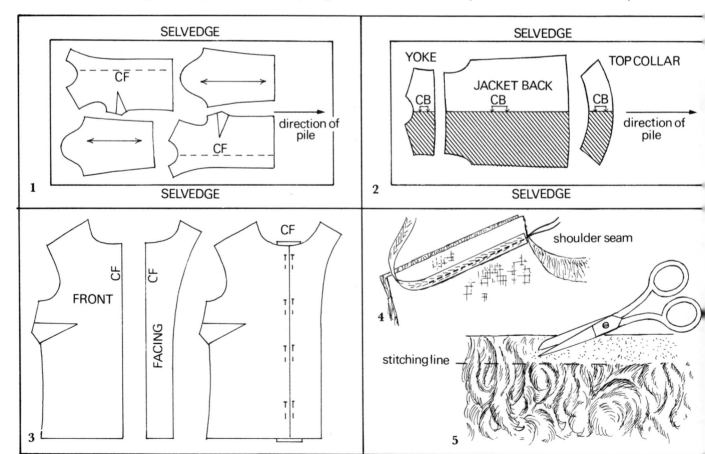

before you begin making up the garment. Pin and tack the garment, using a thick, soft tacking cotton which will stay in position better than a thin silky thread. On very long pile fabrics it is recommended that a zigzag stitch is used and that the pile face of the fabric is cut away from the backing by hand, using a small, sharp pair of scissors, from the seam allowance up to the stitching lines (Fig. 5). This helps to eliminate bulk and also prevents the long hairs of the fabric being caught and hidden in the seams which gives that flat look on all the style lines. Tease out any fibres that may be caught in the seam with a hairpin or a short knitting needle (Fig. 6).

The bulkiness of darts can be reduced by slashing them and trimming off the pile from the seam allowance after stitching (Fig. 7) Finger press and catch the seam allowance edges to the wrong side of the fabric by hand (Fig. 8). All other seams can be treated in the same way to reduce thickness.

Coat hems are less bulky if kept to a minimum width and treated like a false hem with wide bias binding cut from the lining fabric or pre-shrunk grosgrain ribbon (Fig. 9). Remember to match the ribbon shade to your lining fabric to give your garment a professional finish.

Mitred corners on any vents or front edge hem lines also help to eliminate bulk (Fig. 10).

Buttonholes

Avoid machine or handmade buttonholes and consider the possibilities of other forms of buttonhole.

A bound buttonhole using suede or leather could be very attractive in conjunction with matching buttons, bound edges and a leather tie belt.

Remember that it is also possible to use suede and leather type fabrics and vinyl faced cloths as design features.

Zip fasteners

An open ended zip fastener at the front of a jacket presents few problems if planned specifically for pile fabrics.

The possibility of the pile being caught in the zip every time the jacket is opened or closed must be avoided.

It is possible to set the zip into a plain fabric so that the teeth are not adjacent to the pile cloth. Alternatively, zigzag stitch a 1.5cm ($\frac{5}{8}$ inch) grosgrain ribbon to the length of the zip tapes leaving a 2.5cm (1 inch) extension at each end (Fig. 11a). Stitch the other edge of the ribbon to the right side of the fabric 1.5cm ($\frac{5}{8}$ inch) beyond the stitching line of the seam (Fig. 11b). Trim away the seam allowance to 0.6cm ($\frac{1}{4}$ inch). Turn back and hand stitch the seam allowance to the garment (Fig. 11c). The ribbon now forms a facing between the zip and the pile cloth. Tuck under the extension of the ribbon at both ends and hand stitch neatly in place (Fig. 11d).

Pressing

Avoid steam and pressure on all pile fabrics as an excess of either can permanently distort the fibres of the cloth.

Some short pile fabrics like velvet can be pressed on a wire board, but generally great care must be taken to avoid damage. Finger pressing and inside stitching can hold the garment in shape very well, whereas normal pressing methods do not have a lasting effect on pile fabrics.

It is useful to remember that in the event of any marking or spotting during making (or wearing) your fur fabric garment, careful sponging with a mild detergent and luke-warm water, followed by a quick blow-dry with a hair dryer will remove all but the most persistent marks. Whole garments require specialist cleaning, so enquire when purchasing the fabric about the fibre content and manufacturer's cleaning recommendations.

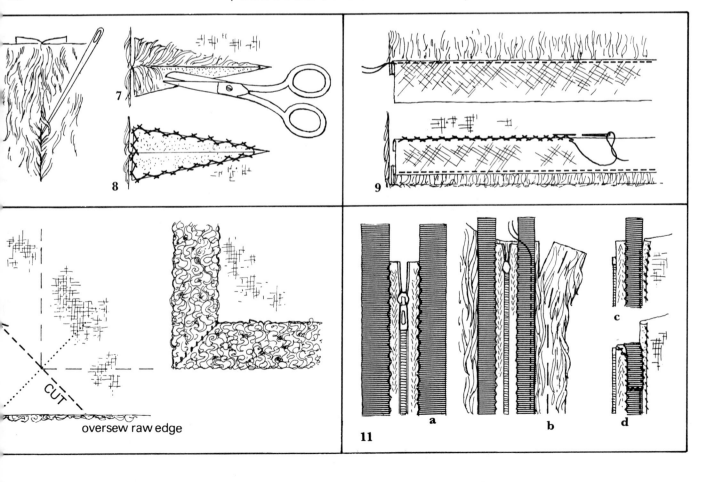

oversew raw edge

Working with leather & suede

Leather and suede are always fashion news. The pattern companies are including in their range more patterns suitable for leather and suede, and developments in the tanning industry have made a wide variety of skins available to the home dressmaker. Elaborate equipment is not necessary for home leatherwork.

Equipment

The following is a list of the essential tools for leatherwork. There are also many gadgets available which you may want to try.

- [ ] Sharp scissors
- [ ] Clear adhesive tape (to secure the pattern when cutting)
- [ ] Stapler (to secure seam allowances when stitching), and staple remover. Paper clips can also be used
- [ ] Adhesive or rubber solution glue (for sticking down seams)
- [ ] Brown paper (for pressing)
- [ ] Tissue paper (for use when stitching seams)
- [ ] Medium/heavy sewing machine needles or special, triangular leather needles
- [ ] Glover's needles (as used for glove making) for hand-sewing
- [ ] Pure silk thread or synthetic thread (the thread must have some elasticity as skins stretch slightly)
- [ ] Ball-point, felt tip pen or tailor's chalk (for marking pattern details)

Preparing for cutting

If you are not sure whether the pattern will fit you it is a good idea to make a mock garment in cotton calico first, as any adjustments made on leather after machining will be unsightly.

If you are using a commercial paper pattern, trim all seam allowances on the pattern tissue to 0.6cm ($\frac{1}{4}$ inch).

If any pattern piece is larger than the skin, decide where it would be best to have a join in the garment and cut the pattern accordingly, adding a 0.6cm ($\frac{1}{4}$ inch) seam allowance to both pieces.

Where a left and right pattern piece is required, make a copy of that pattern piece and mark one 'left', and the other 'right'. This will also allow you to juggle the pieces around on the skin in the same way making another half of any pattern piece where the layout calls for placing on a fold.

Cutting out

When placing the pattern pieces on the skin, ensure that the maximum area is utilised, at the same time noting any blemishes on the right side.

If you are working with suede, you will have to decide whether it is necessary for all the pattern pieces to run in the same direction. On a good suede it may be possible to ignore the nap as the surface is very flexible and it is difficult to detect the direction of the pile.

Secure pattern pieces on the wrong side of skin with clear adhesive tape.

Mark all the cutting lines and darts.

Cut from the neck edge of the skin using very sharp scissors.

Place corresponding pieces together when cut and staple the seam edges together within the seam allowance. Or, if there is no seam allowance, hold the pieces together with paper clips.

Fitting

Try on the 'stapled together' garment for fit and adjust if necessary. This is a very crucial moment as you cannot erase the marks made by a line of stitching if alterations prove necessary at a later stage. The first row of stitches must be the final one.

Stitching

- [ ] Use tissue paper under the leather when stitching. This will prevent the feed teeth of the machine from damaging the skin.
- [ ] Reduce the pressure on the presser foot and do not force the leather under the needle. You will either break the needle or damage the skin.
- [ ] Use a sewing machine needle of medium to heavy thickness or a special leather needle. Change the needle immediately it shows signs of becoming blunt.
- [ ] Use longer stitches than for fabric, about 8 to 10 stitches to 2.5cm (1 inch), and stitch slowly without stretching.
- [ ] Do not stitch sharp corners but round them off very slightly. This will make it easier to turn the corners out.
- [ ] Staple the seam allowances together when stitching. Remove the staples after stitching.
- [ ] For topstitching you will find a roller foot a useful attachment.
- [ ] For all hand-sewing use glover's needles, which will facilitate safe and less strenuous effort on these difficult fabrics.

Finishing

Seams and darts. Make plain seams and where seams are subject to strain or stretch, stitch narrow straight tape into those seams.

1. An alternative and less bulky way to finish a seam is to lap the seam allowances and topstitch them.

Cut darts open. To remove excess bulk on seams and darts pare away (or skive) the under surface of the seam allowance, either with a razor blade or by using one of the scissor blades turned on its side.

Press plain seams and darts open. If you are using a bulky skin it will help if you first pound the seams open with a heavy wooden object such as a rolling pin or a meat hammer; for fine skin, just finger press the seams open. Then press with a warm iron over brown paper or a dry pressing cloth (a hot iron will stretch the skin). Use no moisture. The seam allowance can then be topstitched or stuck down with adhesive.

Edges. Where an edge is curved, cut V-shaped notches into that edge to enable it to lie flat (2).

Hems. Hems can be left raw as leather does not fray, or they can be turned in and glued down. If you decide to leave a hem raw, cut back the seam allowance as shown (3).

Facings. On unlined garments facings can be used to give body.

4. To reduce bulk on the faced edge, trim the seam allowance on the facing to the seam line before stitching and turn in the seam allowance on the garment edge. Place the raw edge of the facing seam line to the folded garment edge and topstitch. This method can be used for the edges of collars, revers and pocket flaps. Alternatively you can omit facings altogether, turn in the raw edges and either topstitch or glue them down.

Sleeves. With many skins it is possible to set in sleeves in the normal way, even to ease in the skin around the sleeve head. Also, you should have no problem in machining the armhole seams. If however, you do find there is too much bulk for machining, sew in the sleeves by hand using a very firm back stitch.

Interfacings. Where the pattern calls for interfacing, use a non-woven type, such as Vilene, appropriate in weight to the skin you are using. In some cases a pre-shrunk tailor's canvas may be suitable. It is always best to ask advice when buying.

Linings. Stitching a lining into a leather garment can be tricky as you cannot slip stitch successfully onto skin. The answer is to stitch tape to the seam or hem allowance, or facing, and slip stitch the lining to the tape.

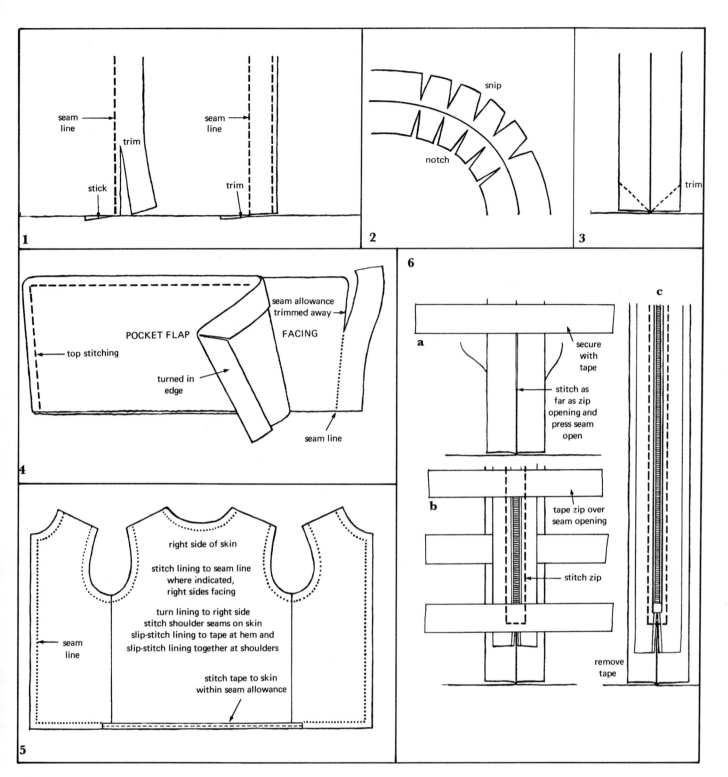

1

seam line → trim

stick

seam line → trim

2

snip

notch

3

trim

4

top stitching

POCKET FLAP

turned in edge

seam allowance trimmed away →

FACING

seam line

5

right side of skin

stitch lining to seam line where indicated, right sides facing

turn lining to right side
stitch shoulder seams on skin
slip-stitch lining to tape at hem and
slip-stitch lining together at shoulders

seam line

stitch tape to skin within seam allowance

6

a

secure with tape

stitch as far as zip opening and press seam open

b

tape zip over seam opening

stitch zip

c

remove tape

5. Alternatively make an edge-to-edge lining as shown.

Use a strong, durable lining such as Tricel, otherwise you will find that the skin outlasts the lining. Even so, you may have to replace the lining.

Make skirt linings fractionally narrower than the skirt to prevent seating.

Zips. Zips can be inserted in the normal way by machining or hand-sewing.

6a, b, c. To hold the zip in place while stitching use clear adhesive tape on the wrong side of the garment.

Buttonholes and eyelets. You can make bound buttonholes quite successfully in soft leather or suede, or the buttonhole edges can be zigzagged by machine.

Alternatively, if buttons are part of the finished effect you may find it easier to dispense with buttonholes altogether and use covered buttons with press studs on the reverse side.

Eyelets used in conjunction with thonging can make a very attractive fastening. This type of fastening is especially suitable for casual garments. You can buy an eyelet making kit in most large department stores, or alternatively a large saddler.

Interfacing may be used around the wrong side of the shape of the buttonhole to prevent stretching.

Working with sequined fabrics

Do not be put off when buying exotic sequined fabrics by their intricate and expensive appearance. They are surprisingly easy to handle, and made up into even the simplest garment the effect is really stunning. Here are a few points to watch when using sequined fabrics.

BUYING THE FABRIC

The cost of all sequined fabrics is relatively high, but some are twice as expensive as others, so make sure that the chosen fabric is not more extravagant than necessary. The sequins catch the light and shine, so even a small area of fabric will show up well (Fig. 1.)

A short length can be used effectively and economically for a yoke or midriff on a bodice, or as the front of a waistcoat or jacket. The halter top of a formal dress could glitter attractively and contrast with a soft matt crepe or floating chiffon skirt. There are exciting border designs available which will make a full length dress with an eye catching skirt cut in a very simple style. These fabrics are usually wide enough for the plainer edge to be used to make the bodice. Some sequined fabrics such as lamé jerseys can also be purchased plain so this makes a combination design possible.

A glittery cardigan over a plain halter topped cat suit would make an effective outfit.

Sequins are attached to the background fabric with a machine stitch which may hold them on individually or catch a continuous strip of them at regular intervals (Fig. 2).

Sequined fabrics tend to be heavy and they should always be lined. Buy a good quality lining fabric to complement the basic fabric.

Checking the fit

If the pattern is cut out first in the lining fabric this can be tacked up and the garment can have a thorough preliminary fitting (Fig. 3). This will simplify the work on the sequined fabric which should be handled as little as possible. If the lining needs any adjustments, make sure that they are clearly marked with tacking thread. The lining can then be taken apart and used as the pattern for cutting out the sequined fabric.

Cutting the fabric

This needs careful planning as each section

should be cut singly to avoid the risk of the scissors slipping on two layers of sequins. The advantage of using the lining as a pattern is that the complete layout can be checked with both halves of each section in place (Fig. 4).

Any stripe in the sequin design must be balanced and the grain lines must be accurate.

Cut out with a pair of heavy shears which will go through the sequins. Beware of flying chips of sequin, as damaged ones will fall away from the cut edges.

The thread securing the sequins to the fabric should be sufficiently locked for there to be no risk of them falling off beyond the 1.5cm ($\frac{5}{8}$ inch) seam allowance. If they seem rather insecure, a thin strip of adhesive tape can make a temporary finish until the seams have been stitched. Or, if the sewing machine can cope with sewing the fabric singly, without getting tangled in the sequins, a line of straight stitching round all the cut edges will anchor the threads which hold on the sequins before starting to make up the garment.

SEWING SEQUINED FABRIC

Choose a fine synthetic sewing thread and do not machine with too many stitches to the inch.

If sequins are mounted on jersey then the seams must be sewn with a stretchy zig-zag stitch. Always make a test seam and then experiment with pressing it as soon as scraps of spare fabric are available.

Pressing

Darts and seams must be pressed as soon as they have been stitched. This should be done first with the fingers (Fig. 5), checking for sharp edges and removing any broken or loose sequins. Sequins are made of a slightly pliable plastic which can be bent, so a certain number may be flattened by folding them between the finger and thumb. But any which are awkwardly placed must be carefully removed (Fig. 6). When the seams have been checked press open carefully with a cool iron.

Use a dry pressing cloth to ensure that the sequins do not stick to the iron and never press from the right side as the heat will damage the surface of the sequins.

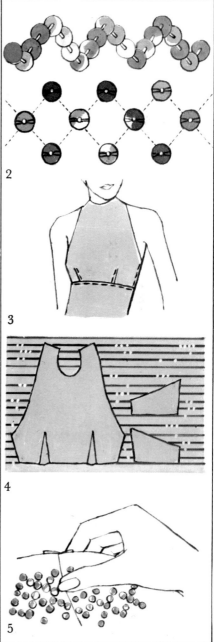

Replacing sequins

Do not reduce the 1.5cm ($\frac{5}{8}$ inch) seam allowance more than necessary, to avoid the danger of the threads holding the sequins pulling loose from the seam stitching. If, where damaged sequins have been removed, bare patches are evident on the garment, they must be replaced. Use spares from the fabric scraps and sew them on carefully by hand (Fig. 7). Try to match the direction and the pattern of the stitches used to attach the sequins, and if it is possible to unravel some of the thread originally used, this should make the repair invisible.

Alternatively, one of the 'invisible' sewing threads might blend in well, especially on light coloured sequins.

If darts seem bulky, the sequins inside should be removed before stitching, without cutting the anchoring threads.

Lining and facings

The lining is slipped into the completed garment with wrong sides together, so that the raw edges will all be concealed and protected from fraying. It should be possible to make the lining act as the facing to most edges, but whether the edges are faced or lined, under stitching will be needed to ensure that they lie flat and are concealed (Fig. 8). However, it may be more comfortable to plan a design which has a binding or faced edging in plain fabric to prevent the sequined fabric feeling rough in wear (Fig. 9).

If there is a raw edge which will not be covered by the lining, either at the hem or round an armhole, this should be neatened with a narrow flat binding cut from bias strips of lining fabric (Fig. 10).

Zip fasteners

For most evening dresses a zip fastener is essential. If this has to go into the sequined fabric it must be sewn in after the lining. Take the lining right to the edges of the opening to face them so that the slider does not get in the sequins. Then the zip is sewn in by hand with tiny spaced back stitches which are concealed between the sequins (Fig. 11). The ends and edges of the tapes can then be oversewn to the lining.

Buttonholes

A simple bound buttonhole may be successfully incorporated in the garment, if sequins are removed from the area and the buttonhole is then made in plain fabric (Fig. 12).

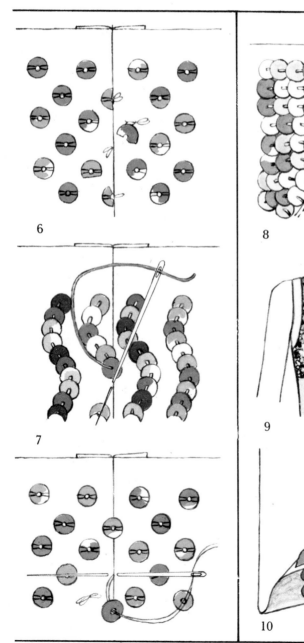

6

7

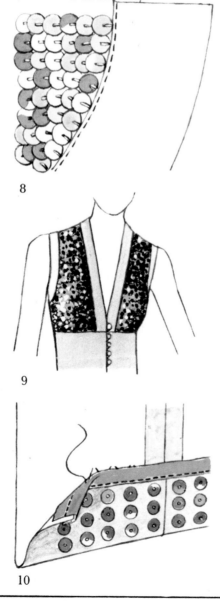

8

9

10

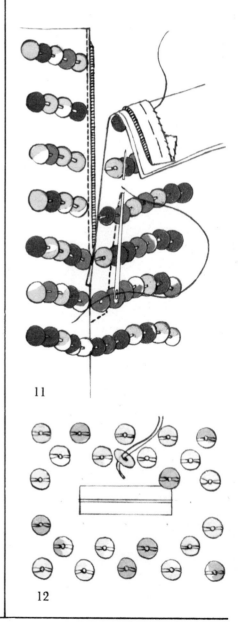

11

12

Enlarging a Pattern

Whether you create your own patterns or wish to copy them from a book or magazine it is important to know how to enlarge them, and this is necessary for all the patterns in the second section of this book.

Materials required:

Tracing paper
Graph or squared paper
Rubber and ruler
Felt tipped pen
Soft pencil
Carbon paper

Extend the two adjacent sides of the rectangle to the final size you want, then draw lines at right angles from the ends of the extended sides to meet at the diagonal line.

5. Count the number of squares in the small rectangle and divide the largest rectangle into the same number of squares to form a grid. Draw this in pencil as you may wish to rub out and re-draw some of the lines of the design to improve its shape. Now, in pencil carefully copy the pattern onto a larger grid. It is best to make tiny marks on each square where the lines of the pattern cross the square then you can simply join up these marks.

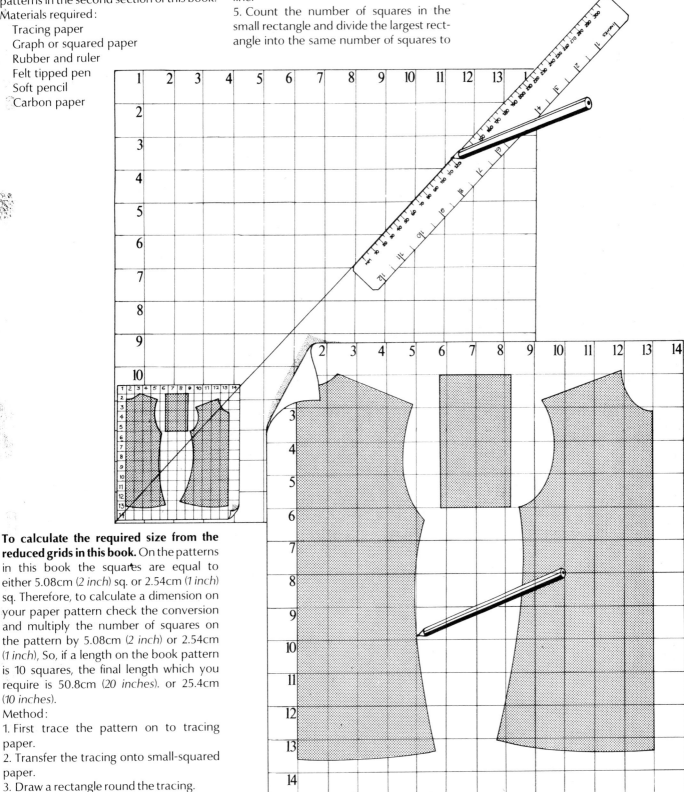

To calculate the required size from the reduced grids in this book. On the patterns in this book the squares are equal to either 5.08cm (*2 inch*) sq. or 2.54cm (*1 inch*) sq. Therefore, to calculate a dimension on your paper pattern check the conversion and multiply the number of squares on the pattern by 5.08cm (*2 inch*) or 2.54cm (*1 inch*), So, if a length on the book pattern is 10 squares, the final length which you require is 50.8cm (*20 inches*). or 25.4cm (*10 inches*).

Method:

1. First trace the pattern on to tracing paper.
2. Transfer the tracing onto small-squared paper.
3. Draw a rectangle round the tracing.
4. Draw a diagonal through the tracing.

101

Sample standard size chart in centimetres (inches in brackets)

UK sizes	10	12	14	16	Grade		
Bust	83 (32½)	87 (34)	92 (36)	97 (38)	3.8 (1½)	5 (2)	5 (2)
Waist	64 (25)	67 (26½)	71 (28)	76 (30)	3.8 (1½)	3.8 (1½)	5 (2)
Hips	88 (34½)	92 (36)	97 (38)	102 (40)	3.8 (1½)	5 (2)	5 (2)
Back waist length	40.5 (16)	41.5 (16¼)	42 (16½)	42.5 (16¾)	0.6 (¼)	0.6 (¼)	0.6 (¼)
Measurements not taken on the body							
Across back	34.5 (13½)	35.5 (14)	37 (14½)	38 (15)	1.3 (½)	1.3 (½)	1.3 (½)
Across chest	35.5 (14)	37 (14½)	38 (15)	39.5 (15½)	1.3 (½)	1.3 (½)	1.3 (½)
Armhole depth (scye)	20 (7¾)	20.5 (8)	21 (8¼)	21.5 (8½)	0.6 (¼)	0.6 (¼)	0.6 (¼)
Shoulder length	11.5 (4½)	12 (4¾)	12.5 (5)	13.5 (5¼)	0.6 (¼)	0.6 (¼)	0.6 (¼)
Neck width	6.5 (2½)	7 (2¾)	7.5 (3)	8 (3⅛)	0.3 (⅛)	0.3 (⅛)	0.3 (⅛)
Sleeve length	62.5 (24½)	63.5 (25)	65 (25½)	66 (26)	1.3 (½)	1.3 (½)	1.3 (½)
Shoulder to elbow	35 (13¾)	35.5 (14)	36 (14¼)	37 (14½)	0.6 (¼)	0.6 (¼)	0.6 (¼)
Elbow to wrist	27.5 (10¾)	28 (11)	28.5 (11¼)	29.5 (11½)	0.6 (¼)	0.6 (¼)	0.6 (¼)
Sleeve width	34.5 (13½)	35.5 (14)	37 (14½)	38 (15)	1.3 (½)	1.3 (½)	1.3 (½)
Wrist width	15 (6)	16.5 (6½)	18 (7)	19 (7½)	1.3 (½)	1.3 (½)	1.3 (½)

SECTION 2
Patterns for the advanced dressmaker

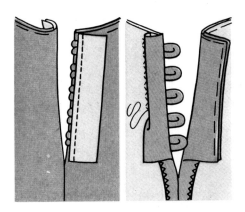

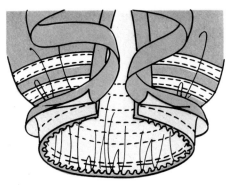

The section that follows is designed to enable you to put into practical use the various skills described in Section I.
As well as designs for women, ranging from lingerie to a complete wedding ensemble, there are clothes to make for men, children and babies. Each is complete with a graph pattern and carefully-detailed step-by-step diagrams, and any unusual techniques required or materials used are explained fully in Section I.

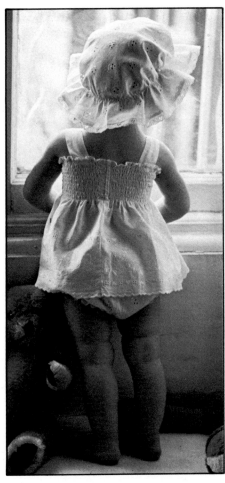

Slip and panties

... cut on the cross for a close clingy fit.

Making up the slip

1 Cut two strips of wide lace the length of the centre-front yoke. Pin the lace centrally on the right side of the yoke, edge to edge. Cut two shorter strips and attach either side of the central lace. Pin-stitch or zig-zag lace to the yoke. Cut strips of lace and pin-stitch to the top edges of the front and back bodices.

| | right side | | wrong side |

2 With right sides together and matching notches tack and stitch the front yoke to the front bodice, easing the bodice on to the yoke slightly. Trim turnings and neaten together. Press onto bodice. With right sides together and matching notches tack and stitch the front and back bodices together on the right hand side only. Press turnings open and neaten.

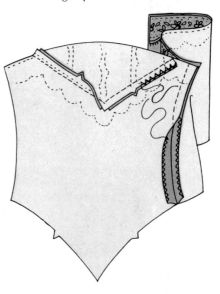

3 With right sides together and matching notches tack and stitch the front and back skirts together at the side seams

Sizes
10, 12, 14 and 16

Fabric required
For sizes 10 and 12: 3.20 metres (3½ yards) of 114cm (45 inch) wide fabric
For sizes 14 and 16: 3.45 metres (3¾ yards) of 114cm (45 inch) wide fabric

You will also need
- ☐ Graph paper for making the pattern
- ☐ Matching thread
- ☐ 2.75 metres (3 yards) of 7.5cm (3 inch) wide lace
- ☐ 3.65 metres (4 yards) of 1.3cm (½ inch) wide lace for edging
- ☐ 3 hooks and eyes
- ☐ 12 press studs
- ☐ 0.90 metre (1 yard) of 0.6cm (¼ inch) wide ribbon
- ☐ 0.25 metre (¼ yard) of interfacing

Making the pattern
Using graph paper and following the colour indicating the size required draw each pattern piece to scale. One square = 2.54cm square (1 inch square). An allowance of 1.6cm (⅝ inch) has been made on all seams and hems except where otherwise stated. Cut out the pattern pieces and mark all dots, notches and the straight grain line.

Cutting out the slip and pants
Cut a 2.25 metre (2¼ yard) section from the fabric and lay out flat for the slip. Following the cutting layout place the pattern pieces as indicated, making sure that the straight grain line lies on the straight grain of the fabric. Pin into place and cut out.
Fold the remaining fabric in half and following the cutting layout place the pattern pieces for the pants as indicated. Pin into place and cut out. Transfer all markings from the pattern pieces to the fabric.

105

leaving an opening above the dot on the left seam. Press turnings open and neaten.

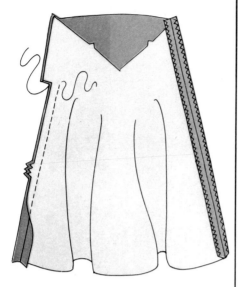

4 Matching side seams, centre-front, and back, pin the bodice to the skirt with right sides together. Tack and stitch. Trim turnings and neaten together. Press on to skirt.

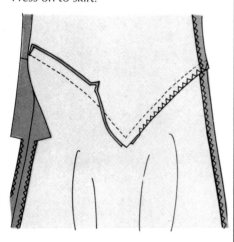

Shoulder straps

5 Cut two pieces of ribbon approximately 42cm (16½ *inches*) long. Tack the ends of each shoulder strap on to the front yoke 6.5cm (2½ *inches*) in from the seams.

Facings

6 Using the appropriate pattern pieces, cut a front and back facing in inter-facing. Attach to the wrong side of the facings. With right sides together stitch the front and back facings together at the right side. Trim turnings and press open.

7 With right sides together and matching seams tack and stitch the facing to the bodice sandwiching the shoulder straps in between. Trim and layer turnings. Neaten raw edge of facing, turn to the wrong side and press downwards.

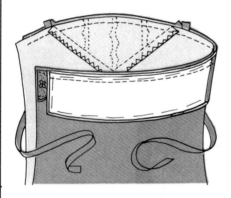

Try on the slip and check the length of the straps. Hand-stitch the remaining ends to the back bodice so that they are 16.5cm to 18cm (6½ *inches to 7 inches*) apart.

8 Cut two strips of fabric on the straight grain both 34.5cm (13½ *inches*) long and one 4cm (1½ *inches*) wide and the other

7cm (2¾ *inches*) wide. Turn over 0.6cm (¼ *inch*) on all short ends to the wrong side and press.

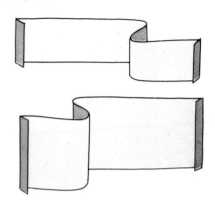

9 With right sides together tack and stitch one long edge of the wider strip to the back edge of the opening taking 1.6cm (⅝ *inch*) turnings. Make a turning of the same amount on the remaining edge, turn over and slip-stitch on to the stitch line. Slip-stitch the short ends together.

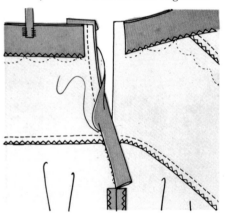

With right sides together tack and stitch the narrow strip to the front edge of the opening in the same way. Make a 0.6cm (¼ *inch*) turning on the remaining edge, turn the strip to the wrong side on the seam line and slip-stitch to the slip.

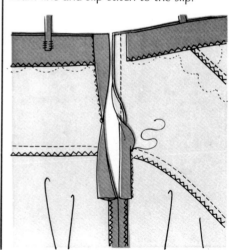

10 Sew a hook and eye to the top of the opening and on the seam joining bodice and skirt. Attach six press studs at regular intervals between the hooks.

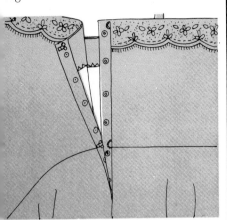

Hem

11 Try on the slip and check the length. Turn up and cut off any excess fabric, leaving a 1.6cm ($\frac{5}{8}$ *inch*) turning. Tack and stitch one edge of the narrow lace on to the right side through all thicknesses, to hold the hem in place also. Remove all tacking and press slip on the wrong side.

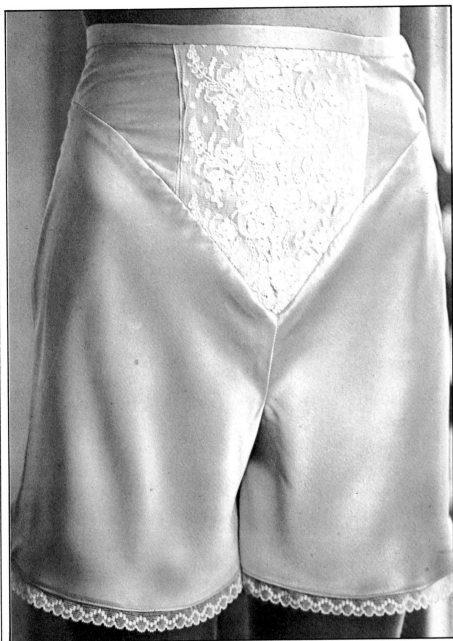

Pants

12 Attach lace to the front yoke as on the slip using two lengths only. With right sides together and matching notches tack and stitch the front and back yoke together at the right side seam only.

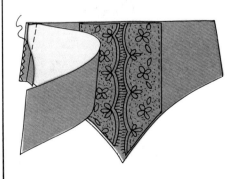

Tack and stitch the back and front leg pieces together on both seams but leaving

open above the notch on the left hand side. Trim turnings, press open and neaten.

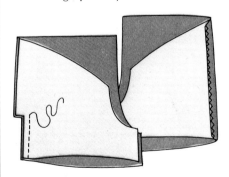

13 With right sides together and matching notches tack and stitch each inside leg seam. Trim turnings, press open and neaten. Turn one leg inside out and slip inside the other leg so that right sides are together with matching notches and

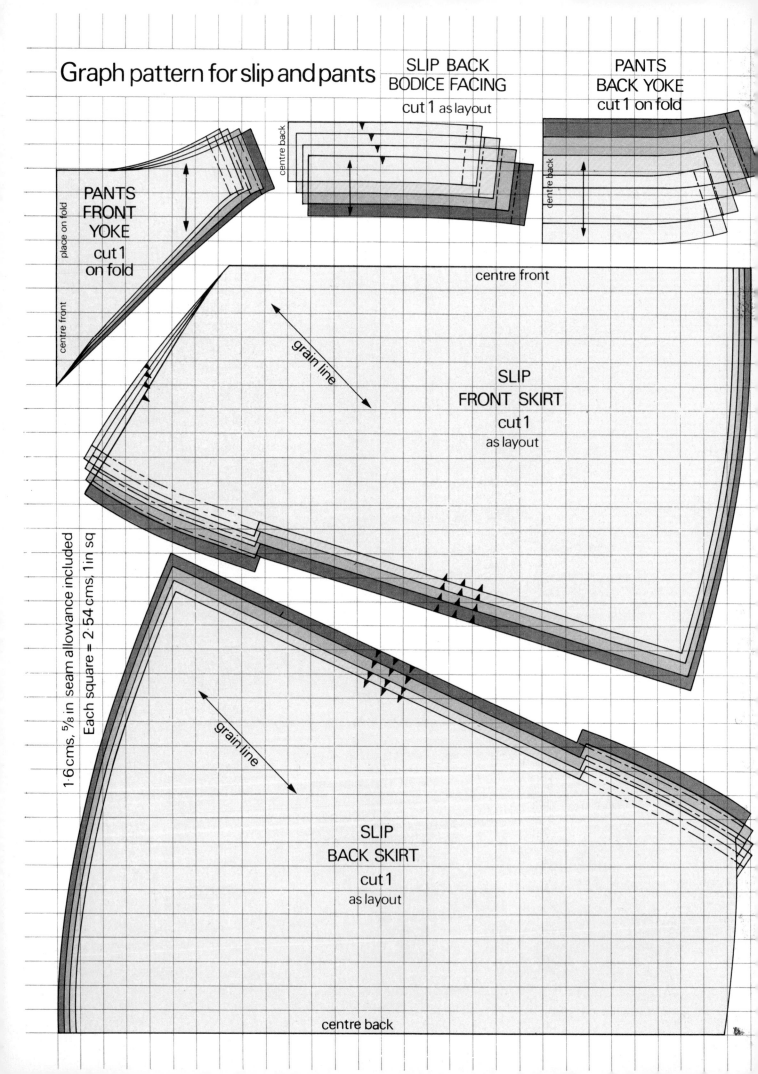

Graph pattern for slip and pants

SLIP BACK BODICE FACING
cut 1 as layout

PANTS BACK YOKE
cut 1 on fold

centre back

centre back

PANTS FRONT YOKE
cut 1 on fold

place on fold

centre front

centre front

grain line

SLIP FRONT SKIRT
cut 1 as layout

1·6 cms, 5/8 in seam allowance included
Each square = 2·54 cms, 1 in sq

grain line

SLIP BACK SKIRT
cut 1 as layout

centre back

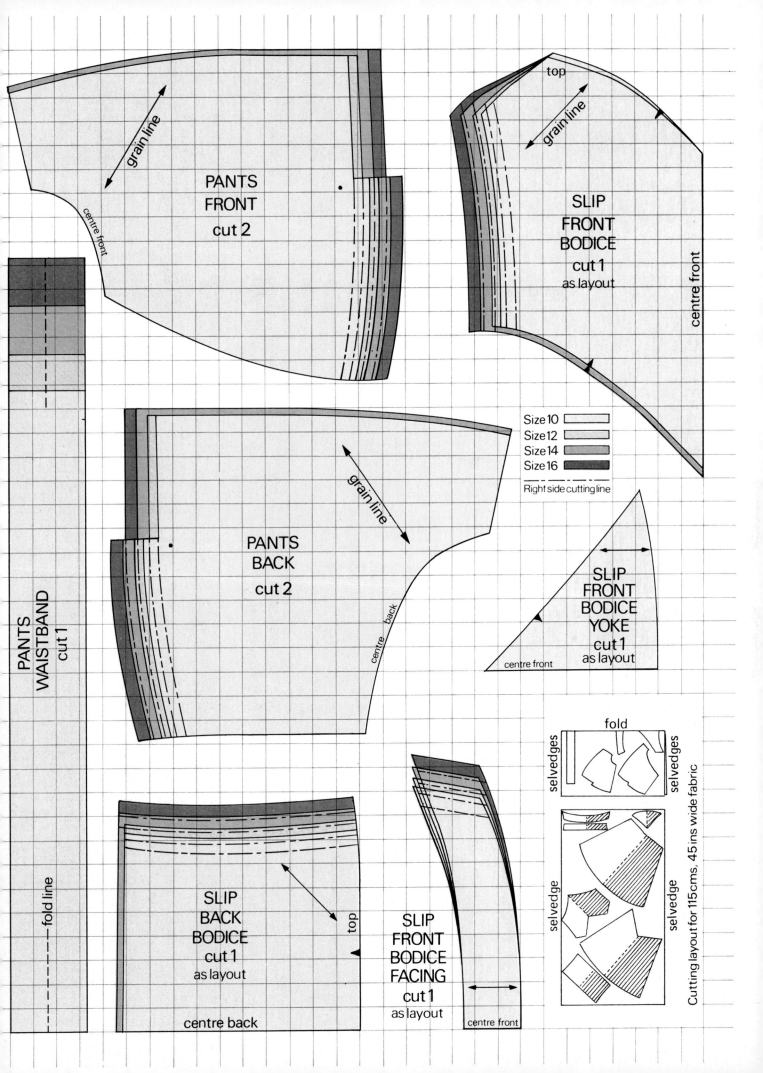

PANTS
FRONT
cut 2

grain line

centre front

SLIP
FRONT
BODICE
cut 1
as layout

top

grain line

centre front

PANTS
WAISTBAND
cut 1

fold line

PANTS
BACK
cut 2

grain line

centre back

Size 10	
Size 12	
Size 14	
Size 16	

Right side cutting line

SLIP
FRONT
BODICE
YOKE
cut 1
as layout

centre front

SLIP
BACK
BODICE
cut 1
as layout

top

centre back

SLIP
FRONT
BODICE
FACING
cut 1
as layout

centre front

fold

selvedges

selvedges

selvedge

selvedge

Cutting layout for 115cms, 45ins wide fabric

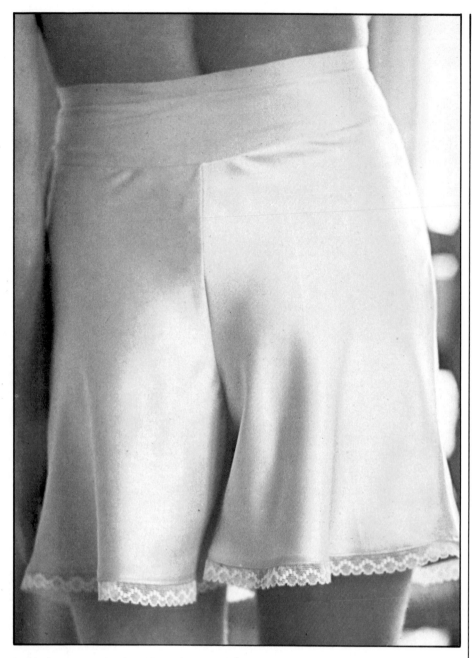

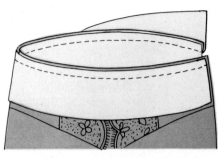

of the pants. Fold over, make a hem of 1.6cm ($\frac{5}{8}$ *inch*) turning on the remaining edge and slip-stitch on to the stitch line.

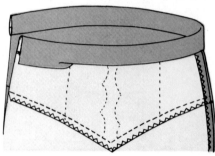

16 Cut two strips of fabric 24cm ($9\frac{1}{2}$ *inches*) long and 5.5cm ($2\frac{1}{4}$ *inches*) wide and the other 4cm ($1\frac{1}{2}$ *inches*) wide. Work in the same way as the slip opening. Then attach a hook and eye to the top of the opening and six press studs at regular intervals down the opening.

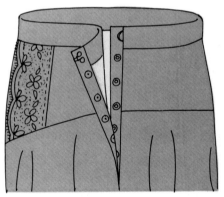

17 Work the hems and attach the lace as above.

inside leg seams. Tack and stitch around crotch. Trim turnings and clip if they pull and neaten.

14 Tack the yoke carefully to the pants matching the side seams. Stitch,

trim turnings and neaten together. Press on to pants.

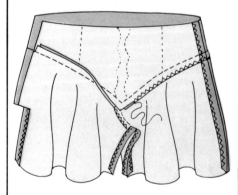

15 Cut a piece of interfacing and attach to the wrong side of the waistband. With right sides together tack and stitch the waistband to the top edge

Velvet coat

. . . to give your long
dresses a luxury look.

Sizes

10, 12, 14 and 16

Fabric required

All sizes take 10.20 metres (11⅓ yards) of 91cm (36 inch) fabric 9.90 metres (11 yards) of 91cm (36 inch) lining

You will also need

☐ Graph paper for making the pattern
☐ Matching thread
☐ 1.65 metres (1¾ yards) of 91cm (36 inch) interfacing
☐ 10 × 1.6cm (⅝ inch) buttons

Making the pattern

Using graph paper and following the colour indicating the size required draw each pattern piece to scale. One square= 5.08cm square (2 inch square).

An allowance of 1.6cm (⅝ inch) has been made on all seams and a 4cm (1½ inch) hem has been allowed.

Cut out the pattern pieces and mark all dots and notches and the straight grain line.

Cutting out the coat

Following the cutting layout place the pattern pieces for the back, side back, front, side front, sleeve, sleeve facing, front facing and front yoke on to single fabric as indicated. Take care that the grain line on the pattern lies on the straight grain of the fabric. Pin into place and cut out. Reverse these pattern pieces and cut out once more.

With the fabric folded pin the pattern pieces for the back yoke, top collar and back neck facing to the fold, again taking care that the grain is correct. Pin into place and cut out. Cut out the under-collar with the centre-back placed to a bias fold of fabric as indicated.

For the lining place the pattern pieces for the back, side back, front, side front, sleeve, yokes and pocket as indicated. Pin into place and cut out, following the cutting lines for the lining marked on the pattern pieces. Reverse the pattern pieces and cut out once more. Cut out two more pockets.

For the interfacing cut out two front facings, two sleeve facings and one under-collar. Transfer all markings from the pattern pieces to the fabric.

Note

Methods for working with velvet has been explained.

Making up

1 With right sides together and matching notches tack and stitch a pocket piece to the pocket extension on each front. Press turnings towards the pocket. With right sides together and matching notches tack and stitch a pocket piece to the pocket extension on each side front. Press turnings towards the pocket.

▬ right side ☐ wrong side

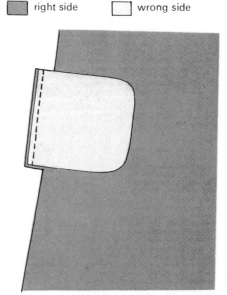

2 On the side fronts clip across to the dots at each side of the pocket extension. With right sides together and matching notches tack and stitch the side fronts and pockets to the fronts. Press the seams open above and below the pockets.

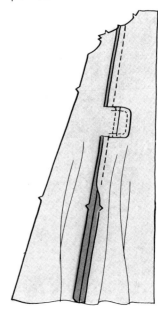

3 Run a gathering thread along the top edges of the coat fronts between the notches. With right sides together and matching notches tack and stitch the fronts to the front yokes, distributing the fullness evenly. Press the turnings towards the yoke.

Tack interfacing to the wrong sides of the fronts, placing the front edges together.

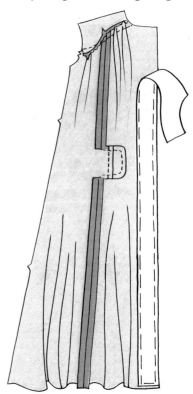

4 With right sides together and matching notches tack and stitch the centre-back seam. Press open. With right sides together and matching notches tack and stitch the side backs to the back. Press the seams open.

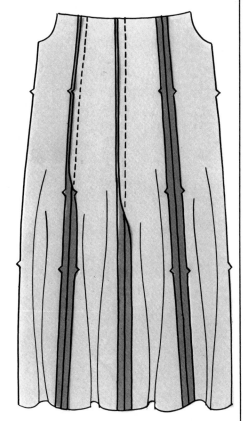

5 Run a gathering thread along the top edge of the coat back between the notches. With right sides together and matching notches tack and stitch the back to the back yoke, distributing the fullness evenly. Press the turnings towards the yoke.

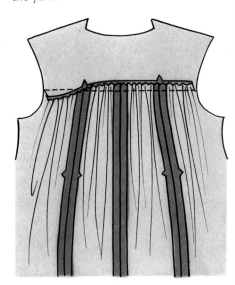

With right sides together and matching notches tack and stitch the fronts to the back at the side and shoulder seams. Press the seams open.

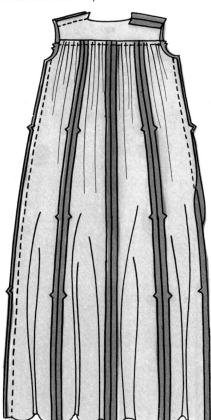

6 Tack interfacing to the wrong side of the under-collar. With right sides together tack and stitch the top collar to the under-collar around the outer edges. Trim and clip the turnings, turn the collar to the right side, tack close to the edge and press. Tack the neck edges together.

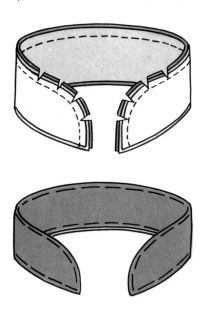

7 With right sides together and matching notches and centre-front dots tack the collar to the neckline.

With right sides together tack and stitch the front facings to the back neck facing at the shoulder seams. Trim the turnings to 1cm ($\frac{3}{8}$ inch) and press open

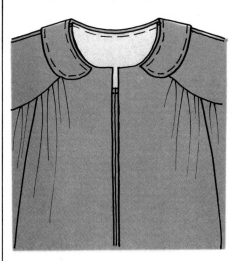

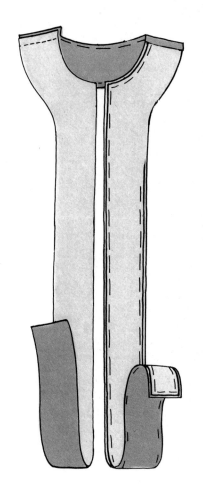

8 With right sides together and matching notches and shoulder seams tack and stitch the facing to the coat at the fronts and neckline. The collar will be sandwiched between. Trim the turnings and clip the neckline curve. Turn the facing to the right side, tack close to the edge and press. Catch the facing to the coat on the shoulder seams. Make 10 bound button-

holes on the right front where indicated. Tack the facing to the coat temporarily.

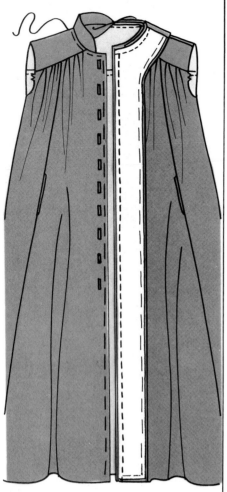

Sleeves

9 Tack interfacing to the wrong side of the sleeve at the lower edge. With right sides together and matching notches tack and stitch the underarm seam. Press open.

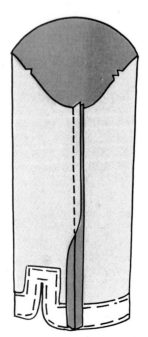

With right sides together tack and stitch the underarm seam of the sleeve facing. Trim turnings to 1cm ($\frac{3}{8}$ *inch*) and press open. With right sides together and matching notches and underarm seams tack and stitch the sleeve facing to the sleeve. Trim the turnings and clip where necessary. Turn the facing to the inside of the sleeve, tack close to the lower edge and press. From the wrong side lightly catch the facing to the sleeve. The stitches should not be visible on the right side.

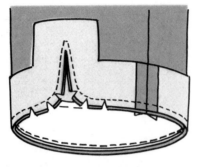

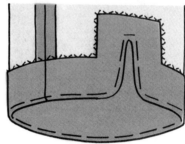

10 Run a gathering thread over the sleeve head between the notches. With right sides together and matching notches and underarm seams pin the sleeve into the armhole, distributing the fullness evenly. Tack and stitch. Trim the turnings to 1cm ($\frac{3}{8}$ *inch*) and press towards the sleeve.

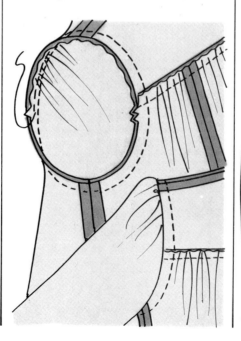

11 Try on the coat and check the length. Turn up the hem and tack close to the fold line. Press. Slip-stitch the hem into place. Slip-stitch the hem folds of the front facings to the front coat.

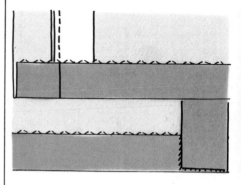

Lining

12 Omitting the pockets tack and stitch the panel and side seams of the lining as for the coat. Press all seams open. Tack and stitch the shoulder seams of the yoke lining. Press open. Run gathering threads along the top edges of the lining fronts and back between the notches. With right sides together and matching notches tack and stitch the fronts and back to the yoke, distributing the fullness evenly. Press the turnings towards the yoke.

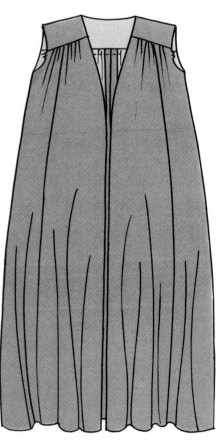

13 With wrong sides together pin the lining into the coat around the armhole. Hand stitch the turnings together close to the seam line.

Lift up the lining and loosely catch the turnings of the lining and coat together at the side seams from the armhole to 5cm (2 inches) above the hem.

14 Turn under the seam allowance around the front, neck and lower edges of the lining and tack to the coat. Take care to ease the lining on to the coat. Slip-hem into place. Press.

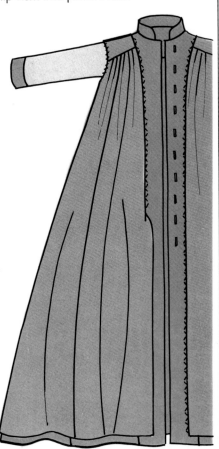

Sleeve lining

15 With right sides together and matching notches tack and stitch the underarm seam of the sleeve lining. Press open. Run a gathering thread over the sleeve head between the notches. Turn the coat-sleeve inside out and with wrong sides together and matching notches and underarm seams pin the sleeve lining to the armhole, pulling up the fullness to match the sleeve. Turn under the seam allowance and hem securely to the stitching line. Press.

16 Turn under the seam allowance at the lower edge of the sleeve lining. Tack to the sleeve facing and slip-hem into place. Press.

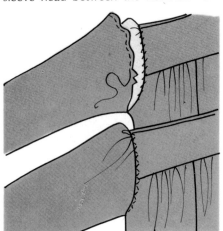

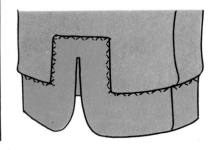

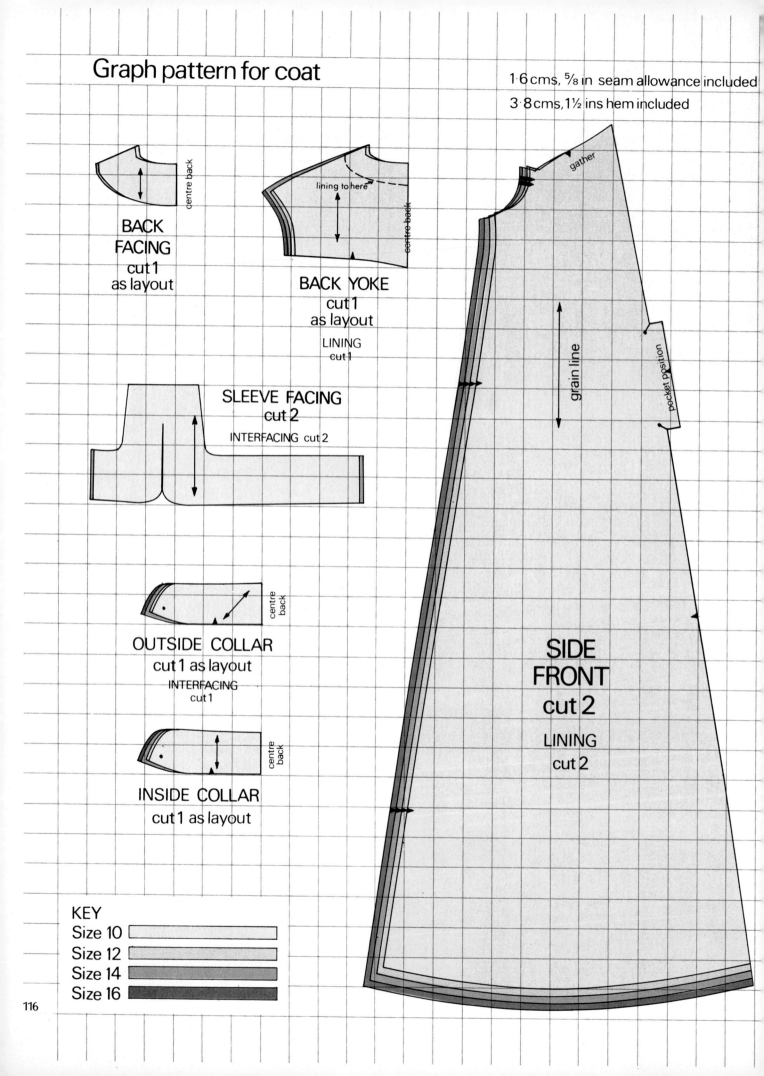

Graph pattern for coat

1·6 cms, ⅝ in seam allowance included

3·8 cms, 1½ ins hem included

BACK
FACING
cut 1
as layout

centre back

BACK YOKE
cut 1
as layout

LINING
cut 1

lining to here

centre back

SLEEVE FACING
cut 2

INTERFACING cut 2

OUTSIDE COLLAR
cut 1 as layout

INTERFACING
cut 1

centre back

INSIDE COLLAR
cut 1 as layout

centre back

gather

grain line

pocket position

SIDE
FRONT
cut 2

LINING
cut 2

KEY
Size 10
Size 12
Size 14
Size 16

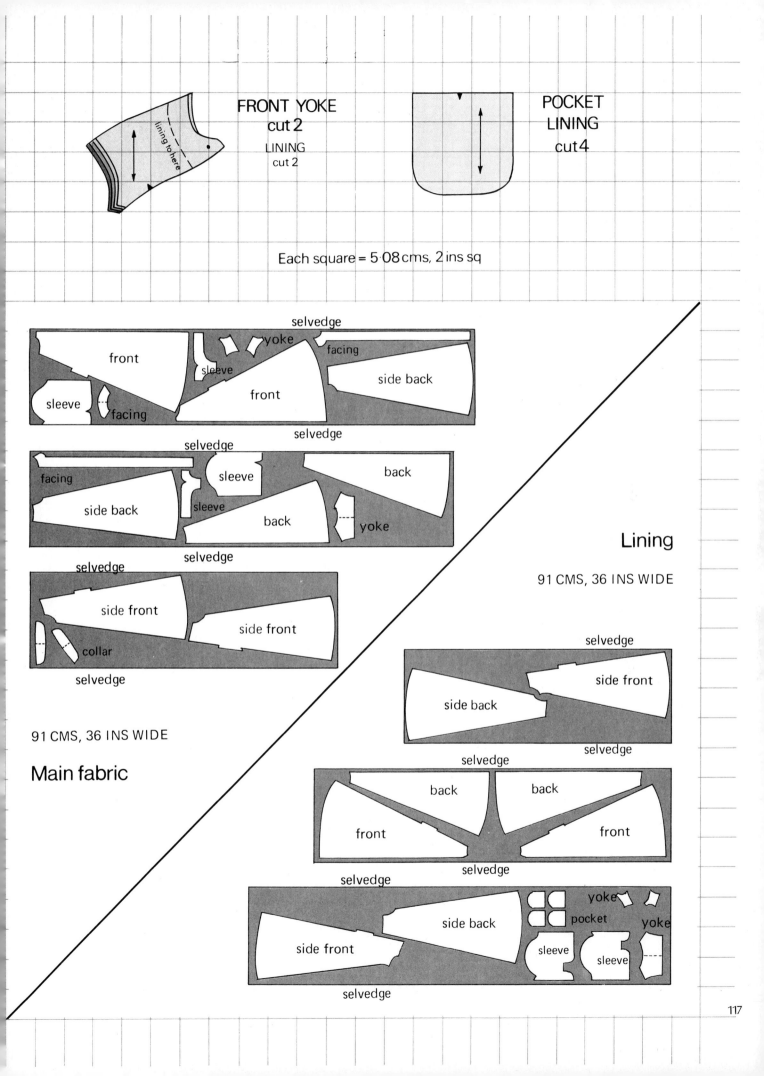

FRONT YOKE
cut 2

LINING
cut 2

POCKET
LINING
cut 4

Each square = 5·08 cms, 2 ins sq

Lining

91 CMS, 36 INS WIDE

91 CMS, 36 INS WIDE

Main fabric

117

Graph pattern for coat

Each square = 5·08 cms, 2 ins sq

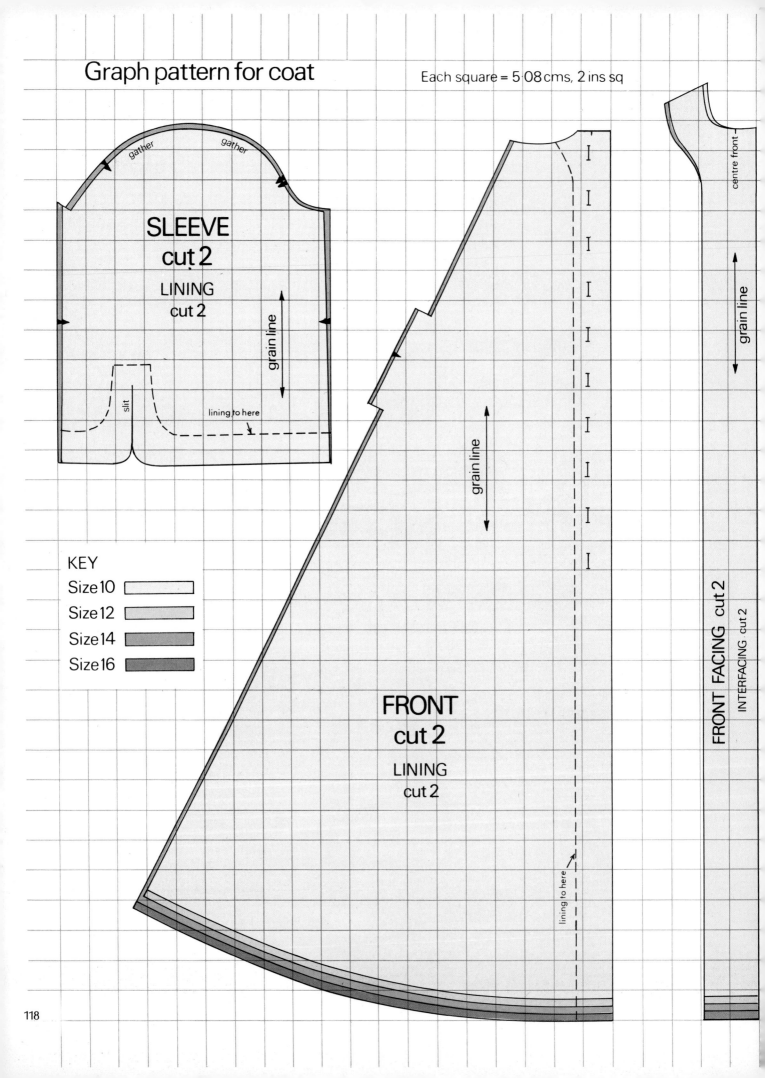

SLEEVE
cut 2

LINING
cut 2

gather   gather

grain line

slit

lining to here

KEY

Size 10
Size 12
Size 14
Size 16

grain line

grain line

lining to here

FRONT
cut 2

LINING
cut 2

centre front

grain line

FRONT FACING cut 2

INTERFACING cut 2

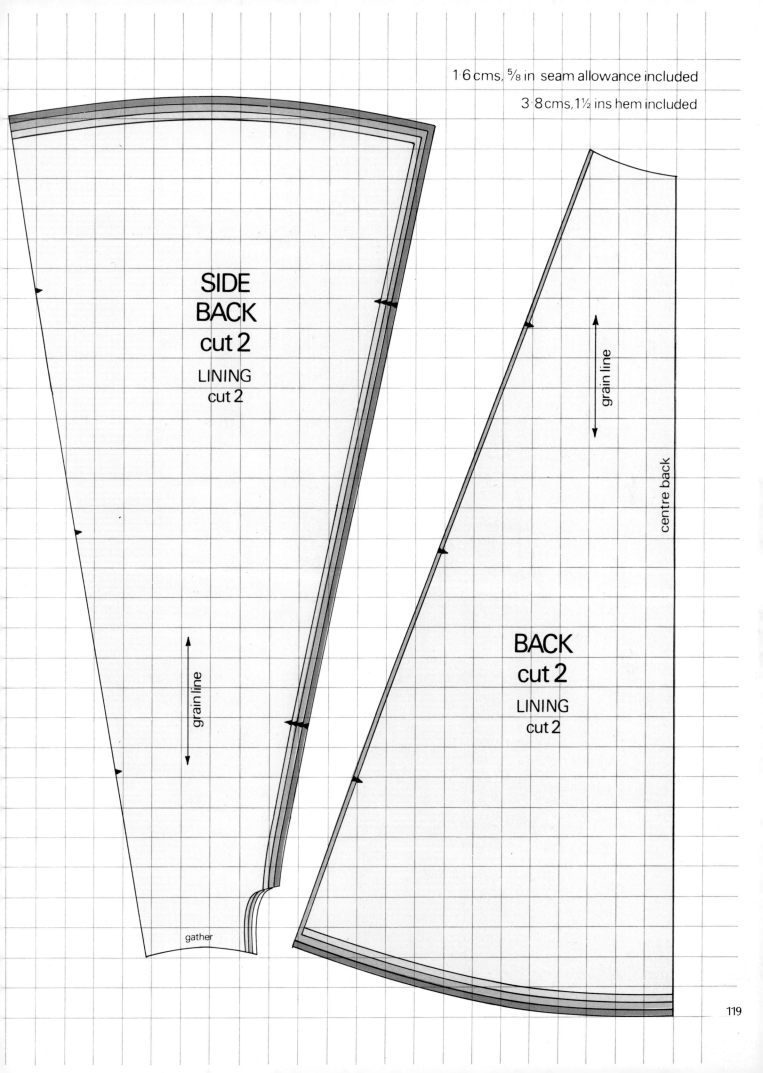

SIDE
BACK
cut 2

LINING
cut 2

grain line

gather

BACK
cut 2

LINING
cut 2

grain line

centre back

1·6 cms, ⅝ in seam allowance included

3·8 cms, 1½ ins hem included

Gorgeous dress

Tiered, plain over print in filmy, floating chiffon.

Sizes

10, 12, 14 and 16

Fabric required

All sizes take 5.95 metres (6½ yards) of 114cm (45 inch) plain silk chiffon and 5.95 metres (6½ yards) of 114cm (45 inch) printed crepe or georgette

You will also need

- [ ] Graph paper for making the pattern
- [ ] Matching thread
- [ ] 14 small buttons or button moulds for covering
- [ ] 13½ metres (14¾ yards) of 1cm (⅜ inch) dark tone satin ribbon
- [ ] 12½ metres (13½ yards) of 1cm (⅜ inch) light tone satin ribbon

Making the pattern

Using graph paper and following the colour indicating the size required draw each pattern piece to scale. One square= 5.08cm square (2 inch square).

An allowance of 1.6cm (⅝ inch) has been made on all seams and on the hem.

Cut out the pattern pieces and mark the position of the sleeve opening, all notches and the straight grain line.

Cutting out the dress

Following the cutting layout with the plain chiffon folded and selvedges together place the pattern pieces for the front and back overdress and sleeve as indicated. Take care that the grain line on the pattern lies on the straight grain of the fabric. Pin into place and cut out. With the printed fabric folded and selvedges together place the two pattern pieces for the underdress as indicated. Pin into place and cut out. Cut off the extension on the centre-back opening on the right back of both dresses. Transfer all markings from the pattern pieces to the fabric.

Making up

1 With right sides together and matching notches tack and stitch the centre-back and centre-front seams of the underdress, leaving the centre-back open above the dot. Press open and neaten. With right sides together and matching notches tack and stitch the side seams of the underdress. Press open and neaten.

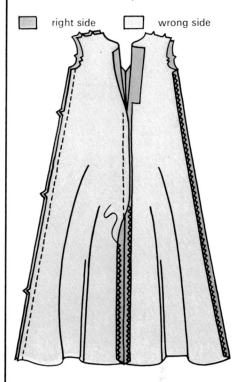

▨ right side	☐ wrong side

2 Leaving the centre-back open above the dot join the centre-front and centre-back seams of the overdress with French seams. It helps to use tissue paper under the fabric when stitching chiffon. Press the seams to one side. Join the side seams of the overdress with French seams. Press towards the centre-back.

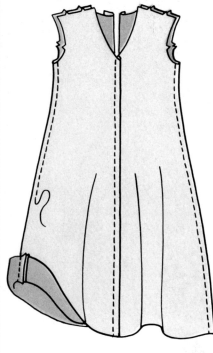

121

3 Place the overdress over the underdress and tack together around the
armholes, shoulders and neckline.
With right sides together tack and stitch
the shoulder seams, stitching the two
dresses as one. Press open and neaten.

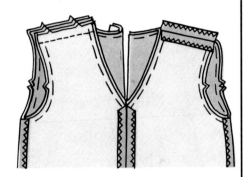

4 To make the buttonholes, use a bias strip
of plain fabric and make a length of fine
rouleau as shown on page 49. Cut the strip
into pieces the correct size for the buttonholes plus turnings. Place on the right side
of the right back with the loops towards
the armhole and raw edges together.
Tack securely on the centre-back line.

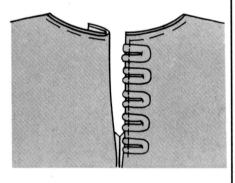

Cut a straight piece of printed fabric 4cm
(1½ *inches*) wide by the length of the
opening plus turnings. With right sides
together tack and stitch the strip to the
centre-back of the right back.
The loops will be sandwiched between.
Trim the turnings and turn the strip to the
inside of the dress. Turn under the raw
edge and slip-stitch to the underdress.
Press.

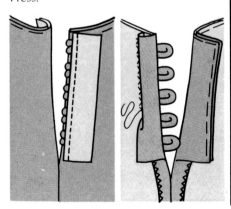

5 Neaten the raw edge of the left side of
the centre-back opening. Turn under
along the fold line, tack and press. Slip-
stitch into place.

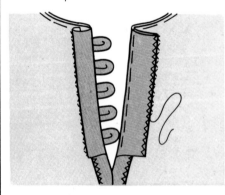

6 Stay-stitch the neckline on the seam
line. Cut away the turnings close to
the stay-stitching. From the printed fabric
cut a bias strip 2.54cm (1 *inch*) wide by the
length of the neckline plus turnings. With
right sides together tack and stitch the

strip to the neckline, taking 0.6cm (¼ *inch*)
turnings. Press towards the strip. Turn
under and press the centre-back turnings
of the bind. Fold the bind over the raw
edges, turn under the raw edge of the bind
and slip hem to the wrong side on the
stitching line. Press.

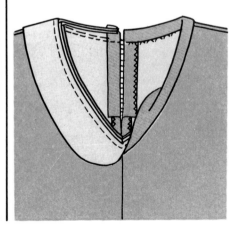

Sleeves

7 Tack and stitch the underarm seam, using a French seam. Press. Cut an opening on the line marked.

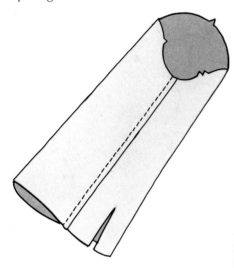

8 On the right side tack three rows of ribbon around the lower edge, starting and finishing at the opening. From the wrong side stitch both edges of the ribbon into place. Press.

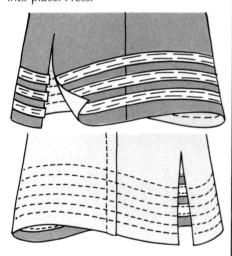

9 Cut a straight piece of plain fabric twice the length of the opening by 2.54cm (*1 inch*) wide. With right sides together tack and stitch the strip to the opening, taking 0.6cm ($\frac{1}{4}$ *inch*) turnings.

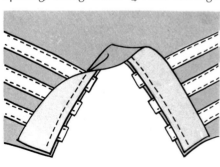

Press the turnings towards the bind. Fold the bind over the opening, turn under the raw edge and slip-hem to the back of the stitching line. Press.

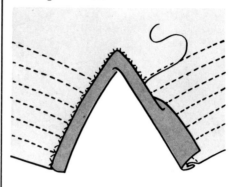

10 Run a gathering thread along the lower edge of the sleeve and draw up to 12.5cm (*5 inches*). Cut a straight piece of plain fabric 5cm (*2 inches*) wide by approximately 114cm (*45 inches*). With right sides facing tack and stitch the short ends and long sides of the strip together, leaving an opening in the elastic for the gathered edge of the sleeve. Turn the strip to the right side, tack and press.

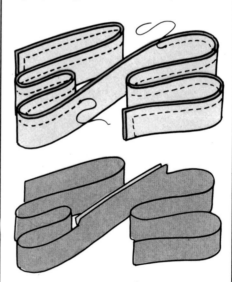

With right sides together tack and stitch the bottom of the sleeve to one side of the strip opening, distributing the fullness

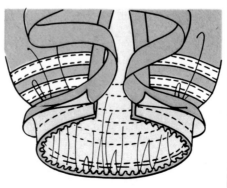

evenly. Trim the turnings and press towards the strip. Turn under the remaining raw edge of the strip and slip-hem to the stitching line. Press.

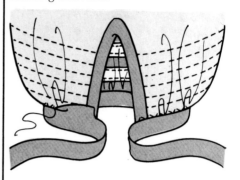

11 With right sides together and matching notches and underarm seams tack and stitch the sleeve into the armhole. Trim the turnings to 1cm ($\frac{3}{8}$ *inch*), neaten together and press towards the bodice. Catch into place so that they do not show through the sleeve on the right side.

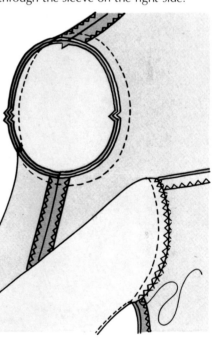

12 Try on the dress and check the length of both hems. Make a narrow rolled hem on the overdress.
Turn up the hem on the underdress, tack close to the fold and press. Neaten the raw edge and slip-stitch the hem into place.

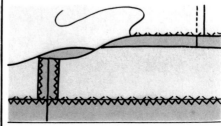

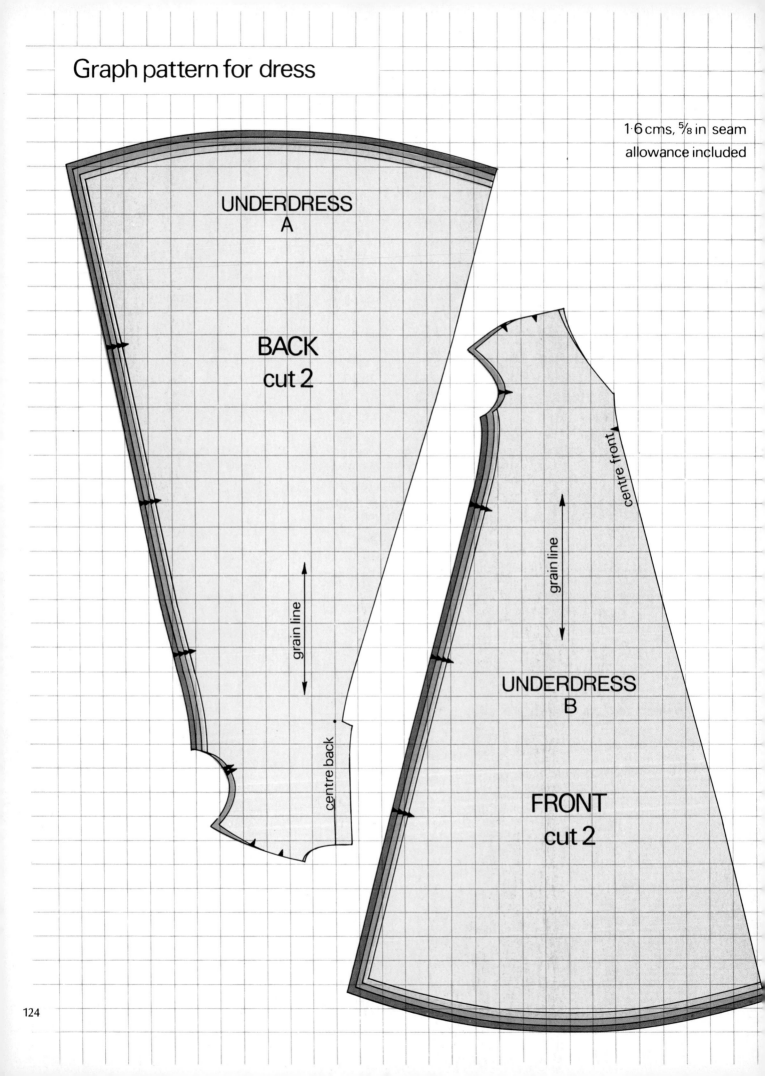

Graph pattern for dress

1·6 cms, ⅝ in seam
allowance included

UNDERDRESS
A

BACK
cut 2

grain line

centre back

UNDERDRESS
B

centre front

grain line

FRONT
cut 2

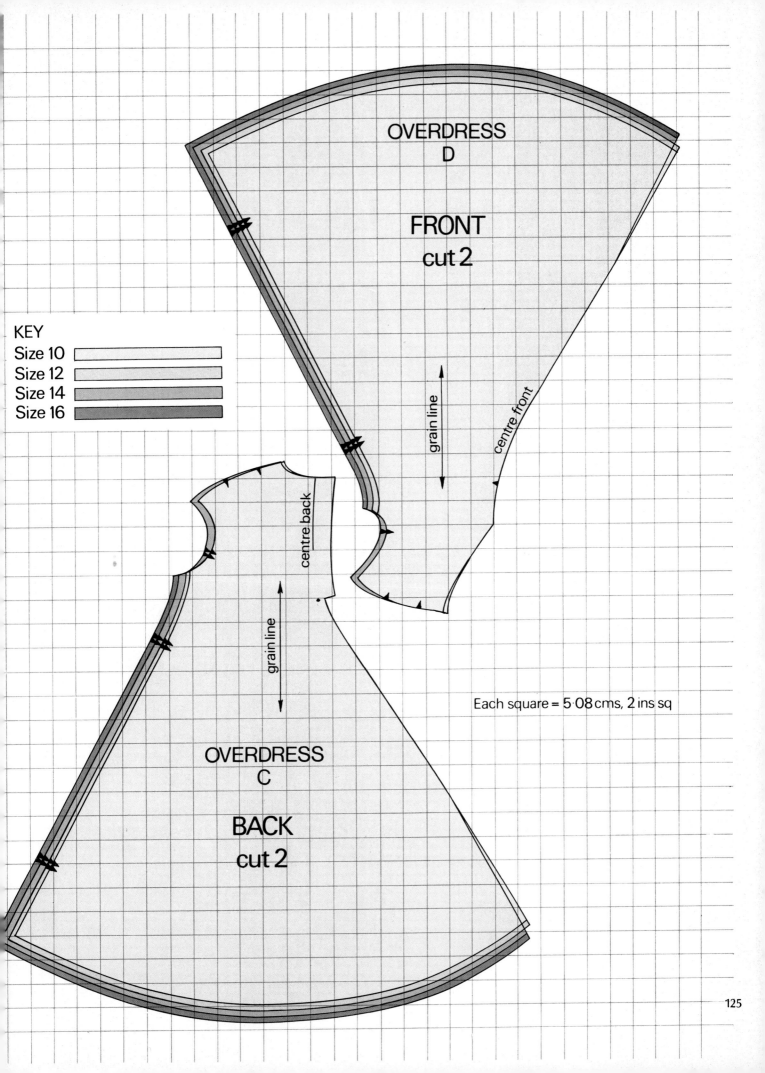

OVERDRESS
D

FRONT
cut 2

KEY
Size 10
Size 12
Size 14
Size 16

grain line

centre front

centre back

grain line

OVERDRESS
C

BACK
cut 2

Each square = 5·08 cms, 2 ins sq

125

Graph pattern for dress

SLEEVE
cut 2

OVERDRESS
E

grain line

KEY
Size 10	
Size 12	
Size 14	
Size 16	

1·6 cms, ⅝ in seam allowance included

Each square = 5·08 cms, 2 ins sq

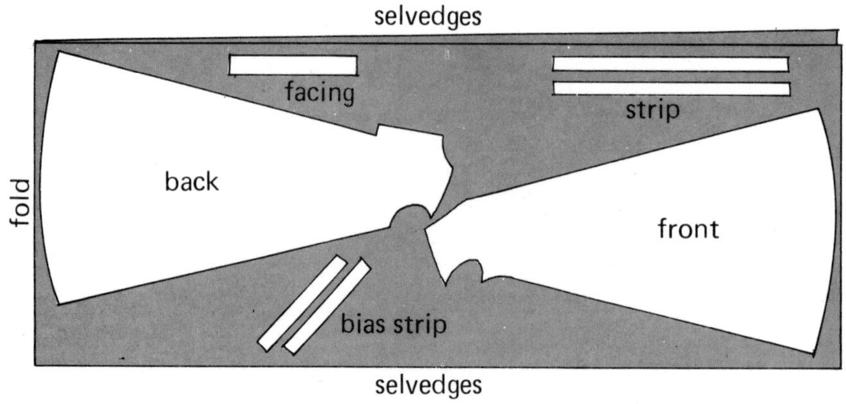

selvedges

facing

strip

back

front

fold

bias strip

selvedges

CUTTING
LAYOUT FOR
114 CMS, 45 INS
WIDE FABRIC

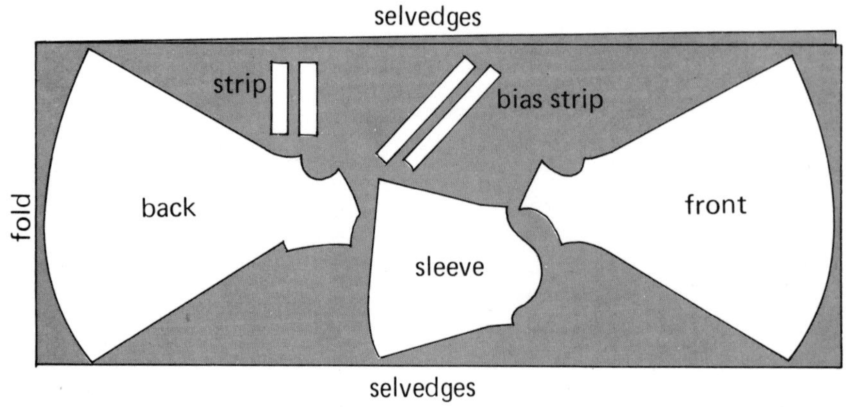

selvedges

strip

bias strip

back

sleeve

front

fold

selvedges

CUTTING
LAYOUT FOR
114 CMS, 45 INS
WIDE FABRIC

Sew four rows of ribbon around the lower edge of the overdress as for the sleeve.

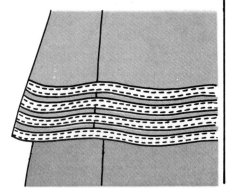

13 Sew buttons to the left side of the centre-back opening to correspond with the buttonholes.

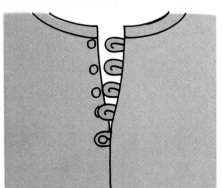

Camisole top

Close fitting with a neat flattering waistline.

Sizes
10, 12, 14 and 16

Fabric required
All sizes take 1.40 metres (*1½ yards*) of 91cm (*36 inch*) fabric

You will also need
☐ Graph paper for making the pattern
☐ Matching thread
☐ 3.65 metres (*4 yards*) of 1.6cm (*⅝ inch*) lace
☐ 15cm (*6 inches*) of 91cm (*36 inch*) light-weight interfacing
☐ 6 hooks

Making the pattern
Using graph paper and following the colour indicating the size required draw each pattern piece to scale. One square = 2.54cm square (*1 inch square*).
An allowance of 1.6cm (*⅝ inch*) has been made on all seams.
Cut out the pattern pieces and mark the centre-front, all notches and the straight grain line.

Cutting out the camisole top
Following the cutting layout place all five pattern pieces as indicated. Take care that the grain line on the pattern lies on the straight grain of the fabric. Pin into place and cut out.
For the shoulder straps cut four bias strips approximately 61cm (*24 inches*) long by 2.5cm (*1 inch*) wide.
From the interfacing cut one front facing and one back facing.
Transfer all markings from the pattern pieces to the fabric.

Making up
1 With right sides together tack and stitch the two front bodice darts. Press towards the centre-front and neaten. On the right side of the front bodice tack and stitch two rows of lace each side of the centre-front approximately 0.6cm (*¼ inch*) apart with the straight edges of the centre rows almost meeting.

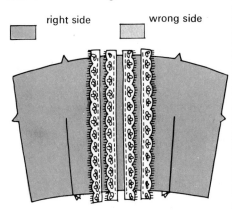

right side   wrong side

2 With right sides together tack and stitch the two back bodice darts. Press towards the centre-back.
With right sides together and matching notches tack and stitch the front bodice to the back bodice at the right side seam.

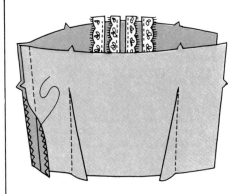

Shoulder straps
3 With right sides facing fold strap in half lengthways. Tack and stitch the long edges together, taking 0.3cm (*⅛ inch*) turnings. Pull through to the right side and press. Fold in the raw edges on one end of the strap and hand stitch together. Make three more straps in the same way.

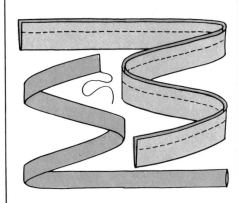

4 On the right side of the bodice tack one strap in line with each dart, placing the raw edges of the strap and top of bodice together.

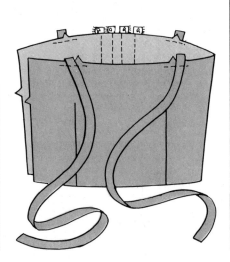

5 Tack interfacing to the wrong sides of the front and back facings. With right sides together tack and stitch the front facing to the back facing at the right side seam. Trim the turnings to 1cm (*⅜ inch*) and press seam open. With right sides together and matching notches and side seams tack and stitch the facing to the bodice along the top edge with the shoulder straps sandwiched between. Trim the turnings, turn the facing to the inside, tack and press. Neaten the raw edge of the facing.

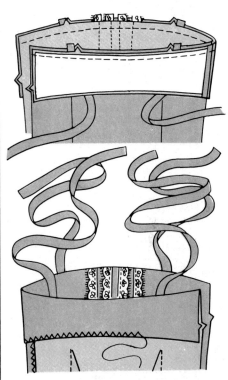

6 Turn under and press the turning allowance on the left side of the back and front. Neaten the raw edges and slip-stitch into place. Turn under and slip-stitch the sides of the facing to the inside of the left side turnings. Catch-stitch the facing to the turning allowance of the right side seam.

Peplum

7 With right sides together tack and stitch the two peplum pieces together at the right side seam. Press open and neaten. From the wrong side tack and stitch a narrow hem on the left side of the back and front peplum. Press.

8 With right sides together tack and stitch the peplum to the bodice at the waist, easing the peplum on the back. Trim the turnings to 1cm ($\frac{3}{8}$ inch), press towards the bodice and neaten together.

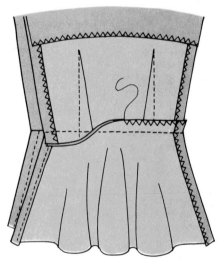

9 Turn under and tack a narrow hem on the peplum. Press. From the right side tack lace to the lower edge with the straight edge of the lace in line with the top fold of the hem. Machine stitch into place through all thicknesses.

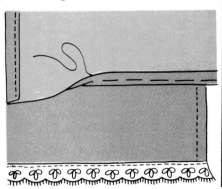

10 Sew six evenly spaced hooks to the left side of the bodice front and work loops on the back to correspond.
Try on the top and tie the front and back straps together on the shoulders.

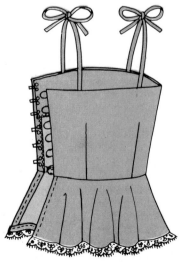

Graph pattern for top

1·6 cms, ⅝ in seam allowance included

Each square = 2·54 cms, 1 in sq

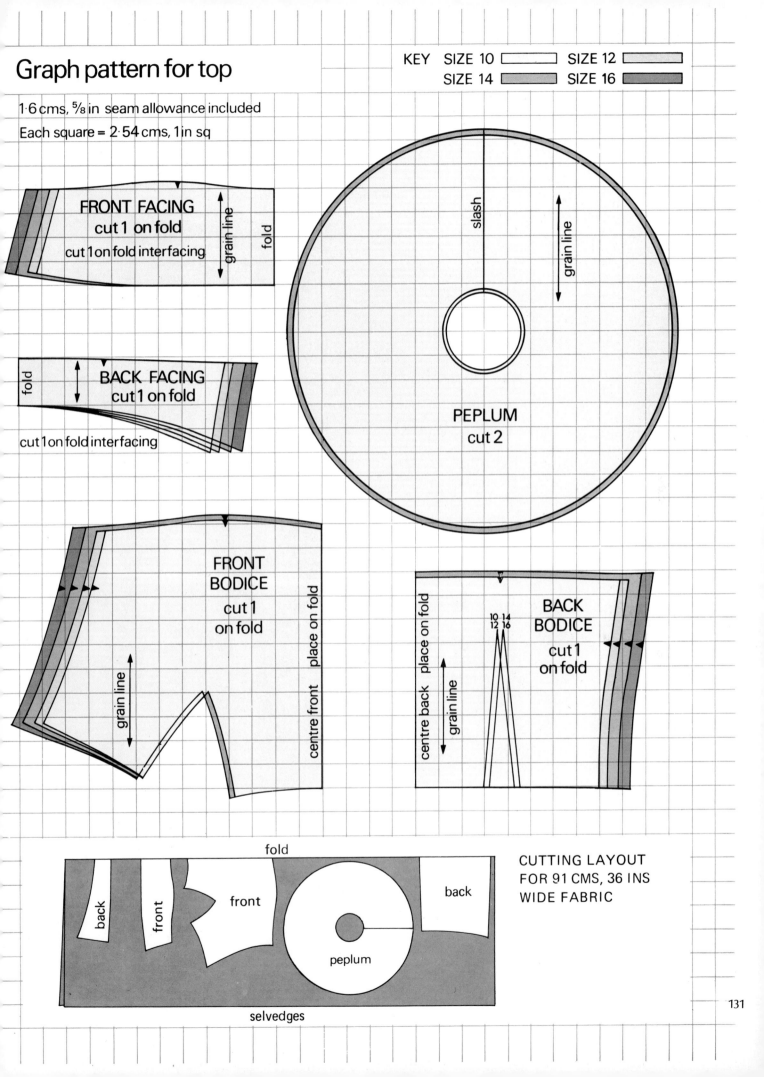

FRONT FACING
cut 1 on fold
cut 1 on fold interfacing

grain line   fold

BACK FACING
cut 1 on fold

fold

cut 1 on fold interfacing

slash

grain line

PEPLUM
cut 2

FRONT BODICE
cut 1
on fold

grain line

centre front   place on fold

BACK BODICE
cut 1
on fold

centre back   place on fold   grain line

10 14
12 16

CUTTING LAYOUT FOR 91 CMS, 36 INS WIDE FABRIC

fold

back   front   front   back

peplum

selvedges

Circular skirt

With a full swing and lace-edged to match the camisole top.

Sizes

10, 12, 14 and 16

Fabric required

All sizes take 3.65 metres (*4 yards*) of 91cm (*36 inch*) fabric

You will also need

☐ Graph paper for making the pattern
☐ Matching thread
☐ 1 × 18cm (*7 inch*) zip fastener
☐ A piece of interfacing 5cm (*2 inches*) wide and 91cm (*36 inches*) long
☐ 1 hook
☐ 2 metres (*2¼ yards*) lace

Making the pattern

Using graph paper and following the colour indicating the size required draw each pattern piece to scale. One square = 5.08cm square (*2 inch square*).

An allowance of 1.6cm ($\frac{5}{8}$ *inch*) has been made on all seams and on the hem. Cut out the pattern pieces and mark all notches and the straight grain line.

Cutting out the skirt

Following the cutting layout place the skirt pattern piece as indicated. Take care that the grain line on the pattern lies on the straight grain of the fabric. Pin into place and cut out. Cut out another skirt as indicated. Cut out one waistband from single fabric. From the interfacing cut out one waistband to the fold line only.

Transfer all markings from the pattern pieces to the fabric.

Making up

1 With right sides together and matching notches tack and stitch the side seams leaving the left side open above the single notch. Press open and neaten.

▨ right side		☐ wrong side	

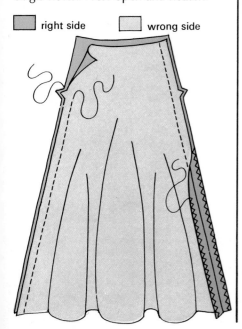

2 Tack and stitch the zip into the opening on the left side.

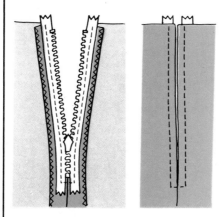

Waistband

3 Place interfacing to the wrong side of the waistband with one edge to the fold line. Tack into place. With right sides together fold the waistband in half lengthways and tack and stitch the ends and the underwrap as far as the notch. Trim the turnings to 0.6cm ($\frac{1}{4}$ *inch*), turn to the right side and press.

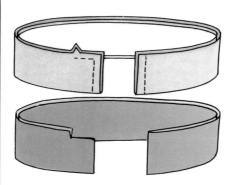

4 With right sides together and making sure that the wrap is on the back of the skirt and the other end is level with the opening, place one edge of the waistband to the top of the skirt. Tack and stitch. Trim the turnings to 0.6cm ($\frac{1}{4}$ *inch*) and press towards the waistband. Turn under the seam allowance on the other edge of the waistband and slip-stitch to the skirt along the seam line. Press.

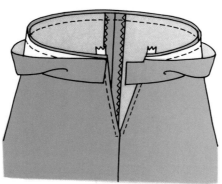

Sew a hook to the wrong side of the front waistband and work a bar on the right side of the back band to correspond.

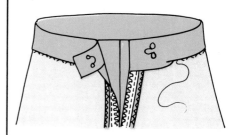

Hem

5 Let the skirt hang for at least twenty-four hours. Try on the skirt and check the length. Adjust and level if necessary. Turn under and tack a narrow hem. Press. From the right side tack lace to the lower edge with the straight edge of the lace in line with the top fold of the hem. Machine stitch into place through all thicknesses.

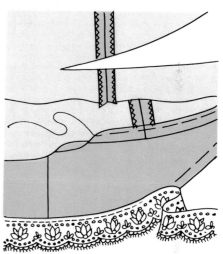

Graph pattern for skirt

Each square = 5·08 cms, 2 ins sq

KEY
SIZE 10
SIZE 12
SIZE 14
SIZE 16

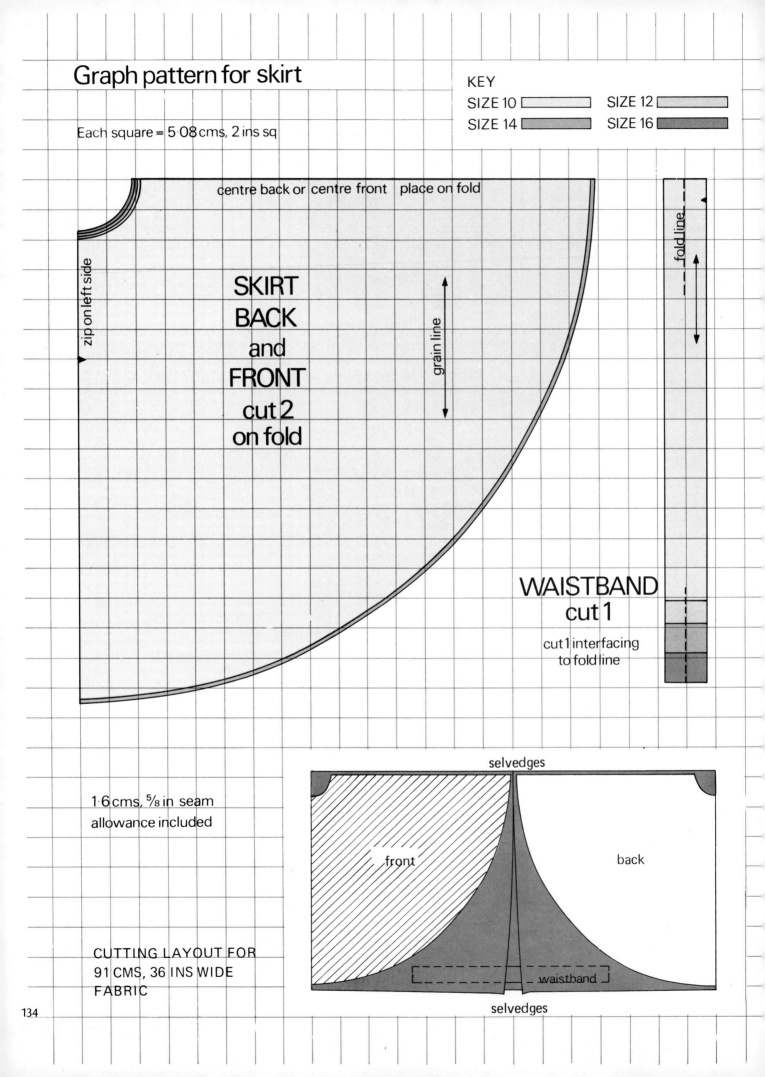

centre back or centre front   place on fold

fold line

zip on left side

**SKIRT
BACK
and
FRONT
cut 2
on fold**

grain line

**WAISTBAND
cut 1**

cut 1 interfacing
to fold line

1·6 cms, ⅝ in seam
allowance included

selvedges

front

back

waistband

CUTTING LAYOUT FOR
91 CMS, 36 INS WIDE
FABRIC

selvedges

134

Overdress

Tabard style, slim, but easy enough to wear over the sweater dress.

Sizes

10, 12, 14 and 16

Fabric required

All sizes take 2.30 metres (2½ yards) of 137cm (54 inch) fabric

You will also need

- ☐ Graph paper for making the pattern
- ☐ Matching thread
- ☐ Matching buttonhole twist
- ☐ 0.45 metre (½ yard) of 91cm (36 inch) iron-on interfacing
- ☐ 8 × 2.2cm (⅞ inch) buttons
- ☐ 1 press stud

Making the pattern

Using graph paper and following the colour indicating the size required draw each pattern piece to scale. One square = 5.08cm square (2 inch square).

An allowance of 1.6cm (⅝ inch) has been made on all seams and a 5cm (2 inch) hem has been allowed.

Cut out the pattern pieces and mark the position of the buttonholes, all notches and the straight grain line.

Cutting out the tabard

Following the cutting layout place the pattern pieces for the back bodice, back skirt and back bodice facing to the fold of the fabric as indicated. Take care that the grain line on the pattern lies on the straight grain of the fabric. Pin into place and cut out. Open the fabric and place the remaining eight pattern pieces as indicated, again taking care that the grain is correct. Pin into place and cut out.

From the interfacing cut out the five pieces as indicated on the layout.

Transfer all markings from the pattern pieces to the fabric.

Making up

1 Tack and stitch the two darts on the front bodice. Press towards the centre-front. Tack and stitch the two darts on the back bodice. Press towards the centre-back.

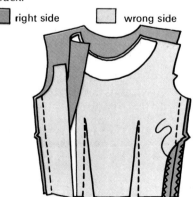

▬ right side   ▫ wrong side

With right sides together and matching notches tack and stitch the front bodices to the back bodice at the side seams. Press open and neaten.

2 Iron interfacing to the wrong side of the back and front bodice necklines.

3 Iron interfacing to the wrong side of the two waistband pieces. With right sides together tack and stitch the front waistband to the back waistband at the right side seam. Press open and neaten.

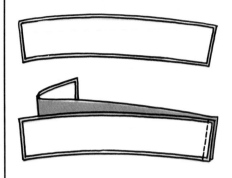

With right sides together and matching notches and side seams tack and stitch the waistband to the bodice. Press turnings towards the waistband and neaten together.

4 With right sides together tack and stitch the underarm seams of the bodice facings. Trim turnings and press open. With right sides together and matching notches tack and stitch the bodice facings to the bodice at the side opening,

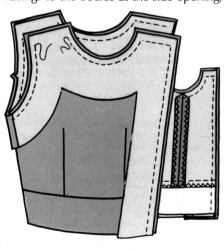

around the armholes and neckline and across the left shoulder. Leave the right shoulder open, finishing the stitching at the seam lines. Trim and clip the turnings, turn the facings to the wrong side, tack the edges and press.

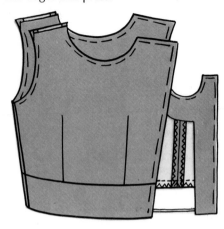

5 With right sides together tack and stitch the back to the front at the right shoulder seam on the line indicated. Trim turnings and press open. Trim the shoulder seam turnings of the facing to 1cm (⅜ inch), turn under and slip-stitch the folded edges together. Press. Neaten the raw edges of the facings.

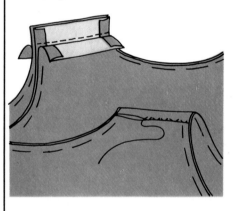

6 From the right side work four equally spaced rows of top stitching around the neckline and armholes.

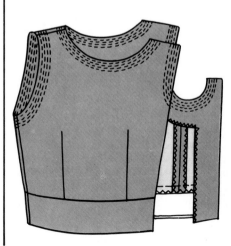

7 Tack and stitch the two darts on the back skirt. Press towards the centre-back. With right sides together and matching notches tack and stitch the front skirts to the back skirt at the side seams. Press open and neaten.
Iron interfacing to the wrong side of the right front skirt, under the buttonhole positions, placing one edge to the fold line.

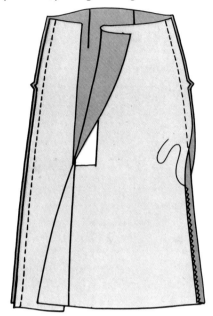

8 With right sides together and matching side seams tack and stitch the skirt to the bodice. Press the turnings towards the waistband and neaten together.
Turn the skirt facings to the inside along the fold lines. Tack close to the folds and press. Neaten the raw edges of the skirt facings.

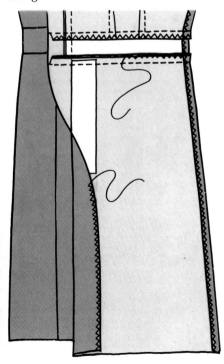

9 From the right side and with facings and turnings free work four equally spaced rows of top stitching on the waist-band.

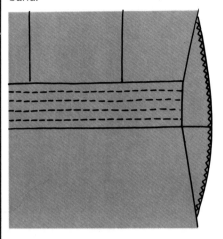

10 Work six buttonholes on the front opening and two on the left front shoulder. Sew on buttons to correspond.

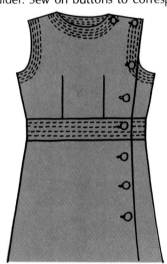

11 Try on the tabard and check the length. Adjust if necessary. Turn up the hem with the facings opened flat and tack close to the fold. Press. Neaten the raw edge and slip-stitch the hem into place. Fold the facings back into position. From the right side work four equally spaced rows of top stitching around the lower edge of the skirt.

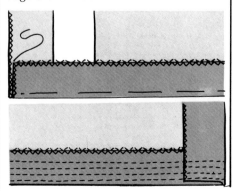

12 At the left armhole sew a press stud to the top of the opening to hold the underwrap in place.

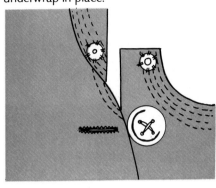

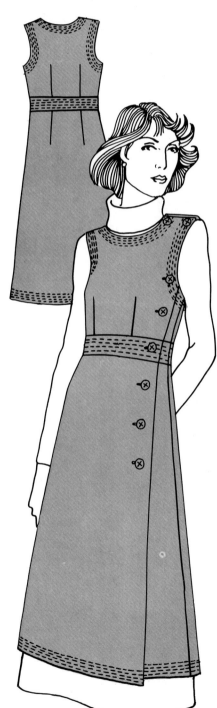

137

Graph pattern for overdress

Each square = 5·08 cms, 2 ins sq

1·6 cms, ⅝ in seam allowance included

5·08 cms, 2 ins hem included

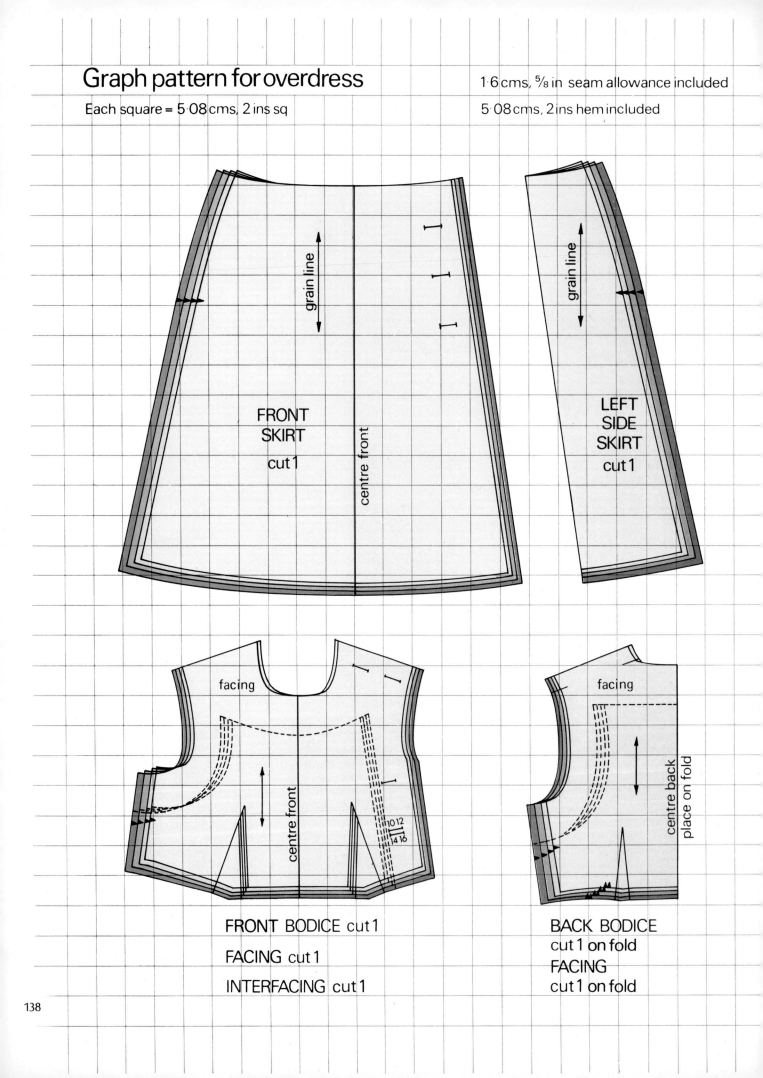

grain line

FRONT
SKIRT
cut 1

centre front

LEFT
SIDE
SKIRT
cut 1

grain line

facing

centre front

facing

centre back
place on fold

10 12
14 16

FRONT BODICE cut 1

FACING cut 1

INTERFACING cut 1

BACK BODICE
cut 1 on fold
FACING
cut 1 on fold

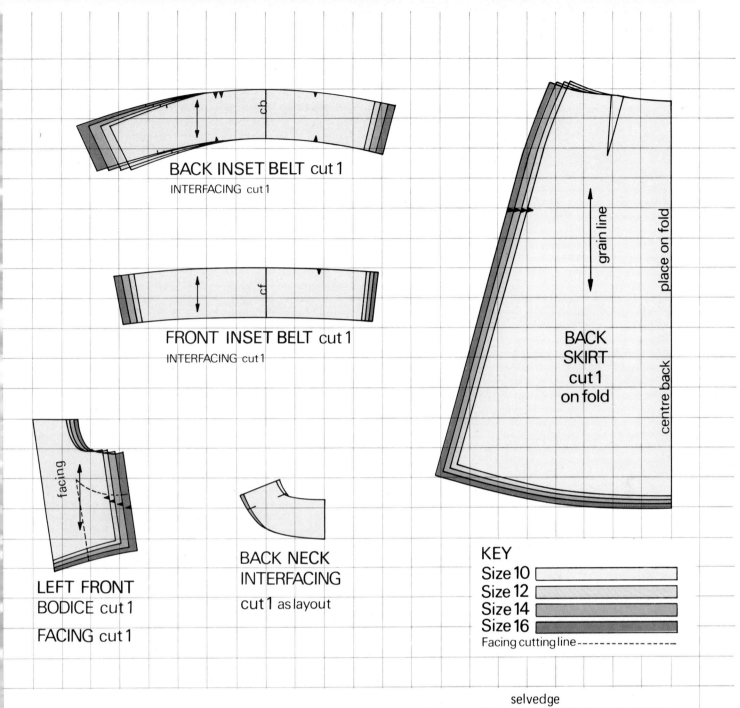

BACK INSET BELT cut 1

INTERFACING cut 1

FRONT INSET BELT cut 1

INTERFACING cut 1

cb

cf

grain line

place on fold

centre back

BACK SKIRT cut 1 on fold

facing

LEFT FRONT BODICE cut 1

FACING cut 1

BACK NECK INTERFACING

cut 1 as layout

KEY
Size 10
Size 12
Size 14
Size 16
Facing cutting line - - - - - - - - - - - - - - -

CUTTING LAYOUT FOR 137 CMS, 54 INS WIDE FABRIC

CUTTING LAYOUT FOR 91 CMS, 36 INS WIDE INTERFACING

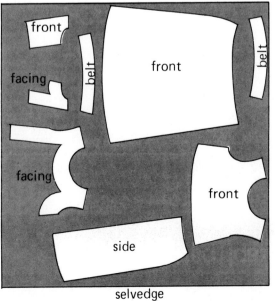

selvedge

front

belt

front

facing

belt

facing

front

side

selvedge

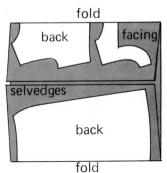

fold

back

facing

selvedges

back

fold

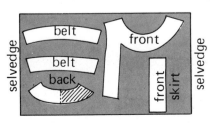

selvedge

belt

front

belt

back

selvedge

front skirt

139

Sweater dress

A sleek shape in fine soft jersey.

Sizes

10, 12, 14 and 16

Fabric required

For sizes 10 and 12: 2.30 metres (2½ yards) of 137cm (54 inch) fabric
For sizes 14 and 16: 2.55 metres (2¾ yards) of 137cm (54 inch) fabric

Note

An extra 60cm (24 inches) will be required for a scarf

You will also need

☐ Graph paper for making the pattern
☐ Matching thread
☐ Matching buttonhole twist
☐ 11.5cm (⅛ yard) of 91cm (36 inch) iron-on interfacing for the belt
☐ 1 × 56cm (22 inch) zip
☐ 2 × 2cm (¾ inch) buttons
☐ 4 hooks
☐ 60cm (24 inches) fringing

Making the pattern

Using graph paper and following the colour indicating the size required draw each pattern piece to scale. One square= 5.08cm square (2 inches square).
An allowance of 1.6cm (⅝ inch) has been made on all seams and a 5cm (2 inch) hem has been allowed.
Cut out the pattern pieces and mark all notches, dots and the straight grain line.

Cutting out the dress

Following the cutting layout place the pattern pieces for the back and front bodice, back and front skirt and sleeve as indicated on double fabric. Take care that the grain line on the pattern lies on the straight grain of the fabric. Pin into place and cut out. Open the remaining fabric and cut out one collar and one belt as indicated.
Transfer all markings from the pattern pieces to the fabric. Using the belt pattern piece cut 1 in interfacing.

Making up

1 With right sides together and matching dots tack and stitch the four tucks on

▓ right side	▒ wrong side

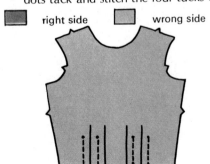

the front bodice. Press towards the centre-front.
With right sides together and matching dots tack and stitch the two tucks on each back bodice. Press towards the centre-back.

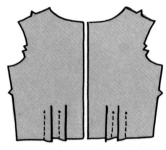

2 With right sides together and matching notches tack and stitch the bodice backs to the bodice front at the side seams. Press open and neaten. With right sides together and matching notches tack and stitch the shoulder seams. Press open and neaten.
Stay-stitch the neckline 1.3cm (½ inch) from the neck edge.

3 Tack and stitch the darts in the back skirt. Press towards the centre-back. With right sides together tack and stitch

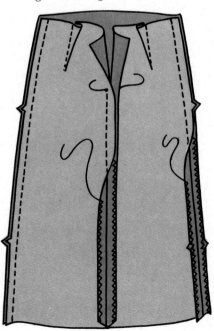

the centre-back seam of the skirt below the dot. Press open and neaten. With right sides together and matching notches tack and stitch the front skirt to the back skirt at the side seams. Press open and neaten.

4 With right sides together and matching side seams and centre-front tack and stitch the skirt to the bodice easing the skirt on to the bodice. Trim turnings to 1cm (⅜ inch), press towards the skirt and neaten together.

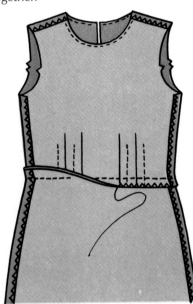

5 Insert zip in the centre-back opening.

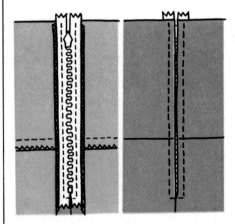

Collar

6 Fold the collar on the fold line with right sides together. Tack and stitch the

Graph pattern for dress

Each square = 5·08 cms, 2 ins sq

1·6 cms, ⅝ in seam allowance included

5·08 cms, 2 ins hem included

grain line

place on fold

FRONT
SKIRT
cut 1
on fold

centre front

grain line

centre back

BACK
SKIRT
cut 2

fold line

fold line

BELT cut 1

INTERFACING cut 1

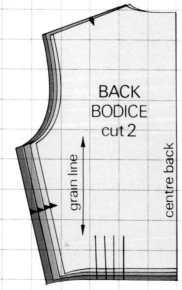

BACK
BODICE
cut 2

grain line

centre back

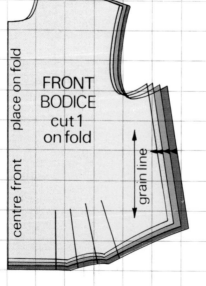

place on fold

centre front

FRONT
BODICE
cut 1
on fold

grain line

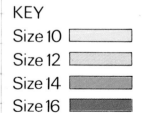

KEY

Size 10

Size 12

Size 14

Size 16

142

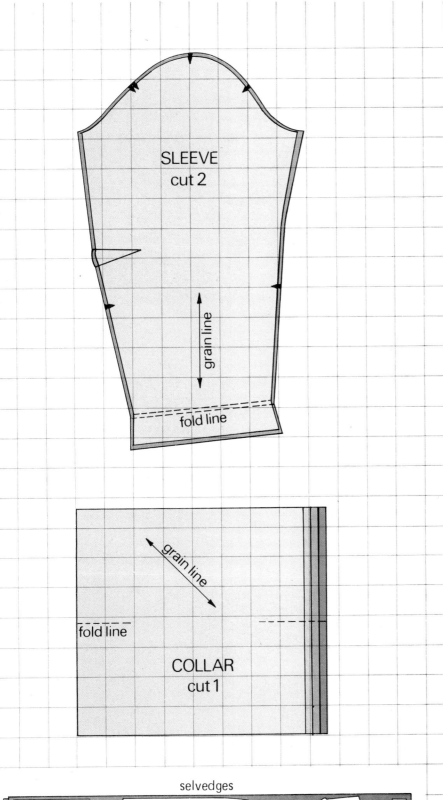

SLEEVE
cut 2

grain line

fold line

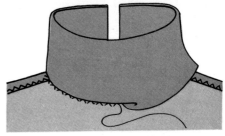

grain line

fold line

COLLAR
cut 1

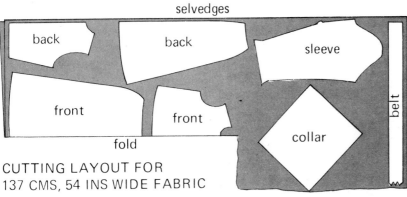

selvedges

back

back

sleeve

front

front

collar

belt

fold

CUTTING LAYOUT FOR
137 CMS, 54 INS WIDE FABRIC

two ends, trim turnings, turn to the right side and press. With right sides together tack and stitch one edge of the collar to the neckline of the dress, easing slightly. Trim and clip turnings and press towards the collar. Turn under the remaining raw edge of the collar and slip-stitch on to the seam line. Press.

Stretch the outer edge of the collar carefully so that it covers the neckline seam when folded over.

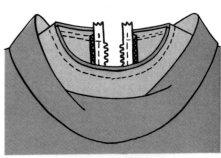

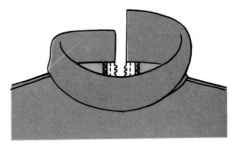

Sleeves

7 Tack and stitch the elbow dart and press towards the wrist. With right sides together and matching notches tack and stitch the underarm seam. Press open and neaten.

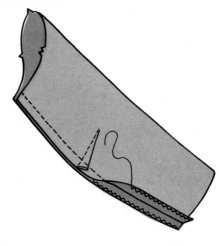

8 Run a gathering thread between notches over the sleeve head. With right sides together and matching notches and underarm seams pin sleeve into the armhole. Pull up the gathering thread evenly to ease the head of the sleeve. Tack and stitch. Trim turnings to 1cm ($\frac{3}{8}$ *inch*), press towards the sleeve and neaten together.

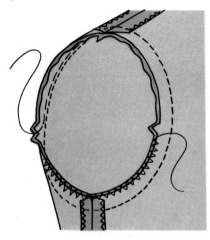

9 Turn under the hem of the sleeve and tack close to the fold. Press. Neaten the raw edge and slip-stitch the hem into place. From the right side work three rows of top stitching 1cm ($\frac{3}{8}$ *inch*) apart, the first row 1cm ($\frac{3}{8}$ *inch*) from the fold.

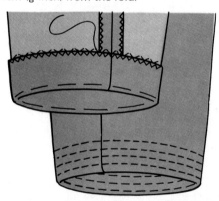

10 Try on the dress and check the length. Adjust if necessary. Turn up the hem and tack close to the fold. Neaten the raw edge and slip-stitch the hem into place. Press. Work three rows of top-stitching 1cm ($\frac{3}{8}$ *inch*) apart, the first row 1cm ($\frac{3}{8}$ *inch*) from the fold.

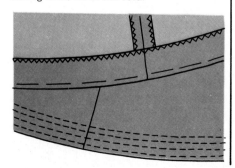

At the centre-back sew hooks to one side of the collar and work loops on the other side to correspond.

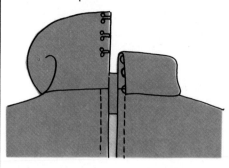

Belt

11 Iron interfacing to the wrong side of the belt. With right sides facing tack and stitch the long edges together. Trim turnings and press the seam open. With right sides together and the seam at the centre of the belt tack and stitch the pointed end. Trim turnings, turn the belt to the right side and press. Turn in the raw edges of the straight end and slip-stitch the folds together. Press. From the right side work a row of top stitching in the centre of the belt and another row 1cm ($\frac{3}{8}$ *inch*) from this each side.

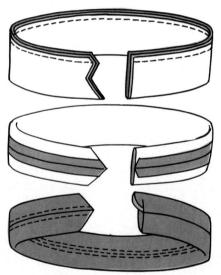

12 Work two buttonholes at the pointed end of the belt and sew two buttons on the other end to correspond.
At the waist work belt carriers at the side seams.

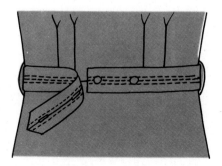

Scarf

13 With right sides together tack and stitch the long edges together, turn through and press to one side. Neaten the ends together and stitch on fringing.

Hooded coat

Unlined, for a lightweight look and an easy shape to sew.

Sizes
10, 12, 14 and 16

Fabric required
All sizes take 4.85 metres ($5\frac{1}{4}$ *yards*) of 137cm (*54 inch*) fabric

You will also need
☐ Graph paper for making the pattern
☐ Matching thread
☐ Matching buttonhole twist
☐ 45cm ($\frac{1}{2}$ *yard*) of 91cm (*36 inch*) iron-on interfacing
☐ A piece of lining 40.5cm (*16 inches*) square for the front pocket bags
☐ 5 × 2cm ($\frac{3}{4}$ *inch*) buttons
☐ 1 press stud

Making the pattern
Using graph paper and following the colour indicating the size required draw each pattern piece to scale. One square= 5.08cm square (*2 inch square*).
An allowance of 1.6cm ($\frac{5}{8}$ *inch*) has been made on all seams and a 6.5cm ($2\frac{1}{2}$ *inch*) hem has been allowed.
Cut out the pattern pieces and mark all dots and notches and straight grain line.

Cutting out the coat
Following the cutting layout with the fabric folded place the pattern pieces for the front, back, front facing, back neck facing, pocket and hood back as indicated. Take care that the grain line on the pattern lies on the straight grain of the fabric. Pin into place and cut out. Cut out another hood back. Place the pattern pieces for the fly and sleeve on to single fabric as indicated. Pin into place and cut out. Cut out another sleeve with the pattern reversed. From the lining fabric cut out another two pocket bags.
For the interfacing cut one fly to the fold line only, two pieces 56cm × 4cm (*22 inches × $1\frac{1}{2}$ inches*) for the front pocket opening, two pieces for the front coat and two for the cuff to the lines marked on the pattern pieces.
Transfer all markings from the pattern pieces to the fabric.

Making up
1 At the back cut away the excess fabric on the left side of the vent on the line marked.
With right sides together tack and stitch the centre-back to the large dot. Clip across the seam allowance to the small dot on the right back. Press the centre-back seam open and neaten.
Turn the left side of the vent to the wrong side on the fold line, tack close to the fold and press. Neaten the raw edge. Turn the

right side of the vent to the wrong side on the fold line. Tack close to the fold line and press. Neaten the raw edge

■ right side   ■ wrong side

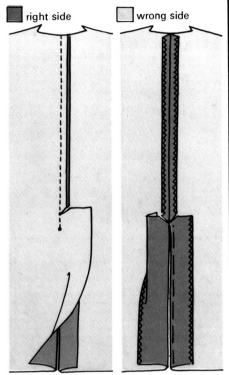

2 On the wrong side tack and stitch the top edges of the vent together across to the large dot. Tack into position on the coat. From the right side top-stitch the vent into place taking the stitching diagonally to the centre-back.

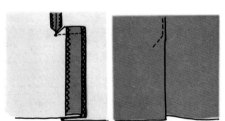

3 Stay-stitch the corners of the back and front armhole on the seam line 2.5cm (*1 inch*) each side of the dots. Clip to the dots.

4 With right sides together and matching notches tack and stitch the pocket bags to the back pocket extensions. Press open and neaten.

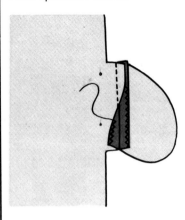

5 Iron interfacing to the wrong side of the front at the centre-front and in line with the pocket opening in the positions marked. With right sides together and matching notches tack and stitch the pocket lining to the front pocket extension. Press towards the pocket bag.

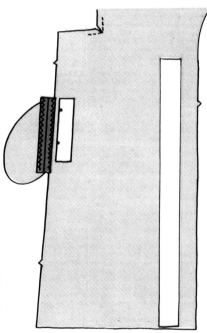

6 Iron interfacing to the wrong side of the sleeve at the lower edge to the fold line as indicated.

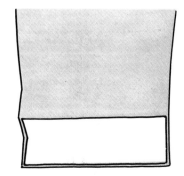

With right sides together tack and stitch the shoulder seam. Press open.
With right sides together and matching notches tack and stitch the sleeve into the armhole, swivelling at the corners. Press turnings towards the coat and neaten together. From the right side work a row of top stitching on the coat 1cm ($\frac{3}{8}$ *inch*) from the seam line.

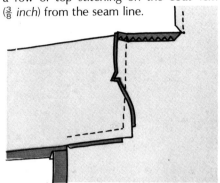

7 With right sides together and matching notches and underarm seams tack and stitch the front to the back at the side and underarm seams, leaving an opening for the pocket between the dots.
Press open and neaten. Tack close to the fold line of the pocket opening on the front and press.
Tack the pocket bags together around the outer edges and neaten. Tack the pocket into position on the wrong side of the front.

8 From the right side work two rows of top stitching 1cm ($\frac{3}{8}$ *inch*) apart to hold the pocket in place.

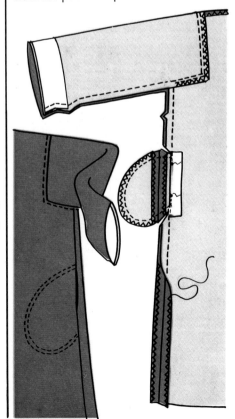

12 With right sides together tack and stitch the back neck facing to the front facing at the neckline and shoulders, swivelling at the corners. Trim and clip the seams open and press open.

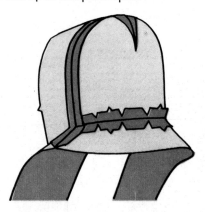

With right sides together and matching notches tack and stitch the facing to the coat. Trim turnings, clip where necessary, turn to the right side, tack close to the edge and press. Neaten the raw edges of the facing.

9 Turn the hem of the sleeve to the wrong side and tack close to the fold line. Press. Neaten the raw edge and slip-stitch the sleeve hem into place. Fold the cuff into position and press. Work a row of top stitching 1cm ($\frac{3}{8}$ *inch*) from the cuff fold.

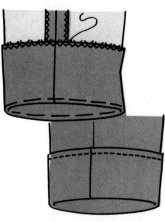

10 With right sides together and matching notches tack and stitch one hood back to the front. Press the seams open. Tack and stitch the centre-back seam of the hood. Press open.

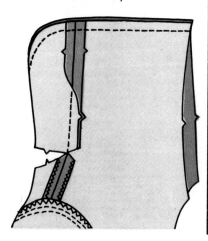

With right sides together and matching notches tack and stitch the neck edge of the hood to the back neckline. Trim and clip the seam and press open.

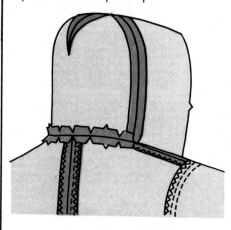

11 Stay-stitch the shoulder corners of the front facing 2.5cm (*1 inch*) each side of the dots. Clip to the dots. With right sides together and matching notches tack and stitch the other hood back to the front facing. Press seams open. With right sides together tack and stitch the centre seam of the hood. Press seam open.

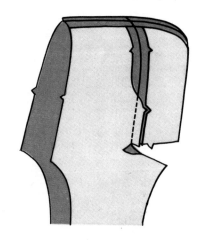

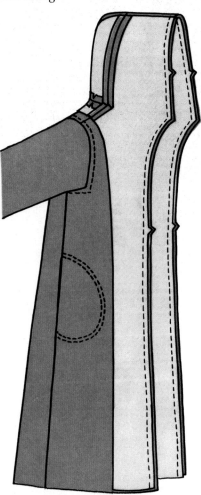

Lift the back neck facing and lightly stitch the turnings to the neckline turnings of the coat.
From the right side work a row of top

Sew buttons to the left front to correspond with the buttonholes. Sew a press stud to the front opening 2cm ($\frac{3}{4}$ *inch*) above the top button.

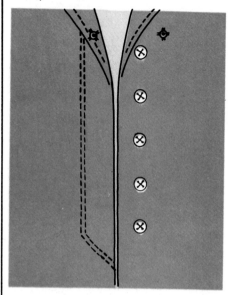

15 Try on the coat and check the length. Turn up the hem and tack close to the fold. Neaten the raw edge and slip-stitch the hem into place. Fold the facings and vent into place and loosely slip-stitch to the coat.

stitching on the hood 1cm ($\frac{3}{8}$ *inch*) from the outer edge, starting at the curve of the collar.

13 Iron interfacing to the wrong side of the fly, placing one edge to the fold line. Fold the fly on the fold line with wrong sides together and press. Tack the

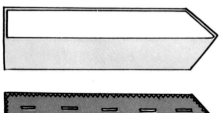

raw edges together and neaten. Work five buttonholes on the fly. Tack the fly to the right side of the right front facing in the position marked. Stitch to the facing horizontally between each buttonhole.

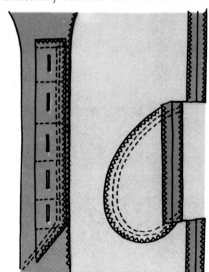

14 From the right side work two rows of top stitching 1cm ($\frac{3}{8}$ *inch*) apart, through the coat and facing to hold the fly in place. Stitch diagonally across to the outer edge as indicated.

Graph pattern for coat

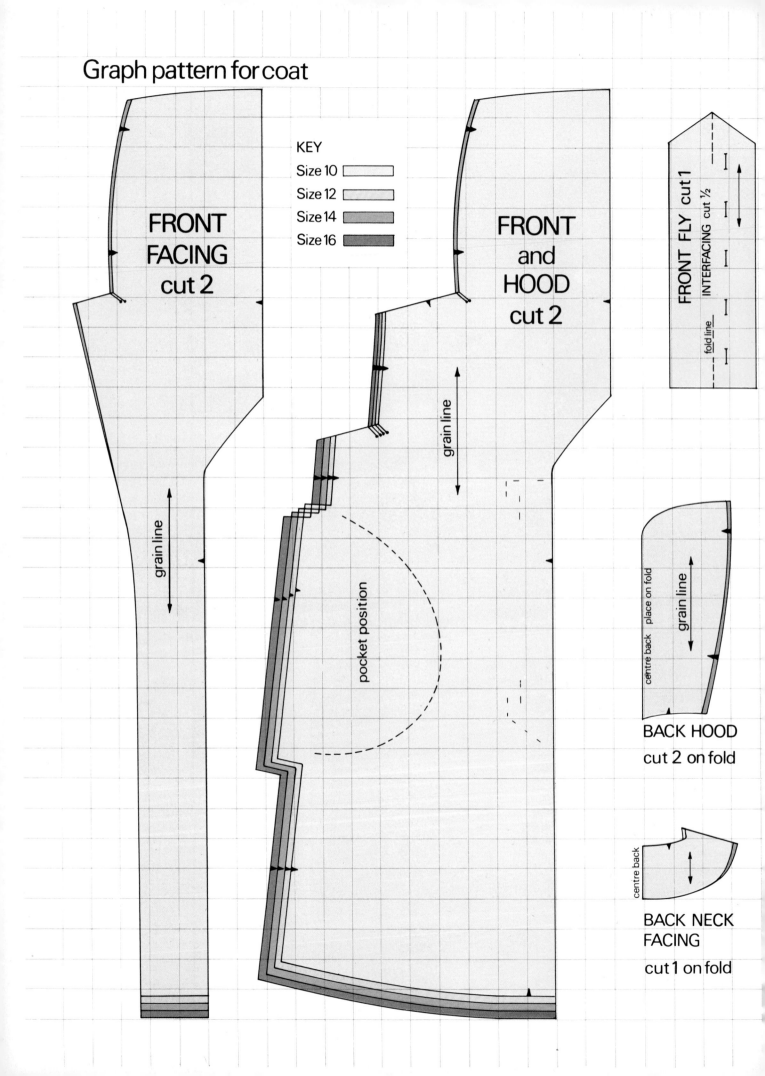

KEY

Size 10	
Size 12	
Size 14	
Size 16	

FRONT
FACING
cut 2

grain line

FRONT
and
HOOD
cut 2

grain line

pocket position

FRONT FLY cut 1
INTERFACING cut ½

fold line

BACK HOOD
cut 2 on fold

centre back   place on fold

grain line

BACK NECK
FACING
cut 1 on fold

centre back

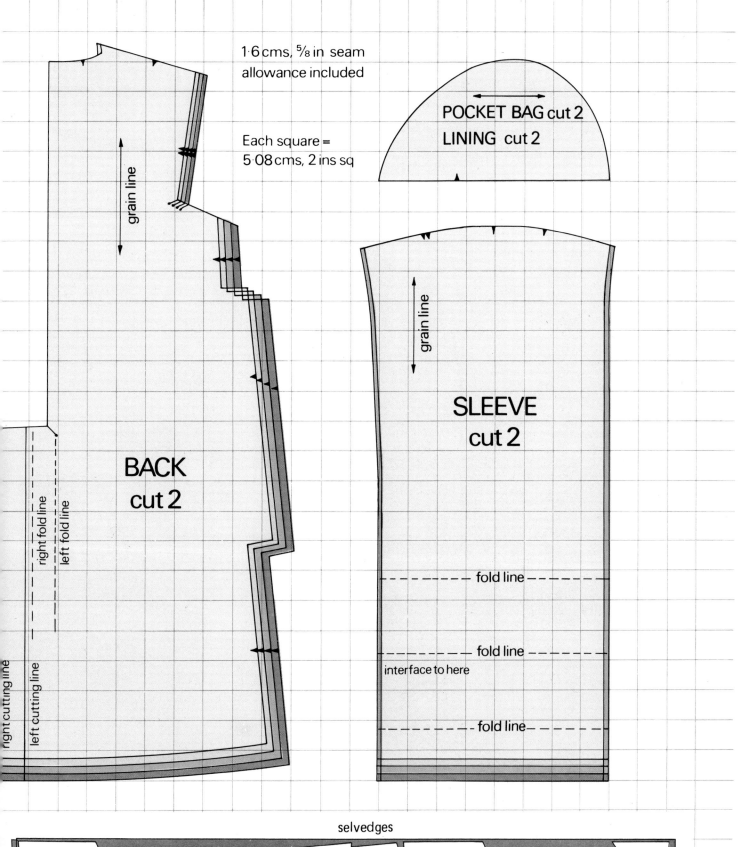

1·6 cms, ⅝ in seam
allowance included

Each square =
5·08 cms, 2 ins sq

POCKET BAG cut 2
LINING cut 2

grain line

BACK
cut 2

right fold line
left fold line

right cutting line
left cutting line

SLEEVE
cut 2

grain line

fold line

fold line

interface to here

fold line

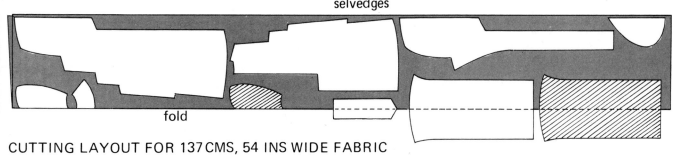

selvedges

fold

CUTTING LAYOUT FOR 137 CMS, 54 INS WIDE FABRIC

Sporting jacket

Crisp, white, a winner for out and about wear.

Sizes
10, 12, 14 and 16

Fabric required
All sizes take 2.10 metres (2¼ yards) of 152cm (60 inch) wide fabric

Note If the jacket is made up in a white fabric it is advisable to mount each piece on lining fabric. You will need 2.10 metres (2¼ yards) of 152cm (60 inch) wide lining.

You will also need
- ☐ Graph paper for making the pattern
- ☐ Matching thread
- ☐ 0.90 metre (1 yard) of interfacing
- ☐ 6 × 2.5cm (1 inch) buttons

Making the pattern
Using graph paper and following the colour indicating the size required draw each pattern piece to scale. One square = 2.54cm square (1 inch square). An allowance of 1.6cm (⅝ inch) has been made on all seams and 4cm (1½ inches) for the hem. Cut out the pattern pieces and mark all dots, notches and the straight grain line.

Cutting out the jacket
Following the cutting layout fold the fabric and place the pattern pieces as indicated. Make sure that the straight grain line on the pattern lies on the straight grain of the fabric. Pin into place and cut out. Cut one of each collar only. Cut two front facings, one back neck facing, one top collar, two top pocket flaps and two lower sleeve facings in interfacing.

Making up
1 With right sides together and matching notches tack and stitch the fronts to the back at the shoulder and side seams

as far as the dots. Press turnings open, including the slit facing extension, and neaten.

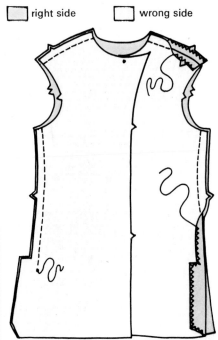

☐ right side   ☐ wrong side

2 Tack interfacing to the wrong side of the back neck facing and front facing. With right sides together tack and stitch the back neck facing to the front facing at the shoulder seams. Trim turnings and press open.
With right sides together and matching notches, tack and stitch the facings to the centre-front edges from the dot.

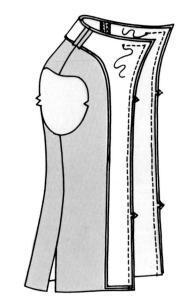

Collar
3 Tack interfacing to the wrong side of the top collar. With right sides together and matching notches tack and stitch the under-collar and top collars together all round, leaving the neck edge open. The under-collar will need to be stretched on to the top collar slightly. Trim turnings

and turn through the stitched edge and press. Tack the neck edge of the collar.

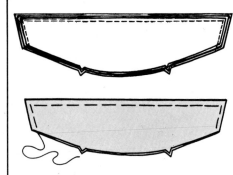

4 Matching notches to shoulder seams and centre-backs tack collar to neck edge with top collar facing up. Tack facing to neck edge, sandwiching the collar in-between the facing and jacket. Machine stitch all round. Clip and layer turnings. Neaten the edge of the facing. Turn facing on to the wrong side and catch-stitch on to shoulder seams.

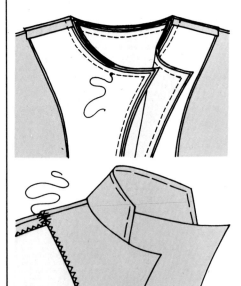

Pockets
5 With right sides together tack and stitch the two top pocket pieces together leaving an opening along the top edge to turn through. Slip-stitch opening together and press.

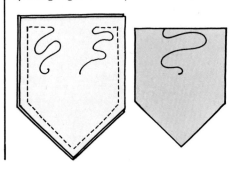

6 Place interfacing to the wrong side of one pocket flap. With right sides together tack and stitch the two pocket flaps together leaving one long edge open to turn through. Trim turnings and turn through. Tack the raw edges together along the seam line. Trim the edges to 0.6cm ($\frac{1}{4}$ *inch*) and neaten. Press. Top-stitch close to the edge and 1.3cm ($\frac{1}{2}$ *inch*) from the edge. Work a buttonhole on the pocket flap by machine or hand. Make another pocket in the same way.

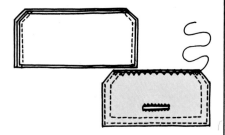

7 Position the pockets on the line indicated on each front jacket and tack. Top-stitch close to the edge around the pocket leaving the top edge open. Work another row of top-stitching 1.3cm ($\frac{1}{2}$ *inch*) in from the edge.

Place the neatened raw edges of the pocket flap to the line indicated above the top edge of the pocket. Tack and stitch. Fasten off ends securely and press the pocket flap down on to the pocket. Top-stitch close to the edge and 1.3cm ($\frac{1}{2}$ *inch*) from the edge.

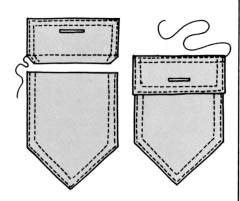

8 With right sides together tack and stitch two large pocket pieces together leaving an opening at the bottom to turn through. Trim turnings, turn through and slip-stitch the opening. Tack and press stitched edges.

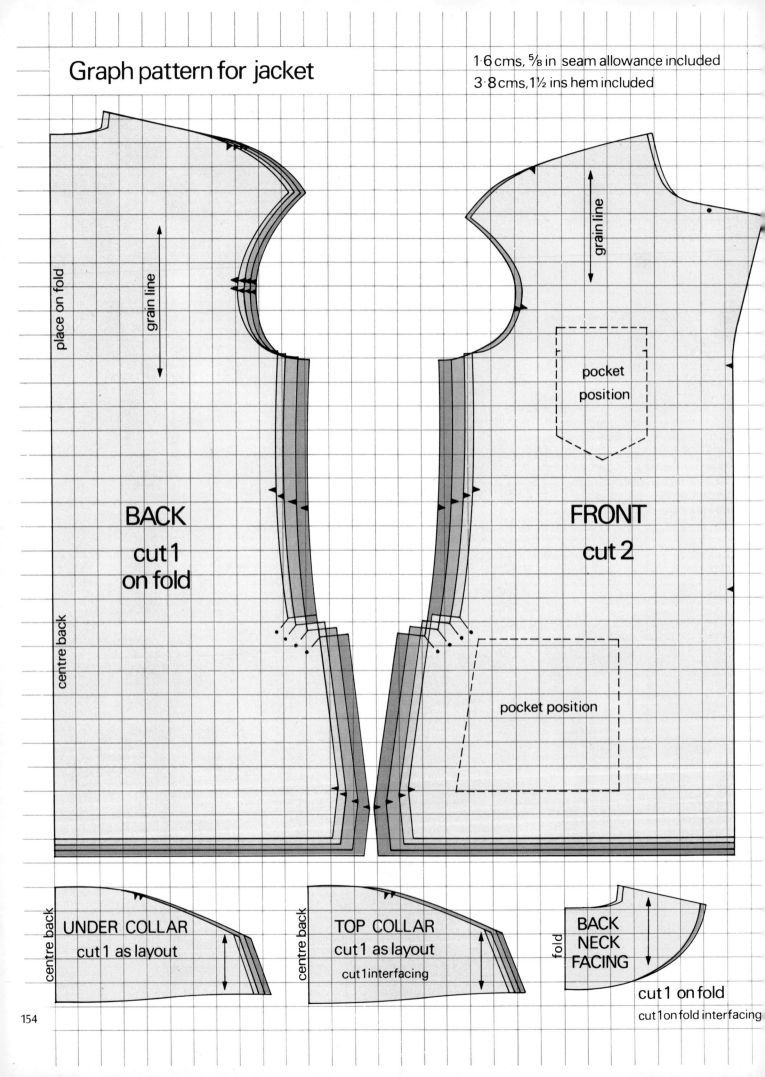

Graph pattern for jacket

1·6 cms, ⅝ in seam allowance included

3·8 cms, 1½ ins hem included

place on fold

grain line

centre back

BACK

cut 1

on fold

grain line

pocket position

FRONT

cut 2

pocket position

centre back

UNDER COLLAR

cut 1 as layout

centre back

TOP COLLAR

cut 1 as layout

cut 1 interfacing

fold

BACK NECK FACING

cut 1 on fold

cut 1 on fold interfacing

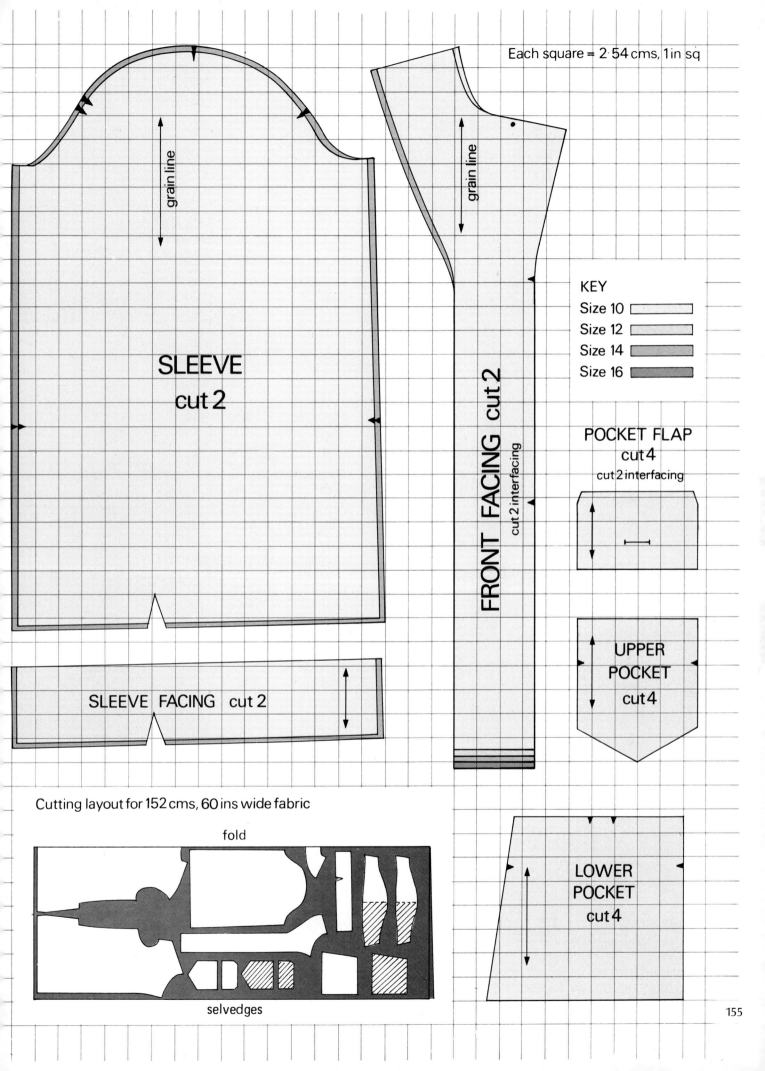

Each square = 2.54 cms, 1 in sq

grain line

SLEEVE
cut 2

FRONT FACING cut 2

cut 2 interfacing

grain line

KEY

Size 10
Size 12
Size 14
Size 16

POCKET FLAP
cut 4
cut 2 interfacing

UPPER
POCKET
cut 4

SLEEVE FACING cut 2

Cutting layout for 152 cms, 60 ins wide fabric

fold

selvedges

LOWER
POCKET
cut 4

9 Place one pocket on each front jacket so that the slanted edge lies down the fold of the slit in the side seam and the lower pocket edge lies 4cm (1½ inches) above the lower edge of the jacket, leaving the top edge free. Top-stitch close to the edge and then work another row of stitching 1.3cm (½ inch) from the edge. Fasten off ends securely and press.

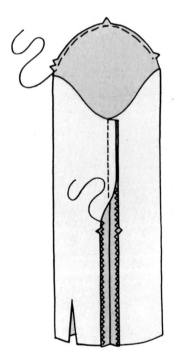

Sleeves

10 Work a gathering thread between the notches on the sleeve head. With right sides together and matching notches tack and stitch the underarm seam. Press turnings open and neaten.

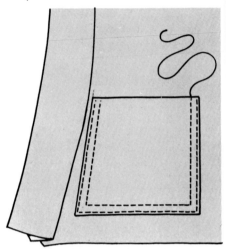

11 With right sides together, matching notches and underarm seams pin the sleeve into the armhole. Pull up the gathering thread and ease the sleeve head into the armhole, making sure that no gathers show on the right side. Tack and

stitch. Trim turnings, neaten together and press towards the jacket.

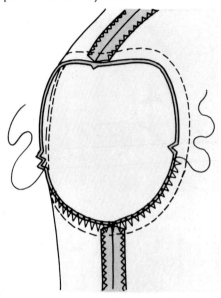

12 Tack interfacing to the wrong side of the lower sleeve facing. With right sides together tack and stitch across the short ends of the facing. Trim turnings and press open. With right sides together and matching seams tack and stitch the facing to the lower sleeve edge. Trim turnings. Neaten the raw edge of the facing.

Turn the facing on to the wrong side and tack around the stitched edge. Press. Top-stitch close to the edge and then work another row of top-stitching 1.3cm (½ inch) from the edge. Catch-stitch the facing on to the underarm seam on the wrong side.

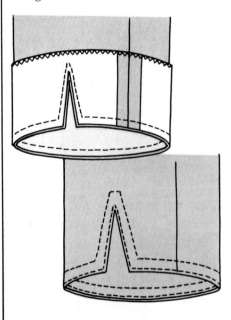

Hem

13 Neaten the lower edge of the jacket. Lay the front facing and side seam slits out flat. Turn up a 4cm (1½ inch) hem

and slip-stitch into place. Turn back the slit turnings and front facings and slip-stitch into place. Press.

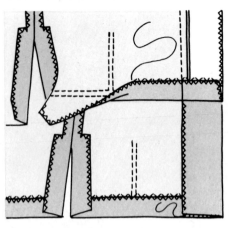

Top-stitch around the collar and down the centre-fronts close to the edge, and then 1.3cm (½ inch) away from the edge. Sew one button on to each top pocket to correspond with the buttonholes. Sew a button each side of the 'V' on the lower sleeve edges as indicated.

Button-through skirt

. . . softly gathered on to a neat waistband with side-placed pockets

Sizes
10, 12, 14 and 16

Fabric required
All sizes take:
1.60 metres (1¾ yards) of 152cm (60 inch) wide fabric

Note
If the skirt is made from white fabric, it is advisable to mount each piece on lining fabric. You will need the same amount of lining as main fabric.

You will also need
☐ Graph paper for making the pattern
☐ 0.45 metre (½ yard) of 91cm (36 inch) wide iron-on interfacing
☐ 0.25 metre (¼ yard) of 91cm (36 inch) wide lining for the pockets
☐ Matching thread
☐ 6 buttons each 2.5cm (1 inch) diameter

Making the pattern
Using graph paper and following the colour indicating the size required draw each pattern piece to scale. One square= 2.54cm square (1 inch square).
An allowance of 1.6cm (⅝ inch) has been made on all seams and 5cm (2 inches) for the hem.
Cut out the pattern pieces and mark all notches, dots, fold lines, buttonholes and the straight grain line.

Cutting out the skirt
Following the cutting layout fold the fabric and place the pattern pieces as indicated.
Take care that the grain line on the pattern lies on the straight grain of the fabric. Pin into place and cut out.
Transfer all markings from the pattern pieces to the fabric.
Fold the lining selvedge to selvedge and

cut the pocket lining pattern piece once from the double fabric.
Cut interfacings from the pattern pieces marked pocket flap, waistband and front facing to the fold lines only.

Making up

1 Iron interfacing in position with one edge to the fold line on the wrong side of each pocket flap. With right sides together fold each flap in half along the fold line, tack and stitch across the short ends. Trim turnings, turn through to the right side and press. Tack the raw edges together. Top-stitch the sides and folds of the flaps 1cm (⅜ inch) away from the edge.
With right sides together and matching notches tack each flap to a pocket lining.

☐ right side   ☐ wrong side

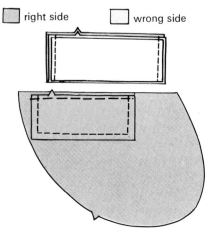

2 With right sides together tack and stitch each pocket flap and lining to the skirt fronts between the dots with the flap between the skirt and the pocket lining. Neaten the turnings together and press towards the pocket.

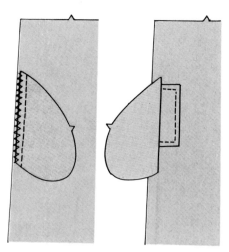

3 With right sides together and matching dots and pocket pieces tack and stitch the front skirts to the side fronts swivelling the machine needle at the dots and stitching round the pockets. Clip

across seam allowance to dots on the side fronts and press seams open above and below the pockets and the remainder of the turnings towards the pockets. Neaten turnings neatening the raw edges of the pockets together. Catch-stitch the short edges of the pocket flaps to the skirt side fronts.

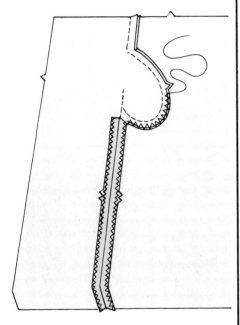

4 With right sides together and matching notches tack and stitch the back to the fronts at the side seams. Press seams open and neaten turnings.

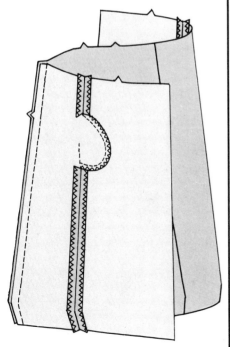

5 Iron interfacing in position with one edge to the fold line on skirt front facings. Turn facings under to the inside

along the fold line and press. Tack across the waist edge.

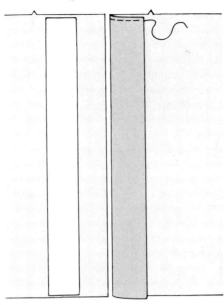

6 Iron interfacing in position with one edge to the fold line on the wrong side of the waistband. With right sides together fold the waistband in half along the fold line and tack and stitch the short ends. Turn through to the right side and press.

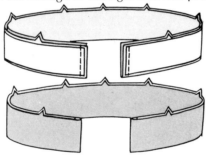

7 Work a row of gathering stitches along the waist edge of the skirt between the dots omitting the centre-back section of the skirt. With right sides together and matching centre-backs and front edges tack and stitch the interfaced edge of the waistband to the skirt. Trim turnings and press towards the waistband.

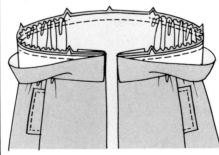

Turn under remaining edge of waistband and slip-stitch to the skirt along the first line of stitching. Press. Working from the

right side top-stitch all around the waistband 1cm ($\frac{3}{8}$ *inch*) away from the edges.

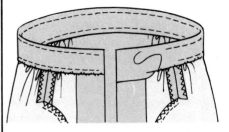

8 Neaten the hem edge. Turn hem up and tack and slip-stitch in position. Turn facings back on inside and slip-stitch in position over the hem.

9 Top-stitch the front edges of the skirt 1cm ($\frac{3}{8}$ *inch*) away from the fold. Work five vertical buttonholes down the right centre-front and one horizontal one on the waistband as indicated on the pattern. Sew buttons down the left centre-front to correspond.

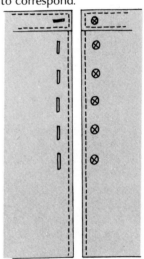

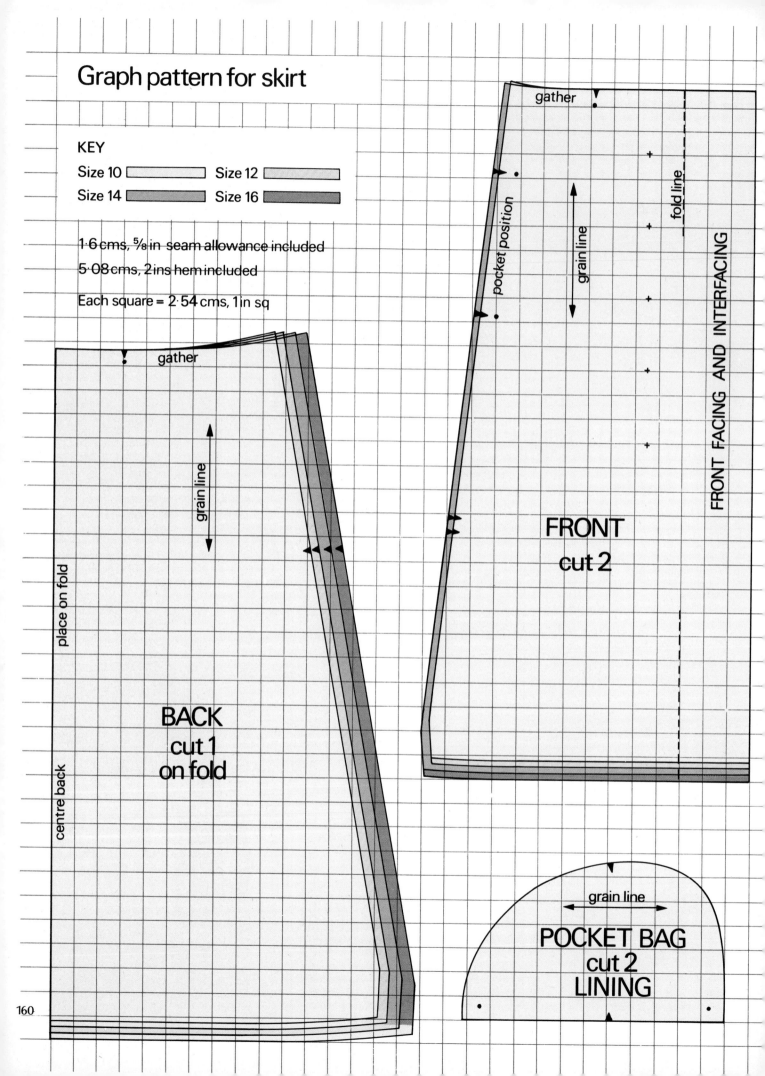

Graph pattern for skirt

KEY

Size 10 ▭ Size 12 ▭
Size 14 ▭ Size 16 ▭

1·6 cms, ⅝ in seam allowance included

5·08 cms, 2 ins hem included

Each square = 2·54 cms, 1 in sq

gather

grain line

place on fold

centre back

BACK
cut 1
on fold

gather

pocket position

grain line

fold line

FRONT FACING AND INTERFACING

FRONT
cut 2

grain line

POCKET BAG
cut 2
LINING

160

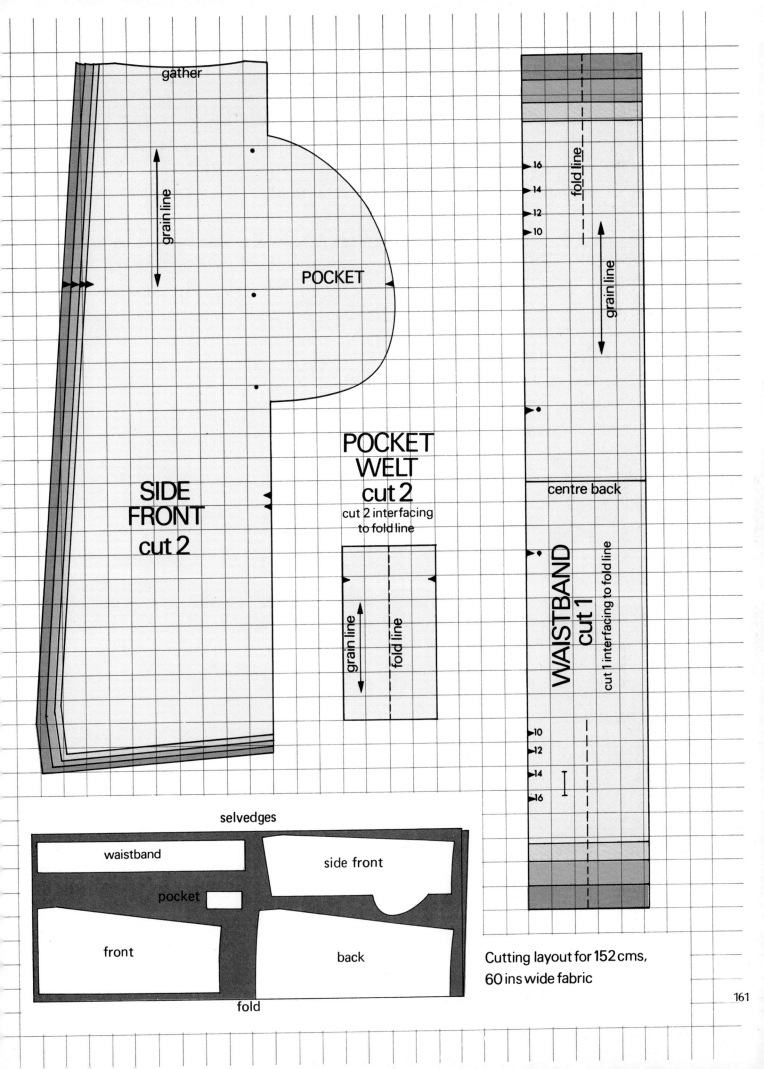

gather

grain line

POCKET

SIDE
FRONT
cut 2

POCKET
WELT
cut 2

cut 2 interfacing
to fold line

grain line

fold line

16
14
12
10

fold line

grain line

centre back

WAISTBAND
cut 1

cut 1 interfacing to fold line

10
12
14
16

selvedges

waistband

side front

pocket

front

back

fold

Cutting layout for 152 cms,
60 ins wide fabric

161

Stretch jacket

A classic shape in soft stretch towelling

Sizes

10, 12, 14 and 16

Fabric required

For sizes 10 and 12:
1.65 metres (1¾ yards) of 152cm (60 inch) fabric
For sizes 14 and 16:
1.85 metres (2 yards) of 152cm (60 inch) fabric

You will also need

☐ Graph paper for making the pattern
☐ Matching thread
☐ 0.45 metre (½ yard) interfacing
☐ 1 × 40cm (16 inch) open ended zip
☐ 1.15 metres (1¼ yards) of 6.5cm (2½ inch) wide elastic

Making the pattern

Using graph paper and following the colour indicating the size required draw each pattern piece to scale. One square= 2.54cm square (1 inch square). An allowance of 1.6cm (⅝ inch) has been made on all seams. Cut out the pattern pieces and mark all dots, notches and straight grain lines.

Cutting out the jacket

Following the cutting layout fold the fabric and place the pattern pieces as indicated. Make sure that the straight grain line on the pattern lies on the straight grain of the fabric. Pin into place and cut out. Transfer all markings from the pattern pieces to the fabric. Fold the interfacing in half and using the appropriate pattern pieces, cut a back yoke, front yoke, upper collar and two pocket flaps.

Making up

1 Tack interfacing to the wrong side of one back and one front yoke. With right sides facing tack and stitch the yokes together at the shoulder seams. Press turnings open. Tack and stitch the two remaining yokes together at the shoulder seams and press turnings open.

☐ right side   ☐ wrong side

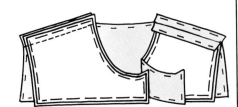

2 Interface two of the pocket flap pieces. With right sides together tack and

stitch one interfaced pocket flap to an uninterfaced flap.
Leave the straight edge unstitched. Trim turnings, turn through and press. Top-stitch the width of the machine foot from the stitched edges. Repeat with other flap. Position one pocket flap on each interfaced front yoke between the dots with raw edges together and the interfaced side facing down. Tack securely.

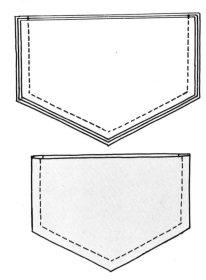

3 With right sides together and matching notches tack and stitch the jacket fronts to the front yokes sandwiching the pocket flaps in between, and the back to the back yoke. Trim turnings and press on to yoke.

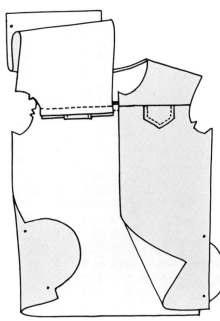

Collar

4 Tack interfacing to the wrong side of the upper collar. With right sides together tack and stitch the under-collar to the upper-collar leaving the neck edge open. Trim turnings and turn collar

through. Press and top-stitch the width of the machine foot from the stitched edges. Tack raw edges together.

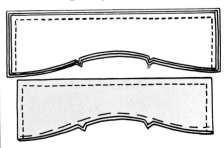

5 Tack the collar to the neck edge making sure that the interfaced side is facing up. Position the yoke facing over the collar and top yoke. With right sides together tack and stitch around the neck edge, sandwiching the collar in between. Trim and clip turnings and turn the yoke facing to the wrong side. Make a 1.6cm (⅝ inch) turning on the lower edges of the yoke facings and slip-stitch on to the stitch line. Top-stitch the back and front yokes the width of the machine foot from the stitch line, through all thicknesses.

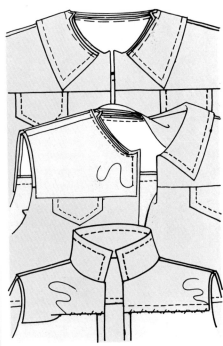

6 With right sides together tack and stitch the straight edge of one pocket piece to the jacket front at the side seam between the dots. Trim turnings.

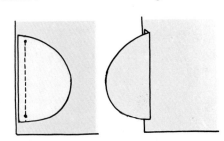

Graph pattern for jacket

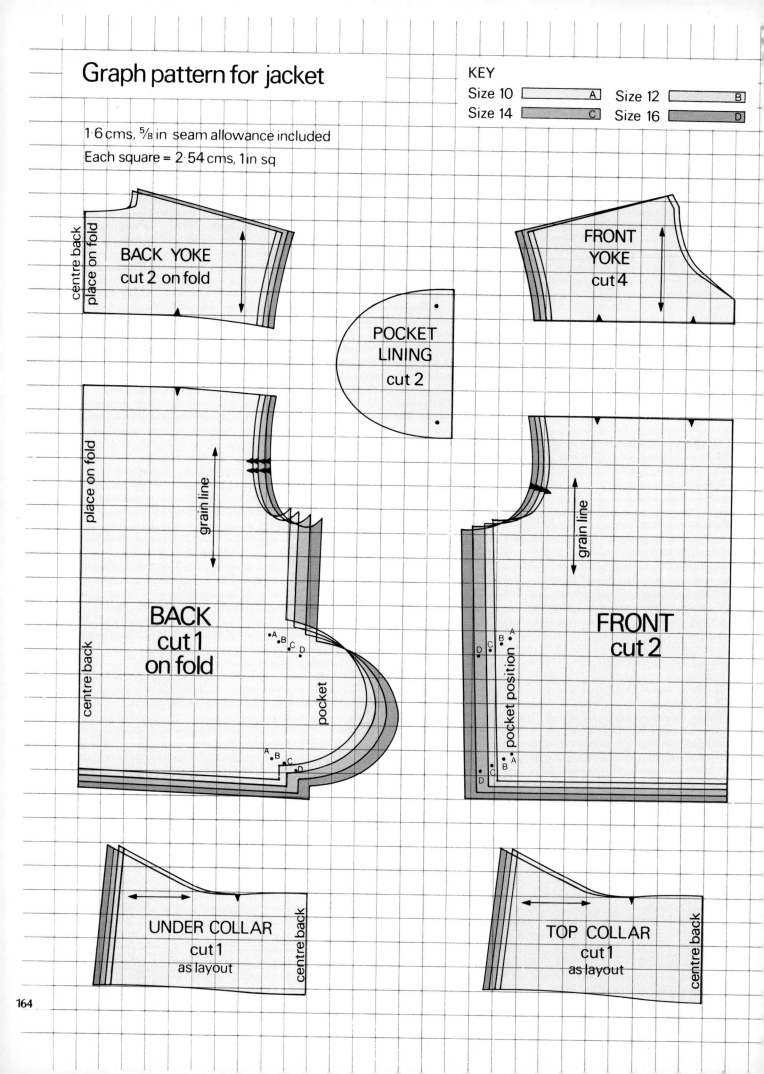

KEY

Size 10 ▭ A	Size 12 ▭ B
Size 14 ▭ C	Size 16 ▭ D

1·6 cms, ⅝ in seam allowance included

Each square = 2·54 cms, 1in sq

BACK YOKE
cut 2 on fold

centre back
place on fold

FRONT YOKE
cut 4

POCKET LINING
cut 2

place on fold

grain line

BACK cut 1 on fold

centre back

pocket

A B C D

A B C D

grain line

FRONT cut 2

D C B A
pocket position
A B C D

UNDER COLLAR
cut 1
as layout

centre back

TOP COLLAR
cut 1
as layout

centre back

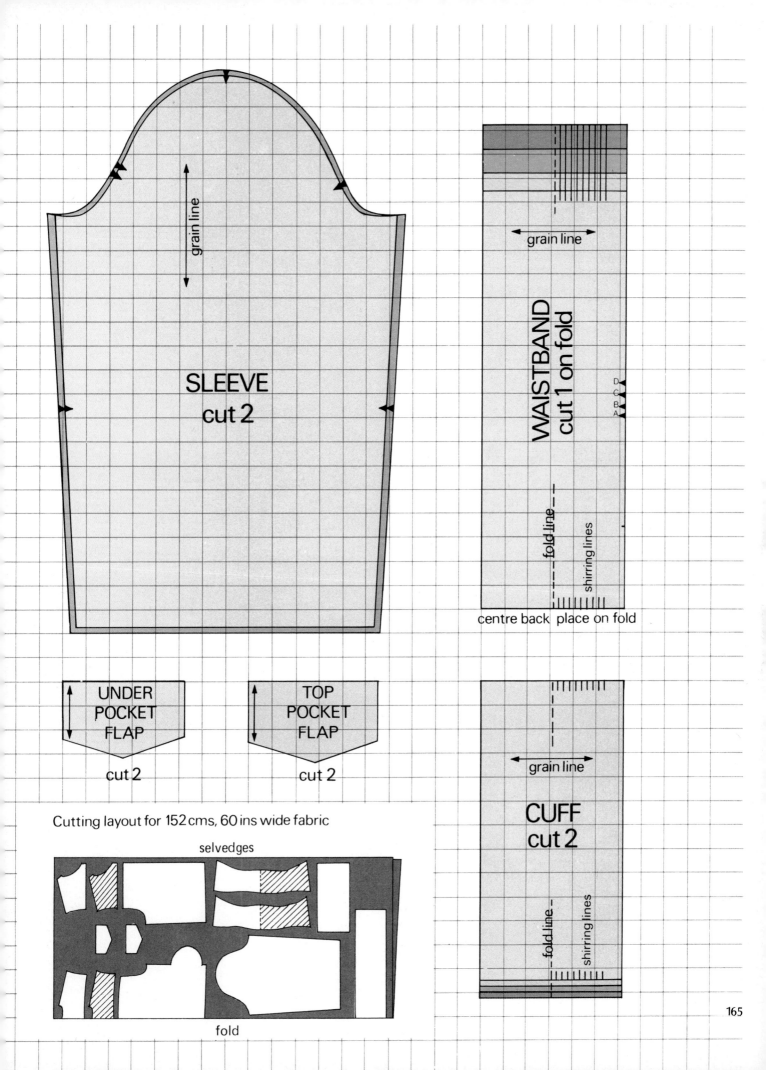

SLEEVE
cut 2

grain line

WAISTBAND
cut 1 on fold

grain line

D
C
B
A

fold line

shirring lines

centre back place on fold

UNDER
POCKET
FLAP

cut 2

TOP
POCKET
FLAP

cut 2

CUFF
cut 2

grain line

fold line

shirring lines

Cutting layout for 152 cms, 60 ins wide fabric

selvedges

fold

7 With right sides together and matching notches tack and stitch the front to the back at the side seam and the pocket pieces together around the outside edge. Trim turnings and clip around pocket turnings at regular intervals. Clip into the corner where the pocket meets the side seam. Neaten. Turn the jacket right side out and push the pocket in.

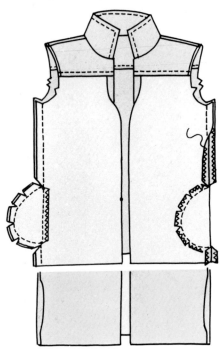

Sleeves

8 With right sides together and matching notches tack and stitch the underarm seam. Press turnings open and neaten. Work a gathering thread between the notches on the sleeve head. With right sides together, matching notches and underarm seams, tack and stitch the sleeve to the armhole, distributing the

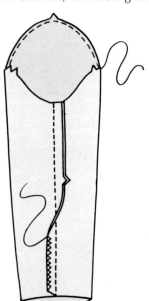

fullness evenly. Trim turnings and neaten together. Press turnings towards sleeve.

Cuffs

9 Fold the cuff in half with right sides together and stitch across the short ends to form a circle. Press turnings open. With wrong sides together fold the cuff in half on the fold line.

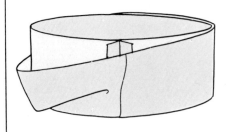

10 Cut a piece of elastic three quarters the length of the cuff. Overlap the ends and sew together firmly. Place elastic to the inside of the cuff with one edge to the fold line. Tack. Work eight rows of top stitching the width of the machine foot apart around the cuff, stretching as you stitch.

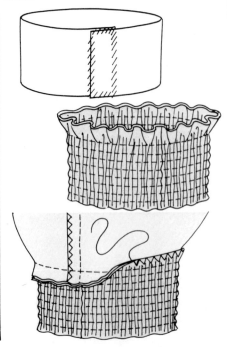

With right sides together and matching seams, tack and stitch the cuff to the sleeve. Neaten all edges together.

11 Cut a piece of elastic three quarters the length of the waistband. Place on the wrong side of the waistband so that one edge lies along the fold line and secure at the ends. This will mean stretching the elastic slightly. With right sides together fold the waistband in half on the fold line and stitch across the ends. Turn to the right side and work eight rows of top-stitching the width of the machine foot apart, stretching the waistband as you sew. Neaten the edges and attach to the lower edge of the jacket in the same way as the cuff.

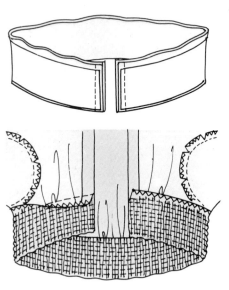

12 Insert the zip into the centre-front seam. Stitch one button on to each pocket flap through all thicknesses.

Safari jacket

Give him style with this smart safari jacket. It's an all-season classic.

Sizes
91cm (*36 inch*), 96.5cm (*38 inch*), 101.5cm (*40 inch*) chest

Fabric required
All sizes take 3 metres ($3\frac{1}{4}$ *yards*) of 114cm (*45 inch*) fabric

You will also need
- ☐ Graph paper for making the pattern
- ☐ 0.70 metre ($\frac{3}{4}$ *yard*) interfacing
- ☐ Matching thread
- ☐ 11 buttons 1.3cm ($\frac{1}{2}$ *inch*) diameter

Making the pattern
Using graph paper and following the colour indicating the size required draw each pattern piece to scale. One square = 5.08cm square (*2 inch square*). An allowance of 1.6cm ($\frac{5}{8}$ *inch*) has been made for all seams and the hem. 3cm ($1\frac{1}{4}$ *inches*) has been allowed on the top pocket edges. Cut out the pattern pieces and mark all dots, notches, buttonhole positions, fold lines and the straight grain line.

Cutting out the jacket
Following the cutting layout fold the fabric lengthways and place all thirteen pattern pieces as indicated. Take care that the grain line on the pattern lies on the straight grain of the fabric. Pin into place and cut out.
Transfer all markings from the pattern pieces to the fabric.

Making up
1 Pocket flaps. These are in two sizes the upper flaps are smaller than the lower. From the flap pattern pieces cut two upper and two lower pieces in interfacing. To make each flap, tack interfacing to one flap piece on the wrong side.

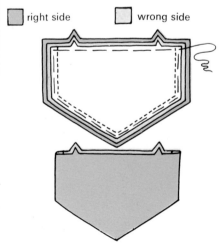

☐ right side   ☐ wrong side

2 Place two flap pieces together with right sides together. Tack and stitch leaving the top long straight edge open.

Trim the turnings, tapering at the corners, and turn through. Press and top-stitch 1cm ($\frac{3}{8}$ inch) from the stitched edge.

3 Pockets. The upper and lower pockets are worked in the same way. Fold the pocket in half lengthways. Tack along the tuck line marked. Press the tuck on the right side so that the centre lies on the seam underneath.

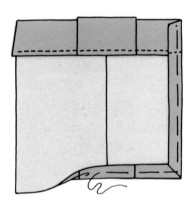

4 Make a small hem of 3cm ($1\frac{1}{4}$ inches) on to the wrong side on the top edge of the pocket and machine stitch close to the lower edge. Turn 1.6cm ($\frac{5}{8}$ inch) on the remaining three edges to the wrong side. Mitre the corners, press the turnings and tack.
Position the pockets on the fronts where indicated, making sure the smaller upper and larger lower pockets are not confused. Tack and stitch on the pockets close to the fold on three edges.

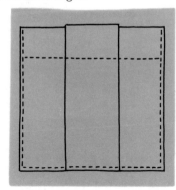

5 With right sides together and the flap pointing upwards place the raw edge of the lower pocket flap to the top of the pocket. Tack and stitch 1.6cm ($\frac{5}{8}$ inch) from the edge. Trim the turnings to 0.6cm ($\frac{1}{4}$ inch) and press flap down over turnings. Work a row of stitches 1cm ($\frac{3}{8}$ inch) from the seam line to hold down the flap.

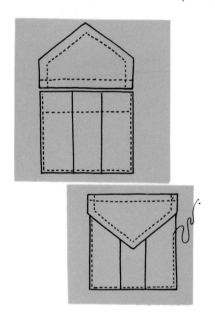

6 Matching the notches place the raw edges of the upper flap on to the top edge of the front with the flap facing down over the pocket. With right sides together and matching notches, tack and stitch the front yokes to the fronts enclosing the flaps. Trim the yoke and flap turnings to 0.6cm ($\frac{1}{4}$ inch). Neaten the raw edge of the front turning and press all the turnings upwards. From the right side stitch 1cm ($\frac{3}{8}$ inch) above the seam line on the yoke. This will hold down the turnings making a stitched lapped seam.

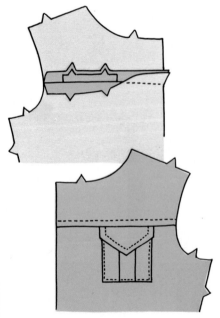

7 With right sides together tack and stitch a dart on each side of the back at the waist.

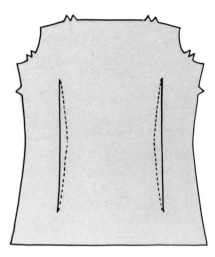

8 With right sides together tack and stitch a pleat in the centre-back starting at the yoke edge and matching the stitch lines, then stitch diagonally across to the fold.

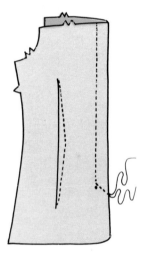

Press the pleat to one side and from the right side top-stitch the distance of the machine foot away from the seam line finishing off at an angle.

9 With right sides together and matching notches tack and stitch the back yoke to the back in the same way as for the front.

10 With right sides together and matching notches tack and stitch the front and back together at the side seams. Press open and neaten turnings together.

11 Belt. Cut a strip of interfacing the length of the belt and 6.3cm (2½ inches) wide. Tack centrally to the wrong side of the belt. Turn the seam allowance on the long edges of the belt to the wrong side. Tack and press.

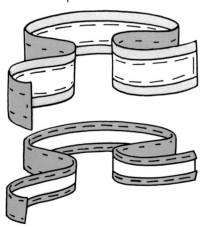

12 Place the lower edges of the belt on to the line indicated, starting at the front edge on the right hand side and finishing at the dots on the left hand side. Tack into place and stitch 1cm (⅜ inch) from either edge.

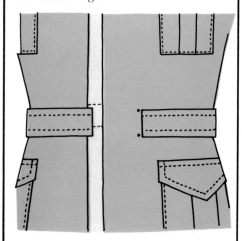

13 Cut a strip of interfacing the length of the front strap and 5cm (2 inches) wide. Tack to the wrong side of the centre-front on the right hand side, with one long edge of the interfacing to the raw edge of garment and the other edge of the interfacing to the fold line. Fold the facing back on the fold line and press.

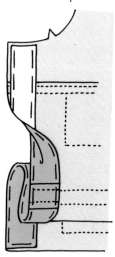

14 Cut a strip of interfacing the length of the centre-front strap and 3.8cm (1½ inches) wide. Tack centrally to the inside of the front strap.

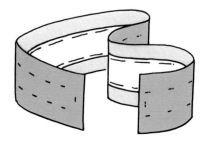

15 Fold the left hand side front facing on the jacket to the inside on the fold line and press.
Place the strap on top of this matching the notches and with one edge on the centre-front fold. Tack and stitch on 1cm (⅜ inch) from the edge down both sides.

16 With right sides together and matching notches tack and stitch the front and back together at the shoulder seams. Press, trim and neaten turnings.

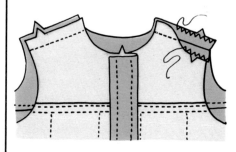

17 From the pattern piece marked collar cut a piece of interfacing and tack it to the wrong side of one collar piece. With right sides together and matching notches, tack and stitch the collar pieces together leaving the neck edge open. Trim and clip to the dots. Turn to the right side and tack around the edge to hold the seam in place.

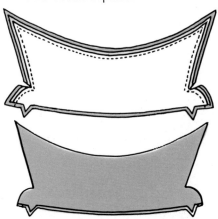

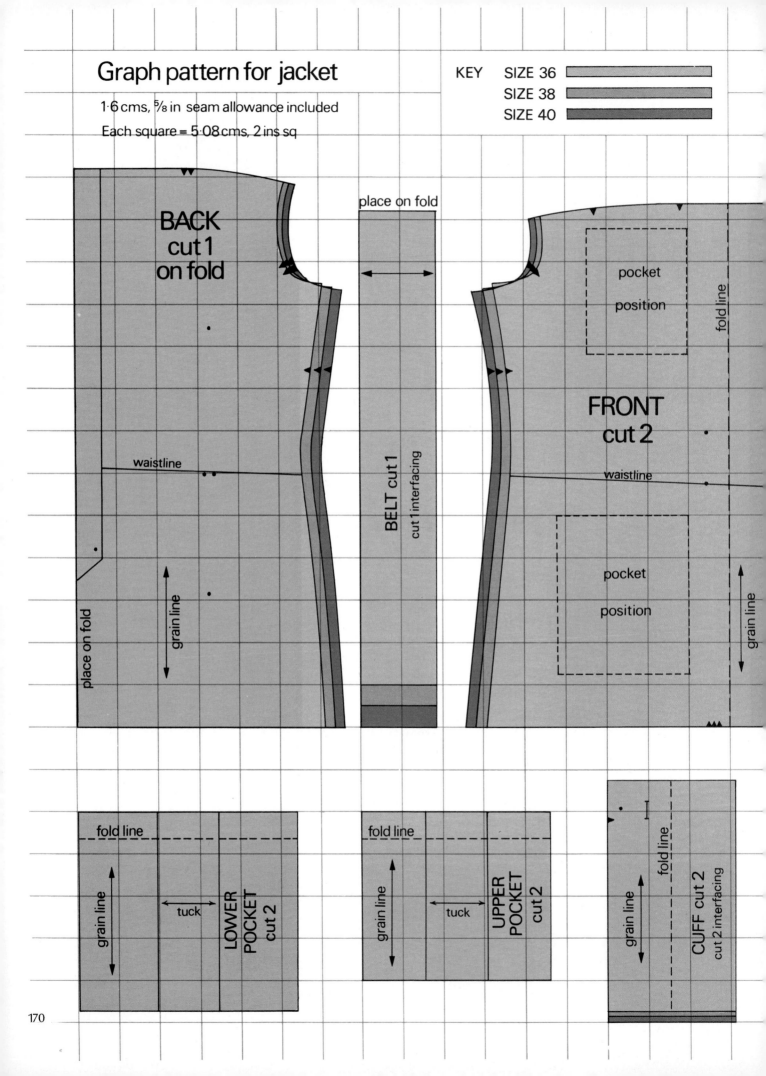

Graph pattern for jacket

1·6 cms, ⅝ in seam allowance included

Each square = 5·08 cms, 2 ins sq

BACK
cut 1
on fold

place on fold

waistline

grain line

place on fold

grain line

BELT cut 1

cut 1 interfacing

FRONT
cut 2

pocket

position

waistline

pocket

position

fold line

grain line

fold line

grain line

tuck

LOWER
POCKET
cut 2

fold line

grain line

tuck

UPPER
POCKET
cut 2

grain line

fold line

CUFF cut 2

cut 2 interfacing

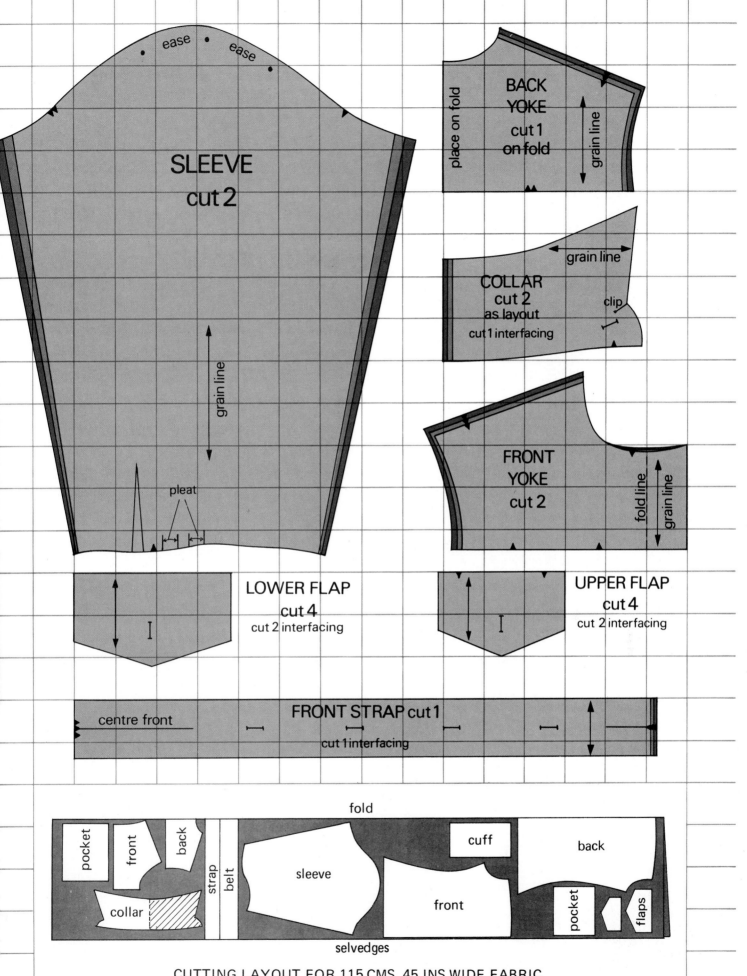

SLEEVE
cut 2

ease • • ease

grain line

pleat

BACK YOKE
cut 1
on fold

place on fold

grain line

COLLAR
cut 2
as layout
cut 1 interfacing

grain line

clip

FRONT YOKE
cut 2

fold line

grain line

LOWER FLAP
cut 4
cut 2 interfacing

UPPER FLAP
cut 4
cut 2 interfacing

FRONT STRAP cut 1

centre front

cut 1 interfacing

fold

pocket

front

back

strap

belt

collar

sleeve

cuff

front

back

pocket

flaps

selvedges

CUTTING LAYOUT FOR 115 CMS, 45 INS WIDE FABRIC

18 Make turnings of 1.6cm ($\frac{5}{8}$ *inch*) on both collar neck edges. Tack. Place to the jacket with the fold lines of the collar on either side of the stitch line of the neck edge. Tack and stitch close to the edge through all thicknesses. Top-stitch around the other edges of the collar, the width of the machine foot from the edge.

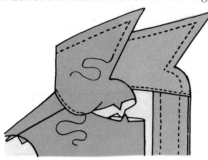

19 Cut two facings for the sleeve slits 15cm (6 *inches*) by 7.5cm (3 *inches*). Neaten two long edges and one short edge on each piece.
Tack one piece to the right side of the lower sleeve with the unneatened edge to the sleeve edge. Make sure that the slit is positioned centrally underneath. Tack and stitch on the lines indicated. Cut the slit open almost to the stitches at the point and turn the facing on to the wrong side. On the right side tack and stitch on the edge around the slit.

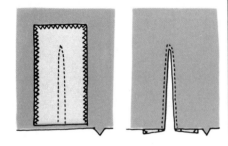

20 With right sides together and matching notches, tack and stitch the sleeves together on the underarm seam. Press, trim and neaten the turnings.

21 Cut a piece of interfacing the width of the cuff. Cut this in half length-ways. Tack one piece to each cuff on the wrong side with one edge on the fold line of the cuff. Fold the cuff with right sides together and tack and stitch at the ends and as far as the dot along one edge. Clip to the dot. Trim the turnings and turn the cuff through. Press.

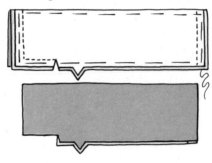

22 On the right-side make two pleats where indicated on the lower sleeve edge and press towards the sleeve slit opening. Tack and stitch the cuff in the same way as the collar. Stitch close to the edge and top-stitch around the three outer edges.

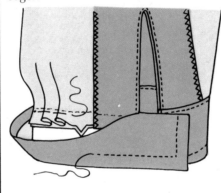

23 Work two rows of gathering between the dots on the sleeve head. With right sides together, matching notches and underarm seams, pin the sleeve into the armhole. Pull up the gathering threads evenly to ease the head of the sleeve. Tack and stitch. Trim and neaten the turnings and press towards the sleeve.

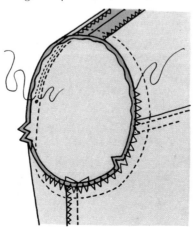

Hem

24 Make a double turning of 1.6cm ($\frac{5}{8}$ *inch*) around the lower edge of the shirt and stitch close to the fold.

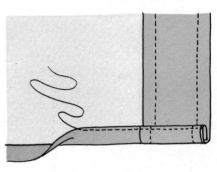

25 Work buttonholes where indicated on the left front strap, collar and cuffs and also on the pocket flaps. Sew on the buttons to correspond.

Soft shirt

A slim line shirt to sew that's as sleek as a second skin.

Sizes

91.5cm (36 inch) 96.5cm (38 inch) 101.5cm (40 inch) Chest

Fabric required

All sizes take 1.85 metres ($2\frac{1}{4}$ yards) of 1.52 metre (54 inch) wide fabric

You will also need

☐ Graph paper for making the pattern
☐ Matching thread
☐ 8 buttons
☐ 0.45 metre ($\frac{1}{2}$ yard) of light-weight or iron-on interfacing

Making the pattern

Using graph paper and following the colour indicating the size required, draw each pattern piece to scale. One square= 2.54 cm square (1 inch square). 1.6cm ($\frac{5}{8}$ inch) has been allowed on all seams and hem.
Cut out the pattern pieces and mark all notches, dots, the straight grain lines and the position of the buttonholes.

Cutting out the shirt

Following the cutting layout fold the fabric and place all ten pattern pieces as indicated, using the collar pattern piece twice. Take care that the grain line on the pattern lies on the straight grain of the fabric. Pin into place and cut out. Transfer all marking from the pattern pieces to the fabric.

Making up

1 Taking 1.6cm ($\frac{5}{8}$ inch) turnings and with right sides together matching the notches, tack and stitch the two side back pieces to the centre back. Trim the turnings on the centre back piece to 0.6cm ($\frac{1}{4}$ inch) press turnings towards the centre-back and top-stitch on the right side 0.6cm ($\frac{1}{4}$ inch) from the stitch line. This is a stitched lapped seam.

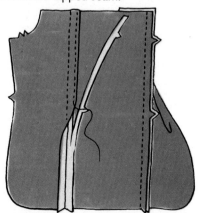

2 With right sides together tack and stitch the two side-front pieces to the fronts using the same method.

3 With right sides together, matching the notches, tack and stitch the front yoke to the front. Trim and press turnings up. Top-stitch.

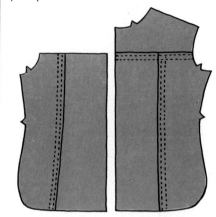

4 Place the back yoke to the back matching the notches and with right sides together. Tack and stitch in the same way.

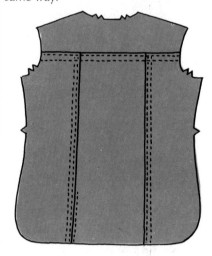

5 With right sides together tack and stitch the shoulder seams and the side seams as far as the dot. Trim and neaten together by hand or zig-zag machine. Press.

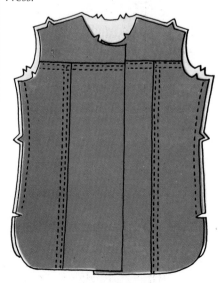

6 Cut three pieces of interfacing from the pattern piece marked front strap. Tack or press one piece of interfacing to the wrong side of the front strap. Press the turnings on the two long edges to the wrong side.

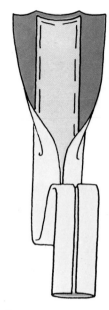

7 Trim the two remaining interfacing straps to a 5cm (2 inch) width and place on to the inside left and right front with one edge to the fold line the other to the raw edge. Tack or press into place.

8 Press the front facing on the left front to the inside on the fold line. Place the front strap on to the left front, with the wrong side of the strap to the right side of the front shirt and the edges together. Tack and stitch 0.6cm ($\frac{1}{4}$ inch) from fold down both sides of the strap.

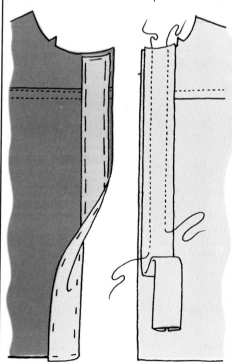

Collar

9 Cut a piece of interfacing from the pattern piece marked collar and tack or press it to the wrong side of one collar piece.

With right sides together tack and stitch the two collar pieces together. Trim turnings to 0.6cm ($\frac{1}{4}$ inch) and clip to dot. Turn the collar to the right side. Tack and press the outside edge.

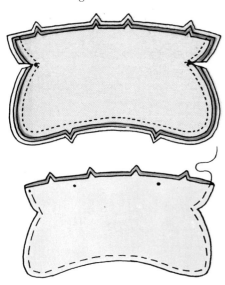

10 Place one edge of the collar to the shirt with the right side of the collar to the wrong side of the shirt matching the dots to the shoulder seams and matching the notches. Tack and stitch. Trim and press turnings on to collar. Turn in the seam allowance on the other edge of the collar and tack over the stitch line. Stitch on the edge of this fold.

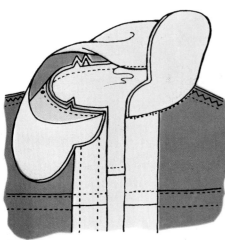

Sleeves

11 Cut two pieces of fabric for the sleeve slit facing 7.5cm (3 inches) × 17.5cm (7 inches). Neaten each piece on the two long edges and one short edge.

With right sides together place facing over the slit in the sleeve with the raw edge of the facing to the edge of the sleeve. Make sure that the slit is central and taking 0.6cm ($\frac{1}{4}$ inch) turnings at the cuff edge, tapering to a point at the top of the slit, tack and stitch. Snip slit close to stitches at point. Turn the facing to the wrong side and press. Machine stitch on the edge of the fold.

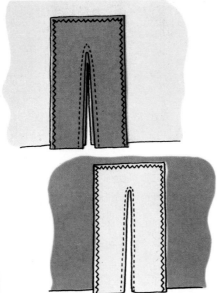

12 With right sides together tack and stitch the sleeve seam. Trim and neaten together by hand or on a zig-zag machine. On the right side make two small pleats towards the slit on the sleeve. Tack.

Cuffs

13 Using the pattern piece marked cuff cut a piece of interfacing. Cut this in half lengthways. Place one on to the inside of cuff with one edge to the fold line. Tack or press into place. With right sides together fold cuff in half lengthways. Tack and stitch the short ends and 2cm ($\frac{3}{4}$ inch)

along the edge towards the single notch. Snip, trim and turn.

14 With right sides together place the stiffened side of the cuff to the sleeve edge matching the notches and easing any fullness. Tack and stitch. Trim turnings. Turn in the seam allowance on the other edge of the cuff, tack and slip-stitch along the stitch line. Top-stitch all round the cuff 0.6cm ($\frac{1}{4}$ inch) from the edge.

Work two buttonholes on the cuff front, one on the collar and three on the shirt. Stitch on buttons to correspond.

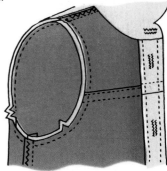

15 Right sides together, matching notches and dot to shoulder seam, tack and stitch sleeve into armhole, neaten and press.

Hem

16 Turn 1.6cm ($\frac{5}{8}$ inch) to the inside. Tack and machine stitch round the curves to the point of the slit. Press.

175

Graph pattern for mans shirt

1·6 cms, ⅝ in seam allowance included

Each square = 2·54 cms, 1 in sq

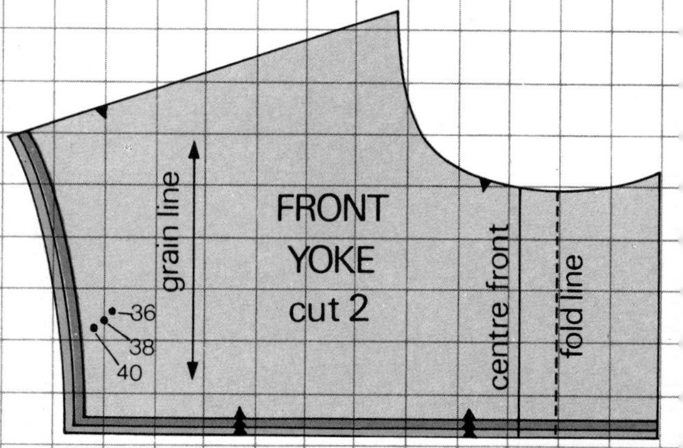

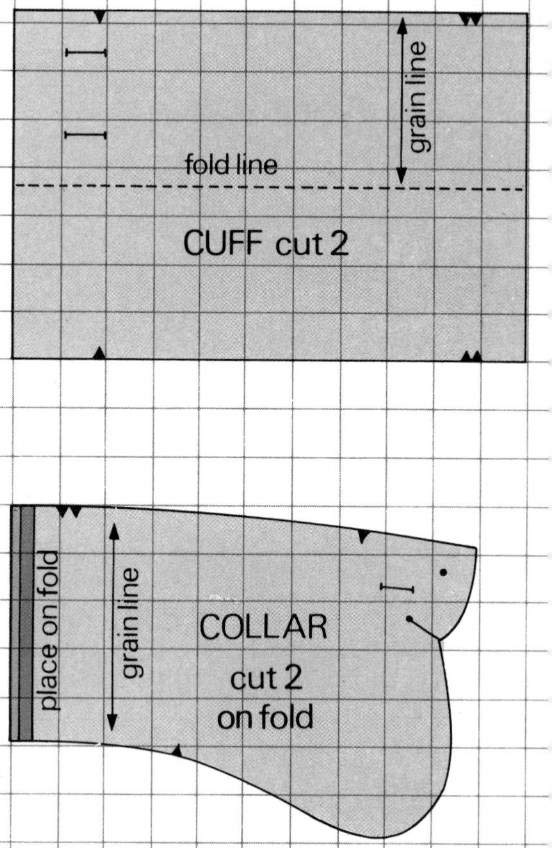

grain line

FRONT YOKE cut 2

centre front

fold line

•36
•38
40

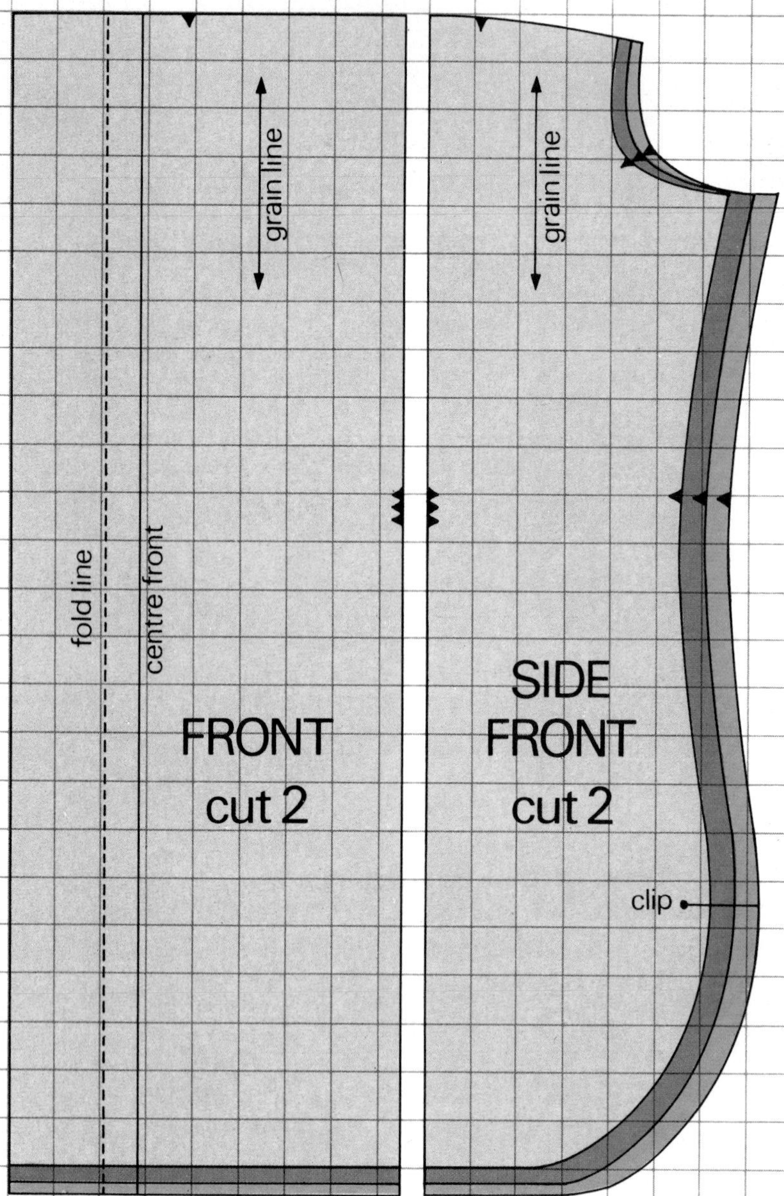

grain line

I

I

fold line

grain line

CUFF cut 2

grain line

fold line

centre front

FRONT cut 2

grain line

SIDE FRONT cut 2

clip •

place on fold

grain line

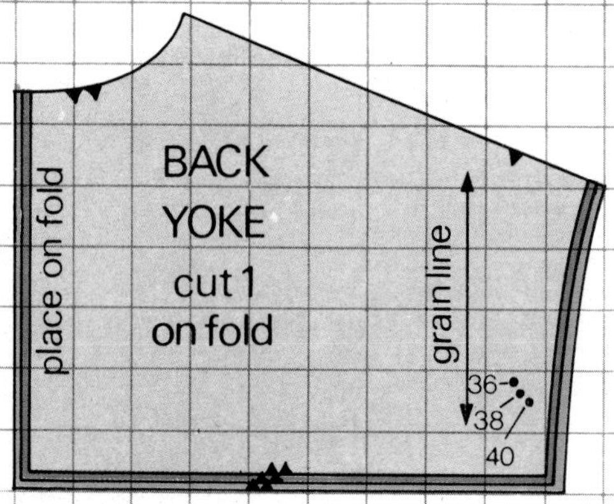

I

•

COLLAR cut 2 on fold

place on fold

BACK YOKE cut 1 on fold

grain line

36•
38•
40

CUTTING LAYOUT FOR 137·16 CMS, 54 INS WIDE FABRIC

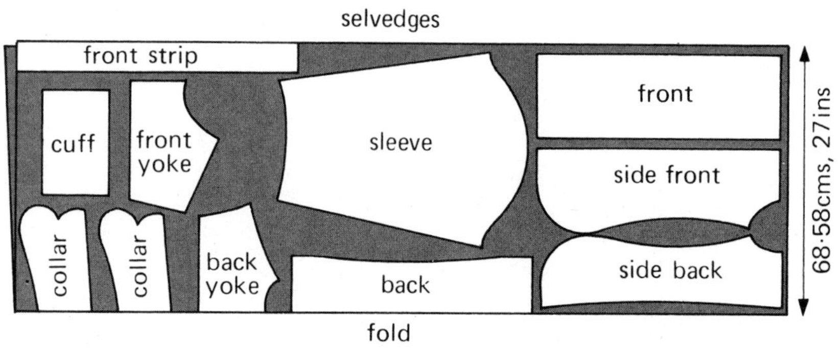

selvedges

front strip

cuff

front yoke

sleeve

front

side front

collar

collar

back yoke

back

side back

fold

68·58cms, 27ins

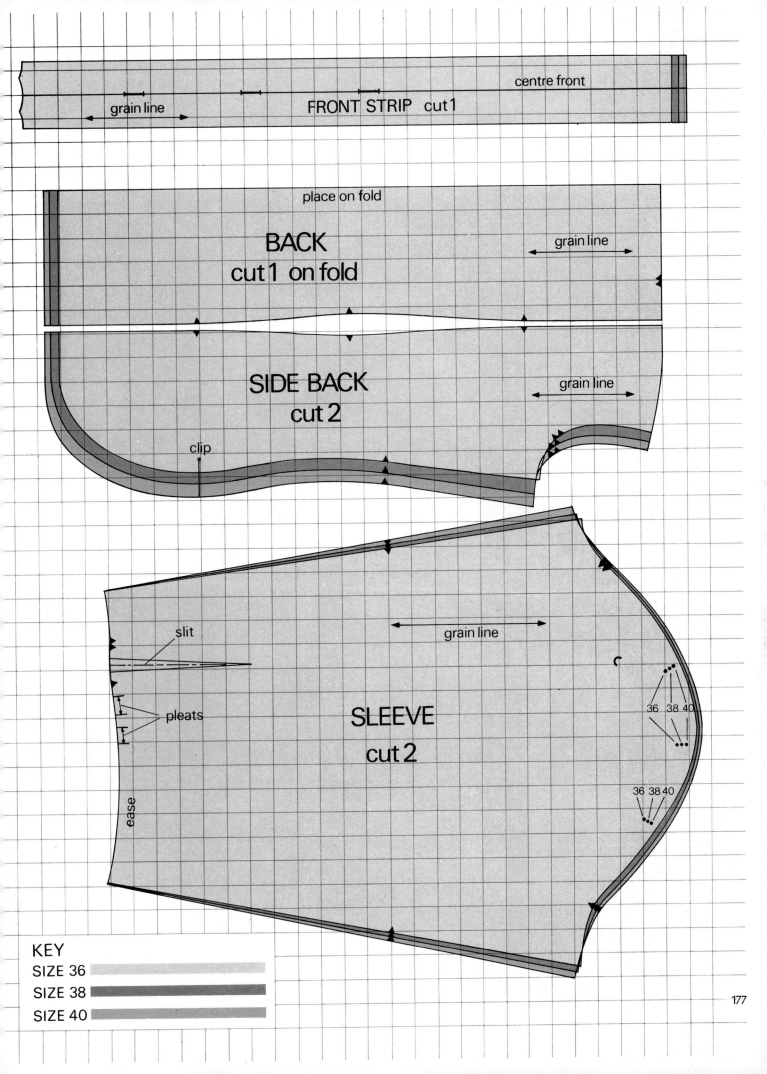

centre front

grain line

FRONT STRIP   cut 1

place on fold

BACK
cut 1 on fold

grain line

SIDE BACK
cut 2

grain line

clip

slit

grain line

pleats

SLEEVE
cut 2

36 38 40

36 38 40

ease

KEY
SIZE 36
SIZE 38
SIZE 40

Wrap-around coat & pull-on hat

**Tie belt, patch pockets and big, bold buttons give this coat an easy elegance.
Pull-on hat makes your outfit complete.**

The Coat

Sizes

10, 12, 14 and 16.

Fabric required

All sizes take 2.75 metres (3 yards) of 1.75 metre (68–70 inch) fabric
25cm ($\frac{1}{4}$ yard) of lining for shoulder pads

You will also need

☐ Graph paper for making the pattern
☐ Matching thread
☐ 7.30 metres (8 yards) of narrow braid
☐ 4 × 3.8cm ($1\frac{1}{2}$ inch) buttons
☐ 4 dress-size foam shoulder pads
☐ 2.55 metres ($2\frac{3}{4}$ yards) jersey or iron-on interfacing

Making the pattern

Using graph paper, and following the colour indicating the size required, draw each pattern piece to scale. One square = 5.08cm square (2 inch square).
1.6cm ($\frac{5}{8}$ inch) has been allowed on all seams. A 3.8cm ($1\frac{1}{2}$ inch) allowance has been made on hem of coat and a 5cm (2 inch) allowance for sleeve hem.
Cut out the pattern pieces and mark all notches, the straight grain line, the pocket position and the position of the button-holes.

Cutting out the coat

Following the cutting layout, fold the fabric and place all twelve pattern pieces as indicated, cutting the collar twice. Take care that the grain line on the pattern lies on the straight grain of the fabric. Pin into place and cut out.
Transfer all markings from the pattern pieces to the fabric.

Making the shoulder pads

For each pad, take two dress-size shoulder pads, place one on top of the other, and stab-stitch through both to keep them together.
Cut a 20cm (8 inch) square of lining fabric. Fold the fabric in half over the pad to make a triangle. Pin and tack the fabric round the edges of the pad. Trim away surplus fabric and sew with a zig-zag stitch.

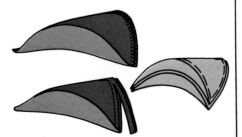

Making up

1 With right sides together, and matching notches, tack and stitch side-back pieces to centre-back panel. Press seams open.

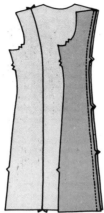

2 With right sides together, and matching notches, tack and stitch side-front panels to centre-front pieces. Press seams open.

3 With right sides together, matching notches, tack and stitch the front and back together at the side and shoulder seams. Snip curves and press open.

Sleeves

4 With right sides together, and matching notches, tack and stitch the top and under-sleeve pieces together. Snip and press seams open.

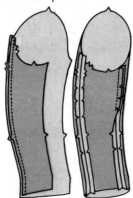

5 Turn the sleeve right side out. Run a small gathering stitch from back sleeve seam to front sleeve seam. Pull up thread gently to ease head of sleeve to fit the coat armhole perfectly.
With right sides together, and matching notches, pin sleeve into armhole. Tack and stitch in place.

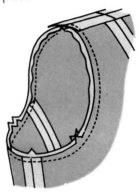

Collar

6 Place collar interfacing to the wrong side of the top collar. Tack all round. Pin, tack and stitch two rows of braid around the long curved edge of top collar, the first row 3cm ($1\frac{1}{8}$ inches) from the raw edge and the second 1.3cm ($\frac{1}{2}$ inch) in from the first.

7 With right sides together tack and stitch the top- and under-collar together around the long curved edge. Trim to 0.6cm ($\frac{1}{4}$ inch), turn through, tack around the edge and press.

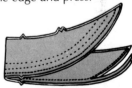

8 Place the collar, with the under-collar to the right side of the coat, matching the notches on the collar to the shoulder seams and front edges.
Tack, easing slightly.

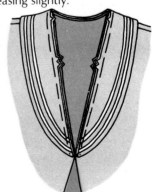

Facings

9 Place interfacing to the wrong side of the two front facings. Tack all round. Tack and stitch the centre-back seam with the right sides together and press open.

10 With right sides together, and matching the notches, tack and stitch the facing to the coat over the collar and from the collar, down each front, to 3.8cm (1½ inches) from bottom edge, then across the facing on the hem line.

Cut away the fabric below the stitching at the hem and trim all round to 0.6cm (¼ inch).

Turn facing to the inside. Tack and press.

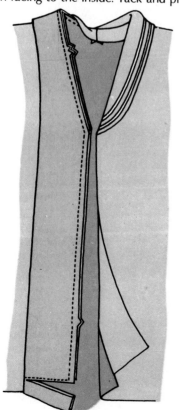

11 Turn up hem of coat, neaten the edges and catch-stitch into place. Press.

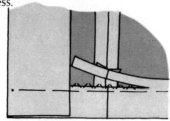

Pockets

12 Tack interfacing to the wrong side of pocket flap and stitch 2 rows of braid on the right side around the curved edge as on collar.

With right sides together, place the pocket flap to the top of the pocket, matching the curved edges. Tack and stitch together at curved edge and short straight edge. Trim, turn and press.

Tack and press the turnings on the remaining edges of the pocket to the wrong side.

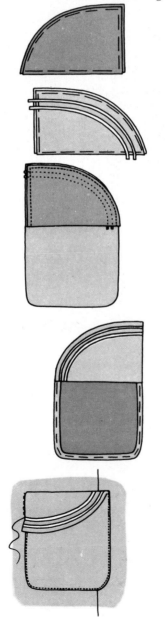

Make a second pocket in the same way. Place the pockets to the coat in the position marked on the pattern, with the long straight edges towards the sides. Tack and machine stitch from the fold line at one side, round the pocket, to the fold line at the other.

Press the pocket flap on to the pocket on the fold line and slip-stitch the short, straight edge on to the pocket.

Buttonholes

13 Make two machine-embroidered buttonholes on the right front where indicated. Sew two buttons on to the left front to correspond and two on the right front. Sew a large press stud behind top button on right front and on left front edge.

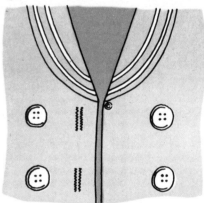

To insert the shoulder pads

14 Put on the coat and insert the pads, pushing them out 1cm (⅜ inch) into sleeve beyond the shoulder seam line. Catch by hand at either side of pads, at armhole seams and at shoulder seams. Catch facing over pads at shoulder seams.

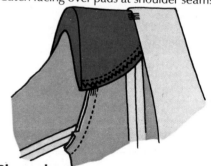

Sleeve hem

15 Adjust sleeve length and turn up hem. Tack and catch-stitch into place.

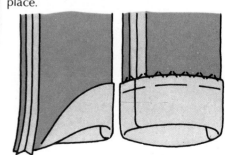

Graph pattern for coat and hat

Each square = 5·08 cms, 2 in. sq.

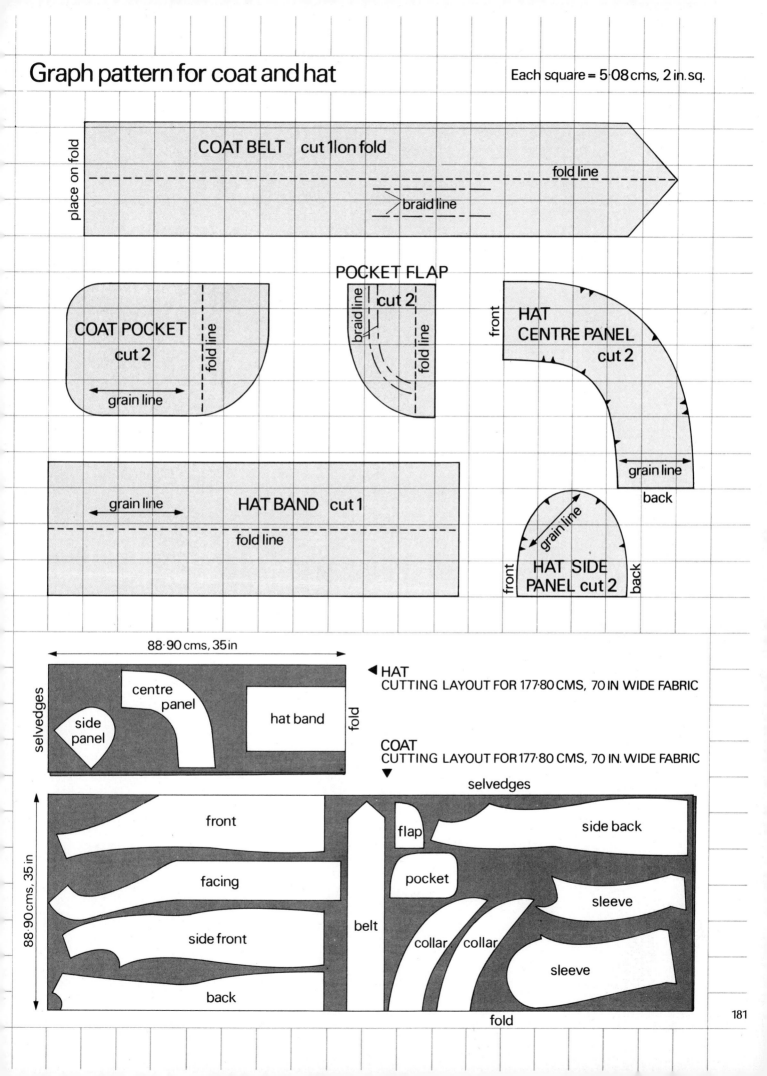

COAT BELT   cut 1 lon fold

place on fold

fold line

braid line

POCKET FLAP

COAT POCKET
cut 2

grain line

fold line

braid line

cut 2

fold line

front

HAT
CENTRE PANEL
cut 2

grain line

back

grain line

HAT BAND   cut 1

fold line

front

grain line

back

HAT SIDE
PANEL cut 2

88·90 cms, 35 in

selvedges

centre
panel

side
panel

hat band

fold

◀ HAT
CUTTING LAYOUT FOR 177·80 CMS, 70 IN WIDE FABRIC

COAT
CUTTING LAYOUT FOR 177·80 CMS, 70 IN. WIDE FABRIC
▼

selvedges

88·90 cms, 35 in

front

facing

side front

back

belt

flap

pocket

collar   collar

side back

sleeve

sleeve

fold

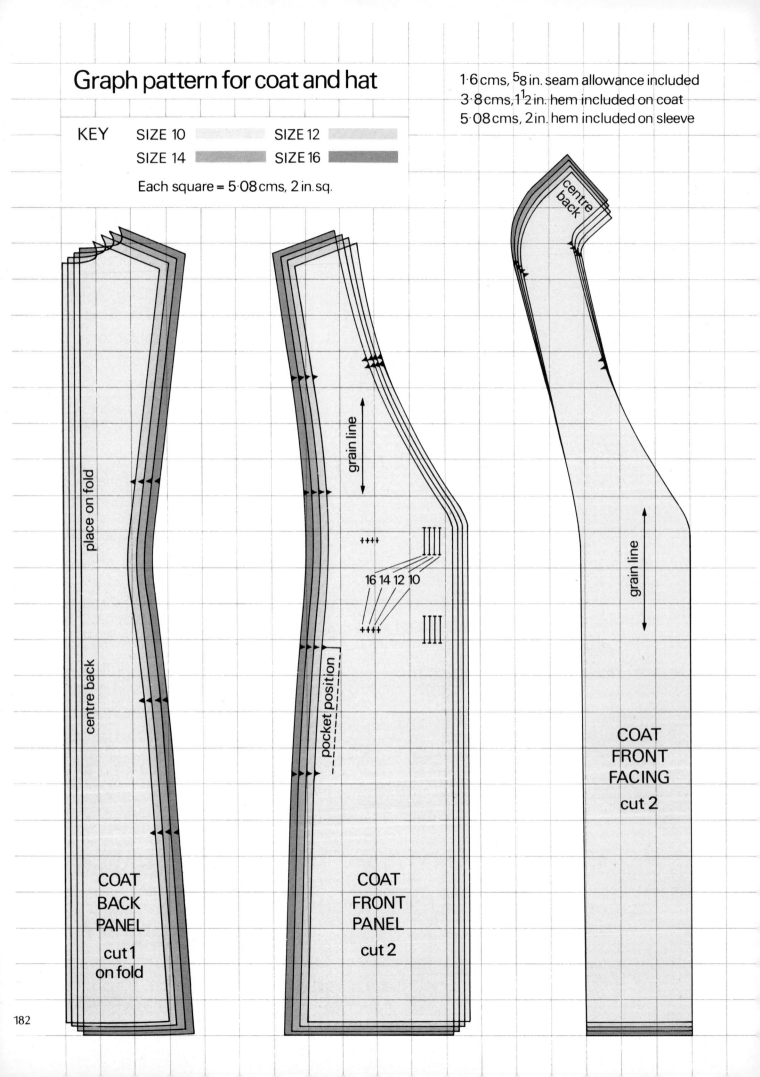

Graph pattern for coat and hat

1·6 cms, $\frac{5}{8}$ in. seam allowance included
3·8 cms, 1$\frac{1}{2}$ in. hem included on coat
5·08 cms, 2 in. hem included on sleeve

KEY   SIZE 10   SIZE 12
       SIZE 14   SIZE 16

Each square = 5·08 cms, 2 in. sq.

centre back

place on fold

centre back

COAT
BACK
PANEL

cut 1
on fold

grain line

16 14 12 10

pocket position

COAT
FRONT
PANEL

cut 2

centre back

grain line

COAT
FRONT
FACING

cut 2

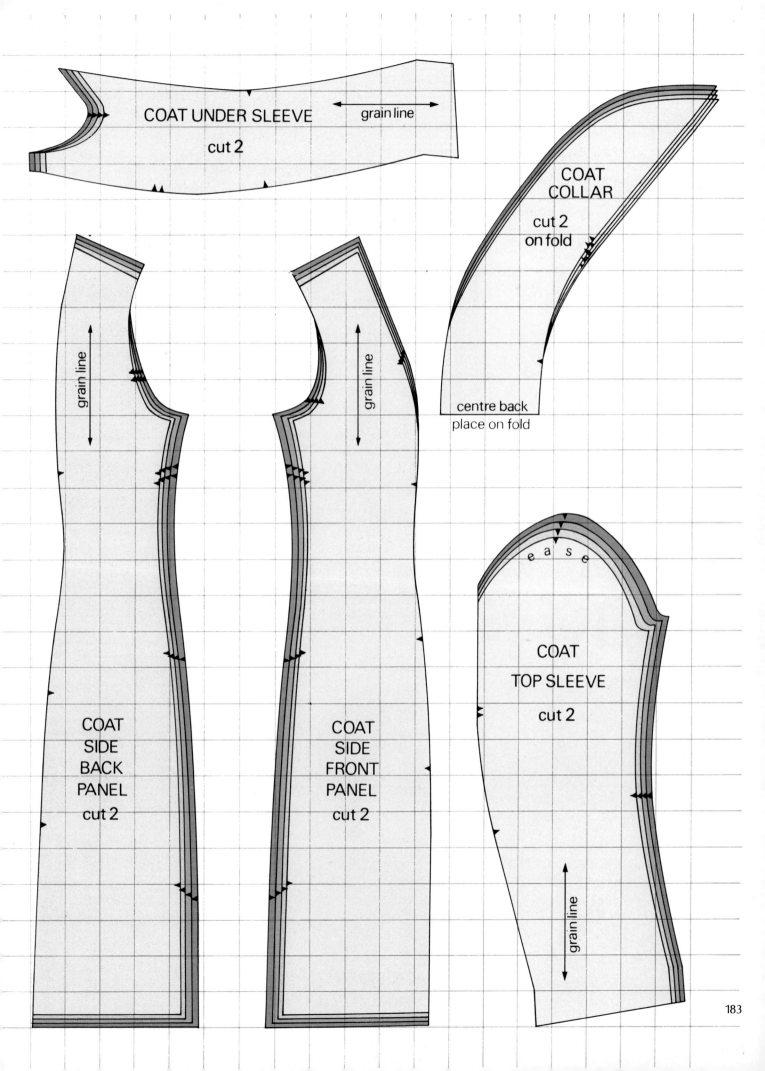

COAT UNDER SLEEVE

cut 2

grain line

COAT
COLLAR

cut 2
on fold

centre back
place on fold

grain line

grain line

e a s e

COAT
TOP SLEEVE

cut 2

grain line

COAT
SIDE
BACK
PANEL
cut 2

COAT
SIDE
FRONT
PANEL
cut 2

183

Belt

16 Place interfacing to one side of belt with one long edge to the fold line, and tack all round. Tack and stitch braid where indicated on the pattern taking the braid right to the end of the belt.
Fold the belt in half lengthways and stitch the diagonal ends and the long edge, leaving an opening through which to turn the belt. Trim seams to 0.6cm ($\frac{1}{4}$ inch), turn through, press and slip-stitch opening.
Make loops at either side of coat, on side seams, and thread belt through.

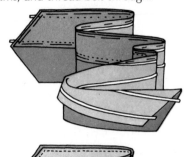

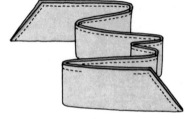

The Hat

Sizes

To fit an average head

Fabric required

30cm ($\frac{1}{3}$ yard) of 1.75 metre (68–70 inch) fabric

You will also need

- ☐ 90cm (1 yard) of braid
- ☐ Matching thread
- ☐ Interfacing
- ☐ Graph paper for making the pattern

Making the pattern

Using graph paper draw each pattern piece to scale. One square = 5.08cm square (2 inch square).
1.6cm ($\frac{5}{8}$ inch) has been allowed on all seams.
Cut out the pattern pieces and mark all notches and the straight grain line.

Cutting out the hat

Following the cutting layout, fold the fabric and place all three pattern pieces as indicated. Make sure the grain line on the pattern lies on the straight grain of the fabric. Pin into place and cut out.
Transfer all markings from the pattern pieces to the fabric.

Making up

1 With right sides together, tack and stitch the two centre panels together. Snip seam and press open.
With right sides together tack and stitch the side panels to the centre panels, matching notches. Trim and snip the seams. Press open.

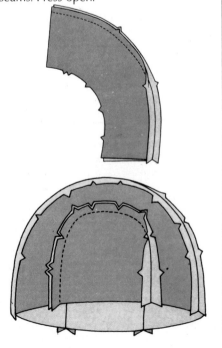

2 Cut a strip of interfacing half the width and the full length of the hatband. Place it to the inside of the band, with one edge to the centre fold line, and tack all round. Catch-stitch along the fold line. Machine stitch braid on to the right side of the hatband 1.3cm ($\frac{1}{2}$ inch) from the fold line.

3 With right sides together, stitch the two short ends of the hatband. Press the seam open.
Fold the hatband in half, with the wrong sides together. Tack the raw edges. Press.

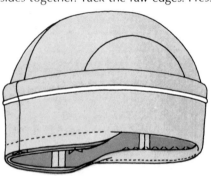

4 Place the hatband to the hat with the unbraided side of the band to the hat and raw edges together. Tack and stitch. Trim and neaten edges together. Press up into the hat and catch-stitch all round.

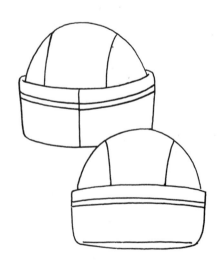

Straight-cut trousers

Slim-line trousers to team with the belted coat and hat.

The Trousers

Sizes
10, 12, 14 and 16

Fabric required
☐ All sizes take 1.40 metres (1½ yards) of 1.75 metre (68–70 inch) fabric

You will also need
☐ Graph paper for making the pattern
☐ Matching thread
☐ 1× 20cm (8 inch) zip fastener
☐ 1× 1.6cm–2cm ($\frac{5}{8}$–$\frac{3}{4}$ inch) diameter button
☐ 23cm ($\frac{1}{4}$ yard) jersey or iron-on interfacing

Making the pattern
Using graph paper and following the colour indicating the size required, draw each pattern piece to scale. One square = a 5.08cm square (2 inch square).
1.6cm ($\frac{5}{8}$ inch) has been allowed on all seams and 5cm (2 inches) for the trouser leg hems.
Cut out the pattern pieces and mark all darts, notches and the straight grain lines.

Cutting out the trousers
Following the cutting layout, fold the fabric and place the three pattern pieces as indicated. Take care that the grain line on the pattern lies on the straight grain of the fabric. Pin into place and cut out. Transfer all markings from the pattern pieces to the fabric.

Making up

1 With right sides together, tack and stitch a dart on each back and front trouser piece. Press darts towards centre.

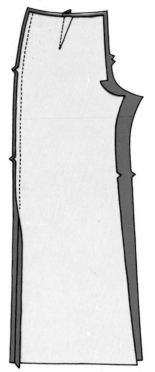

2 With right sides together, and matching notches, tack and stitch the front trouser to the back trouser on the side seams. Neaten and press seams open.

3 On the right side of the garment, pin braid down the sides to cover the seams. Tack and machine stitch.

4 With right sides together, and matching notches, tack and stitch the front trouser to the back trouser on the inside leg. Neaten and press seams open. Turn one leg through.

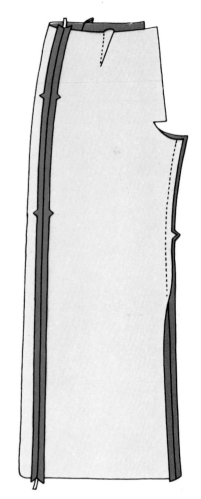

5 With right sides together, slip one leg inside the other, and matching notches and crotch seam, stitch from centre-back waist to point of zip insertion. Clip curves and press seam open.

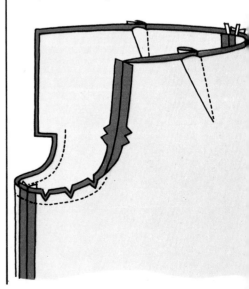

Graph pattern for trousers

KEY

SIZE 10		SIZE 12	
SIZE 14		SIZE 16	

1·6 cms, $\frac{5}{8}$ in. seam allowance included

Each square = 5·08 cms, 2 in. sq.

CUTTING LAYOUT FOR 177·80 CMS, 70 IN. WIDE FABRIC

5·08 cms, 2 in. hem included

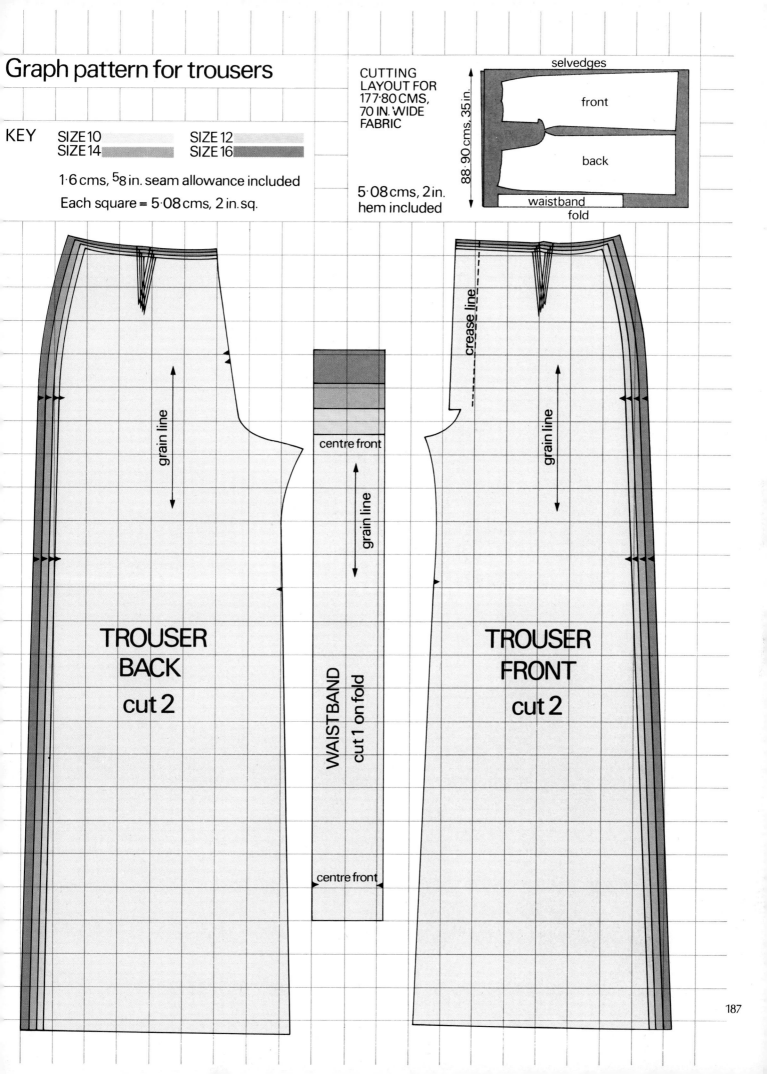

selvedges

front

back

88·90 cms, 35 in.

waistband

fold

TROUSER BACK
cut 2

grain line

WAISTBAND
cut 1 on fold

centre front

grain line

centre front

crease line

TROUSER FRONT
cut 2

grain line

187

6 Inserting the zip. Press the facings on the centre-front opening to the inside along the fold line, clip to stitch line and tack.

Place the zip to the inside and pin into place, overlapping the right side over the left about 0.3cm (⅛ inch). Tack firmly over the zip. Then machine stitch the left side close to the fold and the right side 2.54cm (1 inch) from the fold line, stitching across to the centre-front seam at the bottom of the zip in a curve.

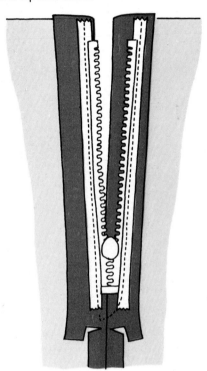

7 Waistband. Cut a piece of interfacing 5.0cm (2 inches) wide and the full length of the waistband. Place to the inside of the waistband with one edge of the interfacing to the centre fold. Tack into place.

With right sides together, fold the waistband in half lengthways and stitch the ends and 3.8cm (1½ inches) along the edge at one end. Trim to 0.6cm (¼ inch) and turn to the right side. Press.

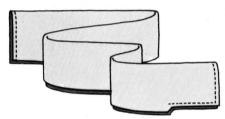

8 With right sides together, and making sure that the 3.8cm (1½ inch) buttonhole extension is on the right front of the trousers and that the other end is level with the opening on the left, place one edge of the waistband to the top of the trousers. Tack and stitch. Press turnings up on to the waistband.

Turn the seam allowance on the other edge of the waistband to the inside and slip-stitch along the stitch line. Press.

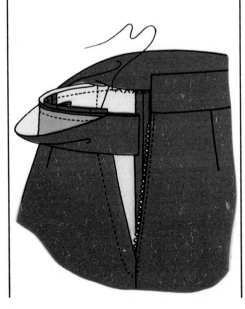

9 Make a buttonhole on the waistband extension and sew the button on to the other side to correspond.

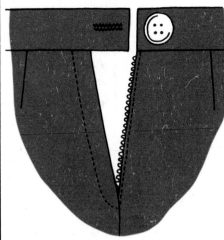

10 Turn the 5cm (2 inch) hem allowance to the inside of trouser legs. Tack and catch-stitch into place. Press.

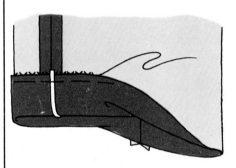

back view

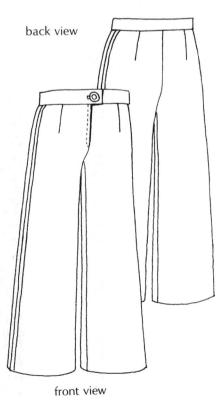

front view

Fitted jerkin

**Stitched and seamed
to match the skirt**

Sizes
10, 12, 14 and 16

Fabric required
All sizes take 0.85 square metre (*9 square feet*) of suede
Note Take the pattern pieces along when purchasing suede

You will also need
☐ Graph paper for making the pattern
☐ Matching thread
☐ Contrasting thread
☐ Suitable glue for leather
☐ 4 gripper snap fasteners

Making the pattern
Using graph paper and following the colour indicating the size required draw each pattern piece to scale. One square = 2.54cm square (*1 inch square*). An allowance of 1.3cm (*½ inch*) has been made on all seams. Cut out the pattern pieces and mark dots and notches.

Cutting out the jerkin
Lay the skins out flat with right sides facing down. Position the pattern pieces allowing enough room to reverse the back, back facing and waistband pieces and to cut two (reversing the pieces) of the side back, side front and front pieces. It is not necessary to find the straight grain but pieces should lie with the top edge nearest the neck edge of the skin and avoiding any weak areas in the skins. Draw round the pattern pieces and cut out.
Transfer all markings from the pattern pieces to the skins with chalk, on the wrong side.

Making up
Note Decorative stitching is worked throughout on this garment. If a machine which works decorative stitching is not available top stitching can be worked instead.

1 With notches matching place the front panels over the side front panels overlapping by 2.5cm (1 inch) and glue. Work stitching down the seams. Overlap the back panel on to the side back panels and stitch in the same way.

■ right side ■ wrong side

2 With notches matching place the fronts to the back, overlapping by 2.5cm (1 inch). Glue and stitch at the side and shoulder seams.

Facings

3 Using the facing pattern pieces, cut out in canvas and glue on to the wrong side of the facings, and waistband. Glue

the back neck facing to the back and the left front facing to the front so that the facings overlap at the shoulder seam.

4 Glue the outside edge of the right front facing only. Then stitch all around the outside edge of the facings, leaving the inside edge free.

5 Insert gripper snap fasteners, where indicated, under the facing on the right front. Then lay the facing flat all around and stitch on the inside edge.

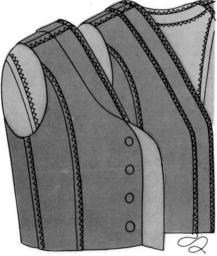

6 Glue the waistband into position and stitch. Insert the remaining halves of

the fasteners, where indicated, on the left front.

7 Glue and stitch the sleeve facings on in the same way starting at the back underarm and working round so that the front overlaps the back.

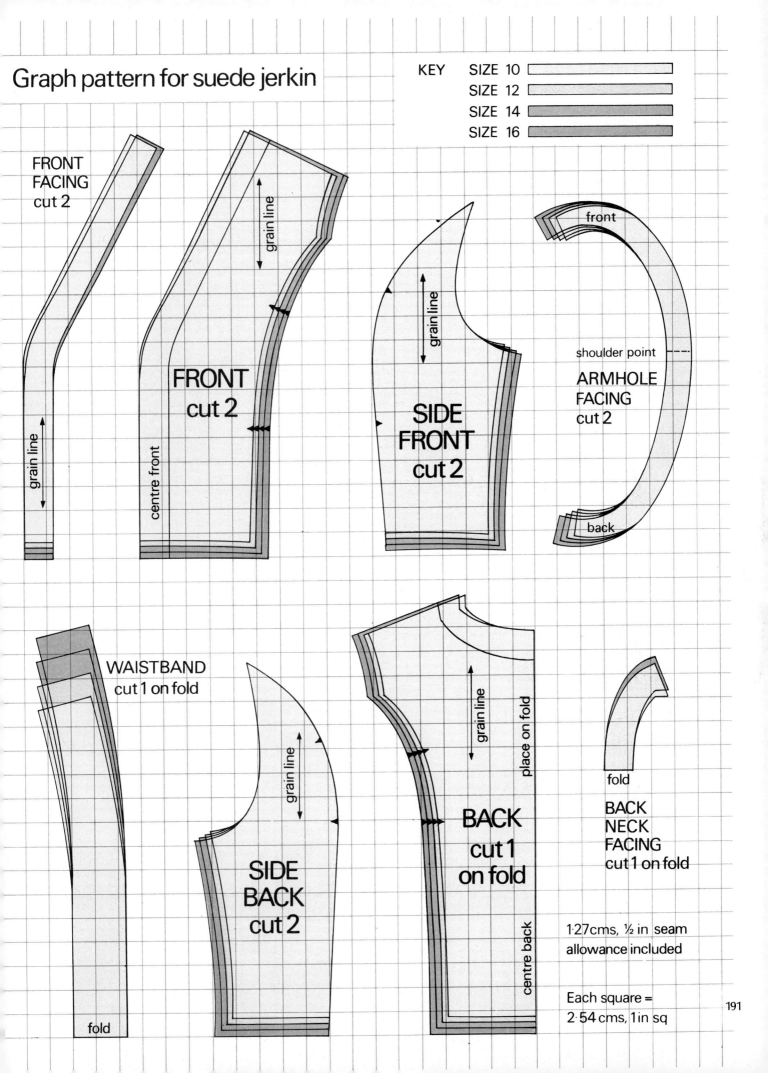

Graph pattern for suede jerkin

KEY
SIZE 10
SIZE 12
SIZE 14
SIZE 16

FRONT
FACING
cut 2

grain line

grain line

FRONT
cut 2

centre front

grain line

SIDE
FRONT
cut 2

front

shoulder point

ARMHOLE
FACING
cut 2

back

WAISTBAND
cut 1 on fold

grain line

grain line

place on fold

BACK
cut 1
on fold

fold

BACK
NECK
FACING
cut 1 on fold

SIDE
BACK
cut 2

centre back

fold

1·27cms, ½ in seam
allowance included

Each square =
2·54 cms, 1 in sq

191

Panelled skirt

The seams are finished with decorative stitching.

Sizes
10, 12, 14 and 16

Fabric required
All sizes take approximately 1.49 square metres (*16 square feet*) of suede
Note Take pattern pieces along when purchasing suede.

You will also need
☐ Graph paper for making the pattern
☐ Matching thread
☐ Contrasting thread
☐ 2 hooks and bars
☐ 1 × 20cm (*8 inch*) zip
☐ Glue suitable for leather (check the label before buying)
☐ 0.15 metre ($\frac{1}{8}$ *yard*) of 91cm (*36 inch*) wide heavy-weight interfacing
☐ Light-weight hammer

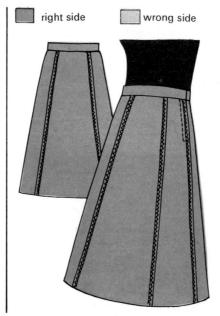

right side   wrong side

Making the pattern
Using graph paper and following the colour indicating the size required draw each pattern piece to scale. One square = 2.54 cm square (*1 inch square*).
An allowance of 1.3cm ($\frac{1}{2}$ *inch*) has been made on all seams. There is no allowance for the hem as it is trimmed to the required length.
Cut out the pattern pieces and mark all notches and dots.

Cutting out the skirt
Check the paper pattern for length before cutting out the skirt. Lay the skins out flat with the right sides facing down. Lay on the pattern pieces placing the waistband, side front and side back pieces twice reversing them once. Draw round the pattern pieces with chalk. It is not necessary to find the straight grain but pattern pieces should lie with the top edge to the top of the skin avoiding any weak areas in the skins. Cut out the pieces and transfer all markings.
Cut one waistband section in interfacing.

Making up
Note If a machine which works decorative stitching is not available top stitching can be worked instead of decorative stitching.

1 Snip through seam allowance to dot on left side back skirt only. Fold the seam allowance above dot under to wrong side and stick it to the skirt using glue. Hammer firmly in position from the wrong side.

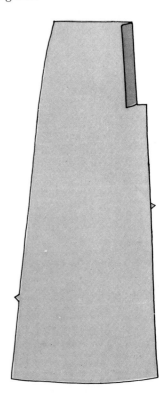

2 Glue the right side of the zip to the wrong side of the left side back skirt so that the centre of the zip teeth are in line with the side seam line. Machine stitch with a straight stitch 0.6cm ($\frac{1}{4}$ *inch*) from the fold.

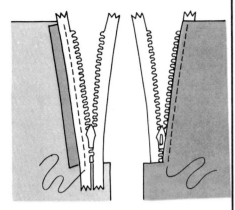

3 Cut a strip of suede 2.5cm (*1 inch*) wide and 24cm (*9$\frac{1}{2}$ inches*) long and glue to the left side front skirt matching side edges to form a facing. From the right side using contrasting thread work decorative stitching 1cm ($\frac{3}{8}$ *inch*) in from the edge starting at base of opening and finishing at waist edge.

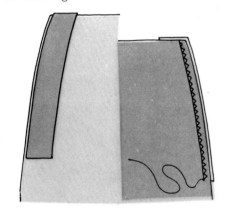

4 Place left side front panel over left side back panel overlapping by 1.3cm ($\frac{1}{2}$ *inch*) and glue the remaining side of the zip in position to the facing. Using a straight stitch sew the zip to the left side front skirt and facing 2cm ($\frac{3}{4}$ *inch*) from the edge.

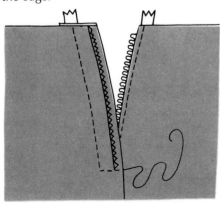

5 Glue the remaining side seam allowance of the left side front over the left side back overlapping by 2.5cm (*1 inch*) matching notches and work decorative stitching 1cm ($\frac{3}{8}$ *inch*) from the edge on the right side of the side front skirt starting from the base of the opening.

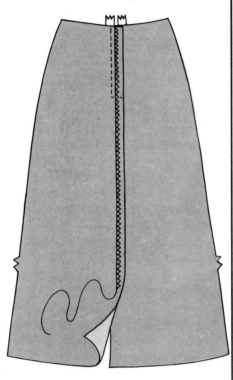

6 Overlapping the seams in the same way, glue and stitch (using decorative stitching) the right side front skirt to the right side back skirt, the front skirt to the left and right side fronts and the back skirt to the left and right side backs matching all notches.

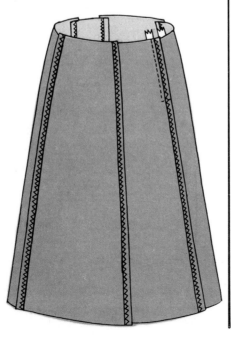

7 Glue the interfacing on to the wrong side of one waistband section. With right sides together stitch the short ends, the top edge and along the extension as far as the dot. Trim seam, clip into corners and turn through to the right side. Hammer firmly.

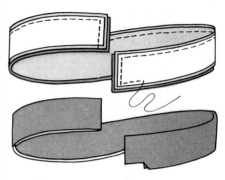

8 With right sides together and matching centre-front and centre-back stitch the edge of the interfaced waistband section to the skirt so that the extension comes on the skirt back. Trim the turnings, glue them to the waistband and hammer firmly.

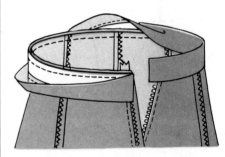

9 Clip the seam allowance on the waistband facing level with the edge of the zip tape. Turn the seam allowance under on back extension to dot and on the front from end of band to clip and slip-stitch.

10 Apply glue to remaining skirt waist seam allowance and press the waistband facing firmly into position. Work a row of straight stitching through the skirt and the waistband facing from the right side as close to the waistband as possible.

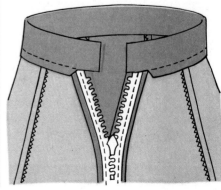

11 Either trim hem to required length fastening off seam thread ends on the wrong side, or turn the hem under to the wrong side, glue to the skirt and hammer firmly in position.

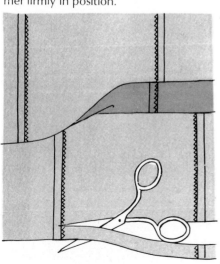

12 Sew two hooks on wrong side of front waistband opening and two bars on the right side of the back waistband to correspond.

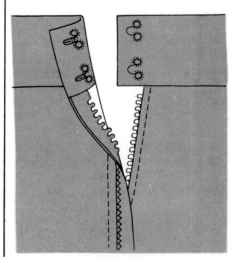

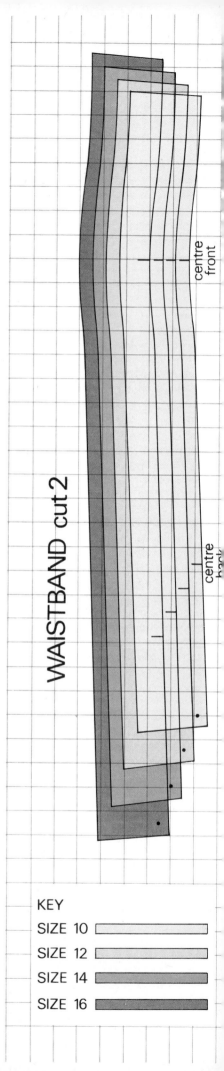

WAISTBAND cut 2

centre front

centre back

KEY

SIZE 10

SIZE 12

SIZE 14

SIZE 16

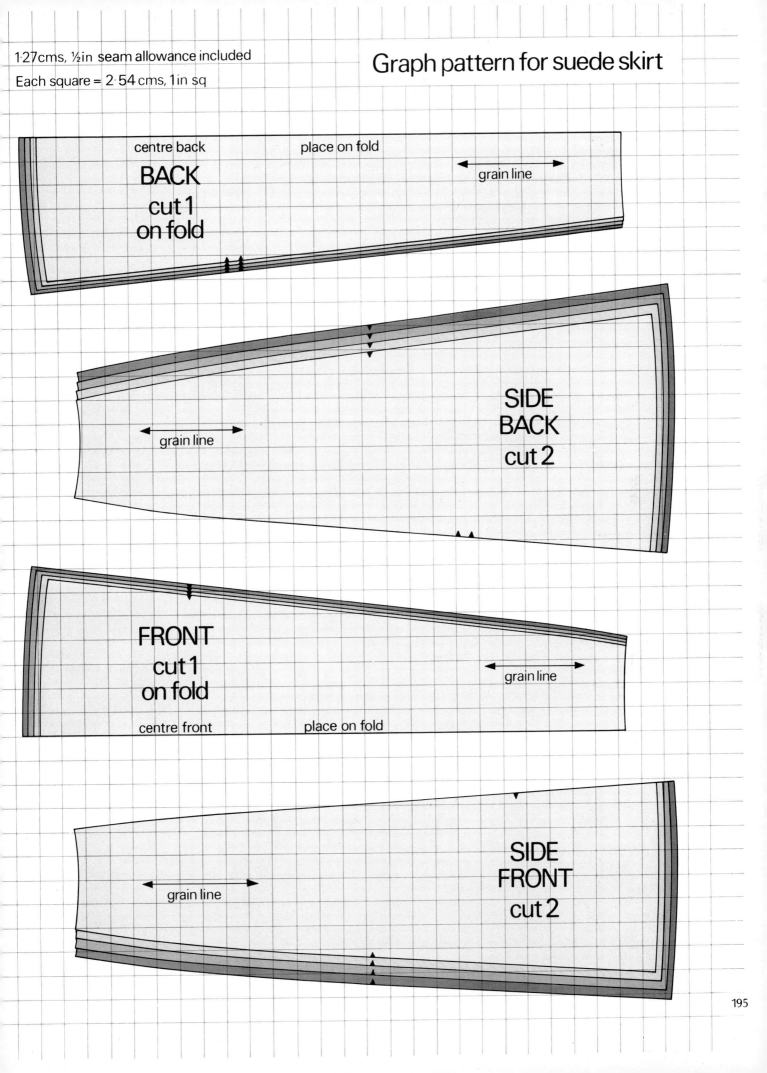

1·27cms, ½in seam allowance included

Each square = 2·54 cms, 1in sq

Graph pattern for suede skirt

centre back   place on fold

grain line

BACK
cut 1
on fold

grain line

SIDE
BACK
cut 2

FRONT
cut 1
on fold

grain line

centre front   place on fold

grain line

SIDE
FRONT
cut 2

Top-stitched jacket

A short, waisted style with attractive yoke detail.

Sizes

10, 12, 14 and 16

Fabric required

All sizes take approximately 2.32 square metres (*25 square feet*) of suede

Note Take pattern pieces along when purchasing suede

You will also need

☐ Graph paper for making the pattern
☐ Matching thread
☐ 7 gripper snap fasteners
☐ Canvas interfacing for the waistband, collar and centre-front straps
☐ Glue suitable for leather
☐ Light-weight hammer

Making the pattern

Using graph paper and following the colour indicating the size required draw each pattern piece to scale. One square = 2.54cm square (*1 inch square*).

An allowance of 1.27cm (*½ inch*) has been made on all seams. Cut out the pattern pieces and mark all dots and notches.

Cutting out the jacket

Lay the skins out flat with right sides facing down. Place the waistband and back yoke pieces on to the skins and chalk around them. Reverse both pieces from the centre-back and chalk again. Cut out, then cut another waistband. Cut all other pieces twice by reversing them once. It is not necessary to find the straight grain, but pattern pieces should lie with the top edge to the neck of the skin, avoiding any weak areas.

After cutting out, transfer all markings from the pattern pieces to the skins. Cut one waistband, one collar and two front straps in interfacing.

Making up

1 With right sides together and matching notches tack and stitch the fronts

right side	wrong side

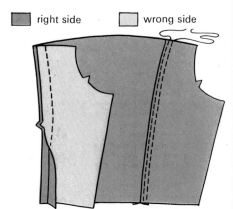

to the side fronts and the back to the side backs. Gently hammer open all turnings and glue flat. From the right side work two rows of top-stitching 0.6cm (*¼ inch*) apart close to the seam.

2 With right sides together and matching notches tack and stitch the front yokes to the front and back yoke to the back. Gently hammer open all turnings and glue flat. From the right side work two rows of top-stitching above each seam line 0.6cm (*¼ inch*) apart.

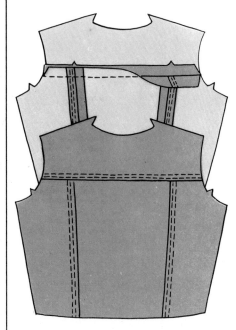

3 With right sides together and matching notches tack and stitch the fronts to the back at the side and shoulder seams. Hammer open turnings and glue.

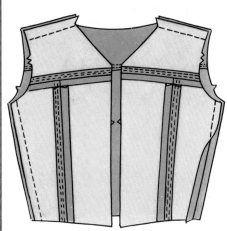

4 Glue canvas on to the wrong side of both front straps. With right sides together and matching notches tack and

stitch the front straps to the centre-fronts. Hammer open turnings and glue.

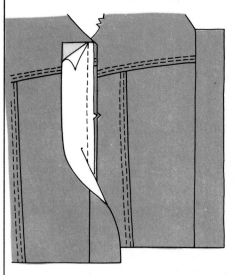

5 With right sides together stitch facings at centre-back seam. Hammer open turnings.

Collar

6 Glue interfacing on to the wrong side of one collar piece. With right sides together stitch the two collar pieces together around the outside edge leaving the neck edge open. Trim turnings, turn through and hammer all around stitched edges. Work two rows of top-stitching 0.6cm (*¼ inch*) apart close to the stitched edges.

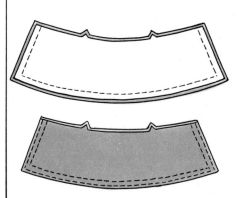

Graph pattern for suede jacket

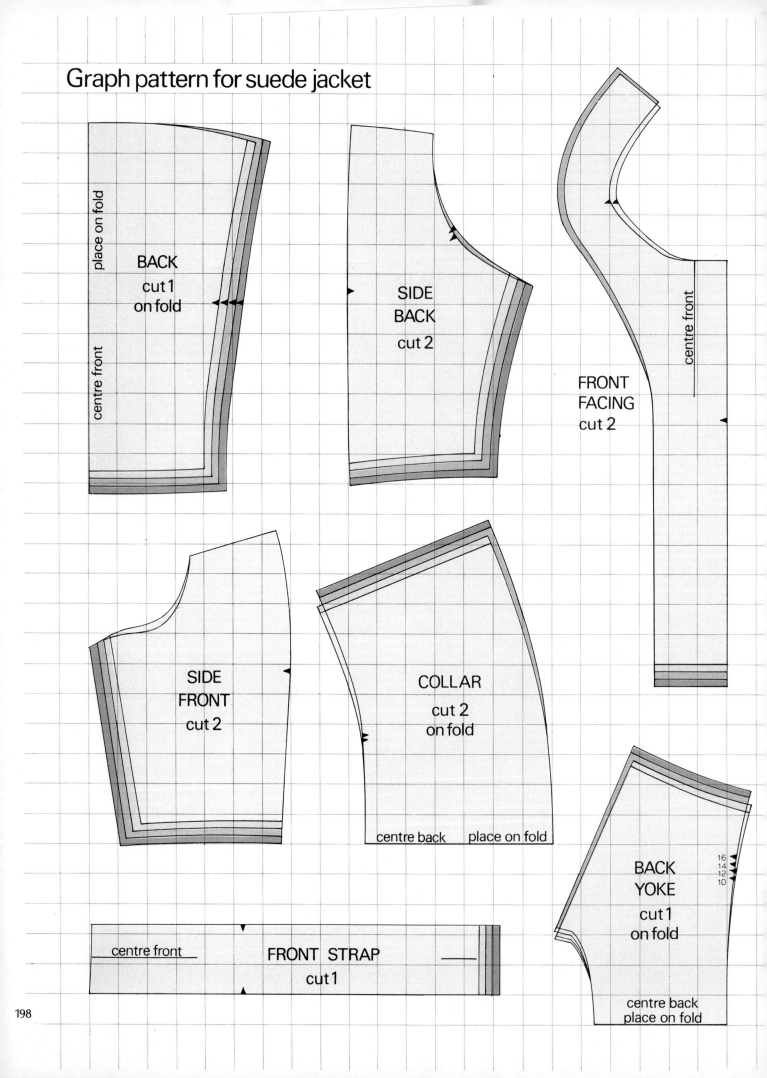

place on fold

centre front

BACK
cut 1
on fold

SIDE BACK
cut 2

FRONT FACING
cut 2

centre front

SIDE FRONT
cut 2

COLLAR
cut 2
on fold

centre back   place on fold

BACK YOKE
cut 1
on fold

16
14
12
10

centre back
place on fold

centre front   **FRONT STRAP**
cut 1

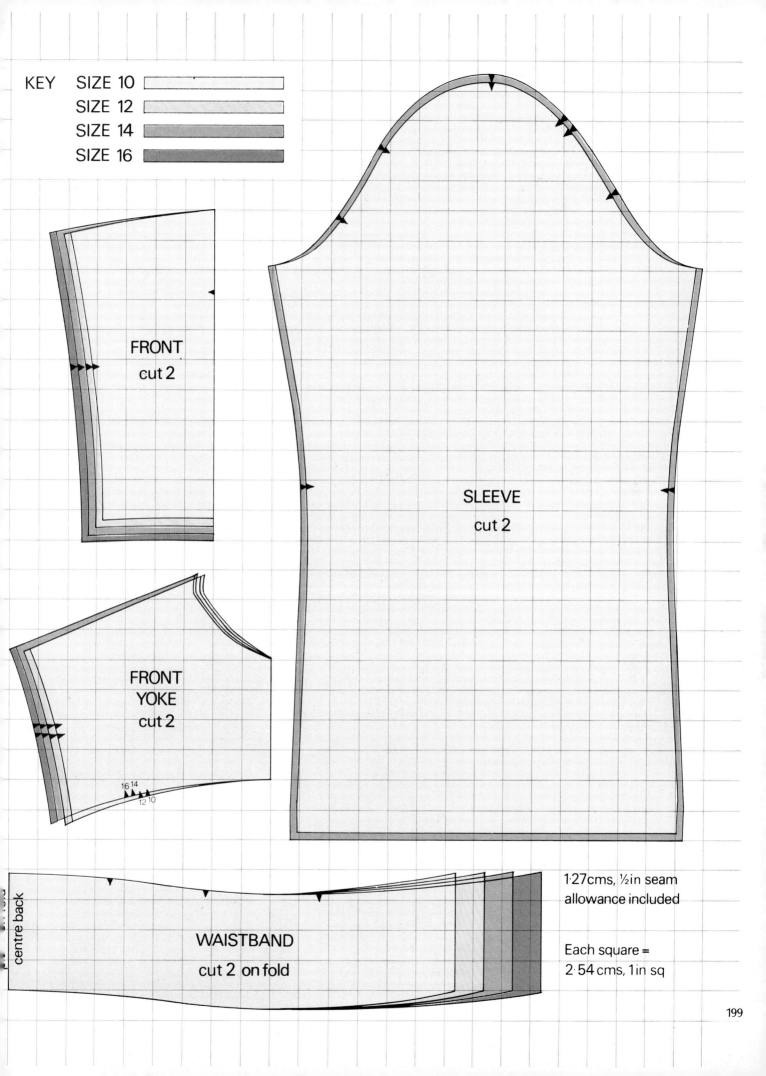

KEY   SIZE 10
       SIZE 12
       SIZE 14
       SIZE 16

FRONT
cut 2

FRONT
YOKE
cut 2

16 14
12 10

SLEEVE
cut 2

centre back

WAISTBAND

cut 2 on fold

1·27cms, ½in seam
allowance included

Each square =
2·54cms, 1in sq

199

7 Tack collar to neck edge with notches to shoulder seams and interfaced side uppermost. With right sides together and matching notches tack the facing to the neck edge and centre-fronts with the collar in between. Stitch through all thicknesses. Trim and layer turnings.

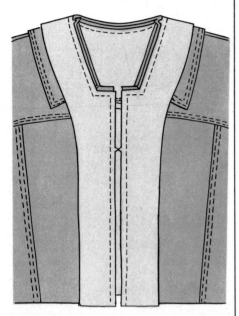

8 Turn facing on to the wrong side. Work two rows of top-stitching 0.6cm ($\frac{1}{4}$ inch) apart down both sides of each centre-front strap.
Work one row of stitching along the back neck 1.6cm ($\frac{5}{8}$ inch) below the seam line to hold the facing flat.

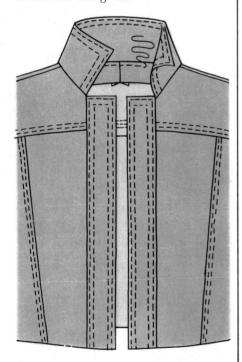

9 Glue canvas on to the wrong side of one waistband. With right sides together and matching notches, tack and

stitch the two waistbands together leaving one long edge open. Trim turnings and turn through.

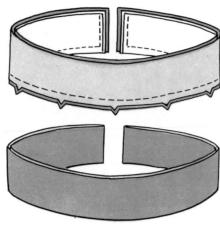

10 With right sides together and raw edges facing the same way tack and stitch the interfaced waistband to the lower edge of the jacket. Hammer turnings open.

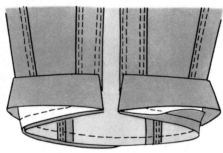

11 Turn down the waistband. Lay the other side of the waistband flat. On the wrong side work two rows of top-stitching 0.6cm ($\frac{1}{4}$ inch) apart through all thicknesses just below the seam line and all around the edges of the waistband.

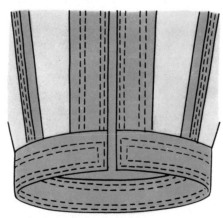

Sleeves

12 With right sides together tack and stitch the underarm seams. Gently

hammer turnings open. Work a double gathering thread between the notches on the sleeve head.

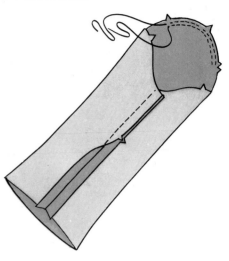

13 With right sides together and matching notches pin the sleeve into the armhole. Pull up the gathering threads and ease the fullness so that no tucks show on the right side. Tack and stitch. Trim turnings to 0.6cm ($\frac{1}{4}$ inch). Try on the jacket and turn up the lower sleeve edges to the required length and glue. Insert the press studs down centre-front as indicated with the top of stud on the right strap and the bottom of stud on the left strap.

Easy dress

Easy fitting, over a shirt
or on its own.

Sizes

10, 12, 14 and 16

Fabric required

Approximately 2.32 square metres (25 square feet) of suede in skins as large as possible

You will also need

- [ ] Graph paper for making the pattern
- [ ] Matching thread
- [ ] Glue suitable for leather
- [ ] 7 buttons 1cm ($\frac{3}{8}$ inch) wide
- [ ] 5 press studs
- [ ] 1 buckle
- [ ] Strip of canvas 91cm × 10cm (36 inches × 4 inches)
- [ ] Light-weight hammer

Making the pattern

Using graph paper and following the colour indicating the size required draw each pattern piece to scale. One square = 2.54cm square (1 inch square). An allowance of 1.3cm ($\frac{1}{2}$ inch) has been made on all seams. Cut out the pattern pieces and mark all darts, dots, notches and fold lines.

Cutting out the dress

Lay the skins flat with right side down. Position the pattern pieces allowing enough room to reverse them but avoiding any weak areas in the skins. The neck binding is reversed at the centre-back to avoid a join. Secure the pattern pieces with sticky tape and draw around with chalk marking in all darts, dots and notches. Reverse the pieces and cut out using sharp shears.

Making up

Note Never use pins on suede as they leave marks. Hold the pieces together with sticky tape.

1 With right sides together stitch the darts on the back yoke. Slit open and glue turnings down on the wrong side. Hammer gently. With right sides together and matching notches stitch centre-back seam on bodice. Glue and hammer turnings gently. Work a gathering thread along the top edge of the bodice.

■ right side		□ wrong side

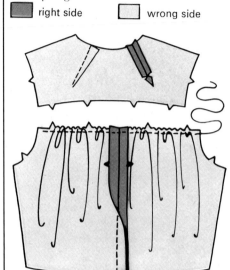

2 With right sides together and matching notches tape the back yoke to the back bodice. Pull up gathering thread and distribute gathers evenly. Stitch. Trim yoke turning and glue bodice turning on to yoke. Hammer gently. With right sides together and matching notches stitch the front bodices to the front yokes in the same way.

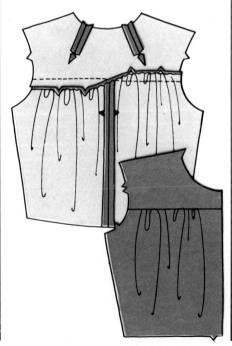

Skirt

3 With right sides together and matching notches stitch the centre-front seam on the skirt. Glue turnings open and hammer gently. Repeat with centre-back seam.

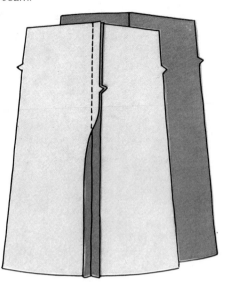

4 With right sides together and matching notches stitch front bodice to front skirt and back bodice to back skirt. Open turnings and glue down.

5 With right sides together stitch the back and front together at the side and shoulder seams. Glue turnings open and hammer gently.

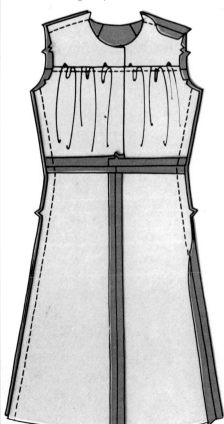

6 Glue one centre-front binding on to the wrong side of the left bodice down the centre-front edge. Insert press studs where indicated on left and right fronts, except for the top left half.

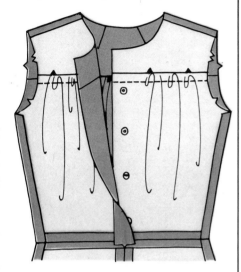

7 Glue a strip of canvas on to the wrong side of the other centre-front binding. Sew the buttons on to the right side of the binding where indicated. Glue the binding on to the centre-front edge of the right bodice. Top-stitch all around the binding 0.3cm ($\frac{1}{8}$ inch) from the edge. Glue and top-stitch neck binding on to the neck edge in the same way. Insert remaining half of top press stud through all thicknesses.

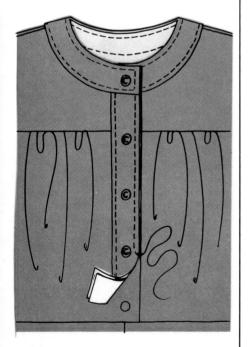

Sleeves

8 With right sides together and matching notches stitch the underarm seam. Glue turnings open and hammer gently. Attach sleeve binding to the right side of the lower sleeve edge so that the ends overlap in the centre with the front over the back. Glue and top-stitch. Sew on buttons as indicated.

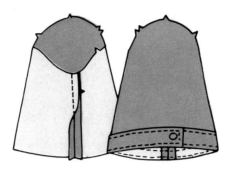

9 Work a gathering thread around the head of the sleeve between notches. With right sides together and matching notches tack the sleeve into the armhole easing the fullness over the head of the sleeve. Stitch.

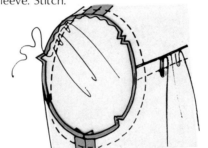

Belt

10 Glue a strip of canvas to the wrong side of one belt piece. With wrong sides together glue the belt pieces together and top-stitch all around 0.3cm ($\frac{1}{8}$ inch) from the edge. Thread the short narrow end of the belt through the buckle, fold back and work four large stitches through all thicknesses. Try on the dress and check the length. Cut off any excess hem and leave a raw edge. Turn up hem and glue into place.

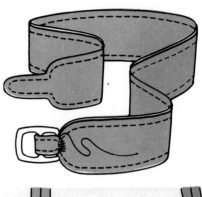

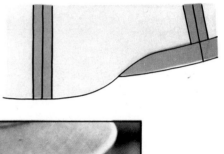

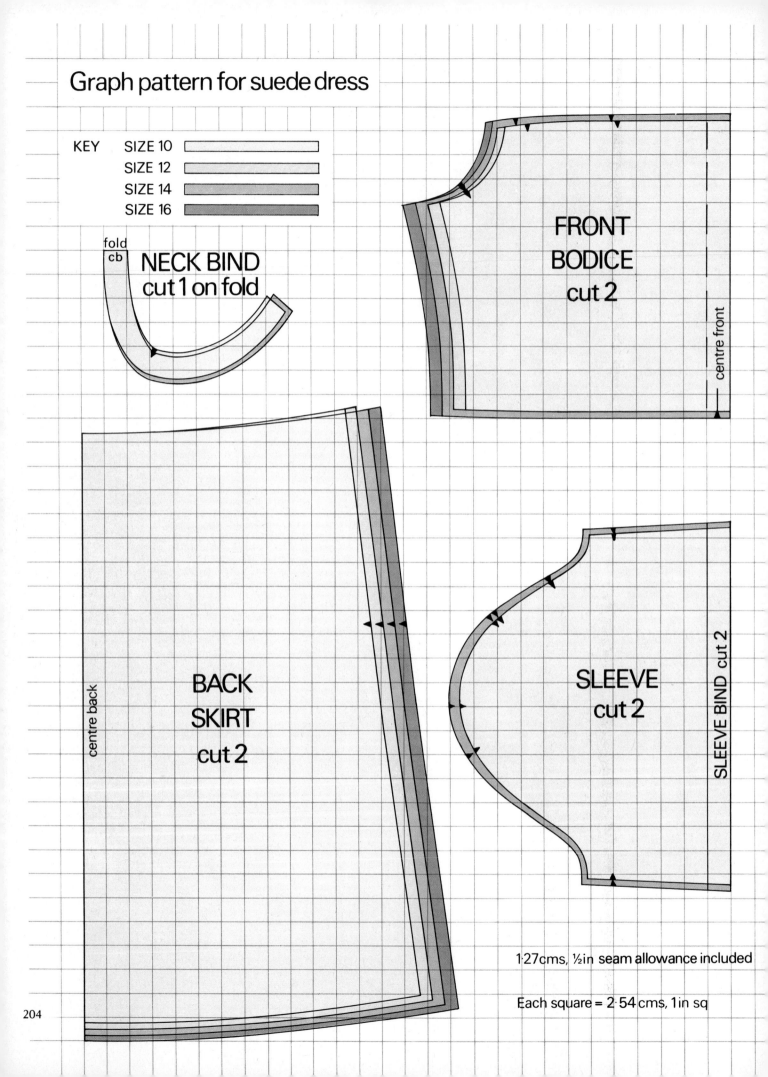

Graph pattern for suede dress

KEY   SIZE 10
       SIZE 12
       SIZE 14
       SIZE 16

fold
cb
NECK BIND
cut 1 on fold

FRONT BODICE
cut 2

centre front

BACK SKIRT
cut 2

centre back

SLEEVE
cut 2

SLEEVE BIND cut 2

1·27cms, ½in seam allowance included

Each square = 2·54 cms, 1in sq

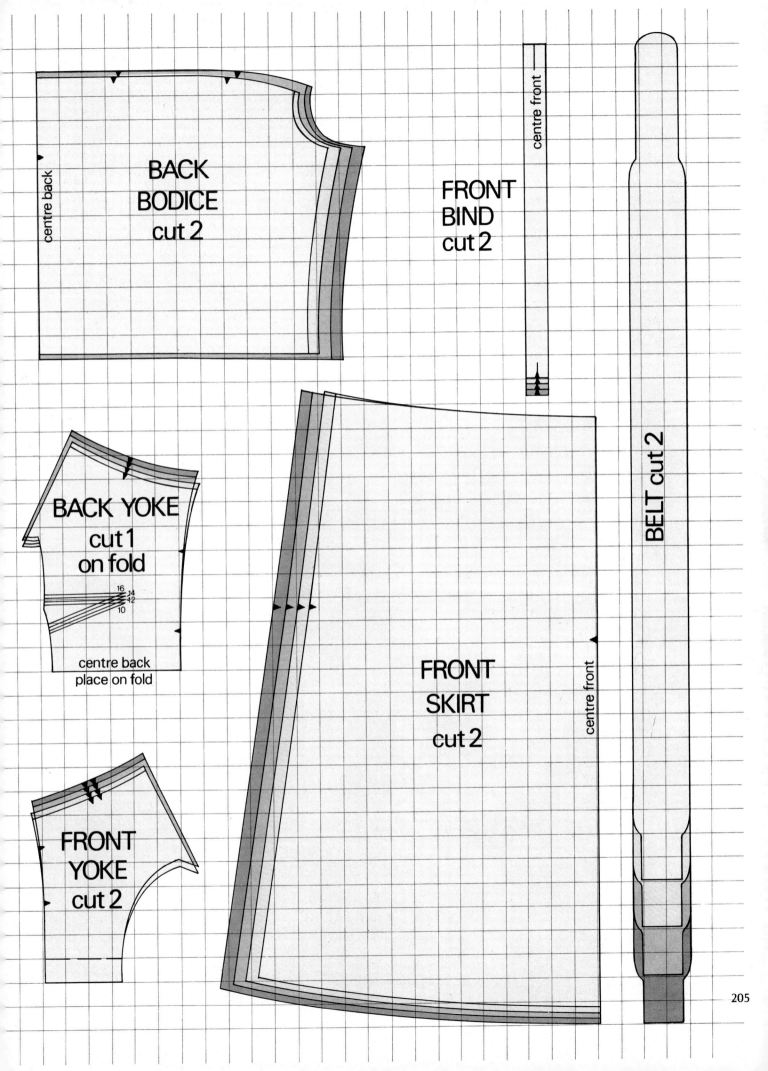

BACK
BODICE
cut 2

centre back

FRONT
BIND
cut 2

centre front

BELT cut 2

BACK YOKE
cut 1
on fold

16 14
12
10

centre back
place on fold

FRONT SKIRT
cut 2

centre front

FRONT
YOKE
cut 2

Wedding dress

A dream of a dress with enchanting cape top, high shirred neckline and waist over an eight panelled skirt with deep frilled hem.

Sizes

10, 12, 14 and 16

Fabric required

12.40 metres (13½ yards) of 91cm (36 inch) wide cotton voile. Other suitable fabrics are crepe de chine, fine silk or any lightweight soft fabric which drapes well. Stiff fabrics such as brocade or satin would be unsuitable.

Yardage suitable for all sizes.

You will also need

☐ Graph paper for making the pattern
☐ Matching thread
☐ Shirring elastic
☐ 2 × 1cm (⅜ inch) diameter buttons
☐ 1 × 20cm (8 inch) zip
☐ 1 hook and eye
☐ Light-weight interfacing 4.5cm × 91cm (1¾ inches × 36 inches)

Making the pattern

Using graph paper and following the colour indicating the size required draw each pattern piece to scale. One square = 5.08 cm square (2 inch square). An allowance of 1.6cm (⅝ inch) has been made on all seams, 1cm (⅜ inch) on the neck and lower sleeve edges, and 0.6cm (¼ inch) on the lower frill and blouse edges. Cut out the pieces and mark all dots, notches, shirring lines and the straight grain line.

Cutting out the dress

Cut a 5.95 metre (6½ yard) length of fabric from the main piece. Following the cutting layout, lay the fabric flat and place the skirt pattern piece eight times as indicated. Cut another length of fabric 3.65 metres (4 yards) long and following the cutting layout place all the other pattern pieces as indicated. Take care that the grain line on the pattern lies on the straight grain of the fabric. Pin into place and cut out.

Transfer all markings from the pattern pieces to the fabric.

The remaining fabric is for the skirt frill.

Making up
Top

1 With right sides together and matching notches tack and stitch the back to the front at one side seam only. Trim turnings to 0.6cm (¼ inch) and neaten together. Alternatively a French seam can be worked on straight seams to re-enforce them and prevent fraying.

Turn a double hem of 0.6cm (¼ inch) on to the wrong side around the lower edge of the top and stitch down with a zig-zag stitch. Press. Thread the spool with shirring elastic and from the right side, work six rows of shirring on and in between the

lines indicated so that they are 1.3cm (½ inch) apart.

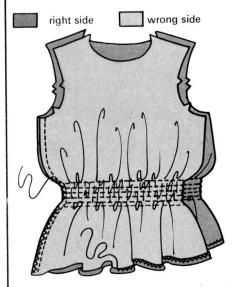

■ right side   ▫ wrong side

2 With right sides together tack and stitch the shoulder darts on the back and press towards the centre-back. With right sides together and matching notches tack and stitch the remaining side seam and shoulder seams. Trim turnings to 0.6 cm (¼ inch) and neaten together. Press.

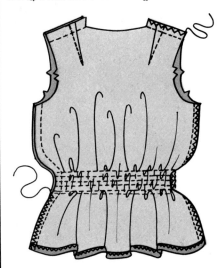

Shoulder cape

3 With right sides together tack and stitch the two cape pieces together across the straight ends. Trim turnings and neaten together. Turn over a narrow hem of 0.6cm (¼ inch) on the outside edge and tack. Then work zig-zag stitch all around. Press.

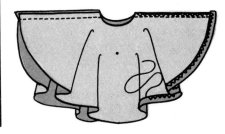

With wrong side of cape to right side of top tack the cape to the top around the neck edge. Tack down either side of the centre-back opening through both thicknesses tapering to the dot and cut the fabric almost to the dot.

Collar

4 Make a double turning of 1cm (⅜ inch) on the top edge of the collar and machine stitch down. Press. Work seven rows of shirring on and in between the two lines indicated so that the rows are 1cm (⅜ inch) apart.

5 With right sides together tack and stitch the collar to the neck edge taking 1.6cm (⅝ inch) turning. Trim turnings to 0.6cm (¼ inch) and neaten together.

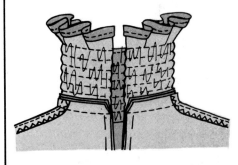

6 Cut a strip of fabric 10cm × 2.5cm (4 inches × 1 inch). Make a turning of 0.6cm (¼ inch) on each long edge. Fold strip in half lengthways and machine stitch down the two edges. Cut the strip in half.

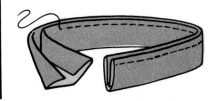

Taking 0.6cm (¼ inch) turning, double each loop and attach to the right side of the left hand centre-back edge of the collar so that one loop is just below the top row of shirring and the other loop is just above the bottom row of shirring.

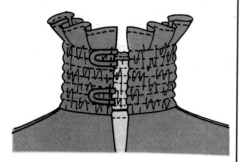

Facing

7 Machine stitch a small narrow hem on all edges of the facing. Make a cut from the top edge almost to the dot. With right sides together place the facing centrally over the centre-back opening so that the top edge of the facing is level with the top row of shirring on the collar. Taking 1cm (⅜ inch) turnings and tapering to the dot, tack through all thicknesses either side of the centre-back opening. Remove all tacking, turn the facing to the wrong side, press and tack around the stitched edges. Sew on buttons to correspond with loops.

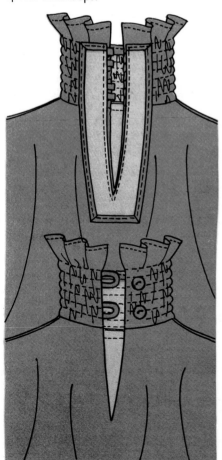

Sleeves

8 With right sides together and matching notches tack and stitch the underarm seams. Neaten and press. Make a double turning of 1cm (⅜ inch) on the lower sleeve edge and machine stitch.

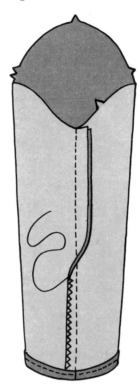

9 Work a gathering thread between the notches on the sleeve head. With right sides together and matching notches and underarm seams pin the sleeve into the armhole. Pull up the gathering thread and ease the sleeve head into the armhole. Tack and stitch. Trim the turnings to 0.6cm (¼ inch) and neaten together.

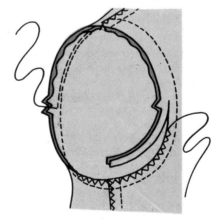

Skirt

10 With right sides together and matching notches tack and stitch all eight skirt panels together leaving a 20.5cm (8 inch) opening at the top of one seam for the zip (do not use French seams as they will pucker). Trim, neaten turnings together, and press to one side. Insert the zip into the opening.

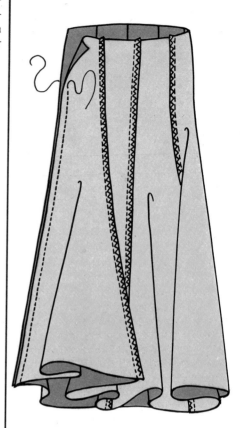

11 Cut a piece of interfacing the length of the waistband by half the width. Tack to the wrong side of the waistband with one edge to the fold line. Fold the waistband in half lengthways with right sides together and stitch across the ends and to the dot on one end. Trim the turnings to 0.6cm (¼ inch) and turn through.

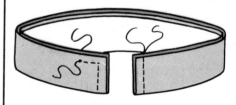

With right sides together place the interfaced half of the waistband to the top of the skirt so that the extension is on the right back.

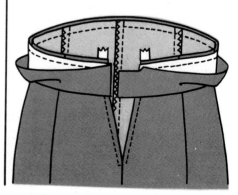

Tack and stitch and trim turnings. Make a turning of 1.6cm ($\frac{5}{8}$ inch) on the free edge and hem-stitch on to the stitch line. Sew the hooks on to the wrong side of the extension and work loops to correspond.

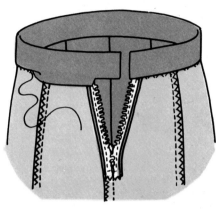

12 Divide the remaining 2.75 metres (3 yards) of fabric into ten equal parts across the fabric. With right sides together tack and stitch all ten pieces together across the short ends. Trim turnings to 0.6cm ($\frac{1}{4}$ inch) and neaten.

13 Work a separate double gathering thread through the top of each panel. Make a turning of 1cm ($\frac{3}{8}$ inch) on the other edge of the frill and machine stitch. Divide the lower edge of the skirt into ten equal parts and mark with pins.

14 With right sides together and the frill seams corresponding with the pins, pin the frill to the skirt. Draw up each set of gathering threads and distribute the gathers evenly. Tack and stitch. Trim turnings to 0.6cm ($\frac{3}{4}$ inch) and neaten.

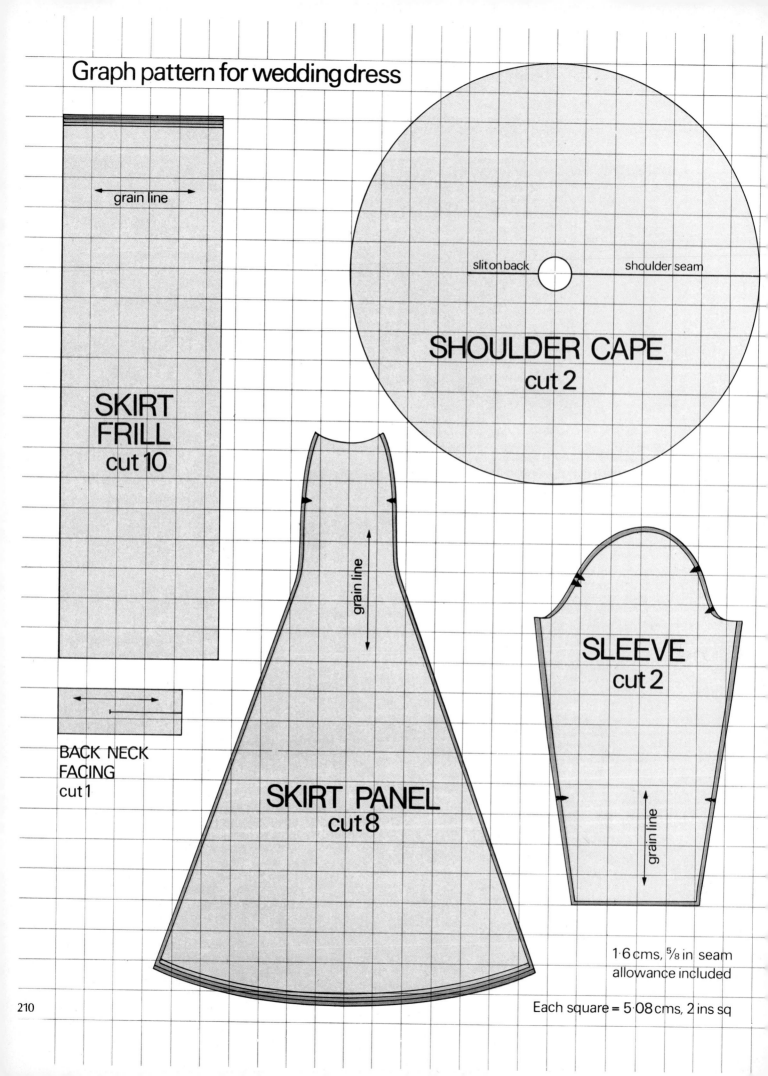

Graph pattern for wedding dress

SKIRT FRILL cut 10

grain line

SHOULDER CAPE cut 2

slit on back   shoulder seam

BACK NECK FACING cut 1

SKIRT PANEL cut 8

grain line

SLEEVE cut 2

grain line

1·6 cms, 5/8 in seam allowance included

Each square = 5·08 cms, 2 ins sq

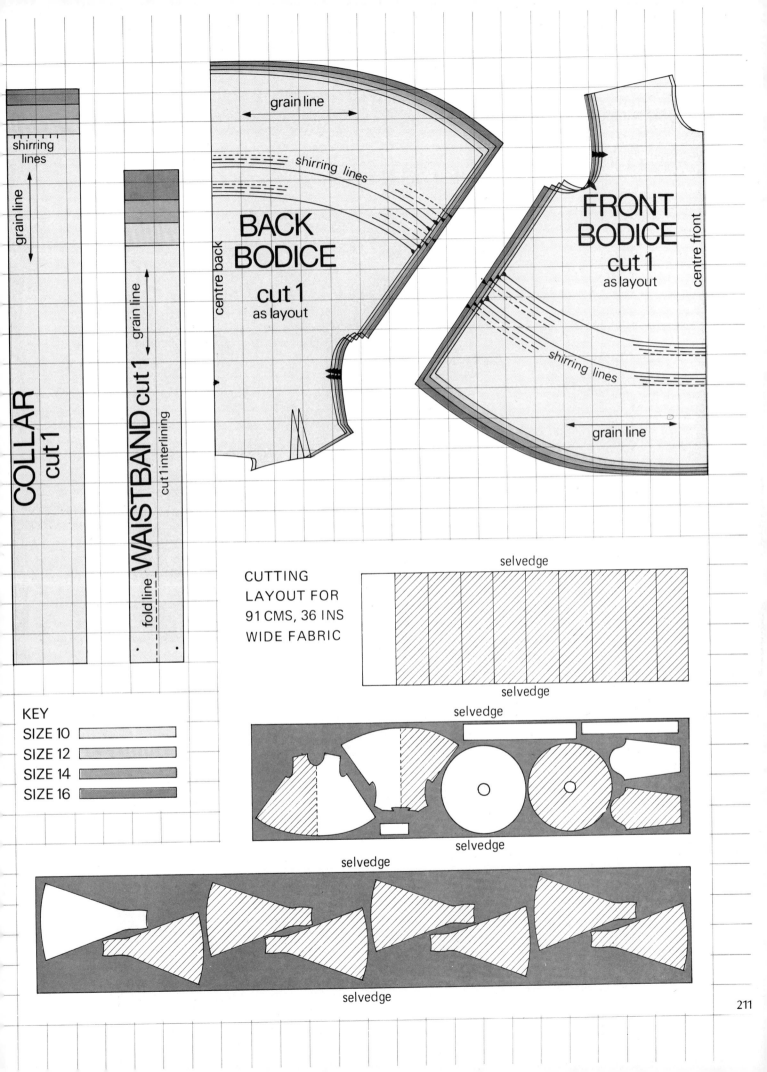

COLLAR
cut 1

WAISTBAND cut 1
grain line
cut 1 interlining
fold line

shirring
lines
grain line

grain line
shirring lines

BACK
BODICE
cut 1
as layout
centre back

FRONT
BODICE
cut 1
as layout
centre front
shirring lines
grain line

CUTTING
LAYOUT FOR
91 CMS, 36 INS
WIDE FABRIC

selvedge
selvedge

selvedge
selvedge

selvedge
selvedge

KEY
SIZE 10
SIZE 12
SIZE 14
SIZE 16

Two-piece dress

Great for going-away — and when you're back.

Sizes

10, 12, 14 and 16

Fabric required

All sizes take 6.20 metres (6¾ yards) of 91cm (36 inch) wide fabric

You will also need

☐ Graph paper for making the pattern
☐ Matching thread
☐ 5 × 1.3cm (½ inch) wide buttons
☐ 1 × 20cm (8 inch) zip
☐ 2 dress size foam shoulder pads
☐ 12.5cm (5 inches) of 91cm (36 inch) wide interfacing

Making the pattern

Using graph paper and following the colour indicating the size required draw each pattern piece to scale: One square = 5.08cm square (2 inch square). An allowance of 1.6cm (⅝ inch) has been made on all seams, 0.6cm (¼ inch) on the belt and neckband turnings and 1cm (⅜ inch) on the lower blouse and skirt hems. Cut out the pattern pieces and mark all dots, notches and straight grain line.

Cutting out the dress

Cut a piece of fabric from the main piece, 1.85 metres (2 yards) long. Following the cutting layout fold the fabric in half and place the six blouse pattern pieces as indicated.

Lay the remaining fabric flat. Place the skirt back and front pieces with one edge on the selvedge and then reverse so that each piece is a semi-circle. Lay the belt piece four times and reverse the front and back skirt yoke pieces once. Pin into place and cut out. Transfer all markings from the pattern pieces to the fabric.

Using the pattern pieces given for the cuffs and centre front facings pin on to interfacing as indicated, and cut two of each.

Making up
Blouse

1 Back

Work a gathering thread between the notches on the top edge of the back.

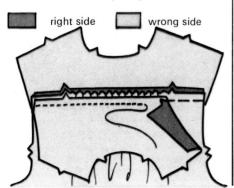

right side ░ wrong side

With right sides together and matching notches pin the yoke to the back. Pull up the gathering thread and distribute the gathers evenly. Tack. With right side of yoke to wrong side of back tack the remaining yoke piece to the top edge of the back.

2 Stitch through all thicknesses. Trim and layer the turnings and press on to the yoke. Work two rows of top-stitching 0.6cm (¼ inch) apart and 0.3cm (⅛ inch) from the seam line.

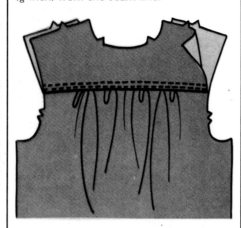

3 With right sides together tack and stitch the darts on the front. Press downwards. With right sides together and matching notches tack and stitch the fronts to the top back yoke only at the shoulder seams. Press turnings towards the back. Make a turning of 1.6cm (⅝ inch) on the shoulder seam of the under-yoke and tack on to the stitch line. From the right side work two rows of top stitching on the yoke 0.6cm (¼ inch) apart and 0.3cm (⅛ inch) from the seam.

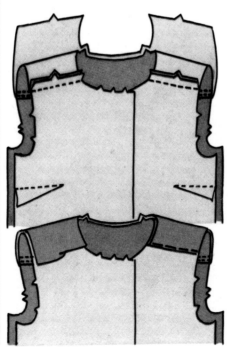

4 With right sides together and matching notches tack and stitch the fronts to the back at the side seams. Trim turnings to 1.3cm (½ inch) and neaten together. Press.

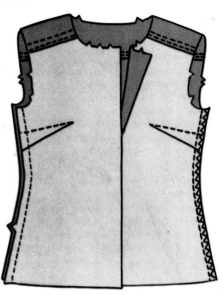

Facings

5 Tack the two pieces of interfacing down the centre fronts 1.6cm (⅝ inch) in from the edge. Turn back the raw edges on to the interfacing and machine stitch close to the fold.

With right sides together fold back both centre-front edges on the fold lines indicated. Machine stitch from the fold line to the dot at the neck edge. Clip to the dot, trim turnings and turn through to the right side. On the right front work two rows of top stitching 0.6cm (¼ inch) apart and 0.3cm (⅛ inch) from the fold. Work another two rows the same distance

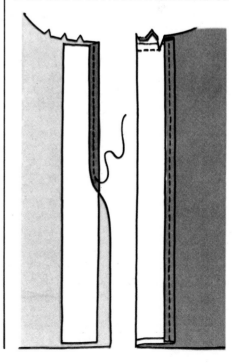

apart, and the outside row 3.8cm ($1\frac{1}{2}$ inches) from the fold. On the left side work one row of top stitching 0.6cm ($\frac{1}{4}$ inch) from the edge.

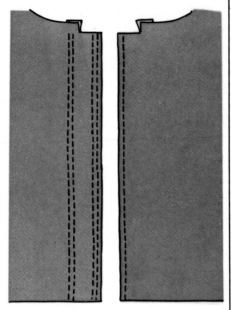

Neckband

6 Place the two neckbands together. Matching dots and with right sides together, tack and stitch the two neck bands together leaving an opening between the dots. Trim turnings. Clip to the dots and turn through.

7 With right sides together tack and stitch one raw edge of the neckband to the neck edge matching the dots. Trim turnings and press on to the neck band. Make a turning of 1.6cm ($\frac{5}{8}$ inch) on the remaining edge of the neckband, turn over and slip-stitch on to the stitch line. Work two rows of top stitching 0.6cm ($\frac{1}{4}$ inch) apart and 0.3cm ($\frac{1}{8}$ inch) from the edge of the neckband and all around the neckband. Press.

Sleeves

8 Work a row of small gathering stitches between the notches on the sleeve head. With right sides together and matching notches tack and stitch the underarm seam. Trim turnings to 1.3cm ($\frac{1}{2}$ inch) and neaten together. With right sides together, matching notches and underarm seams, pin the sleeve into the armhole, easing the fullness over the sleeve head. Tack and stitch. Trim turnings to 0.6cm ($\frac{1}{4}$ inch) and neaten together. Insert shoulder pads centrally over the

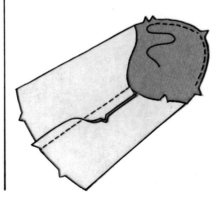

shoulder seam inside the blouse and with the straight edge along the top of the armhole. Catch-stitch all around.

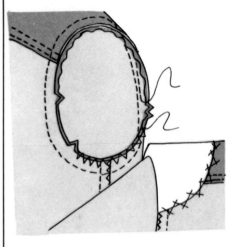

Cuff

9 Tack the interfacing on to the wrong side of the cuff so that one edge lies along the fold line. With right sides together fold the cuff in half with short ends together and stitch across these ends. Trim turnings and press open. Then with wrong sides together fold the cuff with raw edges together and work two rows of top-stitching 0.6cm ($\frac{1}{4}$ inch) apart and 0.3cm ($\frac{1}{8}$ inch) from the fold.

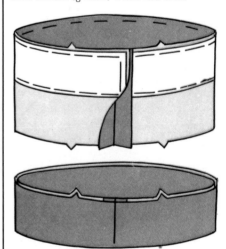

10 Work a gathering thread around the lower edge of the sleeve between the notches. With right sides together and matching notches pin the cuff to the lower

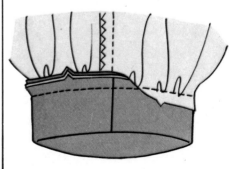

sleeve edge. Pull up the gathering thread and distribute the gathers evenly. Tack and stitch. Trim turnings to 1.3cm ($\frac{1}{2}$ inch) and neaten. Press down on to the cuff. From the right side work two rows of top stitching 0.6cm ($\frac{1}{4}$ inch) apart, the first one close to the stitch line. This will hold the turnings in place.

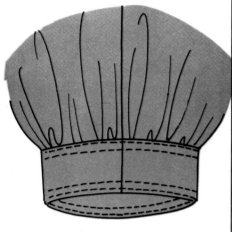

11 Work five vertical buttonholes in the centre of the right hand facing. The top buttonhole should be 0.6cm ($\frac{1}{4}$ inch) below the stitched neck edge and all the rest 7cm ($2\frac{3}{4}$ inches) apart. Sew buttons on to the left side to correspond. Make a double turning of 1cm ($\frac{3}{8}$ inch) on the lower edge of the blouse and machine stitch down. Press.

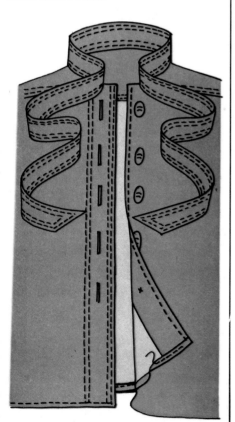

Skirt

12 With right sides together tack and stitch the darts on all four yoke pieces. Press towards the centre front and back. With right sides together and matching notches tack and stitch a front and back together on the right side seam and as far as the notch on the left side seam. Repeat this with the other front and back yoke.

With right sides together and matching seams tack and stitch the two yokes together along the top edge. Trim and clip turnings. Machine stitch the turnings to one side of the yoke close to the stitch line. This will prevent the seam from rolling and must be on the inside of the skirt so that the stitching does not show.

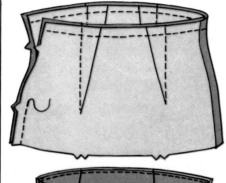

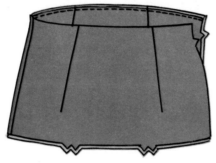

Zip

13 Insert zip into the opening. Lay the zip on the right side of the top yoke with the edge of the tape along one edge of the opening. Stitch close to the teeth.

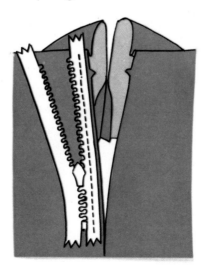

Turn over and attach the other side of the zip in the normal way with the remaining edge of the opening folded over the teeth. Stitch from the right side and across the bottom. Make turnings of 1.6cm ($\frac{5}{8}$ inch) on the edges of the under yoke and slip-stitch on to the zip tape.

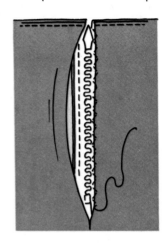

14 With right sides together and matching notches tack and stitch the skirt front and back together at the side seams. Press turnings open. With right sides together, matching notches and seams, tack and stitch the skirt to the top yoke only. Trim and clip turnings and press on to yoke. Make a turning of 1.6cm ($\frac{5}{8}$ inch) on the remaining under-yoke and slip-stitch to the stitch line all round. Press.

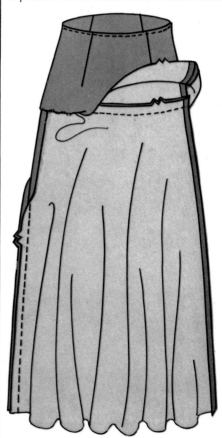

Graph pattern for two piece dress

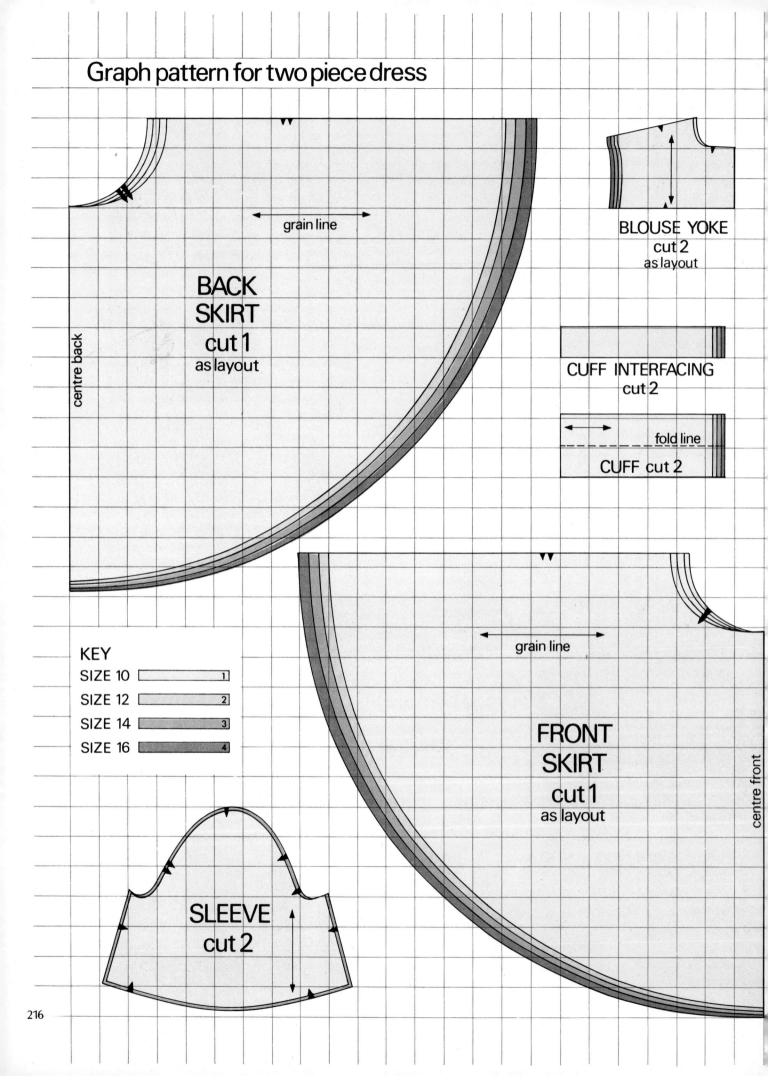

grain line

BACK
SKIRT
cut 1
as layout

centre back

BLOUSE YOKE
cut 2
as layout

CUFF INTERFACING
cut 2

fold line

CUFF cut 2

KEY

SIZE 10		1
SIZE 12		2
SIZE 14		3
SIZE 16		4

grain line

FRONT
SKIRT
cut 1
as layout

centre front

SLEEVE
cut 2

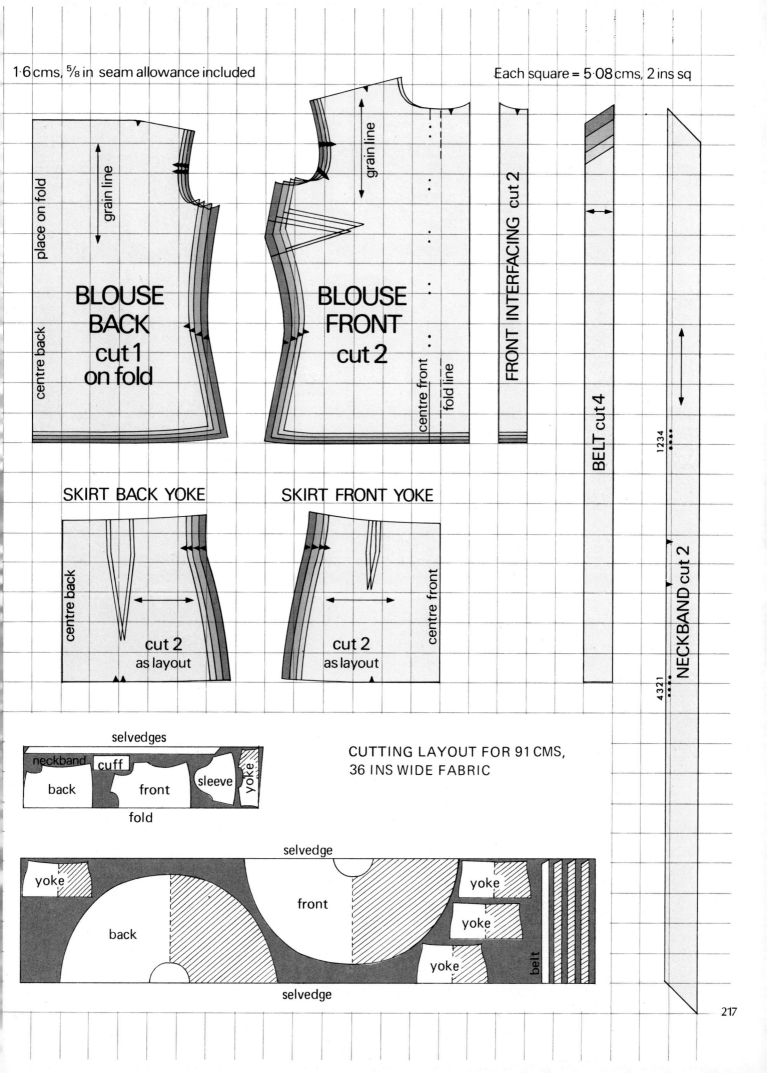

1·6 cms, ⅝ in seam allowance included

Each square = 5·08 cms, 2 ins sq

place on fold

grain line

centre back

BLOUSE BACK cut 1 on fold

grain line

BLOUSE FRONT cut 2

centre front

fold line

FRONT INTERFACING cut 2

BELT cut 4

1234

4321

NECKBAND cut 2

SKIRT BACK YOKE

centre back

cut 2 as layout

SKIRT FRONT YOKE

cut 2 as layout

centre front

selvedges

neckband | cuff

back | front | sleeve | yoke

fold

CUTTING LAYOUT FOR 91 CMS, 36 INS WIDE FABRIC

selvedge

yoke

back

front

yoke

yoke

yoke

belt

selvedge

217

Hem

15 It is important to leave the skirt hanging from the waist for at least three days, or for longer, to allow the hem to drop. Level the hem to the required length. Cut off the excess leaving 1cm ($\frac{3}{8}$ *inch*) to turn up. Make a double turning and machine stitch. Press.

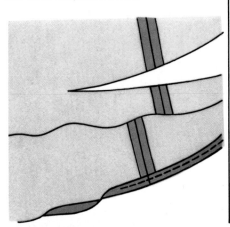

Belt

16 With right sides together tack and stitch the two belt pieces together across the short straight ends. Repeat this with the other two. Press turnings open.

With right sides together and matching seams tack and stitch the two belt pieces together all around leaving an opening to turn through. Trim turnings, turn through and slip-stitch opening. Work top stitching on the belt as on the neckband.

Bridesmaid's dress

Ruched and ribboned, a simple echo of the bride's dress with the same deep frilled hem.

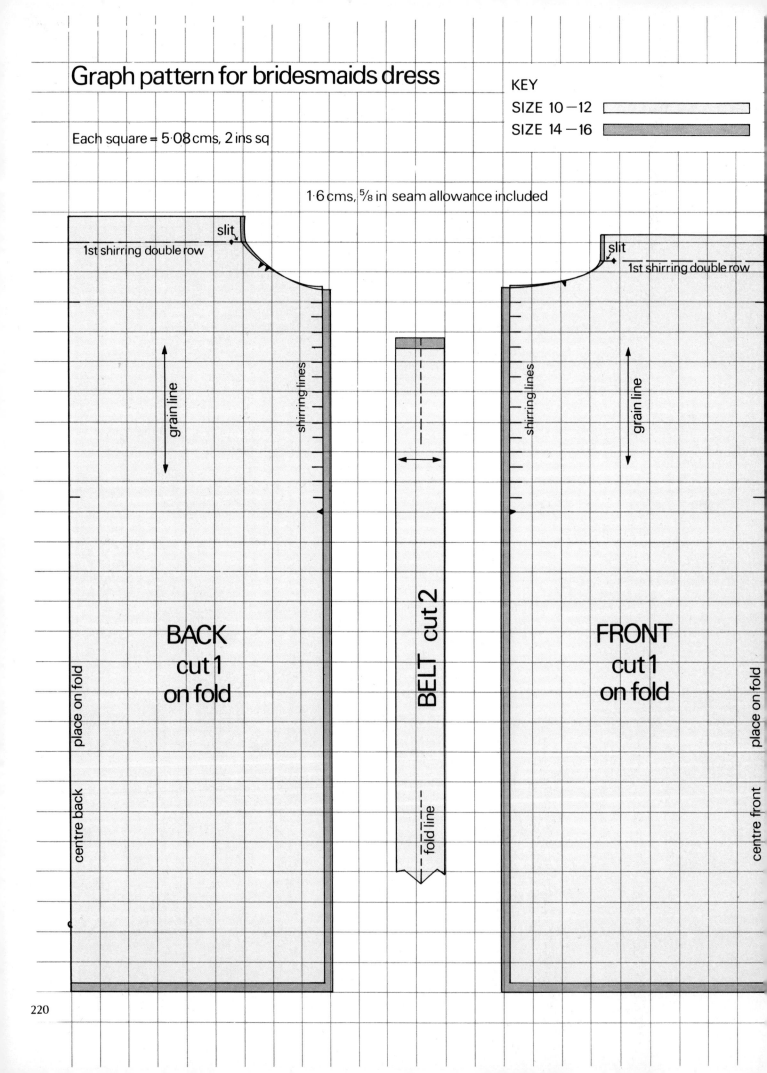

Graph pattern for bridesmaids dress

Each square = 5·08 cms, 2 ins sq

1·6 cms, ⅝ in seam allowance included

slit

1st shirring double row

grain line

shirring lines

BACK
cut 1
on fold

place on fold

centre back

BELT cut 2

fold line

slit

1st shirring double row

shirring lines

grain line

FRONT
cut 1
on fold

place on fold

centre front

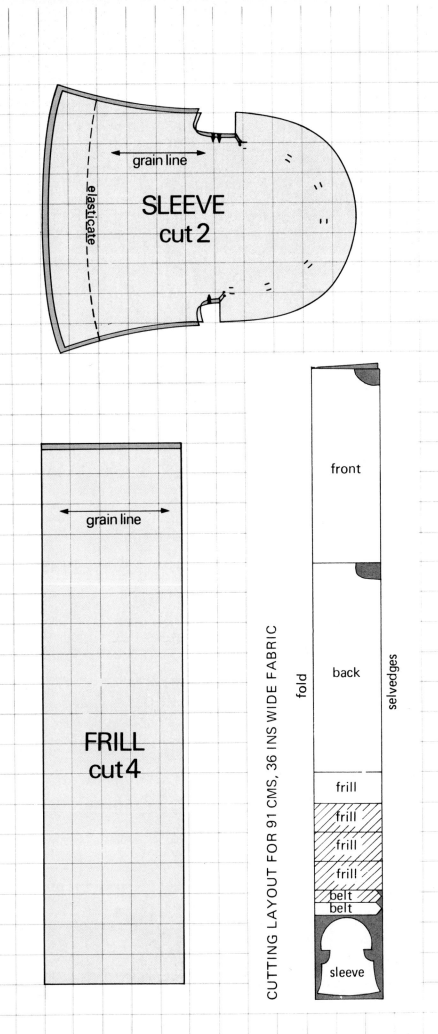

grain line

SLEEVE
cut 2

elasticate

grain line

FRILL
cut 4

CUTTING LAYOUT FOR 91 CMS, 36 INS WIDE FABRIC

fold

selvedges

front

back

frill

frill

frill

frill

belt
belt

sleeve

Sizes
10, 12, 14 and 16

Fabric required
4.60 metres (*5 yards*) of 91cm (*36 inch*) wide cotton voile or fabric suitable for shirring

You will also need
☐ Graph paper for making the pattern
☐ Matching thread
☐ Shirring elastic
☐ 1.85 metres (*2 yards*) of slotted broderie anglaise ribbon 1.3cm (*½ inch*) wide.
☐ 2.75 metres (*3 yards*) of ribbon 0.6cm (*¼ inch*) wide

Making the pattern
Using graph paper and following the colour indicating the size required draw each pattern piece to scale. One square = 5.08cm square (*2 inch square*).

An allowance of 1.6cm (*⅝ inch*) has been made on all seams and 1cm (*⅜ inch*) allowance has been made on the top edges of the front and back, lower sleeve edges and lower frill· edge. An allowance of 0.6cm (*¼ inch*) has been made on the top edges of the sleeves. Cut out the pattern pieces and mark all dots, notches and straight grain line.

Cutting out the dress
Following the cutting layout fold the fabric in half lengthways and place the pattern pieces as indicated. Place the belt piece twice and the frill four times. Make sure that the straight grain line on the pattern lies on the straight grain of the fabric. Pin into place and cut out. Transfer all markings from the pattern pieces to the fabric.

Making up
1 Taking 1cm (*⅜ inch*) turnings, make a small hem on the top edges of the

☐ right side   ☐ wrong side

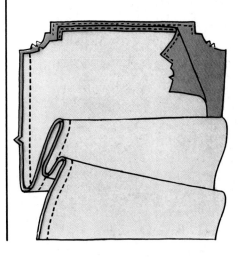

front and back pieces and down the sides as far as the top shirring line. Stitch. With right sides together and matching notches tack and stitch the front to the back down one side seam only. Press turnings open.

2 Thread the spool with shirring elastic. From the right side work the rows of shirring 2.5cm (1 inch) apart, on and in between the top and bottom shirring lines indicated on the pattern. Work two rows of shirring on the top and bottom lines to strengthen. With right sides together, matching notches and shirring lines tack and stitch the remaining side seam. Press turnings open.

Sleeves

3 Taking 0.6cm ($\frac{1}{4}$ inch) turnings, make a small hem on the top edge of the sleeve and stitch down with a zig-zag stitch. Tack and stitch the slotted ribbon on to the right side and on the lines indicated on the top and bottom of the sleeve. Cut two lengths of ribbon 34.5cm (13$\frac{1}{2}$ inches) long. Thread the ribbons through the top row of slotted ribbon from each side of the sleeve so that they meet in the middle. Secure at the ends.

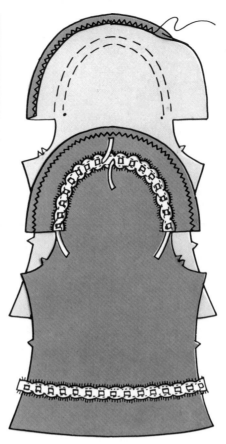

4 With right sides together and matching notches tack and stitch the underarm seam of the sleeve from the base of the underarm curve to the lower sleeve edge. Trim turnings and neaten together. Press. Make a small hem of 1cm ($\frac{3}{8}$ inch) on the lower sleeve edge and stitch. Cut a length of ribbon 68.5cm (27 inches) long and thread through the slotted ribbon on the lower sleeve so that the ends tie in the centre of the sleeve.
Make the other sleeve in the same way.

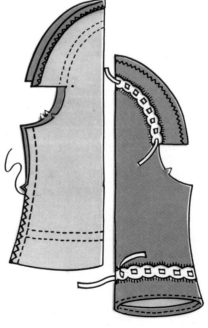

5 With right sides together and matching notches and underarm seams, tack and stitch the sleeve to the armhole around the underarm curve. The top edge of the underarm curve should lie along the top row of shirring and be stitched down. Trim the armhole turnings and neaten.

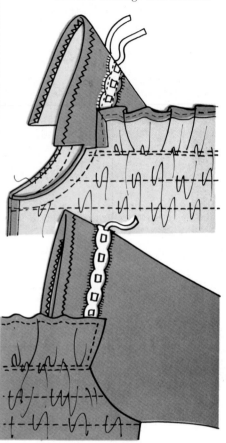

Frill

6 With right sides together tack and stitch the four frill pieces together across the short ends. Press turnings open. Make a small hem of 1cm ($\frac{3}{8}$ inch) around one long edge and machine stitch. Work separate gathering threads through each frill piece along the other long edge.

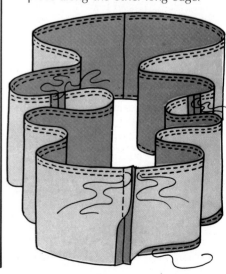

7 Mark the centre-front and back on the lower edge of the dress. With right sides together and matching the seams to the side seams and centre-back and front marks pin the frill to the lower edge of the dress. Pull up each gathering thread and distribute the gathers evenly. Tack and stitch. Trim turnings and neaten together.

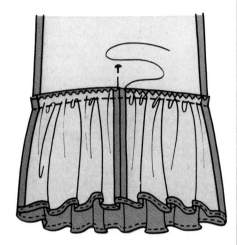

Belt

8 With right sides facing tack and stitch the two tie pieces together across the short straight ends. Press open. With right sides together fold the tie in half length ways. Taking 1.6cm ($\frac{5}{8}$ inch) turnings, stitch the long edge and across the shaped ends leaving an opening to turn through. Trim turnings, turn through and slip stitch opening together. Press.
Try on the dress and tie the ribbons or the shoulders to fit.

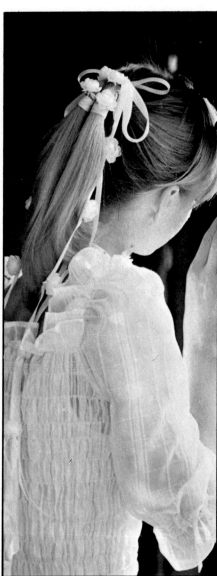

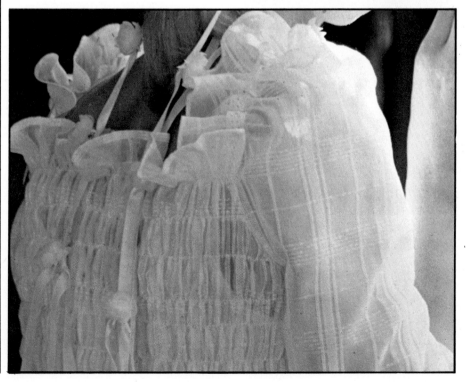

A pretty pair

An enchanting broderie sun set and bonnet to sew.

Cutting out the sun set

Following the cutting layout and using the all-over fabric place the four pattern pieces for the pants and mob cap as indicated. Take care that the grain line on the pattern lies on the straight grain of the fabric. Pin into place and cut out. Cut out the dress from the bordered fabric as indicated.

Transfer all markings from the pattern pieces to the fabric.

Making up
Dress

1 Join the centre-back seam of the dress with a French seam. Press the seam to one side. On the wrong side of the material, turn under and stitch a narrow hem around the top of the dress. Press.

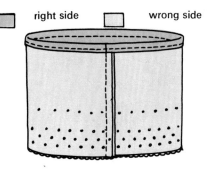

right side   wrong side

2 Shirr the top of the dress on the lines indicated. To shirr:– Hand wind elastic thread on to the bobbin without tension. Use longest stitch setting and for the first row hold material as for ordinary sewing. For second and subsequent rows material must be held taut.

3 Fold the straps in half lengthways with right sides together. Stitch. Press the seams open. Turn the straps to the right side and press with the seams at the

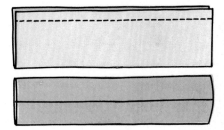

back. Adjust the length of the straps, neaten the raw edges and hand stitch to the wrong side of the dress on the top shirring line.

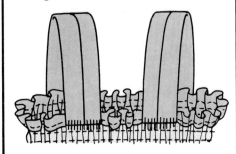

Pants

4 Matching notches join the gusset to the back and front of the pants with narrow French seams. Press to one side. Join the side seams of the pants with French seams. Press.

On the wrong side tack and stitch a narrow hem at the waist, leaving a small opening to thread elastic through. Measure elastic to fit the waist comfortably, thread through the casing and secure the ends. Stitch the opening and press.

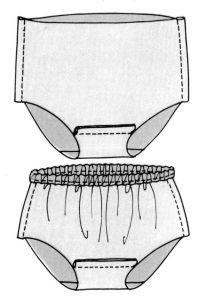

5 Turn under and press a narrow hem around each leg. Tack lace edging to the wrong side and machine stitch with the hems. Work two rows of shirring around the legs just above the hems. Pull up the elastic to the size required and tie the ends together.

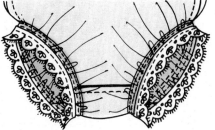

Mob cap

6 Turn under a small hem around the edge of the hat and press. On the wrong side tack lace edging around the edge and machine stitch with the hem. Work two rows of shirring on the lines indicated. Pull up the elastic to fit the head comfortably and secure the ends.

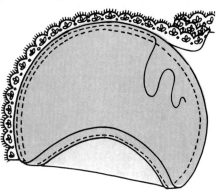

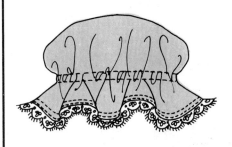

Graph pattern for sun set

1·27cms, ½ in seam allowance included
Each square = 2·54 cms, 1 in sq

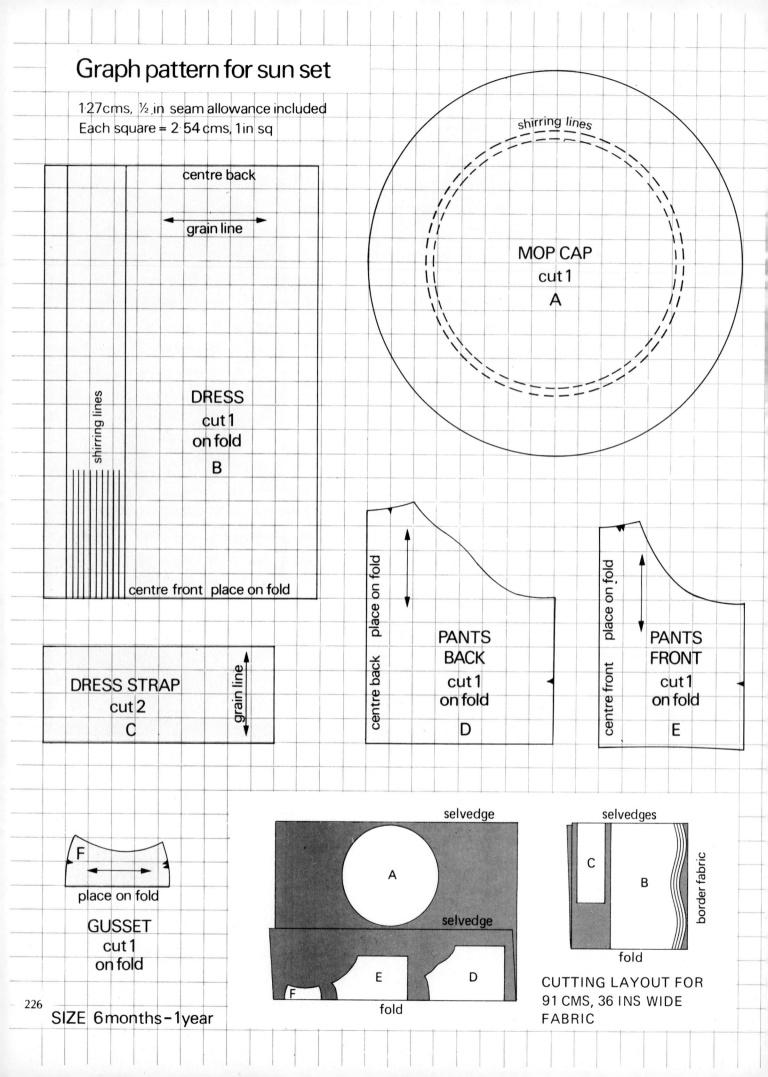

centre back

grain line

shirring lines

DRESS
cut 1
on fold
B

centre front place on fold

MOP CAP
cut 1
A

shirring lines

DRESS STRAP
cut 2
C

grain line

place on fold
centre back

PANTS
BACK
cut 1
on fold
D

place on fold
centre front

PANTS
FRONT
cut 1
on fold
E

F

place on fold

GUSSET
cut 1
on fold

selvedge

selvedge

A

E

D

F

fold

selvedges

C

B

border fabric

fold

CUTTING LAYOUT FOR
91 CMS, 36 INS WIDE
FABRIC

226

SIZE 6 months – 1 year

His and her fur

For him, leather trimmed, for her print lined – cold weather duffles to make from the same easy pattern.

Sizes

3–4 years, 5–6 years and 7–8 years

Fabric required

For size 3–4 years:
0.80 metres ($\frac{7}{8}$ *yard*) of 137cm (*54 inch*) fabric
1.40 metres (*1$\frac{1}{2}$ yards*) of 91cm (*36 inch*) lining
For size 5–6 years:
1.05 metres (*1$\frac{1}{8}$ yards*) of 137cm (*54 inch*) fabric
1.85 metres (*2 yards*) of 91cm (*36 inch*) lining
For size 7–8 years:
1.25 metres (*1$\frac{3}{8}$ yards*) of 137cm (*54 inch*) fabric
2.30 metres (*2$\frac{1}{2}$ yards*) of 91cm (*36 inch*) lining

You will also need

☐ Graph paper for making the pattern
☐ Matching thread
☐ 1.15 metres (*1$\frac{1}{4}$ yards*) of cord
☐ Strips of suede 4cm (*1$\frac{1}{2}$ inches*) wide for boy's coat
☐ 8 toggles

Making the pattern

Using graph paper and following the colour indicating the size required draw each pattern piece to scale. One square = 5.08cm square (*2 inch square*).
An allowance of 1.3cm ($\frac{1}{2}$ *inch*) has been made on all seams. A 5cm (*2 inch*) hem has been allowed.
Cut out the pattern pieces and mark the position of the centre-front, and pockets, all notches and the straight grain line.

Cutting out the coat

Following the cutting layout place the five pattern pieces on the wrong side of single fabric as indicated. Take care that the grain line on the pattern lies on the straight grain of the fabric. Pin into place and cut out the hood, pocket, front and sleeve. Outline the pattern piece for the back with tailor's chalk. Unpin and reverse the pattern, placing the centre-back to the centre-back of the outlined section. Cut out the complete back. Reverse the other pattern pieces, pin into place and cut out.
Transfer all markings from the pattern pieces to the fabric.
Following the cutting layout place the five pattern pieces on the lining as indicated. The back is placed to a fold. Pin into place and cut out.
Transfer all markings from the pattern pieces to the lining.

Making up

1 With right sides together and matching notches, tack and stitch the shoulder and side seams. Press seams open.

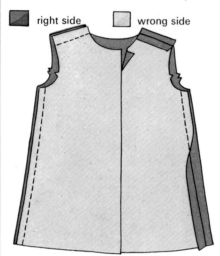

■ right side   ▢ wrong side

Sleeves

2 With right sides together tack and stitch the underarm seam. Press open. Work a gathering thread between the notches on the sleeve head. With right sides together and matching notches pin sleeve into armhole, easing over the

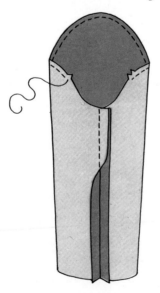

sleeve head. Tack and stitch. Press seam towards the sleeve. Repeat with other sleeve.

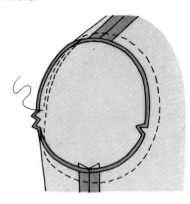

Pockets

3 With right sides of pocket and lining together, tack and stitch along sides, leaving an opening at the bottom edge. Trim turnings and corners and turn through to the right side. Slip-stitch the opening. Press.

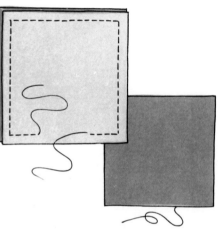

4 On the boy's coat pocket tack a strip of suede on the lining side with the edge to the top of the pocket. Stitch through all thicknesses of fabric. Fold suede over the edge to the right side of the pocket and machine stitch into place through all thicknesses.

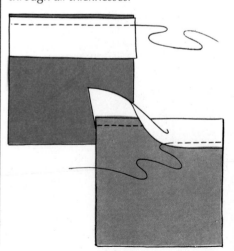

5 Tack pocket into position on the front of the coat. Working from the wrong side back-stitch firmly into place, reinforcing at the corners with tape. Press.

Hood

6 With right sides together tack and stitch the centre-back seams of hood and hood lining. Clip seams and press open. With right sides together stitch lining to hood along the front edge. Turn to the right side and press.
Bind the front edge of the boy's coat hood with suede in the same way as the pocket.

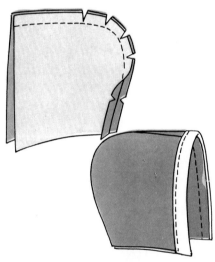

7 With right sides together tack the hood to neckline of coat.

8 For the lining repeat stages 1 and 2.

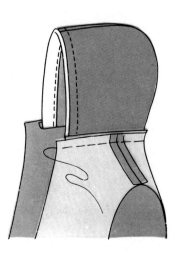

9 With the right sides of lining and coat together tack and stitch front edges and neckline. Clip corners and curve, turn through to the right side and press.

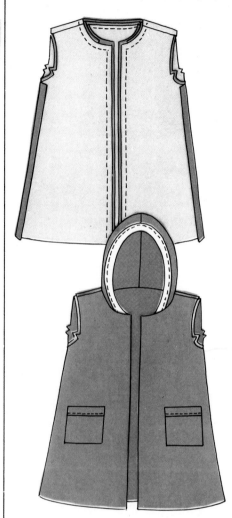

10 Turn up hem on coat and catch-stitch into place. Turn up and stitch hem of lining, making it 2cm ($\frac{3}{4}$ inch) shorter than the coat. Press.
To hold the lining in place, work bar tacks between coat and lining at the side seams.

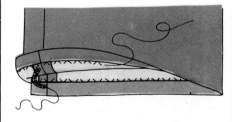

11 Draw sleeve lining through garment sleeve. Turn up sleeve hem and catch-stitch into place. Slip-stitch lining to sleeve hem. Press.

Fastening

12 Wind cord approximately 4cm ($1\frac{1}{2}$ inches) long round one toggle and stitch ends neatly to the coat. Wind cord approximately 21.5cm ($8\frac{1}{2}$ inches) long around another toggle, across centre-front and back again, leaving a loop large enough to slip over the corresponding toggle. Stitch neatly and securely into place.
After completing the garment look over all seams and with a pin gently ease out any of the pile caught in the stitching. Take care not to pull the threads.

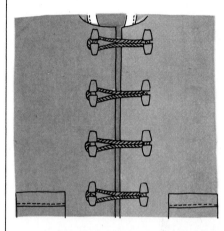

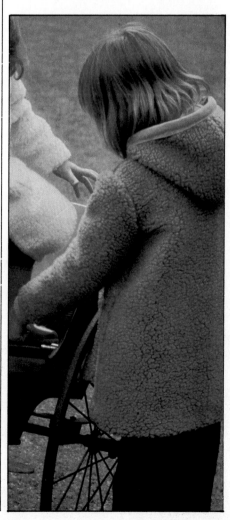

229

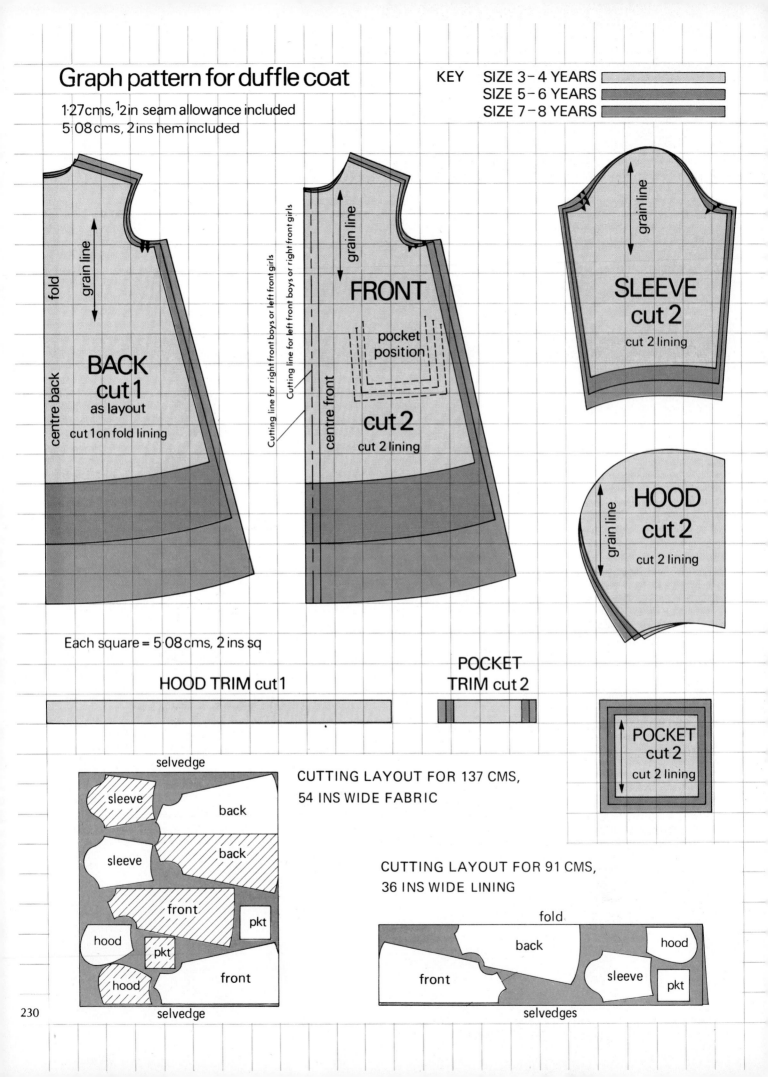

Graph pattern for duffle coat

1·27 cms, $\frac{1}{2}$ in seam allowance included
5·08 cms, 2 ins hem included

KEY
- SIZE 3–4 YEARS
- SIZE 5–6 YEARS
- SIZE 7–8 YEARS

fold
centre back
grain line

**BACK
cut 1**
as layout

cut 1 on fold lining

Each square = 5·08 cms, 2 ins sq

Cutting line for right front boys or left front girls
Cutting line for left front boys or right front girls

grain line
centre front

FRONT

pocket
position

cut 2
cut 2 lining

grain line

**SLEEVE
cut 2**
cut 2 lining

grain line

**HOOD
cut 2**
cut 2 lining

HOOD TRIM cut 1

**POCKET
TRIM cut 2**

**POCKET
cut 2**
cut 2 lining

selvedge

sleeve	back
sleeve	back
front	pkt
hood	pkt
hood	front

selvedge

**CUTTING LAYOUT FOR 137 CMS,
54 INS WIDE FABRIC**

**CUTTING LAYOUT FOR 91 CMS,
36 INS WIDE LINING**

fold

front	back	hood
		sleeve
		pkt

selvedges

230

Rain again . . .

. . . but baby won't care if you make her this gay coat and sou'wester set.

Using plastic or vinyl fabric

Hold the edges together and the pattern pieces in place with sticky tape and not pins which leave marks. Do not tack but if necessary mark any position lines on the wrong side with pencil. To prevent the fabric from sticking to the machine spray the machine bed and needle with a good silicone polish or a specially-made product from a needlework store. If the sticking continues place a piece of tissue paper either side of the fabric and remove after stitching.

Sizes

18 months and 3 years

Fabric required

For both sizes:
1.3 metres (1⅛ *yard*) of 152cm (*60 inch*) fabric or 1.6 metres (1¾ *yards*) of 91cm (*36 inch*) fabric

You will also need

☐ Graph paper for making the pattern
☐ Matching thread
☐ 5 gripper snap fasteners
☐ Carpet or fabric glue

Making the pattern

Using graph paper and following the colour indicating the size required draw each pattern piece to scale. One square = 5.08cm square (*2 inch square*).
An allowance of 0.6cm (¼ *inch*) has been made on all seams and a 2.54cm (*1 inch*) hem has been allowed on the coat and sleeves.
Cut out the pattern pieces and mark the position of pocket and fastenings, all notches, fold and straight grain line.

Cutting out the raincoat and sou'wester

Following the appropriate cutting layout place all seven pattern pieces as indicated. Take care that the grain line on the pattern lies on the straight grain of the fabric. Hold in place with sticky tape and cut out. Cut another collar and two more crown sections.

Transfer all markings from the pattern pieces to the fabric.
For the sou'wester strap cut a strip of fabric 4cm (1¼ *inches*) wide and 45cm (*18 inches*) long.

Making up Raincoat

1 With right sides together and matching notches stitch the underarm seams. Fold the turnings towards the back and from the right side work a row of top-stitching 0.3cm (⅛ *inch*) from each seam line.

2 Turn under and stitch 0.6cm (¼ *inch*) on the front facing edges.
Turn up 2.54cm (*1 inch*) on the lower edge of the coat. Turn under 0.6cm (¼ *inch*) on the raw edge and machine stitch the hem into place.

🟦 right side　　🟦 wrong side

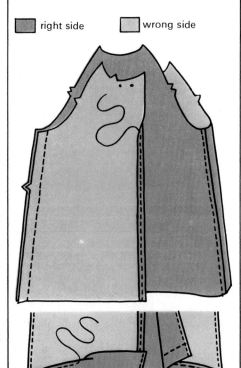

3 With right sides together and matching dots stitch the front facings to the neckline from the fold lines to the centre fronts. Clip at centre-fronts almost to the stitching, turn the facings to the inside and glue to the wrong side of the coat with carpet or fabric glue.

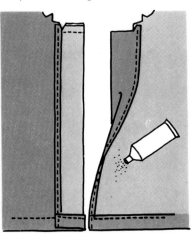

Sleeves

4 With right sides together stitch the dart at the top of the sleeve. Fold towards the back and from the right side work a row of top-stitching approximately 0.3cm (⅛ *inch*) from the dart seam. With right sides together and matching notches stitch the underarm seam. Open the turnings and glue down to the wrong side. Turn up and stitch the lower edge of the sleeve as for the coat hem.

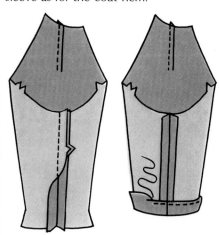

232

5 With right sides together and matching notches and underarm seams stitch the sleeve into the armhole. Fold the turnings towards the sleeve and from the right side work a row of top-stitching 0.3cm ($\frac{1}{8}$ inch) from the seam line.

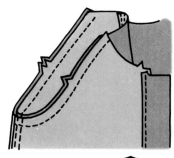

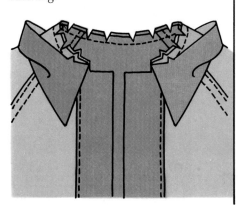

Collar

6 With right sides together and matching notches stitch the two collar pieces around the outer edges. Clip the curve, trim off corners and turn to the right side.

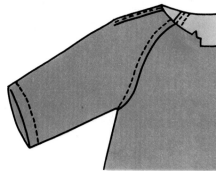

With the right side of the top collar to the wrong side of the coat and matching notches and shoulder dots stitch round the neckline. Clip turnings almost to the stitching.

7 Make small clips on the neck edge of the under-collar, fold under the seam allowance and stitch to the neckline seam. Work a row of top-stitching round the collar 0.3cm ($\frac{1}{8}$ inch) from the edge.

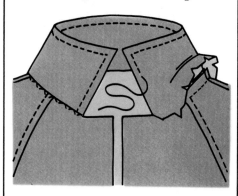

Pockets

8 Turn under and stitch 2.54cm (1 inch) on the top edge of the pocket. Turn under 0.6cm ($\frac{1}{4}$ inch) on the other edges and top-stitch to the front of the coat in the position indicated. Machine stitch a triangle at each corner for extra strength. Attach grip fasteners to the centre-front.

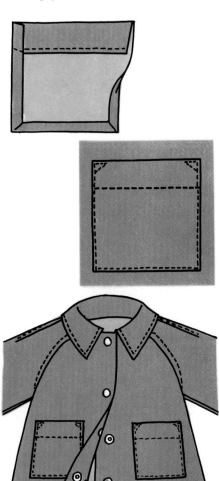

Sou' wester

1 With right sides together and matching notches join two sections of the crown. Fold turnings together to one side and from the right side work a row of top-stitching 0.3cm ($\frac{1}{8}$ inch) from the seam line. Join the other two sections in the same way and then the two sets together.

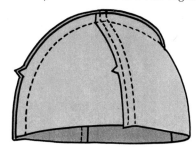

2 With right sides together stitch the centre-back seam of each brim. Glue the seams open. With right sides together and matching seams stitch the upper to the under brim round the outer edges. Clip the curve and turn to the right side. Work a continuous row of machine stitching from the outer to the inner edge, keeping the rows 0.6cm ($\frac{1}{4}$ inch) apart.

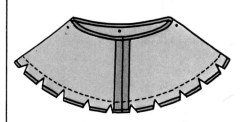

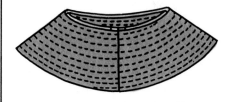

3 With right sides together and matching notches stitch the brim to the lower edge of the crown.

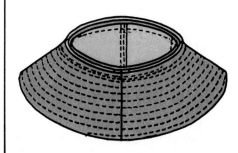

Graph pattern for raincoat

0·6 cms, ¼ in seam allowance included   Each square = 5·08 cms, 2 ins sq

2·54 cms, 1 in hem included

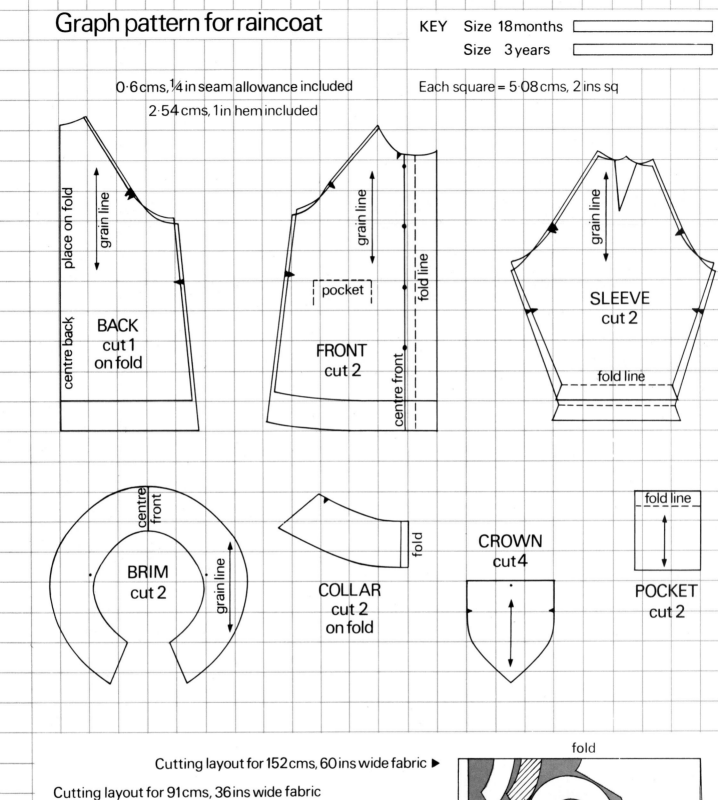

BACK
cut 1
on fold

place on fold

grain line

centre back

FRONT
cut 2

grain line

fold line

pocket

centre front

SLEEVE
cut 2

grain line

fold line

BRIM
cut 2

centre front

grain line

COLLAR
cut 2
on fold

fold

CROWN
cut 4

POCKET
cut 2

fold line

Cutting layout for 152 cms, 60 ins wide fabric ▶

Cutting layout for 91 cms, 36 ins wide fabric
▼

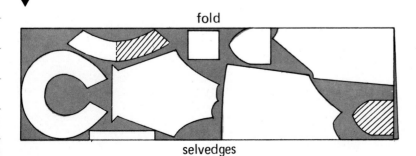

fold

selvedges

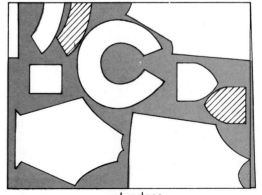

fold

selvedges

234

4 Fold the long sides of the strap to the centre, fold over again and work a row of top-stitching close to each edge. Place the strap on the top of the under brim so that it is half way between the centre-front and centre-back and stitch into place. Turn the hat to the right side and with the turnings of the crown and ends of the strap folded upwards work a row of top-stitching from the right side just above the seam line. Work another row parallel to the first, catching the turnings underneath.

Cut a small strip of fabric approximately 1.3cm ($\frac{1}{2}$ inch) wide by 10cm (4 inches) long. Fold in half lengthways and glue

wrong sides together. Fix under section of snap fastener to one end, place the band round the tie and fix the top half of fastener to correspond, trimming off any surplus fabric.

Housecoat

Soft folds and gathers for a flattering shape
that is also cleverly concealing.

Sizes

10, 12, 14, and 16

Fabric required

For sizes 10 and 12:
5.50 metres (6 yards) of 91cm (36 inch) fabric
For sizes 14 and 16:
5.75 metres (6¼ yards) of 91cm (36 inch) fabric

You will also need

- ☐ Graph paper for making the pattern
- ☐ Matching thread
- ☐ 1 × 55cm (22 inch) open ended zip
- ☐ 0.45 metre (½ yard) of matching seam tape
- ☐ 2 pieces of iron-on interfacing 5cm (2 inches) square

Making the pattern

Using graph paper and following the colour indicating the size required draw each pattern piece to scale. One square = 5.08cm square (2 inch square). An allowance of 1cm (⅜ inch) has been made on the seams of belt and casing, 1.6cm (⅝ inch) on all other seams and 5cm (2 inches) for the hem.
Cut out the pattern pieces and mark the position of belt casing, sleeve shirring, all notches and the straight grain line.

Cutting out the Housecoat

Following the cutting layout fold the fabric in half lengthways and place the pattern pieces for the back, belt and collar as indicated. Take care that the grain line on the pattern lies on the straight grain of the fabric. Pin into place and cut out. Cut another collar. Fold the remaining fabric widthways with the selvedges together. Place pattern pieces for the front, front facing, sleeve and belt casing as shown on the cutting lay-out, again taking care that the grain line is correct. Pin into place and cut out. Pin back neck facing pattern piece to the straight grain fold of double fabric and cut out. Transfer all markings from the pattern pieces to the fabric.

Making up

1 Stay-stitch front and back neck edges with a row of machine stitching.

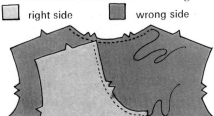

☐ right side ☐ wrong side

2 With right sides together and matching notches tack and stitch side seams. Press open and neaten. With right sides together and matching notches tack and stitch shoulder seams. Press open and neaten. If using knitted fabric, tack narrow matching tape to the seam lines of back shoulders before stitching shoulder seams. This prevents the shoulder seams from stretching.

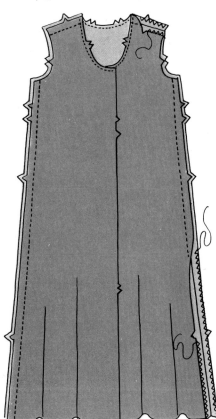

Belt casing

3 Iron small squares of interfacing to wrong sides of fronts, placing centrally over lines indicating openings for belt. Work buttonhole stitch around openings, stitching by hand or machine through fabric and interfacing.

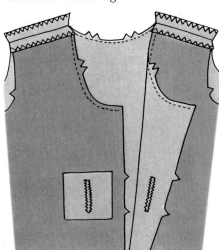

4 With right sides together tack and stitch centre-back seam of belt casing. Press open. On the two long edges of casing turn in and tack 1cm (⅜ inch). Press. With wrong sides together tack casing to garment in position indicated and stitch close to the folded edges. Finish stitching 1.6cm (⅝ inch) from the raw edges of fronts and cut away casing beyond this.

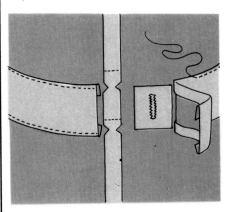

Collar

5 With right sides together tack and stitch outer edges of collar. Trim turnings and clip almost to the stitching line. Turn collar to right side, tack the edge and press. Tack the neck edges of upper and under-collars together. Make two tucks each side of collar on the lines indicated and tack securely. With notches matching tack collar to neckline of garment.

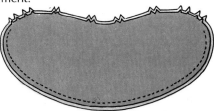

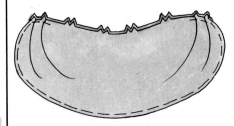

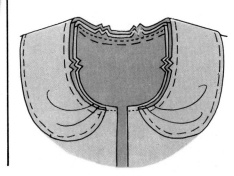

Graph pattern for housecoat

1·6 cms, ⅝ in seam allowance included

5·08 cms, 2 ins hem included

KEY	SIZE 10	
	SIZE 12	
	SIZE 14	
	SIZE 16	

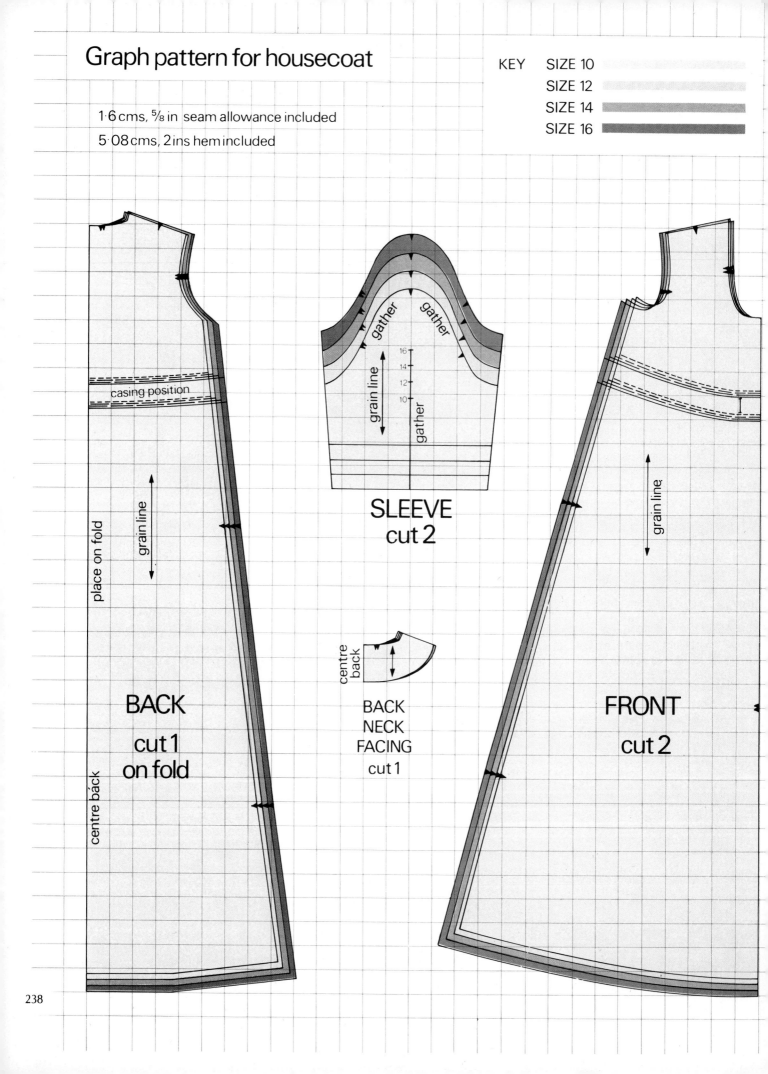

casing position

place on fold

grain line

centre back

BACK

cut 1

on fold

16
14
12
10

grain line

grain line

gather

gather

gather

SLEEVE

cut 2

centre back

BACK
NECK
FACING
cut 1

grain line

FRONT

cut 2

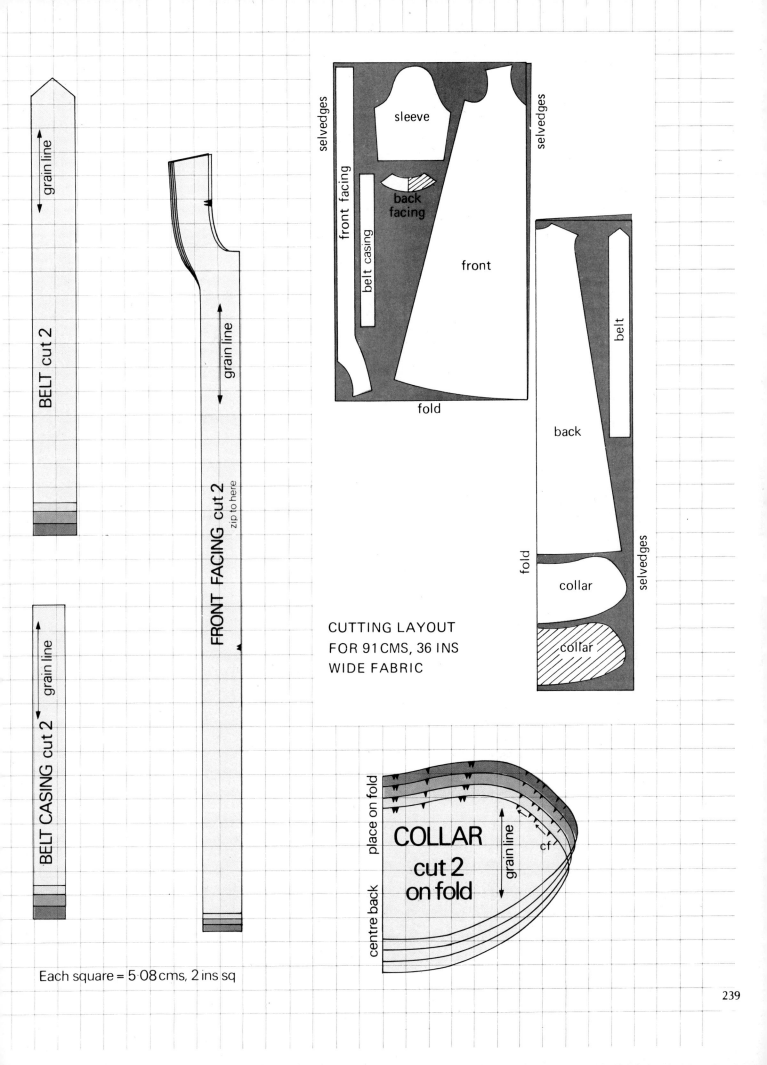

BELT cut 2

grain line

BELT CASING cut 2

grain line

FRONT FACING cut 2

zip to here

grain line

Each square = 5·08 cms, 2 ins sq

selvedges

selvedges

front facing

belt casing

sleeve

back
facing

front

fold

CUTTING LAYOUT
FOR 91 CMS, 36 INS
WIDE FABRIC

belt

back

fold

collar

collar

selvedges

place on fold

COLLAR
cut 2
on fold

centre back

grain line

cf

239

6 With right sides together tack and stitch shoulders of front facings to back neck facing. Press seams open.
With right sides together and matching notches and shoulder seams tack and stitch neck of facing to neck of garment. The collar will be sandwiched between. Trim turnings and clip almost to the stitching line. With right sides together tack and stitch front facing to garment front below zip opening. Trim turnings. Turn facing to inside, tack front edges and press. Tack garment and facing together just below neck seam and press.

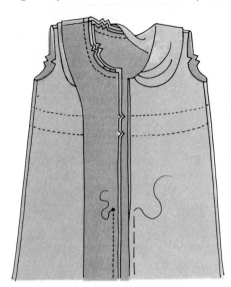

7 Insert zip by hand or machine, following instructions given on the packet. Take care not to catch in the facing. Turn in the facing at the back of the zip and hem on to the zip tape.

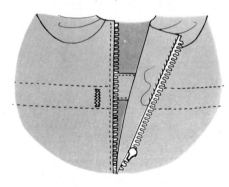

8 Neaten raw edges of facing and catch to garment at shoulder seams and on to the belt casing.

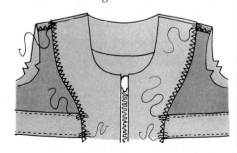

Sleeves

9 With right sides together tack and stitch underarm seam. Press open and neaten. Neaten lower edge of sleeve, turn up hem and slip-stitch into place. Press.

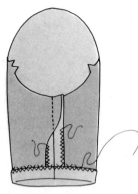

10 Work a row of gathering stitches up from sleeve hem on the line indicated. Draw up to 9cm ($3\frac{1}{2}$ *inches*) and finish off securely.
Tack a stay tape on the wrong side behind the gathers, distributing the fullness evenly on to this. Stitch stay tape into position through the centre line.

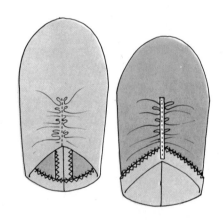

11 Work a gathering thread between the notches over the sleeve head. With right sides together and matching notches pin sleeve into the armhole distributing the fullness evenly. Tack and stitch. Trim turnings to 1cm ($\frac{3}{8}$ *inch*) press towards the sleeve and neaten together.

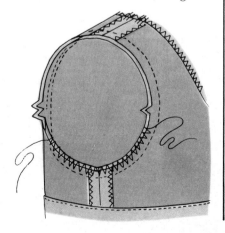

Belt

12 With right sides together tack and stitch centre-back seam of belt. Press open. With belt folded in half lengthways and right sides together tack and stitch the edges, leaving an opening at the centre-back. Trim turnings and pull belt through opening to the right side. Sew sides of opening together by hand, tack edges of belt and press. Thread belt through casing.

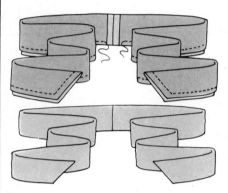

Hem

13 Try on housecoat and check length. Adjust if necessary. With facing opened out, turn up and tack hem, neaten the raw edge and slip-stitch down. Press. Slip-stitch lower edge of facing to wrong side of garment.

Slim line trousers

. . . the sailor style front conceals a neat stretch panel.

Sizes

10, 12, 14 and 16

Fabric required

For sizes 10 and 12:

1.5 metres (1⅝ yards) of 178cm (70 inch) fabric and 35cm (⅜ yard) of 91cm (36 inch) loosely knitted jersey for the under-front.

For sizes 14 and 16:

1.65 metres (1¾ yards) of 178cm (70 inch) fabric and 45cm (½ yard) of 91cm (36 inch) loosely knitted jersey.

You will also need

- ☐ Graph paper for making the pattern
- ☐ Matching thread
- ☐ 6 × 2.25cm (⅞ inch) buttons
- ☐ 45cm (½ yard) of 3cm (1¼ inch) elastic
- ☐ 1 × 18cm (7 inch) zip
- ☐ 25cm (¼ yard) of 91cm (36 inch) light weight woven interfacing

Making the pattern

Using graph paper and following the colour indicating the size required draw each pattern piece to scale.

One square = 5.08cm (2 inch) square. An allowance of 1.6cm (⅝ inch) has been made on all seams and a 7.5cm (3 inch) hem has been allowed.

Cut out the pattern pieces and mark the position of buttonholes, all darts, notches and straight grain line.

Cutting out the trousers

Following the cutting lay-out fold the fabric in half lengthways and place the four pattern pieces as indicated. Take care that the grain line on the pattern lies on the straight grain of the fabric. Pin into place and cut out.

Fold the light-weight jersey fabric as indicated and place the pattern piece for the under-front to the fold. Pin into place and cut out.

For the interfacing cut two back facing pieces, two front flap pieces and one front facing to a fold.

Transfer all markings from the pattern pieces to the fabric.

Making up

1 Tack and stitch the two back darts and two side darts. Press all four darts towards the centre-back.

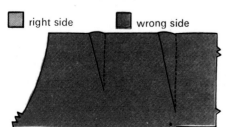

◼ right side ◼ wrong side

2 With right sides together and matching notches tack and stitch the side seams from dots to hem. Press open and neaten. Clip back turning to dot.

With right sides together and matching notches tack and stitch the inner leg seams. Press open and neaten.

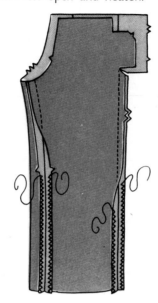

3 Turn one leg through to the right side and slip it inside the other. With right sides together and matching notches and leg seams tack and stitch crotch seam, leaving an opening of 19.6cm (7⅝ inches) for the zip in the centre-back. Work another row of machine stitching 0.6cm (¼ inch) away from the first on the turnings of the curve between notches. Trim turnings close to this stitching and neaten together. Press seams open above the notches and neaten.

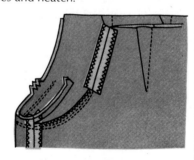

4 Tack interfacing to the wrong side of each front flap, catch-stitching the raw edge into place along the fold line.

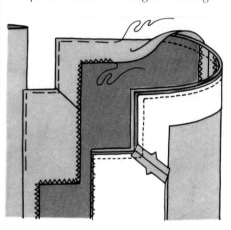

5 Tack interfacing to the wrong side of front facing. With right sides together and matching notches tack and stitch slanted edges of front facing to slanted edges of front flaps. Trim seams to 0.6cm (¼ inch) and press open.

With right sides together and matching notches tack and stitch front facing to front along waistline, down each side and to folds of flaps. Trim turnings and corners. Turn facing to the inside, tack the edge and press. Neaten raw edges of facing.

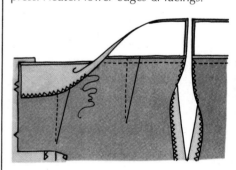

6 Tack interfacing to the wrong sides of back facings. With right sides together tack and stitch back facings to backs. Trim turnings, turn facings to inside of the trousers, tack the edges and press. Neaten lower edges of facings.

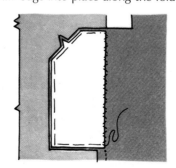

7 With facings lifted up insert zip into centre-back opening. Fold in raw edges of back facings and hem to the back of zip tape. Press.

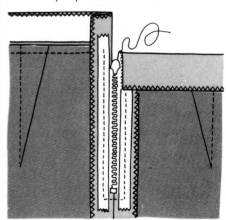

8 Make a hem at the top of the under-front tacking down along fold line. Turn in and stitch the raw edge. Press. Machine stitch 0.6cm ($\frac{1}{4}$ *inch*) from the fold line. Insert the required length of elastic into the casing and stitch the ends securely.

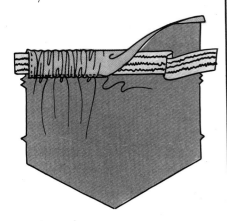

9 With right sides together and matching notches tack and stitch under-front to back extension pieces. Keep facings free. Press turnings towards the back and neaten together. Turn in ends of back facings and hem on to the back of the stitching lines. Neaten lower edges of extensions and under-front.

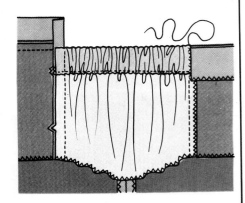

10 Work six buttonholes by hand or machine on the lines indicated. Sew on buttons to correspond.
From the right side work bar tacks on the side seams at the bottom of the front flaps.
At the top of the back opening sew a hook on one side and work a bar to correspond on the other.

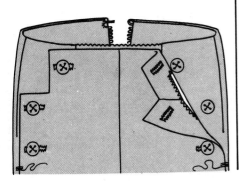

11 Try on trousers and check length. Adjust if necessary. Tack on fold, neaten raw edges and slip-hem into place. Press.

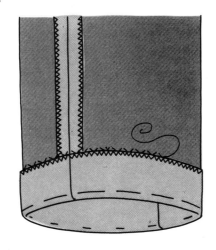

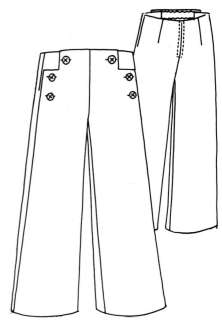

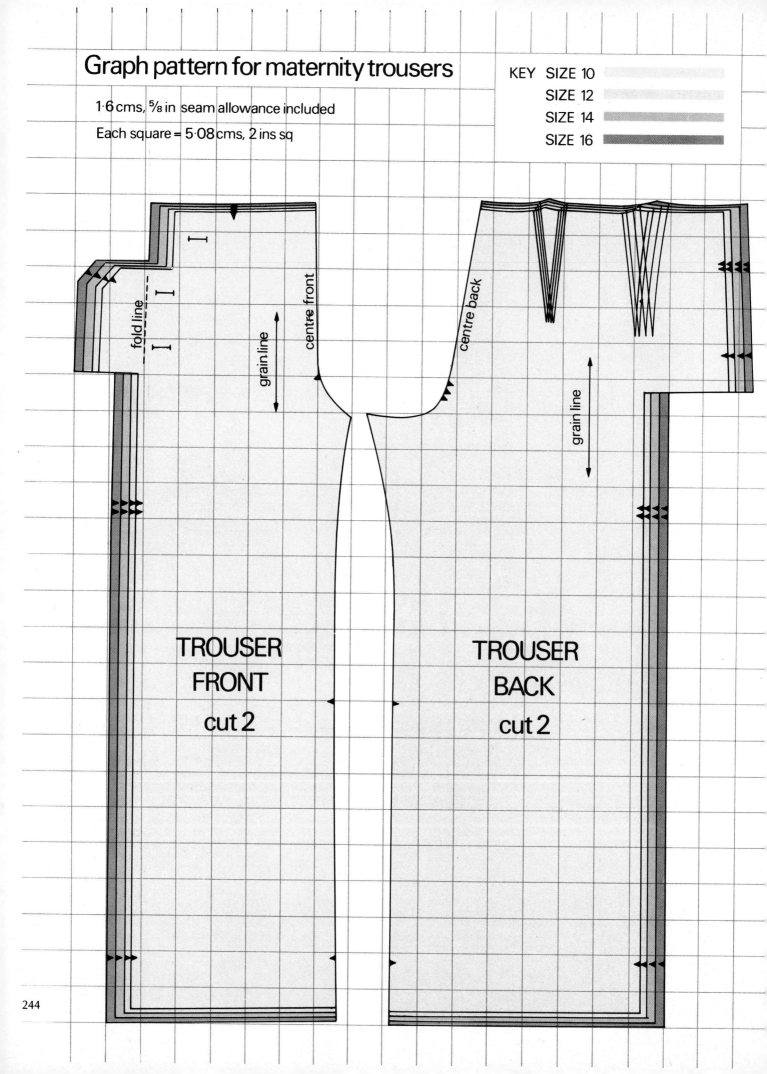

Graph pattern for maternity trousers

1·6 cms, ⅝ in seam allowance included

Each square = 5·08 cms, 2 ins sq

KEY SIZE 10
SIZE 12
SIZE 14
SIZE 16

fold line

grain line

centre front

centre back

grain line

TROUSER
FRONT
cut 2

TROUSER
BACK
cut 2

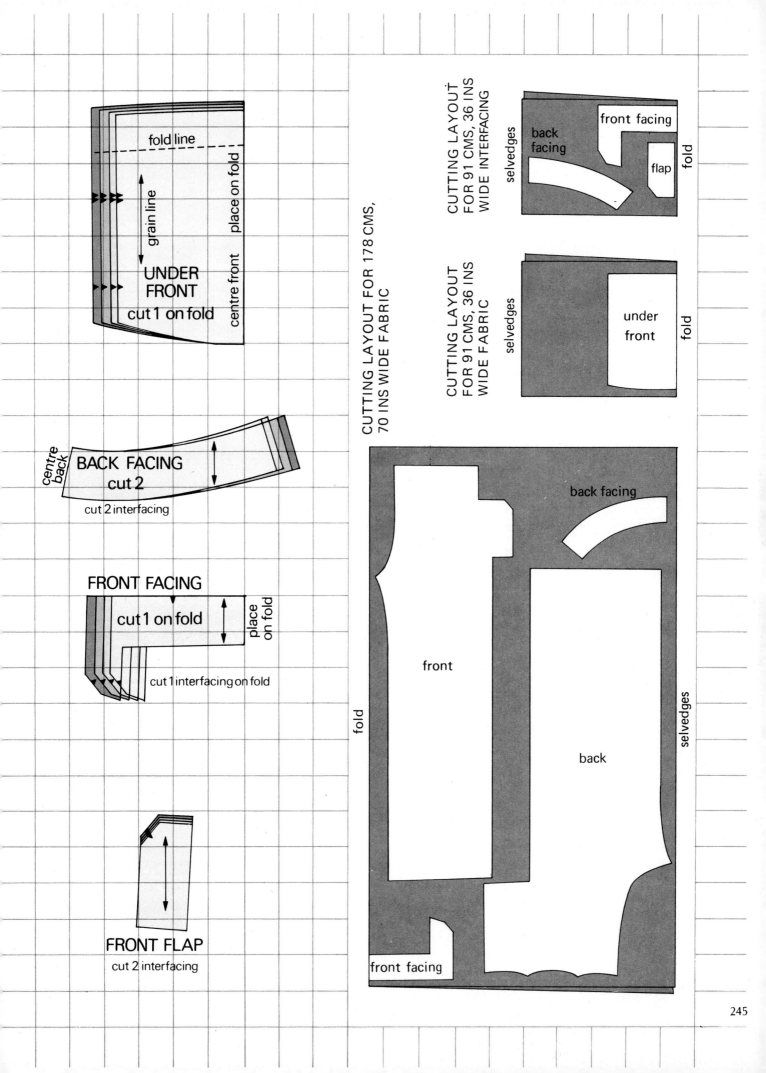

fold line

grain line

place on fold

centre front

UNDER FRONT

cut 1 on fold

centre back

BACK FACING
cut 2

cut 2 interfacing

FRONT FACING

cut 1 on fold

place on fold

cut 1 interfacing on fold

FRONT FLAP

cut 2 interfacing

CUTTING LAYOUT FOR 178 CMS,
70 INS WIDE FABRIC

CUTTING LAYOUT
FOR 91 CMS, 36 INS
WIDE INTERFACING

selvedges

back facing

front facing

flap

fold

CUTTING LAYOUT
FOR 91 CMS, 36 INS
WIDE FABRIC

selvedges

under front

fold

fold

front

back facing

back

selvedges

front facing

Cotton On

Make yourself a crisp cotton hat. It's top-stitched for a really cool shape.

Size
To fit an average head

Fabric required
0.60 metres ($\frac{5}{8}$ *yard*) of 91cm (*36 inch*) cotton
0.25 metres ($\frac{1}{4}$ *yard*) of 91cm (*36 inch*) lining

You will also need
☐ Graph paper for making the pattern
☐ 0.25 metres ($\frac{1}{2}$ *yard*) of tarlatan interfacing
☐ 0.70 metres ($\frac{3}{4}$ *yard*) of 2.5cm (*1 inch*) wide toning milliner's petersham ribbon
☐ Matching thread

Making the pattern
Using graph paper draw both pattern pieces to scale. One square = 5.08cm square (*2 inch square*).
1.6cm ($\frac{5}{8}$ *inch*) has been allowed on all seams.
Cut out the pattern pieces and mark all notches and the straight grain line.

Cutting out
Following the cutting layout, place the two pattern pieces as shown noting that the brim is cut twice and the crown section six times. Taking care that the grain line on the pattern lies on the straight grain of the fabric, pin into place. Cut out. Transfer all markings from the pattern pieces to the fabric.

Cut out six crown sections in lining.
Cut one brim and six crown sections in tarlatan.

Making up
Brim
1 Tack interfacing in place on the wrong side of one brim piece.
With right sides together and matching notches, tack and stitch centre-back seams of both brims. Layer seams and press open.

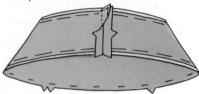

2 With right sides together and matching notches, tack and stitch the two brims together around the outer edge. Trim and snip seam allowance and turn through to right side. Cover the brim all over with tacking to secure the three layers for top-stitching.

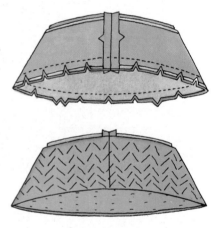

3 Starting at centre-back, machine lines of top stitching parallel to the outer edge, with the width of the machine foot between each line, to cover the brim. Complete each line of top stitching separately. Press.

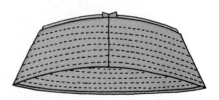

Crown
4a Tack interfacing in place on the wrong side of each crown section. With right sides together and matching notches, tack and stitch three of the sec-

tions together. Layer seam turnings and press open.

4b Top-stitch either side of both seams, the width of the machine foot away from the seam, stitching through the turnings. Press.
Repeat with the other three sections.

5a With right sides together and matching notches, tack and stitch the two halves together. Layer turnings and press open.

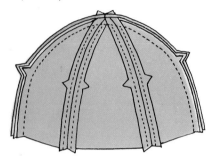

5b Top-stitch either side of seam as before.

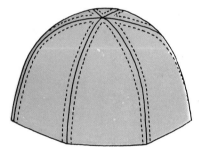

6 With right sides together place centre-back seam of brim to the centre of the edge of one crown section. Tack and stitch brim to crown. Layer seam turnings and press upwards towards crown.

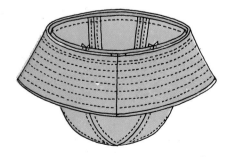

7 Dampen the petersham ribbon and curve it with a hot iron. Neaten one raw end. Sew curved edge to seam line.

Trim off excess ribbon at centre back brim and neaten this raw end as before.

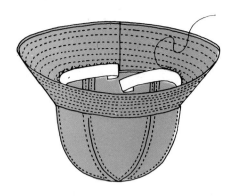

8a Join crown sections of lining as in stages 4 and 5 eliminating interfacing and top stitching.

8b Turn under remaining seam allowance and with wrong sides together catch down to crown section on seam line behind petersham ribbon.

Graph for Hat

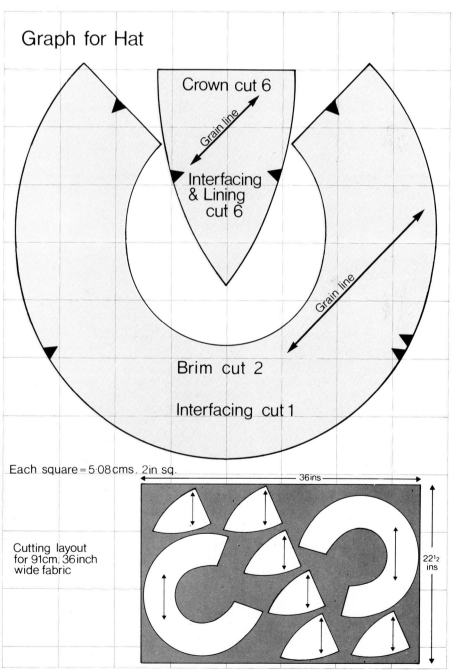

Crown cut 6

Grain line

Interfacing & Lining cut 6

Brim cut 2

Interfacing cut 1

Grain line

Each square = 5·08 cms. 2in sq.

Cutting layout for 91cm. 36 inch wide fabric

36 ins

22½ ins

INDEX

Photography by

John Carter 173.
Roger Charity 128, 130, 132, 135, 140, 145, 146, 148, 149
167, 172, 189, 190, 192, 194, 196, 201, 203.
David Finch 111, 115, 120, 121, 122, 127.
Tony Horth 104, 105, 107, 110, 153, 157, 158.
Chris Lewis 241.
Sandra Lousada 49, 224, 225, 227, 229.
McCalls Patterns 86.
Tony Page 231, 235.
Peter Pugh Cook 236, 243.
Ian Stokes 178, 185, 186.
John Swannell 206, 209, 212, 218, 219, 223.

Illustrations. Terry Evans, Barbara Firth, Garry Shewring.

Cutting Lines

10
12
14
16

16
14